Business Organizations

Business Organizations

Unincorporated Businesses
and Closely Held Corporations
Essential Terms and Concepts

Robert W. Hamilton

Minerva House Drysdale Regents
Chair in Law
University of Texas School of Law

ASPEN LAW & BUSINESS
A Division of Aspen Publishers, Inc.

ISBN 1-56706-488-4

1   2   3   4   5

To Dagmar S. Hamilton, and my children and grandchildren who, by and large, let me work on this book over several summers.

Summary of Contents

PART III:

FINANCIAL TOOLS OF THE TRADE   333

Table of Contents

Chapter 3.   Proprietorships   29

PART III:

FINANCIAL TOOLS OF THE TRADE 333

Chapter 14.   Valuation of Closely Held Businesses   397

Preface

This book about closely held businesses in the United States is designed for the benefit of law students, business students, and others who find that they must know something about business forms and about the management of small firms.

The author is a law professor who first practiced corporate law for several years and since then has taught business-related courses in law schools for more than thirty years. He has also written extensively about legal topics. Given this background, it should not be surprising that the principal emphasis of this book is on legal relationships within firms rather than on business or finance theory.

Regrettably, the law applicable to business and corporate transactions is often complex, uncertain, and (to people in the business world at least) confusing. Indeed, for someone faced with difficult business choices in the face of massive uncertainty, the complexity and uncertainty of legal rules surrounding transactions may be frustrating. Fortunately for the lawyer, business as it relates to law is easier to understand than law as it relates to business. A lawyer should always be able to understand what goal a client is pursuing and the means he or she is using to get there.

This book is divided into three principal parts. Part I deals with legal relationships created by unincorporated business forms. These include not only the traditional forms of a proprietorship, a partnership, and a limited partnership, but also the most important novel business forms invented during the early 1990s. Part II deals at length with closely held corporations, still the predominant business form for closely held enterprises. Part III provides readers with basic tools and information so that they have a working understanding of the most fundamental aspects of business finance: cash-flow analysis, leverage, analysis of financial statements, valuation, the time value of money, and so forth. Every lawyer should have a grounding in these basic concepts.

Part III, however, does not involve financial analysis as it is taught in business schools and some law classes. A formidable theoretical literature exists on business-related topics: management techniques and management goals, financial analysis, portfolio theory, decision analysis under conditions of uncertainty, the theory of the firm, multiple regression analysis, beta values, internal rates of return, efficient capital markets, chaos and "noise" theories, the capital asset pricing model, event studies, and many more. Most of this theoretical literature deals with publicly held corporations— that is, businesses with established markets for their shares—and has limited applicability to closely held businesses. It was largely generated not by legal scholars but by scholars in economics departments, in business schools, and in schools of management.

Without in any way deprecating the importance and usefulness of these concepts in the public corporation context, little attention is given them here because they are rarely encountered when dealing with small firms. On the other hand, every person involved with any business—closely held or publicly held—must have a working understanding of principles of taxation, accounting, cash-flow concepts, leverage, the time value of money, and of how to decipher a financial statement. All of these topics are discussed in Part III of this book.

Finally, the author wishes to thank my research assistant, Alan Bickerstaff, who read the final draft and made many helpful suggestions.

Business Organizations

PART I

THE UNINCORPORATED BUSINESS

1

Of Businesses and Business Forms

§1.1   Introduction
§1.2   Business Forms
§1.3   Default Business Forms
§1.4   The Definitions of "Business" and "Closely Held"
§1.5   Data on the Incidence of Closely Held Businesses

§1.1   INTRODUCTION

This book is about closely held businesses in the United States. A *closely held business* may be defined preliminarily simply as a business with a few owners. While there are technical problems with this preliminary definition (discussed in section 1.4), the basic concept seems clear enough. When there are only a few owners there is no established market for ownership interests in the firm. There are tens of millions closely held businesses in the United States, ranging from a lemonade stand owned by one or two teenagers to a large industrial enterprise such as Brown & Root, Inc., a multibillion dollar construction company that is a wholly owned subsidiary of Halliburton, Inc. Most closely held businesses are small, but some are obviously quite large.

Because of their diversity in size, closely held firms may adopt different legal forms in which to conduct business. In this respect, closely held businesses differ from publicly held firms, virtually all of which are incorporated, and nearly half of which are incorporated in Delaware.

Four factors largely control the structure, management, and operation of closely held businesses: (1) the desire of owners for immunity from liability for the business's obligations, (2) the desire to minimize the total cost of federal income taxes on the firm and on its owners, (3) the desire to participate in management in order to assure (hopefully) the profitable operation of the enterprise, and (4) the desire to be able to exit from the enterprise when circumstances dictate. The unique issues of closely held businesses that are the core topics of this book are, first, the relationships between the business and its owners, and, second, the relationships among the owners themselves.

Major changes are roiling the world of closely held businesses in the 1990s. When I began law practice in the 1950s there were three principal types of business form, each with very well-defined rules and limitations: the partnership (or proprietorship), the limited partnership, and the corporation. Today, in the 1990s, new forms of business enterprise have been created that "mix and match" characteristics in new and challenging ways. New forms of business are being created almost monthly in some state. Further, the basic structure of the federal income tax law—certainly a driving force for change in closely held businesses—is coming under serious legislative scrutiny for the first time this century. The scent of even more major changes in approach is in the air.

This book was written at a time before the outlines of rules for a "brave new world" of closely held businesses have been developed, and the ultimate dimensions of that world are therefore uncertain.

§1.2 BUSINESS FORMS

The phrase *business forms* refers to whether the business is conducted as a proprietorship or a one-person corporation (in the case of a one-owner business), or a partnership, limited partnership, corporation, limited liability company, or some other form (in the case of a multi-owner business). It is sometimes referred to as the *legal form* of the business. The legal form selected for a specific business has a variety of implications and consequences for the business and its owners. It defines the legal relationships between the proprietor or owner of the business and the business itself. In a multi-owner business it defines (or at least has a strong influence on) the rights and responsibilities of the owners to each other, impacts significantly on the federal income tax treatment of both the owners and the business, and largely establishes the extent to which the owners are personally responsible for the debts of the business. The choice of business form also affects or determines what state and local taxes the business is subject to, and what the business must do if it decides to expand its operations into more than one state. Part I of this book describes the traditional and novel business forms in use in the United States of the 1990s.

The most versatile business form in many ways is the corporation. It may be used by a person who is the sole owner of a small business as well as by General Motors or Exxon Corporation, two of the largest American businesses.[1] Virtually all large businesses use the corporate form, whether or not they are publicly held. Chapters 8 through 10 discuss the corporate form of business as it is used in a closely held business with relatively few owners. In other words, these chapters discuss corporations as used in closely held businesses, but ignore the corporate form as used in large publicly held corporations. That topic is simply beyond the scope of this book.

§1.3 DEFAULT BUSINESS FORMS

While this and the following chapters in Part I are largely pitched in terms of selecting a business form, it should be emphasized at the outset that "selection" is not always made consciously or rationally. The law provides for default forms for business. If the parties do not expressly address the form a new business should take but simply start it up, they nevertheless will have selected a business form, for better or worse. The two default forms of business are proprietorships (for one-owner businesses) and general partnerships (for multiple-owner businesses), though other legal relationships (such as debtor/creditor or employer/employee) may sometimes serve as default classifications of uncertain business relationships among multiple owners.

Both proprietorships and partnerships are business forms in which the owners of the business are personally liable for the debts and liabilities of that business. The critical point, therefore, is that if no conscious decision about business form is made, the parties have in fact opted for a form that entails personal liability for business debts on the part of the owners.

§1.4 THE DEFINITIONS OF "BUSINESS" AND "CLOSELY HELD"

The definition of "closely held business" given in the first pararaph of section 1.1 was described as "preliminary." It is desirable to consider further the definitions of both "business" and "closely held."

1. Business. A "business" may be defined as any kind of profit-making endeavor excluding only employment in which one person works for and under the direction of another. A *profit-making endeavor* in turn is an enterprise or activity that promises to throw off money in the future to its owners. The economist uses the word "firm" to refer to the same concept. A business

---

[1]Large publicly held businesses may also be conducted to a limited extent in the form of master limited partnerships. See §5.20. It is also possible that they may be conducted in the form of limited liability companies, though that seems unlikely.

is hopefully a cash-generating machine. That is why, of course, people form businesses and own and manage them.

Personal services in an employment relationship are excluded since typically wages are paid on a fixed basis and are not directly tied to the success of the enterprise.

2. Closely Held. "Closely held" normally signifies that there are only a few owners of the business. The problem with this simple definition is at the margin. When the tens of millions of businesses in the United States are classified solely by the number of owners, they form a continuum from one-owner businesses, at one end of the spectrum, to vast corporations with hundreds of thousands of shareholders at the other. It is not possible to define precisely what is meant by a "few" except on a purely arbitrary basis. Whatever number is chosen to define "few," there will always be indistinguishable businesses that have precisely one more owner than whatever number has been chosen.

A more precise definition may be obtained by first defining the essential characteristic of a "publicly held" business, and then defining a closely held business negatively as all businesses that are not "publicly held". It turns out that this approach leads to a much more useful classification. A *publicly held business* may be defined as one having a sufficiently large number of owners that there has developed an active established market in which ownership interests of the specific business are traded.[2] The existence of an active trading market for ownership interests means that outside investors always have a power to "enter" or "exit" simply by buying or selling ownership interests in these public trading markets. This characteristic sharply distinguishes publicly held businesses from closely held ones, where entrance and exit are usually circumscribed or nonexistent.

Publicly held corporations have two additional subsidiary characteristics that also help to distinguish them from closely held businesses. First, they are subject to the continuous disclosure requirements of the Securities Exchange Act of 1934.[3] In other words, they operate in a goldfish bowl and not as purely private enterprises. Second, the business of a publicly held corporation is usually managed by professional managers who do not own, in the aggregate, a significant percentage of the ownership interests of the

---

[2]The best known such market is the New York Stock Exchange, on which securities issued by more than 2,000 businesses are actively traded. In addition, there are other regional and national securities exchanges, as well as a major over-the-counter market administered by the National Association of Securities Dealers called "NASDAQ" (National Association of Securities Dealers Automated Quotations). More than 10,000 firms have shares with quotations listed on NASDAQ.

[3]Businesses subject to these requirements are those that have made a registered public offering of securities under the federal Securities Act of 1933 or have 500 owners of record and more than $5 million of assets.

business.[4] However, these subsidiary characteristics may exist in many businesses in which there is no active trading market for ownership interests; these businesses may be described typically as being "in between" businesses that have some characteristics of both publicly held and closely held firms. In the classification adopted here they are classified as closely held even though the number of owners may be large, since by definition there is no active trading market in ownership interests.

Under any definition, virtually all closely held businesses will be small and will be owned by one or a few persons. Under the definition adopted here, some closely held businesses may be large in terms of assets and may have a substantial number of passive owners. But so long as there is no active trading market for the ownership interests, the business does not have the most fundamental characteristic of a publicly held business.

§1.5 DATA ON THE INCIDENCE OF CLOSELY HELD BUSINESSES

The most readily available source of information about the incidence of businesses of various types is drawn from information published by the Internal Revenue Service based on filings of income tax returns.

Based on data for the 1992 tax year (that is, returns filed in 1993), the IRS estimates that there were about 15,500,000 active, nonfarm *proprietorships* in the United States. There were about 1,214,000 *general partnerships* and 270,748 *limited partnerships* filing returns for the same year. Finally, there were about 3,868,000 *corporations* that filed income tax returns for the same tax year. These numbers indicate approximately how many active businesses there were in each category in 1992. Proprietorships outnumber all other business forms in a numerical count. Since the novel business forms created in the 1990s are almost all taxed as partnerships, their data is presumably included in the 1.2 million partnerships; however, it is unlikely that their numbers were significant in that year.

From an economic standpoint, corporations are much more important in the American economy than all other business forms put together. Information about gross receipts (also taken from tax returns) may be summarized as follows:

---

[4]In the very largest corporations there may be no identifiable individuals or groups of individuals who may be identified as "principal owners" of the business. No individual shareholder in a major corporation such as General Motors Corporation, for example, may own as much as one percent of the outstanding shares of that corporation. Such businesses inevitably must be managed by professional managers. In some businesses that are clearly publicly held, however, the original founders continue to own an appreciable fraction of the business and are active in its management. Good examples of publicly held corporations that are managed by owners are Microsoft Corporation and Dell Computer Corporation.

Total receipts by proprietorships: $737,000,000,000
Total receipts by partnerships: $46,194,000,000
Total receipts by corporations: $9,965,629,000,000

Thus, the total receipts by corporations account for approximately 93 percent of all business receipts. Further, about $6.3 trillion of the nearly $10 trillion of business receipts by corporations were accounted for by the 5,900 corporations with more than $250,000,000 of receipts. Indeed, the cumulative receipts of the ten largest corporations exceeded the gross receipts of the 15 million-odd proprietorships. Virtually all corporations with more than $250,000,000 of assets are publicly held rather than closely held.

2

Agency and Employment

§2.1 INTRODUCTION

This chapter discusses basic agency and employment relationships underlying virtually all commercial dealings in the modern world. Agency relationships by and large do not themselves create new business forms; rather they are the glue that holds unincorporated businesses together. As such, they define the rights and responsibilities of individuals who work for or on behalf of businesses. It is surprising that this essential subject today receives relatively little attention, since modern business is conducted almost entirely by agents or employees. To take an obvious example, a corporation, an artificial legal construct that has no physical being of its own, can act only through agents for everything it does. Whenever one person performs services for, or acts on behalf of, someone else, the principles of agency define the relationships and the responsibilities of both participants and of persons who deal with them. The most common agency relationship is the employment relationship,[1] but agency law is applicable in many other situations as well.

Thirty years ago, virtually every law school in the country offered a course in agency. In many schools this course was a required course, either in the Spring semester of the first year or a second or third year course that was a prerequisite for graduation. Times certainly have changed.

Today, agency as a separate course has disappeared from virtually all law school curricula. To the extent agency is separately considered at all in law schools, it is usually combined with unincorporated business forms in a course typically called Agency and Partnership, but in fact largely devoted to partnerships and other unincorporated business forms. In other law schools, agency may be tucked into a survey course on "business associations." Agency may also be given some attention in contracts, torts, employment law, or other substantive courses, but there is usually no systematic treatment of the subject. The reasons usually given for downgrading the importance of this subject are that it may be picked up readily from other substantive courses, the concepts are not inherently difficult and are adequately treated in the Restatement of Agency and other treatises, and the subject is a little "thin" for even a two hour, one semester course.

Because of the lack of systematic exposure to agency law, it is not uncommon for a newly minted lawyer to be unable to respond to relatively simple agency questions: for example, an employee acting within the scope of her employment violates specific instructions of her employer, leading to an injury to a third person. Is the employer liable? If the employer has a liability insurance policy that expressly excludes coverage for "intentional torts," and the act of the employee constitutes an intentional tort, (e.g., she falsely imprisons a customer on the belief he is a shoplifter), is the intention of the employee imputed to the employer so that the event is not covered by the employer's insurance? Answers to these questions are not intuitively obvious.[2] This brief chapter is designed to give readers an introduction to agency principles as a separate and coherent subject.

Agency law readily lends itself to illustration by example.

[1] Many aspects of employment law are of course governed by statutes or common law principles independent of agency law. The employment at will doctrine is a common law doctrine that addresses a most basic characteristic of the employment relationship. Statutes of long standing govern such matters as minimum wages, overtime pay, pay periods, and the like. Other statutes govern matters relating to the workplace, e.g., safety, sexual harassment, and a variety of other subjects.

[2] In case you are interested, the answer to the first question is clearly yes. See Restatement (Second) of Agency §219(1) (1957). The answer to the second question is also yes, at least if the action was within the scope of employment and the employee was attempting to benefit the employer. See id. §272.

§2.2 BASIC CONCEPTS

The principal source of agency law today is probably the Restatement of Agency, Second, published in 1957. The Restatement is useful particularly because it provides a comprehensive set of definitions for the subject. It defines *agency* as the "fiduciary relation which results from the manifestation of consent by one person to another that the other shall act on his behalf and subject to his control, and consent by the other so to act."[3] The person who is acting for another is the *agent;* the person for whom the agent is acting is the *principal.*

An agency relationship is based on conduct by the principal and agent, the principal manifesting that he is willing to have another act for him and the agent manifesting a willingness to act. The relationship may be contractual, but it need not be. Persons acting as agents without compensation are still agents.[4] Thus, agency is basically a consensual relationship in which one person agrees to act for the benefit of another.

Artificial entities such as corporations, trusts, partnerships, or limited liability companies may act as principals or as agents. The relationships are not limited to natural persons. An artificial entity can in turn act only through agents. Thus, the law of agency is involved whenever a corporation acts, whether it be writing a check, selling a product, or entering into a multibillion dollar merger. Partnerships similarly involve the law of agency, with each partner being an agent for the partnership. See Chapter 4.

§2.3 FIDUCIARY DUTIES

An agency relationship has the important characteristic of being a *fiduciary* relationship. The agent is a fiduciary with respect to matters within the scope of his agency.[5] Basically, this means that the agent is accountable to the principal for any profits arising out of the transactions he is to conduct on the principal's behalf,[6] and that he breaches his duty to the principal if he acts either to benefit himself or someone else other than the principal.[7] This *fiduciary duty* also prevents an agent either from acting adversely to the interest of the principal[8] or assisting an adverse party to the principal in connection with the agency.[9] An agent also may not compete with his

---

[3]Id. §1.
[4]These agents may be called "unpaid" or "gratuitous" agents.
[5]Id. §13.
[6]Id. §388.
[7]Id. §387.
[8]Id. §389.
[9]Id. §391.

principal concerning the subject matter of the agency.[10] In addition, the agent must act to preserve and protect property entrusted to his care by the principal, and is liable for its loss if he disposes of the property without authority to do so, or it is lost or destroyed because of his neglect or because he intermingles it with his own property.[11] The agent may be required to account for his actions or for property of the principal entrusted to him.

The scope of the agency is usually determined by contract between the principal and agent or by the nature of the instructions given by the principal to the agent. The scope of the agent's fiduciary duty may be shaped by these terms, but the fiduciary obligation exists even though the contract is silent as to the duties of the agent or purports to abolish this duty.

When parties are dealing at arms length, one party usually does not have a duty to volunteer information to the other. This is not true, however, if one owes the other a fiduciary duty.

> *Example*: M is looking for a site for his plant. He learns that O has a site for sale. The asking price is $250,000. M and O negotiate and agree upon a price of $247,500. In this negotiation, O does not disclose that he purchased the site for $150,000 a few days before, information that would have been relevant to M's decision to agree to the $247,500 price. O's failure to disclose this information is not a breach of duty and M may not rescind the transaction.

> *Example*: P retains A to purchase a suitable manufacturing site for him. A owns a suitable site which he offers to P for $250,000, a fair price. A tells P all relevant facts except that a short time previously he purchased the site for $150,000. A has breached his fiduciary duty and the transaction may be rescinded by P.[12]

§2.4 OTHER DUTIES OF THE AGENT

In addition to the broad fiduciary duty, an agent must act with reasonable care in carrying out the agency and must meet at least the standard of competence and skill in the locality for work of the character he is obligated to perform. An unpaid agent may have a lesser duty than one who is paid.

> *Example*: X, a person in the community who does odd jobs for homeowners, agrees to construct a chimney for Y, a homeowner.

[10]Id. §393.
[11]Id. §§402–404A.
[12]Id. §390, illustration 2.

X has not previously had experience building chimneys on his own, though he has assisted other masons in building chimneys. He places a row of bricks incorrectly in the chimney with the result that the chimney does not draw properly. X has breached his duty to Y.

Presumably, if Y knows that X has had no experience building chimneys, a different result would be reached. In that situation, Y reasonably can expect only that X will do the best he can.

§2.5 DUTIES OF THE PRINCIPAL TO THE AGENT

The principal owes duties to the agent. These duties are different from the agent's duties since the basic fiduciary duty only runs from the agent to the principal. A principal must perform his commitments to the agent, act in good faith, cooperate with the agent, and not interfere with or make more difficult the agent's performance of his duties. Implicit in the arrangement may be an obligation by the principal to give the agent work, an opportunity to earn a reasonable compensation, or an opportunity to find additional work.

> *Example*: P employs A as a hatcheck girl, the understanding being that A will be entitled to retain all tips but that P will not pay her a salary. P places A at a secondary entrance which is not heavily used, with the result that A receives relatively few tips. P has breached his duty to A.

In addition, if the agent incurs expenses or spends his own funds on behalf of the principal, the principal may have a duty to repay or indemnify the agent.[13]

§2.6 THE RIGHT TO CONTROL: INDEPENDENT CONTRACTORS AND SERVANTS

In general terms, the principal has the right to control the conduct of the agent with respect to matters entrusted to him.[14] The principal can determine what the ultimate goal is, and the agent must strive to meet that goal. The degree of control that the principal has over the acts of the agent, may vary widely within the agency relationship. In this respect, the Restatement

[13]Id. §§432–469.
[14]Id. §12.

distinguishes between a master/servant relationship and an independent contractor relationship.[15] A *master* is a principal who "employs an agent to perform service in his affairs and who controls or has the right to control the physical conduct of the other in the performance of the service." A *servant* is an agent so employed by a master. In a way, the use of the words master and servant for this relationship is unfortunate, because those words may imply servility, household service, or manual labor. Under these definitions, most employment relationships are technically master/servant relationships.

> *Example*: General Motors Corporation employs an individual to serve as head designer of a new automobile. His salary is $300,000 per year. The designer is a "servant" in the Restatement terminology and General Motors is his "master."[16]

An *independent contractor* is a "person who contracts with another to do something for him but who is not controlled by the other nor subject to the other's right to control with respect to his physical conduct in the performance of the undertaking."[17] An independent contractor may or may not be agent. In other words, he may or may not be subject to the principal's control.

> *Example*: An attorney agrees to represent hundreds of persons on a contingency basis seeking to recover damages for injuries arising from exposure to asbestos. The attorney is an independent contractor, but not an agent.[18]

> *Example*: A builder enters into a contract with the owner of a lot to build a house on the lot in accordance with certain plans and specifications prepared by an architect. The builder is an independent contractor, but he is not an agent. He is employed merely to accomplish a specific result and is not otherwise subject to the owner's control.

---

[15] Id. §2.

[16] Do you have any doubt about the correctness of this conclusion? If you do, consider this possible scenario: The chief executive officer of General Motors comes to the designer and says, "John, the board of directors liked your sketches for the new convertible. They feel, however, that it looks a little boxy and they think the headlights are too conspicuous. Please streamline it a little more and move the headlights into the front fenders." What should the head designer do? He makes the changes that are requested, thereby indicating clearly that he is a servant.

[17] Id. §2(3).

[18] Do you agree that the attorney is not an agent in this situation? Does he "consent to act subject to the control of" the client? See §2.2. The attorney may be an agent in other roles, e.g., when negotiating a contract on behalf of his client.

Example: A broker enters into a contract to sell goods for a manufacturer. His arrangement involves the receipt of a salary plus a commission on each sale, but the broker has discretion as to how to conduct his business. He determines which cities to visit and who to contact. He uses his own automobile to visit prospects. The broker is an agent and an independent contractor. He is not a servant.

Example: A customer of a brokerage firm directs the firm to sell on the New York Stock Exchange at the best price obtainable 100 shares of XYZ Stock owned by the customer. The brokerage firm, when executing this instruction, is also both an agent and an independent contractor.

Example: Acme Superstores, a chain of grocery stores, enters into a contract with Gene's Pheasant Farm, Inc., by which Gene's promises to supply Acme with killed and dressed pheasants for sale by Acme. The contract gives Acme the power to direct Gene's operations to assure a continuing supply of fresh, high-quality pheasants. Acme is the principal and Gene's is an agent. Gene's may also be a servant if the degree of control maintained by Acme means that Acme may "control the physical conduct of" Gene's.

The distinction between an independent contractor who is an agent and one who is not depends on the degree and character of control exercised over the work being done by the independent contractor. In some instances, there may be doubt as to whether an independent contractor is also an agent. Similarly, uncertainty may sometimes exist as to whether an agent is also a servant. The Restatement of Agency contains a somewhat dated provision that gives guidelines as to the latter issue:

In determining whether one acting for another is a servant or an independent contractor, the following matters of fact, among others, are considered:

(a) the extent of control which, by the agreement, the master may exercise over the details of the work;

(b) whether or not the one employed is engaged in a distinct occupation or business;

(c) the kind of occupation, with reference to whether, in the locality, the work is usually done under the direction of the employer or by a specialist without supervision;

(d) the skill required in the particular occupation;

(e) whether the employer or the workman supplies the instrumentalities, tools, and the place of work for the person doing the work;

(f) the length of time for which the person is employed;

(g) the method of payment, whether by the time or by the job;

(h) whether or not the work is a part of the regular business of the employer;

(i) whether or not the parties believe they are creating the relation of master and servant; and

(j) whether the principal is or is not in business.[19]

§2.7 THE RESPONSIBILITY OF A PRINCIPAL FOR HIS AGENT'S TORTS

The classification of an agent as a servant or as an independent contractor is important primarily because different rules apply with respect to the liability of the principal for physical harm caused by the agent's conduct. A master is liable for torts committed by a servant within the scope of his employment, while a principal is not liable for torts committed by an independent contractor in connection with his work.

> *Example*: P, the owner of a successful retail operation with two stores, hires D to drive her delivery truck and deliver goods to her two stores. Before doing so, P checks D's driving record and arranges for him to go to a driving school for truck drivers. D's record shows that he has had no accidents for 20 years, and he completes the driving school program without difficulty. Three weeks later, while driving P's delivery truck, D is negligent and has a serious accident, injuring X. P is liable to X for his injuries.

In this example, D is a servant, and P's liability is independent of whether P exercised due care in hiring D, or even whether she knew that D was her employee at all. P's liability in this situation may be described as "vicarious liability" and the consequence of "respondeat superior." *Respondeat superior* is a Latin phrase that means "let the master respond." It is important to recognize that P's liability only applies to actions within the scope of D's employment, though nice questions about coverage may arise as to whether the specific trip was a "detour" that was nevertheless part of the agent's duties to the principal or a "frolic" by the agent on his own.

> *Example*: D's accident occurs while driving the truck to a family picnic. P has acquiesced in D's using the truck for this purpose.

[19]Id. §220(2). A more modern list might include factors such as whether the employer files a W-4 form for the employee, whether he is listed as an employee on insurance forms, and the like.

P is not liable as a master. She may be liable on other theories, such as negligent entrustment.[20]

Example: The broker who is selling on commission in one of the above illustrations has an automobile accident while driving his own car to visit a prospect. The manufacturer is not liable for injuries to third persons arising from the accident. The same would be true of a person injured by the contractor in the above illustration while working on the owner's house.

Of course, the broker and the contractor would both be personally liable for the injuries in these illustrations. *D*, the servant in the above illustration, would also be personally liable for *X*'s injuries, since he too is a tortfeasor. The reason that respondeat superior is applied in numerous cases is because the chances are very good that the servant is judgment proof, has no insurance of his own, and therefore *X*'s only recourse is against *P*.

§2.8 THE POWER OF AN AGENT TO AFFECT THE PRINCIPAL'S LEGAL RIGHTS AND DUTIES IN GENERAL

An agent has power to affect the legal rights and duties of the principal in various ways. The tort liability of the principal for acts of the agent discussed in the previous section is one illustration. In other respects, to the extent the agent acts within the scope of his agency his acts are viewed as the acts of the principal and therefore affect the contractual or property rights and duties of the principal accordingly. However, the power of the agent is broader than this. An agent may also affect the principal's rights and duties to some extent even when the agent is acting in direct violation of the principal's instructions, or beyond the scope of the agency relationship, or in some cases even when he is not really an agent at all.

The power of the agent to affect the principal's rights and duties is known as the agent's *authority*. The law of agency deals with three quite different, but interrelated, sources of authority that one person may have to bind another. These sources of power are discussed in the following sections.

[20]In some states, *P* may be held directly liable for the negligence of a permitted user of a vehicle under doctrines known as the permissive use doctrine or the family use doctrine. In most states, however, the owner of a vehicle is not liable for the negligence of a person to whom the vehicle is lent, at least in the absence of knowledge that the borrower has a tendency to drive carelessly.

§2.9 ACTUAL AUTHORITY

Actual authority (often described as *express authority* or simply by the words "authority" or "authorized") arises from the manifestation of a principal *to an agent* that the agent has power to deal with others as a representative of the principal. An agent who agrees to act in accordance with that manifestation has actual authority to so act, and his actions without more bind the principal.

> *Example*: P, the owner of two retail stores, employs C to serve as credit manager. C has authority to review and approve requests from customers for the extension of credit. C reviews the application of Y and approves him for the extension of credit. P is bound by C's decision, though that decision may be revoked by P at any time.

When an agent acts within the scope of her authority, she is not personally liable to the third person on the obligation so created (though, of course, the parties may agree otherwise).

> *Example*: C approves of a sale of a washing machine to Z, a customer, for $100 down and $50 per month until a total of $600 is paid. This action is within the scope of C's authority. P, the owner, refuses to deliver the washing machine to Z unless Z pays the $600 in cash immediately. P is liable for breach of contract, but C has no responsibility to Z and is not personally liable when P refuses to permit Z to purchase the machine on the terms agreed upon.

In this situation, P is bound by C's decision even though Z is totally unaware of who P is, or erroneously believes that C is the owner of the stores.

> *Example*: T knows that P owns a horse he is thinking of buying and which A, P's agent, is offering to sell him. A says, "This horse is only three years old and is sound in every respect." On these facts alone, P is liable if A's warranty turns out to be false, but A is not.[21]

Different rules may be applicable if the principal is not known to the third person. These rules are considered briefly below.

[21]Restatement (Second) of Agency §320, illustration 1.

§2.10 APPARENT AUTHORITY

Apparent authority arises from the manifestation *of a principal to a third party* (directly or indirectly) that another person is authorized to act as an agent for the principal.[22] That other person has apparent authority and an act by him within the scope of that apparent authority binds the principal to a third party who is aware of the manifestation by the principal and believes the person is authorized to act on behalf of the principal. The person with power to act in this situation should perhaps be called an "apparent agent" but typically he is simply described as an agent, one with apparent authority to act.

Apparent authority arises when a person represents that someone else is his agent when that is not the case, or, more commonly, creates or permits the creation of the impression that broad authority exists when it in fact does not. The theory is that if a third person relies on the representation or appearance of authority, that person may hold the putative principal liable for the action of the putative agent. The principal is bound by the agent's act within the scope of his apparent authority in this situation even though the act was not in fact authorized by the principal.

> *Example*: P gives A, an agent who is authorized to sell a piece of property on behalf of the principal, specific instructions as to the minimum price ($300,000) P is willing to accept, as well as other terms. P informs possible buyers that A is his agent but obviously does not communicate A's specific instructions to anyone but A (since to do so would be a virtual blueprint to possible buyers as to how to buy the property as cheaply as possible). A has actual authority only to enter a contract to sell the property at a price equal to or higher than $300,000, but he has apparent authority to sell the property at any price since the principal has represented to possible buyers that A is his agent.

> *Example*: A actually signs a contract on behalf of P to sell P's property to TP for $275,000. P is bound on that contract because the action was within A's apparent authority but A has violated his instructions and is liable to P for the loss incurred.

The difference between apparent and actual authority can be most easily envisioned in that actual authority flows directly from the principal to the agent while apparent authority flows from the impression created by (or permitted to exist by) the principal in the mind of a third person.

[22]Id. §27.

Apparent authority *cannot* be created by the mere representation of the putative agent. Not even the most convincing and persuasive person can create an agency or apparent agency relationship entirely on his own.

> *Example*: A approaches John's Buicks, Inc., a new car dealer and falsely explains that he is *P*'s agent, and that *P* desires to test drive a new Buick. Since *P* has been a good customer of John's Buicks in the past, and *A* is unusually convincing, John's entrusts *A* with a new Buick automobile, which *A* misappropriates. *P* is not liable for *A*'s conduct.

> *Example*: Bill is a smooth-talking con man. He becomes friends with X and represents to X that he is an agent for General Motors seeking possible owners of new car franchises. Bill is very convincing, showing forged letters on GM letterhead, a forged identification card, and so forth. He persuades X that he will obtain a franchise for X if X will post $250,000. X does so. Bill converts the money to his own use, and disappears. General Motors is not liable for X's loss.

While the conclusion reached in these two examples may seem self-evident, it is surprising in real life how often a third person relies upon representations by a putative agent of the scope of the agent's authority.

In many instances, the scope of apparent authority is as broad as an agent's actual authority — for example, where identical letters describing the scope of the agent's authority are sent both to the agent and to the third party. However, this is not necessarily so, and it is important to recognize that the power to affect the principal's legal rights and obligations may arise either from statements by the principal to the agent (actual authority) or statements made directly or indirectly by the principal to a third party (apparent authority). Apparent authority is related to concepts of estoppel based on the principal's conduct. In order to establish apparent authority, the third party must establish that it was reasonable for him to believe that the agent was authorized to act, based on what the principal said or on the impression that the principal created. If he can do so, the principal is bound even though he never intended to make A his agent or to enter into a contract with that third person.

In one aspect, apparent authority is broader than traditional estoppel. Liability arises under apparent authority even if the relying party has not changed his position in reliance on the representation. In other words, in the two examples in this section relating to the sale of land where A violates his instructions and sells the land for $275,000 rather than $300,000, P is bound to the contract with TP as soon as it is negotiated between TP and A even though TP has not relied in any material way on the contract and shortly thereafter learns that A was not authorized to sell the land for $275,000.

§2.11 INHERENT AND INCIDENTAL AUTHORITY

Inherent authority arises from the *agency itself and without regard to either actual or apparent authority*. Inherent authority may be viewed as authority arising by implication from the authority actually or apparently granted.[23]

> *Example*: P hires A to operate a branch store of P's retail operations. A has authority to manage the store on a day-to-day basis but is told expressly that he has no authority to mark down the prices of goods without the prior approval of P. A nevertheless marks down slow-moving goods which are sold to third persons. There is neither actual nor apparent authority (because there was no manifestation of authority to the customers) but P is bound since a manager of a store has inherent authority based on his position to set prices of goods.

In many instances actual authority is coextensive with inherent authority based on the nature of the agency, but again this is not necessarily so.

Incidental authority is simply authority to do incidental acts that relate to a transaction that is authorized.[24]

> *Example*: P authorizes A to purchase and obtain goods for him but does not provide him with funds to pay for them. It is implicit that A has authority to purchase goods on P's credit.

Obviously, the lines between apparent, inherent, and incidental authority may not always be clear-cut.

§2.12 IMPLIED AUTHORITY

One complicating factor about the classification of authority as actual or apparent is that in either case the existence of authority may be implied rather than express. Indeed, the same conduct may often be relied upon to prove the existence of implied actual authority and implied apparent authority. Authority may be inferred from a prior course of conduct by the principal. Such conduct may be the basis for implying that the agent has

[23] Id. §8 A.
[24] Id. §35.

continuing actual authority to act on the principal's behalf. If known to a third party, the very same conduct may lead to an inference that apparent authority exists.

> *Example*: P is an elderly person living alone. He is befriended by A, a neighbor. A does errands for P, going to the store, helping P go to the doctor, and so forth. P has long had a charge account at the local grocery store that A has used frequently to charge groceries. Originally, the owner of the grocery store checked with P before accepting the charges but has stopped doing so since the relationship between A and P is well known to the owner. When A charges groceries, P is bound to pay for them. This result may be reached on the basis of either implied actual authority or implied apparent authority. The approval by P of A's prior transactions justifies a conclusion that A has actual authority to buy groceries for P (implied actual authority). The holding out in the past by P of A as his agent to the grocer also justifies an inference by the grocer that authority exists no matter what the actual state of relations is between P and A (implied apparent authority).

Apparent authority is destroyed if the third party knows, or has reason to know that A is no longer authorized to act for P.

> *Example*: P and A have an argument and P tells A that he wants nothing more to do with him. The grocer, knowing this, nevertheless sells groceries to A on credit. P is not obligated to pay for them.

§2.13 DISCLOSED AND UNDISCLOSED PRINCIPALS

This section deals with the common situation in which an agent is dealing with a third party on behalf of a principal under circumstances in which the third party may not know that the agent is acting for someone else. There are basically three different situations: the disclosed principal, the partially disclosed principal, and the completely undisclosed principal.

A principal is *disclosed* if the third party knows the identity of the principal at the time the transaction is entered into. It may be, of course, that in a specific situation, a third person does not actually know who the principal is, but should be able reasonably to infer the identity of the principal from the information on hand. That is still a disclosed principal situation. All of the prior discussion in this chapter has assumed that the principal is disclosed.

When a transaction is entered into on behalf of a disclosed principal, the principal becomes a party to that contract. Equally importantly, the agent does not become a party to such a contract unless there is an agreement to the contrary.

A *partially disclosed principal* is one whose identity is unknown but the third person is on notice that the agent is in fact acting on behalf of some principal.[25]

> *Example*: A offers to sell goods to *TP*, truthfully advising him that he is the manufacturer's representative for a well-known manufacturer. The identity of the manufacturer is not disclosed. The manufacturer is a partially disclosed principal.

Typically, the partially disclosed principal becomes immediately bound to any authorized contracts entered into by the agent. However, the agent also becomes bound to the third party unless there is an agreement by the third party to look solely to the partially disclosed principal. The third party's right to hold the agent responsible on such contracts is based on the commonsense notion that the third party normally would not agree to look solely to a person whose identity is not known for performance of the contract. Thus, in the above example, if A's representation accurately describes his instructions from *P*, and *TP* places an order with A, both A and the manufacturer are personally bound to fill that order. Generally, the agent is not released from liability if *TP* elects to sue the manufacturer for nonperformance — the agent and principal are both liable on the contract, though the third party obviously is entitled to only a single recovery, and in some situations may be required to make an election as to which defendant he prefers to pursue.

A principal is *undisclosed* if the third party is not aware that the agent is acting on behalf of anyone when in fact the agent is acting on behalf of a principal. In effect, the third party is dealing with the agent as though the agent is the sole party in interest.[26] Clearly, in this situation the agent is personally liable to the third person on any contracts negotiated by him since the third party believes he is dealing directly and solely with the agent as the real party in interest. In addition, the agent has the rights and remedies available to any party to a contract, and he may, for example, settle with the third party or release that party from the contract.[27]

The undisclosed principal is also liable on the contract to the third party if the agent was acting within the scope of his *actual* authority. This

---

[25] Id. §321.

[26] Id. §322.

[27] Id. §186, §205 et seq. If the agent violates his instructions when he releases the third party from the contract, the principal is bound by the agent's action but has a claim against the agent for the loss thereby incurred.

is because of the basic agency concept that the authorized act of an agent binds the principal. It may seem a bit odd that the third party may have entered into a contract with a person he is unaware of, and be able to enforce that contract against that person, but it really is not, since that person can ignore the undisclosed principal and hold liable the agent with whom he was actually dealing. On the other hand, the right of the undisclosed principal to directly enforce a claim against the third party is circumscribed: the principal has only the rights an assignee of the contract would have, though, of course, the agent may enforce the contract directly against the third party on behalf of the undisclosed principal.

There is generally no room in the same transaction for concepts of apparent authority and an undisclosed principal. However, an agent for an undisclosed principal may have inherent or incidental power from the agency relationship to bind the principal.

§2.14 TERMINATION OF AGENCY RELATIONSHIPS

As indicated earlier, the relationship between an agent and a principal is a consensual relationship. That relationship terminates when the objective of the relationship has been achieved,[28] when the agent dies or becomes incompetent, or in a variety of other circumstances. The relationship may terminate either when the event occurs or when the other party has notice of the event, depending on how the relationship is formulated.

The relationship also terminates when the principal or agent determines to end it. However, if the relationship is based on contract, the decision to terminate it may be a breach of that contract. Nevertheless, the relationship has ended, even though contractual liability may exist for its termination. Since an inference of apparent authority may be based on the existence of prior actual authority, the termination of the relationship does not of itself eliminate the apparent authority of the agent. Notice may have to be given to third persons who may have dealt with the agent or otherwise believe that the principal has authorized the agent to act.[29]

§2.15 MANAGERIAL EMPLOYEES

A managerial employee — a high-level employee who is typically in charge of a department or division of a firm and oversees the activities of a number of lower-level employees — is technically a "servant" in the quaint

---

[28]Restatement (Second) of Agency §106 et seq.
[29]Id. §125 et seq.

nomenclature of the Restatement of Agency. Theoretically, servants are subject to the right of the master to "control the physical conduct" of the servant's performance. Servants also owe "fiduciary duties" to the master. What do these phrases mean when we are talking about a senior manager that is responsible, say, for the operation of a complex plant with hundreds of employees?

It should be apparent that such an employee is expected to use skilled judgment and discretion in managing his part of the business at a profitable level. It is very unlikely that the "master" (who may be an intangible entity such as a corporation) can oversee and direct in any meaningful way how a managerial-level employee performs his normal work. He is in fact expected to perform much as an owner would in the day-to-day management of his part of the business. This relationship creates problems of *agency cost*[30] as the managerial employee may be tempted to maximize his own personal utility rather than the utility of the owners of the business. Managerial employees lack the incentives of owners to maximize the owners' personal utility.

Employers usually attempt to assure the fidelity of managerial employees through devices that provide incentives to them to perform as though they were owners of the enterprise. Such employees may be given employment contracts that assure some tenure and security even if risks taken by the employees do not work out. Most importantly, at least part of the expected compensation of managerial employees must be based on a series of incentives. The more superior the performance, the greater the income of the employee. In order to have an effective incentive compensation system, there must be a definition of the goal that the managerial employee is to strive for, and some way of measuring how close the employee came to meeting that goal. These arrangements may be difficult to negotiate since there are serious problems of definition and measurement, particularly when other factors beyond the control of the managerial employee may increase the difficulty of achieving his goal.

Of course, it is often possible to place limits on the discretion of even managerial employees. For example, the managerial employee may be instructed that he must obtain approval from one of the owners or an even more senior manager for all transactions that involve more than x thousand dollars. It is also possible to impose external restraints by imposing procedures involving employees not under the control of the managerial employee. Inventory records may be kept by persons not under the direction

---

[30]"Agency costs" is a term coined by economists to describe the costs incurred by a principal who entrusts decision-making to an agent where the agent reaches decisions in light of his own personal preferences and desires rather than those of the principal. Agency costs may be broken down into "monitoring expenditures," "bonding expenditures," and losses incurred from misappropriations by the agent. Agency costs are reduced by various techniques, as described in the text.

of the sales manager, for example. Managerial employees may also be bonded to protect against misappropriation or theft.

Incentive programs can be created for managerial employees without necessarily utilizing formal employment contracts. However, employment contracts are very common. Lawyers are often called upon to draft or review proposed employment contracts for managerial employees, either on behalf of the firm or on behalf of the employee. In considering the terms of such a contract, it must be recognized that the interests of the employer to some extent diverge from the interests of the managerial employee. For example, the employee wishes job security, a form of tenure which assures him that he will keep his job even if things go badly. The employer, on the other hand wishes to have freedom to change managerial employees inexpensively if it loses confidence in the specific managerial employee. These conflicts are right at the surface of the negotiation and must be directly addressed by the firm. All of these methods of providing incentives and ensuring honesty involve real costs from the standpoint of the business.

In addition to managerial employees, similar problems may arise with respect to other classes of employees, particularly purchase agents and individual members of the sales force, since oversight of the activities of these employees is often difficult or impossible. Incentive compensation arrangements are very common to assure that they will exert their best efforts on behalf of their employers. Indeed, compensating sales personnel in part through commissions based on sales volume is probably the norm in most businesses.

These problems are less likely to arise in connection with lower-level employees. They are likely to be employees at will and the terms of their employment are implicit in the job title for which they are hired, or by the instructions of their immediate supervisors. There is not a great deal of discretion involved in most jobs but there is a considerable amount of direct oversight. Even so, dishonesty or theft may be difficult or impossible to discover, and it is customary to bond lower-level employees who have direct access to cash or valuable property. The lower-level employees are expected to follow instructions, work carefully but energetically, pay attention at all times, and so forth. These employees may be compensated at an hourly rate or on a per diem, weekly, or monthly basis. Many low-level employees may be compensated on a piecework basis.

§2.16 EMPLOYMENT AT WILL

Probably the most litigated employment issue is whether an employee has an express or implicit contract of employment. The issue is usually phrased as whether the employee has employment "for a term" or is merely an "employee at will." It is important, however, to understand clearly what is at issue. Even an employee with a contract of employment may be fired; the question is whether the firing was wrongful and a breach of that contract.[31] An employment contract is not enforced by specific performance but by an award of damages that may require the contract employee to mitigate damages by accepting similar employment in the same community.[32] In some instances where the employee breaks an employment contract, he may be enjoined from working elsewhere during the term of the contract. Most employees, however, are *employees at will*, which means that the contract does not include a specific term of the employment, and either party is theoretically free to terminate it at any time without liability.

> *Example*: X is hired as an employee to work in a hardware store. The owner states that he hopes that the employee will remain working at the hardware store for at least a year. The employee is an employee at will.

> *Example*: Y is hired to work as a bookkeeper to fill a job made vacant by an employee who has taken maternity leave for six months. Even though Y "is hired to fill that vacancy" he is still an employee at will.

Even if an employee is clearly hired for a specific term, the statute of frauds will in effect make that relationship an employment at will if the term extends beyond a year and there is no memorandum sufficient to satisfy the statute.

Theoretically, an employee at will may be fired for any cause or for no cause at all. However, a number of statutes protect employees against discrimination based on race, age, sex, or handicaps unrelated to job performance. These statutes provide a fair degree of protection to employees against arbitrary discharge. Labor union contracts also usually provide some protection against arbitrary firings. There may also be some natural judicial sympathy for the long-term employee who is unexpectedly laid off for business retrenchment reasons or for some completely irrational reason unconnected with his or her performance. This sympathy may lead a court to find that a specific employee was not an employee at will at all. For example, some cases have relied on statements in pension-plan brochures or other forms given to new employees to infer that after a "probationary" period, an employee has indefinite tenure, that is, can be fired only "for cause." As a

---

[31] In an employment for a term, the employee also may be fired for cause — e.g., dishonesty or incompetence. If the contract does not expressly reserve the power of the employer to fire a term employee for cause, the power nevertheless exists as an implied term in all employment contracts.

[32] Principles of contracts damages may also permit the defendant a credit for any actual earnings by the fired employee in other employment that was made possible by the release of the employee's time as a result of the breach of the employment contract by the employer.

result, one should not automatically assume that because no specific period of employment is agreed upon an employee is defenseless and can be fired at any time. On the other hand, there clearly is a legal presumption that an indefinite employment is an employment at will.

There are, of course, two sides to the employment at will issue. Sympathy for the laid off employee must be balanced against the need to give employers the economic freedom to structure or restructure their businesses to promote efficiency and profit. Unfortunately, efficiency may dictate a widespread pattern of layoffs that cause significant hardship to employees. A system of permanent employment may lead to significant inefficiencies, as may be evidenced by municipal, state, or federal governmental units in which the procedural obstacles to firing incompetent employees may prevent any person from being fired at all.

3

Proprietorships

§3.1 INTRODUCTION

This chapter deals with the simplest business form, an unincorporated proprietorship. A *proprietorship* is simply a business owned by a single individual. A business owned by a single individual may also be conducted as a corporation, with the individual being the sole shareholder of the corporation.[1] If the business is incorporated, it may be referred to as an "incorpo-

---

[1] In some states a one-owner business may also be conducted in the form of a limited liability company. See §6.13.

rated proprietorship," a "one-person corporation," or, perhaps most commonly, simply as a "corporation." The one-person corporation is discussed in Chapter 8.

§3.2 ENTREPRENEURSHIP

The owner of a proprietorship is sometimes called an entrepreneur, a neutral and more general term that implies economic ownership and control but not a specific type of business form. An *entrepreneur* is an owner of a business who is personally involved in its management and who shares in its profits or losses. Entrepreneurship combines both ownership and management. Even the smallest business may have several entrepreneurs, though probably single-entrepreneur small businesses are more common. Even the smallest business may also have passive owners who do not participate directly in the management of the business and therefore are not entrepreneurs. Passive investors in small businesses are usually contributors of capital. As firms grow in size, multiple owners, some of whom are passive investors, become more common.

§3.3 THE START-UP BUSINESS IN GENERAL

As the name suggests, a *start-up business* is a new business just getting underway, sometimes on a relatively informal basis. The prototype start-up business is the entrepreneur with a good idea attempting to translate it into a viable and profitable business.

In the prototypical start-up business, the entrepreneur is personally and actively involved in the provision of the goods or services that are the backbone of the new business. If the business develops a good reputation for reliability and quality, it is the consequence of the energy and skill of the entrepreneur. Quality control is the responsibility of the entrepreneur who is personally involved in the business. If employees are hired and trained, their activities are closely overseen by the entrepreneur. Equipment is purchased by the entrepreneur, the product is priced by the entrepreneur, and if customer problems develop, the entrepreneur is there to work them out. The success or the failure of a start-up business, in short, depends on the personal abilities of the entrepreneur in providing the goods or services of the business.

Start-up businesses may begin without any real understanding by the entrepreneur that in fact she is beginning a new business. The nine-year-old opening a lemonade stand is the traditional juvenile entrepreneur, but it is not very likely that enterprise will survive for more than a few days.

However, that lemonade stand is certainly a business, as is the paper route, the teenager cutting neighbors' grass in the summer, or the college junior tutoring a freshman for a fee. Businesses may also develop out of a hobby: the accountant who makes candlesticks in his basement in the evenings, gives them for Christmas presents, and sells a few to his friends may shortly become an entrepreneur in a start-up business. In a couple of years he may give up the practice of accountancy and go into the manufacture of candlesticks full-time.

§3.4 START-UP BUSINESSES CREATED BY FORMER EMPLOYEES

Start-up businesses may flower from a variety of vines. Many are unique and individualistic, the accountant who goes into the candlestick-making business as a result of a hobby, or the person who helps friends to redecorate houses and gradually realizes that she has a talent that strangers are willing to pay for. However, certain patterns are recurring. One very common pattern is for a person who is employed by a business eventually to leave the business and form a directly competing business. The employee may originally have accepted employment with the established business with a pre-conceived plan to "learn the ropes" and then to start her own business, in direct competition with her former employer. In other cases, satisfied customers may gradually come to rely more on the employee's skills than on the employer's in deciding to patronize the business. In seeking a better price, customers may urge the employee to do work on her own time directly with the customers rather than on behalf of her employer, even though that may be disloyal and even tortious. Before an employee starts a competing business, she may make quiet inquiries of customers to determine how many customers are willing to shift their patronage to the new business. In some instances, she may "sign them up" to contracts before launching her own business.

Significant legal problems may arise whenever an employee actually breaks off and starts a new business in direct competition with her former employer. Is she appropriating trade secrets or proprietary information that belong to the former employer? Is she using a similar name in an effort to appropriate the goodwill that the former employer has built up? Were there contractual restrictions imposed by the former employer that limit the employee from competing with her former employer? These are potentially important issues familiar to lawyers that depend entirely on the specific facts. One general observation can, however, be made: The American economy is built on an assumption of free enterprise and open competition. In the absence of very specific contractual limitations or the direct use of trade secrets or the former employer's trade name by the former employee, there is nothing to prevent the former employee from opening a competing business.

Successful small businessmen must therefore recognize the possibility that as they train new employees they are also training potential future competitors, that valued and well-treated employees may decide at some point to break off and create their own competing business. There is an incentive, therefore, to try to keep valued employees happy, perhaps with compensation incentives or even by taking them in as co-owners of the business, with all the potential problems that that may later entail. Such arrangements may encourage valued employees to remain with the firm and also induce them to exert greater efforts on behalf of the firm.

If an employee becomes a co-owner of an unincorporated business, a partnership has been created. See chapter 4.

§3.5 START-UP BUSINESSES CREATED BY "MID-CAREER" ENTREPRENEURS

Another variation of a start-up business arises when a mid-career, white collar employee who has spent many years working for a large, well-established firm leaves the security of his position and creates a business on his own. The decision may be entirely a voluntary one on the part of the employee or it may arise because the employee is unexpectedly laid off or fired, events that are quite common in periods of recession such as occurred in the early 1990s. Perhaps the employee has been offered "early retirement" with the implicit threat that he will be laid off if the early retirement offer is not accepted. Many laid off employees of course seek new white collar jobs with other businesses. Some may "downsize" by accepting employment with established small businesses that may be run by family members or friends. A few search unsuccessfully for jobs similar to the one they lost, and end up by taking hourly employment at or close to the minimum wage in order to continue to meet family obligations. However, rather than seeking another white collar job, a former employee in this situation may decide to become his own employer and either start up a business from scratch or purchase an ongoing small business, thereby becoming an instant entrepreneur.

Unfortunately, in many instances, a person in this situation does not have extensive prior experience in the practical problems of creating a start-up or running a small business; his experience is typically as an employee (albeit often a high-level employee with considerable discretion and responsibility) in larger, more bureaucratically organized firms.

Many persons in this category have built up a fair amount of financial resources — hundreds of thousands of dollars is not uncommon — and thus are able to provide substantial initial capital on their own. This capital may be from savings or investments, but most of it typically is a combination of severance payments and mandatory or permissible distributions from retirement or pension-plan funds that become available upon the termination of employment. The decision whether or not to actually withdraw these funds is complex because there are significant tax costs upon withdrawing the money and the loss of these funds is apt to be sorely felt when the employee actually retires many years later. However, it is quite common for a mid-career employee leaving his employment and starting his own business to withdraw substantially all his retirement funds and invest them in the new business, often along with substantially all his other liquid capital. Obviously, in many cases a former employee will launch his new career as an entrepreneur on a reasonably well-financed basis.

Perhaps the most serious problems faced by a person in her 40s or 50s who decides to become an entrepreneur and form a start-up business—even if the business is reasonably successful—arises from the fact the entrepreneur is likely to have a family to support, children to educate, and aged parents to care for. A steady personal cash flow is essential if family needs are to be met, something a start-up business may not be able to provide. In some instances, a spouse or other family members may have a reliable job which provides basic family support during the start-up period.

A particularly serious problem may be health insurance: an employee whose family has been protected for 25 years by employer-provided or employer-subsidized health insurance may be in for a shock when she discovers how valuable this fringe benefit is, and how expensive it is today to provide adequate private health and medical insurance. And, if the former employee's family includes an individual with serious health problems, insurance may not be available at all, or only at exorbitant premiums. In the most extreme situation, an employee may decide to remain with an employer (if that is possible) simply because of the cost of health insurance and the potentially disastrous consequences of loss of coverage. Of course, this problem may become less serious in the future if improvements in the national health care system are made.

§3.6 START-UPS BY LAWYERS

Yet another common variation is the lawyer who hangs out his shingle or who creates a break-off law firm. The most common scenario is that a partner in a law firm, after working for a decade or more in an established firm, decides to form his own firm, taking some portion of the present firm's clients with him. Several other partners and associates may decide to leave the old firm and join the new one at the same time. In the 1980s and 1990s this pattern has become so common that Professor Robert Hillman has written a book on it, originally titled Law Firm Breakups: The Law and Ethics of Grabbing and Leaving, and more modestly entitled Lawyer Mobility in a loose-leaf revised edition. Professor Hillman's introduction graphically describes the quantum change that has occurred in law firms over the last two decades:

> The traditional view of the law firm as a stable institution with an assured future is now challenged by an awareness that even the largest and most prestigious firms are fragile economic units facing a myriad of risks in their quests to survive and prosper. No longer can the law graduate join a major firm with the sanguine assumption that the firm will not experience major upheavals, turnover in lawyers, downsizing, or in extreme cases, receivership. . . . Increasingly, firms are temporary resting places for their partners. Lateral hiring, once confined largely to junior lawyers, now extends through all levels of the partnership.[2]

In recent years, there has been increasing litigation over various aspects of law firm breakups. Courts have split, for example, on the issue whether it is against public policy for law firms to include covenants not to compete in partnership agreements or to provide in partnership agreements that payments to be made after withdrawal may be reduced or eliminated if the withdrawing partner competes directly with his old firm.

In most instances, new firms are formed around one or more partners with independent practices whose practices comprise the new firm's business. Several associates go along to do the detailed work and to provide longer-range continuity for clients. The reasons why these break-offs occur are usually economic. The partners who leave feel they are being undercompensated for the contribution they make to the firm. However, personal antagonisms may be a factor, as may the constraints of large-firm practice, including conflicts of interest and the fear of personal liability for the actions of partners they may barely know.

It is less common, but by no means unknown, for one or more associates in a law firm to break off and form their own firm. One associate may end up dealing virtually exclusively with one major client. Over the years, the relationship between the associate and that client may become so close that the associate is able to leave the firm and open his own office, a one-person practice, with the major client as his principal source of business.[3] The client may transfer all its business to the associate or may continue to use both the original firm and the associate for its work. The larger firm may

---

[2]R. Hillman, Hillman on Lawyer Mobility, 1-1 to 1-3 (1995).

[3]Of course, reliance on a single client or single area of practice is dangerous since an abrupt shift by the client or an unexpected change in law may leave the attorney with substantial fixed costs but no source of income. The danger is a lack of "diversification," or more colloquially, "putting all of one's eggs in a single basket."

send small pieces of legal business that are not economic for that firm to handle to the former associate's firm. Split-offs formed in this way may have a significant capacity for permanence and growth since the associate is obviously a good lawyer to win the complete confidence of a major client.

A graduating law student may also establish a start-up business the hard way: after getting his law license, he may rent an office, hang out a "shingle," and begin the practice of law. At one time, this was an accepted method of starting a practice, particularly in smaller communities, but it has become less common in recent years. Most young lawyers today spend some time under the tutelage of more experienced lawyers before striking out on their own. Legal apprenticeship of this type is doubtless a good idea since law schools do not try to teach students the mundane and nitty-gritty details of practicing law and representing clients.[4] The recent law school graduate may not know where the courthouse is, to use a common expression.

A young lawyer may agree to work for a solo practitioner or in a firm with only one or two lawyers (which amounts pretty much to the same thing). The understanding between the young lawyer and the more senior one (or between the young lawyer and the small law firm he or she joins) may range from a contemplated lifetime commitment to an understanding that the young lawyer will move on in a year or so. Where the senior lawyer has his own clients and is approaching retirement, the understanding may be that the junior lawyer will gradually take over the practice of the more senior one.[5] Again, this pattern is probably most common in very small communities where one- or two-person law firms are the norm.

Most law students assume that lawyers are concentrated in the large cities in firms that have a significant number of lawyers. That is not really an accurate picture of law practice. A surprisingly large number of lawyers are solo practitioners or work in small law firms with less than ten attorneys. The state of Texas is a microcosm of the United States, with several major centers of population, numerous small cities and towns, and substantial farming and ranching areas. In August 1993, there were about 53,000 persons licensed to practice law in Texas (out of a total population of over 17 million). Thirty-one percent of Texas lawyers reported that they were solo practitioners; another 23 percent practiced in firms of two to five members, and an additional 9 percent were in firms of six to nine lawyers. Despite the

---

[4] The so-called McCrate Report, prepared by an American Bar Association Committee, recommends that law schools should provide more detailed and practical training in the nitty-gritty of law practice. The author personally doubts whether the implementation of this program, if approved by the practicing bar, will be successful unless there is a massive change in the composition of most law school faculties. Most law schools, of course, do currently offer some practice-oriented classes.

[5] One should not underestimate the potential problems that may arise when the financial terms under which the senior lawyer will retire are negotiated.

widespread publicity given to the huge law firms in Dallas and Houston and other large Texas cities, more than 60 percent of all Texas lawyers are either solo practitioners or practice in firms with less than ten lawyers!

§3.7 SEPARATION OF PERSONAL AND BUSINESS TRANSACTIONS

In the very smallest proprietorship, at the outset there may be little or no separation between business finances and the personal finances of the entrepreneur. The same checking account may be used for both household and business expenditures. However, if the business has any success at all, the entrepreneur will shortly find it necessary to set up financial books and records for the business separate from her personal books and records. In effect, the business begins to assume an economic existence of its own. An entrepreneur quickly realizes that mixing together business and personal transactions makes it very difficult to see how well either the business or the family is doing from a financial standpoint. And, when funds are commingled, it is very irritating, to say the least, for the spouse of the entrepreneur to discover that the money being set aside for a vacation has been innocently spent for business supplies.

Many people today keep their personal financial records on their computers, using one of a number of user-friendly personal finance programs that are available at a surprisingly low cost. For such persons, the creation of separate accounts for the business simply involves creating a set of new accounts within their finance program, followed by the opening of separate checking accounts at the local bank. Doubtless in many instances, the growth of a start-up business is the first indication to a person that he or she should begin keeping records on a computerized basis.

This segregation of business transactions and business assets from personal ones usually occurs early in the life of start-up businesses. The opening of a separate checking account for the business is often the first tangible step of this separation. Almost from the outset of the smallest start-up, it is viewed by the entrepreneur as an economic entity in some sense distinct from his or her family or persona, with its own cash sources and cash needs.

§3.8 THE ADDITION OF EMPLOYEES

A very important step in the life of a proprietorship occurs when the business takes on its first outside employee. This may be a costly and risky business decision for a new business: for every $1,000 of income paid to an employee in 1992, it has been estimated that the employer incurred additional costs of about $400 in the form of tax obligations imposed by state and federal law and administrative costs.

The entrepreneur must obtain an "employer identification number" (EID) from the Internal Revenue Service. With the addition of the first part-time employee, the entrepreneur becomes enmeshed in the complex federal and state rules applicable to employers generally, including computation of Federal Insurance Contribution Act payments and amounts to be withheld from employee paychecks for federal and state income taxes. Employees must be given W-4 forms to determine the level of withholding required of each employee. Each employer in effect becomes a collection agent for the Internal Revenue Service and state tax authorities with an obligation to make bi-weekly remittances of these amounts to the appropriate authorities.[6] In addition, the entrepreneur is responsible for preparing quarterly reports of payroll and unemployment taxes, overtime pay earned by employees, and the maintenance of various tax and employment-related records. At the end of the year, federal and state employment tax returns must be prepared, and each employee must be given his or her W-2 form. These various requirements are complex and require careful recordkeeping; in most instances, they require professional assistance for satisfactory compliance, since it is not uncommon otherwise for an entrepreneur to spend more than four hours per week on tax related paperwork over and above the operation of her business. Outsourcing these functions to third parties for a fee is very common. Perhaps our accountant-turned-candlestick-maker might be able to do this paperwork in less time, given his earlier experience. But that begs the more basic question, "Is this the most efficient and productive use of the entrepreneur's time?"

A virtually complete set of books and records for the business distinct from the entrepreneur's personal affairs is almost certain to follow shortly after the addition of the first employee, if it has not occurred previously.

The line between employees and owners (or potential owners) of a business is sometimes not clear cut. There is a tradition in some families in the United States of family members working in the family business more as a matter of family responsibility than as employment. The family-run ethnic restaurant or grocery store is a traditional example, but in many small or start-up businesses, family members may "help out" from time to time without compensation and without becoming regular participants in the business. In many businesses, sons and daughters who work in the business may not be viewed as employees at all, but as partial owners, or as potential owners or inheritors of the business. However, that is probably not the typical pattern in small businesses in the United States. Young people tend to be restless and to desire funds of their own. Usually a child who begins

---

[6]I.R.C. §6672 imposes a one hundred percent penalty on persons who fail to pay over amounts so withheld. This is an effective, punitive sanction to assure compliance with this requirement.

working in the family business is treated as an employee no different in principle from employees who are not family members. This also makes sense from an income tax standpoint, since total tax obligations of the family are reduced if the number of taxpaying members is increased.

§3.9 THE GROWTH OF A START-UP BUSINESS

Assume that a start-up business is begun by a single person, perhaps the hypothetical accountant who goes into a successful candlestick-making business. At first he makes candlesticks by hand, cutting metal in his basement workshop, and shaping and welding it by hand as he has always done. As the business grows, the accountant gives up his accounting practice and devotes his full attention to candlestick making. Let us further assume that he opens a small retail candlestick shop down the street from his home; he is in business.

As the business grows, it quickly becomes apparent that the accountant is unable to manufacture enough candlesticks to meet the demand. What should he do? The most obvious suggestion is to hire people to help him in the manufacturing and in the selling. That may well be the best solution. However, it is quite possible that the accountant can take advantage of specialized business entities on a contract basis to perform much of the work he now does by hand. That may be much cheaper than hiring employees, with all the costs and recordkeeping that entails.

There are firms that specialize in metal cutting and metal shaping. Perhaps one of these firms could supply pieces of wrought iron shaped to the accountant's specifications by the hundreds or thousands, for a nominal price. A welding firm three blocks away may be able to weld hundreds of candlesticks together, again following the specifications of the accountant, in a few hours. Alternatively, the accountant might contract with an experienced welder who is interested in "moonlighting" to do the welding in his own basement during the evening hours, saving the accountant hours of work each week. That welder would be an "indepenent contractor," not an "employee." This kind of specialization of function permits tremendous improvement of efficiency over handwork often without the addition of any employees at all and explains why the American economy today bears no relationship to the pre-industrial revolution era.

The accountant may also find methods of distribution that are more efficient and much less expensive than operating a retail store that requires the hiring of a salesperson for at least 40 hours per week. Perhaps the finished candlesticks could be sold "on consignment" to quality retail stores that attract many customers. To the extent the candlesticks sell, the accountant will receive the established retail price minus a fee for the store that displays the candlesticks and handles the details of the sales transaction. Candlesticks that do not sell may be returned to the accountant. Perhaps a mail or telephone ordering system might be substituted for the retail store. Perhaps the accountant is able to take advantage of the increasingly commercial use of the Internet and advertise his wares by electronic communication on a worldwide basis. Thus, growth of a business may not require a proportional increase in employment; growth may often be handled by improving the efficiency of the manufacturing and selling processes.

Until relatively recently, economic theory paid little attention to the internal organization of a firm. It assumed that a firm was composed of some combination of workers, machinery, technology, equipment, and managers. However, the firm itself was viewed as a sort of black box into which various inputs were made at one end and sales of various products came out the other. The firm succeeded or failed depending on whether the manager was able to organize the various inputs in a way that produced the desired output at a profit. Recent analysis indicates that the principal entrepreneurial function is to select the best among alternative combinations of internal efforts and market-available products and services. Of course, entrepreneurs, like everyone else, live in a world of uncertainty. People may make wrong decisions; third-party suppliers that appear competent may make promises they cannot keep. But entrepreneurs, driven by the desire to maximize profits, must select from both internal and external sources of inputs if the business is to succeed in the modern economy.

The services of the person who manages a business is itself an input. Normally, in a small business these services are provided by the owner. However, this is not necessarily so. The owner of the business may hire a manager to provide these services, though some oversight and auditing to assure honesty will always be required.

§3.10 THE LACK OF LEGAL SEPARATION IN A PROPRIETORSHIP

Some degree of economic separation between the personal affairs of a proprietor and her business usually occurs relatively early in the life of a new business. Even a tiny proprietorship normally has its own trade name, bank account, tax employer identification number, and other distinguishing characteristics that separate it from the proprietor's personal economic activities. From a legal standpoint, however, in a proprietorship there is no separation between personal and business affairs.

Legally, the proprietor owns all the property utilized by the business, she is individually responsible for all of the business's debts, and she is personally taxed on the income of the proprietorship. If the business has employees, she (and not the business) is the employer and is responsible for their wages. She is also responsible for their actions under the general principles of agency law discussed in Chapter 2. If the business acquires property or casualty insurance policies, she is the proper named insured. If someone wants to sue the business, the proprietor is the appropriate defendant and the person upon whom papers may be served. Service of process may also be made, however, upon an agent of the proprietor. If the business wants to sue someone else, suit must usually be brought in the name of the proprietor. And so forth.

§3.11 ASSUMED NAMES

Things are sometimes more complicated than they first appear. A proprietor may conduct the business either in her own name or under a trade or assumed name. Let us assume that Mary Jones, the proprietress of a small beauty shop, decides to do business as the Ashton-Smith School of Beauty. Is there anything wrong with that? The black letter rule is that as long as the name does not deceive the public, is not misleadingly similar to the name of a competing business, or is not otherwise used in a fraudulent or deceptive manner, Mary Jones may do business under any name she wishes. And that should probably include the name Ashton-Smith School of Beauty, even though Mary Jones is neither an Ashton nor a Smith. There are a few legal restrictions on the use of specific words in trade names; in most states; for example, terms such as Corporation, Incorporated, or Inc. may not be used because they falsely imply that the business is incorporated. The word Company does not usually carry this implication, and generally may be used by a proprietorship without restriction. Most states prohibit or limit the use of the words Bank or Insurance for similar reasons. Other trade names may be misleading because they imply that the proprietor possesses a license or professional degree that in fact she does not possess or that the business is engaged in activities which in fact it is not engaged in. However, none of these limitations appear to apply to Mary Jones' use of the name Ashton-Smith School of Beauty.[7]

An assumed or trade name may help to increase the appearance of separation between the business and the proprietor, and may improve the business's image and help revenues. Certainly, the name Ashton-Smith School of Beauty has a better cachet in the minds of many than the unimaginative name Mary Jones' Beauty Shoppe, or something like that.

Many states have "assumed name" statutes that require a public disclosure of the identity of a person conducting business in an assumed or trade name, but compliance with those statutes is simple and straightforward. A

---

[7]Is there anything inappropriate about an ordinary business operation calling itself a school? Would a person think that the Ashton-Smith School of Beauty was training beauticians? That there were at least two owners? Even if a person might be misled, would that person be injured by the potential deception of calling a beauty shop a school? The answer to all these questions is probably no.

certificate setting forth the real names of the parties doing business under an assumed name must be filed with the county clerk or some other public office. An unhappy customer of Mary Jones wanting to sue the Ashton-Smith School of Beauty might check the public assumed name filings to determine who is the owner. Doubtless many small businesses adopt assumed or trade names but fail to file assumed name certificates because of ignorance of the requirements. State statutes may make a failure to file a petty or minor misdemeanor criminal offense, and additional penalties may be imposed for an intentional failure to file. However, the level of enforcement appears to vary from low to nonexistent. Texas adopts a somewhat different scheme to enforce its assumed name statute: persons who fail to file assumed name certificates may not utilize the judicial system affirmatively to enforce claims against another until they comply with the statute. They may also be required to pay the legal fees and costs of plaintiffs who may have brought suit against the business not having the benefit of information as to who the real owners of the business are.

Often proprietorships use assumed names but also routinely disclose who the real owner is. Many proprietorships in fact do business and enter into contracts in the form Mary Jones dba Ashton-Smith School of Beauty. *Dba* (or d/b/a) stands for "doing business as." In this way, both the proprietor and the trade name under which she is conducting business appear on most business transactions.

A business operating under an assumed name often enters into transactions only in its assumed name rather than in the name of the owner. Deliveries of beauty supplies may be made to the Ashton-Smith School of Beauty without any reference at all to the name of the owner, Mary Jones. The supplier may not even know who the owner of the Ashton-Smith School of Beauty is. But that does not matter. Mary Jones is still the purchaser, making purchases through one or more authorized agents. She is therefore personally liable on the obligation to pay for those beauty supplies.

In a Texas case, a plaintiff brought suit against Holberg & Co., a proprietorship owned by Robert E. Holberg, naming as the defendant only the business in its assumed name. After obtaining a judgment for over $90,000, the plaintiff moved to add Robert E. Holberg's name individually to the judgment. The trial court did so and Robert E. Holberg appealed on the ground there was no evidence indicating he was personally responsible for the debt. Not only did the appellate court affirm the trial court's action (because of the legal identity between a proprietor and his business), but it also sanctioned the defendant's attorney for filing a frivolous appeal taken "for delay and without sufficient cause."[8] This case is a graphic illustration of the basic legal proposition that a proprietorship does not have a separate legal identity from the proprietor, even if it has its own name.

---

[8]Holberg & Co. v. Citizens National Assurance Co., 856 S.W.2d 515 (Tex. App. Houston (1st Dist.) 1993).

§3.12 THE PROPRIETOR'S INTEREST IN BUSINESS ASSETS

As the sole owner of the business, a proprietor is of course entitled to the fruits of the proprietorship; that is, its income and cash flow. Distributive transactions between the proprietor and the business may be very informal. For example, a proprietor may simply empty the cash drawer of the business to pay for her personal vacation if that does not disrupt business operations and appropriate records are maintained. Similarly, the proprietor may use business assets for her personal benefit. She might decide, for example, to take out a loan secured by a security interest on property used in the business and then use the proceeds of that loan to finance a personal gambling trip to Las Vegas.

   The proprietor's power to use business assets has certain limitations. She may not hide or dispose of property in transactions that are designed to defraud creditors. Such transactions are prohibited in most states by the Uniform Fraudulent Transfers Act or similar statutes or common law rules. She also may not use her power over business assets to transmute personal expenses into business expenses for federal or state income tax purposes. For example, the proprietor of a flower shop and greenhouse might arrange to have fresh flowers delivered to her residence each morning. For income tax purposes, the cost of those flowers should not be viewed as a business expense any more than emptying the cash drawer for a personal vacation should be viewed as a business expense.

§3.13 MORE ON THE PROPRIETOR'S PERSONAL RESPONSIBILITY FOR BUSINESS OBLIGATIONS

As indicated above, for liability purposes a proprietorship is not a separate entity and the proprietor is personally liable for all business debts. There is no difference in parity of treatment between unsecured personal obligations and unsecured business obligations of the proprietor. For example, a proprietor may borrow money on her personal credit either for personal use (e.g., a family vacation) or to raise capital for use in the business. It is not uncommon for struggling proprietors to obtain cash advances on personal credit cards and use the proceeds to pay pressing business obligations. Such advances are unsecured loans, and if not repaid, the lender may collect upon the loan by proceeding against either personal or business assets without regard to whether the loans were originally used for business or personal purposes.[9] Loans may also be obtained solely in the name of, and on the

---

[9]Certain personal assets may be exempt from seizure for either personal or business debts. Many states, for example, exempt a homestead and certain personal property from

credit of, the Ashton-Smith School of Beauty but Mary Jones is also individually liable on such loans whether or not her name appears on the note or whether she actually negotiated the loan and signed the note. That is, of course, precisely Holberg's case.

If a business fails, the proprietor is liable without limit for all the general business debts. Her personal assets—life insurance policies, real estate, furniture, and what have you—may be seized by business creditors (unless the property is exempt from seizure by general creditors by reason of state statute). The collapse of the business therefore often leads to the collapse of the proprietor's personal finances shortly thereafter.

The credit history of the business may appear on the proprietor's personal credit report or it may have its own report in the name of the business (if the business is well established and has had a significant number of reported transactions). If a business obligation remains unpaid, however, the creditor is free to bring suit against the proprietor individually even if it relied solely on the reported credit history of the business. The business cannot itself declare bankruptcy since it is not a separate legal entity; the proprietor must declare personal bankruptcy if she wishes to be discharged from the unpaid business obligations. If a bankruptcy petition is filed by the proprietor it covers her individual assets and liabilities as well as the business's assets and liabilities.

§3.14 SECURED CREDIT

Many suppliers of goods do not realistically expect to go after the proprietor's personal assets if the business fails. They may sell to proprietorships on an open account basis, planning to write off any losses that occur if the proprietorship cannot pay. Or, they may sell to small businesses on credit secured by a lien or security interest on the goods being purchased. Often, the only name on the invoice is the trade or assumed name of the purchaser. While the owner of the business is personally liable on these obligations as well, the secured creditor as a practical matter is likely to look only to the goods securing the loan without trying to levy upon the other assets of the proprietor. The reason for this is that if the proprietor is unable to meet her business obligations, there is likely to be a line of unsecured creditors trying to get satisfaction from her unpledged business and personal assets; a secured creditor has no priority at all with respect to those assets. The cost of "getting in line" to share in the proprietor's other assets may exceed the slight

---

seizure for debts. States may prohibit garnishment for wages, but that is not likely to help a proprietor since she is the owner of the business, not an employee, and as such, any amounts paid to her from the business are not based on an employment relationship.

additional benefit to the secured creditor who has significant protection from his security interest in the specific goods themselves.

The creation of a security interest in goods is quite simple. It usually involves the execution of a security agreement and the filing of a financing statement as required by Article 9 of the Uniform Commercial Code.

Another way of looking at these business practices of creditors is to view them as assuming a certain level of small business defaults in their pricing and electing not to seek personal recoveries from the proprietors. If they can recover the goods or the proceeds from the sale of the goods, so much the better.

§3.15 NONRECOURSE LOANS

A creditor of course may agree to look only to the assets of the business for repayment of its loan and voluntarily give up its right to seek a personal recovery from the proprietor. This is known as a nonrecourse loan and is not very common in normal commercial transactions (even though the practice of many secured creditors described in the previous section essentially creates a de facto nonrecourse loan). Nonrecourse loans are common in commercial real estate transactions, at least during boom periods.

A nonrecourse loan may be effected either by a provision in the transactional documents themselves or by using a "straw party" to execute loan documents that give the creditor a security interest in the business assets. A *straw party* is a person without financial resources who agrees (usually for a nominal fee) to lend his or her name to a transaction, including signing liability-creating documents. A corporation without substantial assets is a perfect straw party, and may be created specifically for that purpose. The willingness of a creditor to grant a nonrecourse loan depends on economic conditions and the assets available in the proprietorship; it is unlikely that trade creditors dealing with an average proprietorship would be willing to voluntarily release the proprietor even if they have no intention of actually pursuing her if the business fails. After all, why should a creditor voluntarily let the debtor off the hook? It may encourage fraud or flimflam on the part of the proprietor, and there is no benefit to the creditor in doing so. Creditors normally will refuse to voluntarily limit their rights unless they receive some substantial benefit in return.

§3.16 OTHER ISSUES RELATING TO THE LEGAL STATUS OF A PROPRIETORSHIP

The principle that a proprietorship is not a separate legal entity is quite consistently followed. If the business becomes involved in litigation, the proprietor is the appropriate plaintiff; if the business is sued, the proprietor is the proper defendant. Procedural statutes or rules of court may set forth the appropriate manner to name a proprietorship and its owner as a defendant. For example, in litigation involving a proprietorship it is customary in many jurisdictions to use the *dba* (doing business as) designation when bringing suit on a business obligation: suit may be filed against Mary Jones dba Ashton-Smith School of Beauty.

A proprietorship may have to obtain local permits to engage in specific businesses or to occupy leased space for commercial purposes. These permits must be applied for by the proprietor; they are usually formally issued in the dba form, though sometimes they may be issued in the name of the proprietor individually, or in the assumed name of the business without a dba notation. It really does not matter. If the proprietorship is engaged in a professional practice such as law, medicine, dentistry, or accounting, both the proprietor and each person having responsibility for providing professional services must be licensed.

By and large, a proprietorship is a private business. There are no general disclosure obligations, no mandatory public reports, no requirements that permission be obtained before a new office or facility is opened, and so forth. Of course, a proprietor must comply with all general statutes involving employees, the purchase and sale of restricted products, and so forth. A proprietorship that conducts a pharmacy or a gun shop must comply with the various legal requirements applicable to such businesses. And so forth.

A proprietorship may open a new office or facility in another state, without obtaining permission or qualifying to transact business. A corporation, on the other hand, may be required to obtain permission to transact business in the second state. Opening an office in another state may subject the proprietor to suit in both states and she may have to file an assumed name certificate in the new state. She may also become liable for state income taxes in the second state and therefore have to file tax returns in the second state.

§3.17 PROPRIETORSHIP EMPLOYEES

A proprietor may employ one or more persons to work in the business. The proprietor is not herself an employee; she is the owner. She may not participate in tax-favored retirement or benefit plans for her employees. For tax purposes, she is *self-employed*. If participation in these plans is important to her, she may be able to become an employee by incorporating the business and hiring herself as an employee.[10]

A proprietorship is usually managed by the proprietor and employees

---

[10]See §8.18.

are hired to assist the proprietor under her direct supervision. However, an employee may be hired as a general manager to direct the affairs while the proprietor is away from the business. Further, the proprietor may hire a general manager and in effect delegate the entire operation of the business to that employee. This may occur when the proprietor owns and operates several independent businesses; however, usually in this situation the proprietor retains some oversight and general review in all the businesses she owns. Managerial employees who are not closely supervised may seek to pursue their selfish interests rather than the interests of the proprietor. The agency problems created by the role of managerial employees apply with equal force to proprietorships and to other business forms.

When a proprietor concludes that she no longer wishes to operate and own a business she may simply close it down. However, employees may desire to continue the business, in effect offering to buy out the proprietor's interest in the business. Assuming that a price can be agreed upon, a further problem arises. Usually, the employees will lack the ready capital to purchase the business for cash so that some kind of deferred payout of the purchase price must be negotiated, with the source of the payments to the former proprietor being from the expected future profits of the enterprise. In effect, the former proprietor and her employees enter into a type of profitsharing agreement that extends over several years. If the business does not do well under the new owners, it is likely that the former proprietor will not receive her expected payments, though she may be able to take the business back if she retained a security interest and the business is still viable. A major issue in this situation is the extent of the former proprietor's responsibility for post-sale obligations. It is relatively easy for a court to recast the transaction as a co-ownership of the business rather than as a sale, with the likely result that the former proprietor may be liable both for ordinary business obligations and for possible tort liabilities.

When employees are working for a sometimes-absent proprietor, there is little incentive for them to maximize their efforts. However, restructuring the ownership so that the employees have an opportunity to own the business outright creates strong incentives on the part of the former employees to make the business a success.

§3.18 THE TAXATION OF A PROPRIETORSHIP

A proprietorship is not a separate taxable entity. Its income or loss is reported on the proprietor's personal income tax return. For example, if a proprietor files a joint return with his or her spouse, the business income or loss of each proprietorship owned by either or both of them must be included in that joint return.

The manner of reporting the income and expenses of a proprietorship is interesting because it reflects a pragmatic compromise between the legal view that a proprietorship is not a separate entity from its owner and the economic view that the proprietorship's financial affairs should not be inter-mixed with the proprietor's personal affairs. The Internal Revenue Code requires an individual taxpayer who is also an entrepreneur to file the long-form personal income tax return — the form 1040. The Internal Revenue Code also requires a separate tax form, Schedule C, to be prepared to record the gain or loss from each business owned by the taxpayer. Schedule C must be attached to the taxpayer's form 1040 and the income or loss of the proprietorship is added to or subtracted from the proprietor's other income in order to determine her final liability to Uncle Sam. A separate Schedule C must be filed for each business. State income taxation works much the same way (though many states base their tax on the taxpayer's federal tax return and do not require a completely separate accounting of income or loss).

In the modern era, adequate record-keeping is an essential ingredient to keeping the entrepreneur out of serious tax trouble. Schedule C requires a detail of reporting that would be difficult to meet if personal and business transactions were commingled. A considerably simpler form, the Schedule C-EZ, is available for the very smallest business that has no employees and less than $25,000 in gross receipts.

The business income reported on Schedule C is not subject to the income tax withholding requirements most readers are familiar with from their employment experience. Rather, the Internal Revenue Code requires the entrepreneur to file quarterly declarations of estimated tax, and to make the payment of estimated tax each quarter reflected on that declaration. The Code also imposes substantial penalties on a taxpayer who is required to file quarterly declarations and fails to do so. These penalties cannot be avoided simply by paying the entire tax amount due when the form 1040 is filed.

Every entrepreneur operating a sole proprietorship must also take into account the requirements of the Self Employment Contributions Act of 1954, imposing a tax on Schedule C income equal (in 1995) to 12.4 percent of proprietorship income up to $61,200 for old age survivors and disability insurance (OASI) and an additional uncapped 2.3 percent for Medicare. If the entrepreneur is also an employee of another firm, the OASI tax is ap-plied first against the salary of the employee and the proprietorship income is taxed only to the extent the salary is less than $61,200.

The technical rules in the Internal Revenue Code strongly encourage the careful separation and reporting of business income and expenses on Schedule C rather than mixing them in with personal income and employ-ment-related deductions. A taxpayer may simultaneously be an employee of one business and a proprietor of another business. Indeed, this happens all the time by persons who are "moonlighters" and run their own business at night rather than holding a second job. It also happens in joint returns when one spouse is an employee and the other is a proprietor of a proprietorship. The tax laws permit an employee to deduct certain employment-related expenses from her income — for example, the cost of uniforms or of driving a personally owned motor vehicle by a salesman in connection with his employment.

These types of expenses are deductible on Schedule B (personal deductions) rather than Schedule C, and are deductible only to the extent they exceed 2 percent of adjusted gross income. They are different from the expenses deductible on Schedule C because they are deductions that relate to the taxpayer's employment rather than to her business. Deduction on Schedule C is always preferable to deduction on Schedule B because most Schedule C expenses may be deducted directly from Schedule C income, dollar for dollar,[11] while Schedule B deductions are subject to the 2 percent floor. Further, Schedule B deductions are folded into the standard deduction and are lost if that deduction is elected; Schedule C deductions are not subject to either of these limitations.

Treating a Schedule C expense as a personal deduction and listing it on Schedule B may therefore result in a higher tax bill than treating the item correctly. In some instances, specific expenses may arguably be listed on either Schedule B or Schedule C. The line between the two may not be clear or the expense may relate both to employment and outside business. Sophisticated taxpayers place such doubtful expenses on Schedule C rather than Schedule B in order to avoid the Schedule B floor.

Practically all adults today (and most children too, for that matter) have social security numbers. These numbers are used by employers to report salary and wages that have been paid to individual taxpayers. They are also used by payers of interest, dividends, and other kinds of distributions when reporting such payments to individual taxpayers on 1099 forms. (The Internal Revenue Service avoids a lot of convenient "forgetting" by taxpayers by matching these 1099s with the reported payments of interest, dividends, and distributions by individuals on their personal income tax returns.)

A business proprietor should not use his or her social security number for business purposes; rather he or she should apply for a separate *employer identification number* (or EIN) to record transactions involving the business. An EIN must be obtained if the proprietorship has employees to whom salary or wages are paid, since the proprietor must withhold funds for employment and income taxes from salary payments, pay them over periodi-

---

[11]If Schedule C expenses exceed Schedule C income, the loss so created may be used to offset other taxable income of the taxpayer.

cally to the Internal Revenue Service, and report the payments to the IRS. A proprietor may also be required to pay taxes imposed by state law for unemployment compensation plans and other programs, to pay for overtime work as required by statute, to provide workers' compensation protection, and so forth.

Some tax advisers recommend that proprietors incorporate their businesses because that creates a much clearer line of separation between transactions that relate to the business and transactions that relate to the taxpayers' employment income and expense. Such incorporated proprietorships may usually elect S corporation tax treatment so that there is no difference in the amount of tax owed following incorporation.[12]

These various tax and related obligations usually require a proprietor to obtain professional assistance in setting up books and records of account, and when employees are hired, assistance in preparing the required tax forms and making tax payments. Much of the separation between business and personal transactions undoubtedly is a result of the fairly complex rules imposed by the tax laws and by the employment-related statutes.

[12]For a description of the S corporation election, see §9.6.

4

General Partnerships

§4.1 INTRODUCTION

A *partnership* is a logical extension of a proprietorship: it is simply an unincorporated business of which there is more than one owner.[1] The owners are of course called "partners." A partnership is sometimes called a "general partnership" to distinguish it from the limited partnership discussed in Chapter 5.[2] Even though the logical extension from one owner to several owners may seem a minor or trivial change, in fact it is the cause of a substantial increase in complexity in the partnership relation as compared to the sole proprietorship.

Partnerships are a very common business form found in every area of the American economy. They vary from the two person "handshake" arrangement by high school students to share a newspaper delivery route after school hours to immense accounting firms that have offices in hundreds of cities and towns across the United States.[3] Law firms also have traditionally conducted business in the form of general partnerships, though important alternative forms of business enterprise for legal practice have surfaced in the last half of this century.[4] Most partnerships are relatively small enterprises with a few partners, but there are also many partnerships with hundreds of partners. Law firms and accounting firms are the principal examples of very large firms that historically have been conducted as general partnerships.

The partnership is the default relationship that arises when two or more persons decide to go into a business together without specifically con-

---

[1] Section 6(1) of the Uniform Partnership Act (1914) states that a partnership "is an association of two or more persons to carry on as co-owners a business for profit."

[2] There has been a proliferation of partnership-type forms created during the 1990s. In addition to the traditional limited partnership discussed in Chapter 5, they include limited liability partnerships and limited liability limited partnerships (both discussed in Chapter 7), and limited liability companies (discussed in Chapter 6).

[3] Many accounting firms have elected to become limited liability partnerships since 1993. Historically, however, all the major accounting firms were general partnerships.

[4] In addition to the modified partnership forms discussed in note 2, law firms in most states may also conduct their business in the form of professional corporations or professional associations (discussed in §8.40).

sidering or designating the business form. Thus, if two or more persons agree that they will create a start-up business on the basis of a handshake, a general partnership will have been formed. One important attribute of the general partnership form of business is that each partner is personally liable for all obligations of the partnership.

The previous chapter describes a single proprietor creating a start-up business on a very informal and tentative basis. Many start-up businesses consisting of two or more persons are created in a similar manner. However, that is often not the case. Because several different owners are involved, it is likely that the roles of individual owners will be specifically addressed. One individual may have the basic idea, a second may provide the start-up capital, the third may provide services — the "sweat equity" — to make the business a success, and so forth. Typically, these roles, and the profitsharing rights to be assigned to each participant, will be the subject of negotiation and bargaining before the venture commences. The result of this negotiation is a business plan that clearly describes the rights and responsibilities of each person. Such a plan may be a relatively formal written document prepared by a lawyer, but it also may be a sketchy memorandum written on a paper napkin, or even an entirely oral understanding.

If the amount of capital being invested is substantial — as may be the case, for example, in a manufacturing start-up — the business plan is usually a formal document that considers specifically how the necessary capital is to be raised, how and where the product is to be manufactured, and how it is to be distributed. In such a start-up, at least some of the participants are usually sophisticated in a business sense, and will insist that lawyers be involved at the outset of the planning process. A commercial supplier of capital will also insist on reviewing a relatively detailed business plan that describes the business in sufficient detail to indicate how borrowed funds will be repaid before approving a loan application.[5] In these situations, extensive planning takes place before the start-up opens its doors and arrangements are formalized through one or more contract documents. Where one participant in a start-up negotiation is represented by a lawyer, usually all participants ultimately find it necessary also to obtain independent legal advice. At one time, it was common for a lawyer to act as "attorney for the situation," and represent all interests in a business. More sophisticated articulation of codes of ethics make it clear that that time has passed.

---

[5] Such a plan will usually address specifically the question of who is to be responsible for the repayment of those funds if the business fails and is unable to repay them.

A. *BASIC PRINCIPLES*

§4.2 THE COMPLEXITY OF GENERAL PARTNERSHIPS

In a proprietorship, the owner calls all the shots and receives all the fruits of the endeavor. In a general partnership, there is more than one owner, and some principles must be established for determining what the rights and duties of the partners are with respect to each other, and what the rights of third persons are with respect to one or more of the partners. If the partners do not reach express agreement on these issues, their relationship will be governed by the default rules provided by the state partnership statute. These default rules may not be ideal for a partnership.

Traditional partnership issues that do not arise in a proprietorship include: What property and/or services are each to contribute? How are the profits of the business to be divided? What are the obligations of individual partners to each other with respect to disclosure? With respect to sharing and use of property? To what extent do the actions of one partner bind the other partners? What rules are to be applied when the venture comes to an end? How is the venture to be taxed under the Internal Revenue Code? If it becomes insolvent, may the venture seek bankruptcy protection without involving the individual partners? All of these issues arise because of the existence of multiple owners of the business.

While a partnership is inherently a much more complex business form than a single person running a proprietorship, the most basic characteristic of an unincorporated proprietorship — that the proprietor is personally responsible for all business obligations — is carried over to a general partnership. Each partner is liable to third persons for all business obligations of the partnership, a fact that partners in several large and prestigious law firms have been unpleasantly reminded of in the 1990s.[6]

In addition to the general liability for partnership obligations, there are six other important economic or business characteristics of a partnership that should be mentioned at the outset.

1. A partnership is a consensual arrangement that may be varied over a broad range as the participants agree. This concept is implicit in

---

[6]There have been several well-publicized failures of major law firms in this decade in which firm liabilities significantly exceeded firm assets. For example, the Boston firm of Gaston and Snow decided to dissolve since potential firm liabilities exceeded firm assets by $50 million. Presumably, each partner of Gaston and Snow was required to make contributions toward this deficit in the future. See §4.14.

the widely quoted statement that "the partnership agreement is the law for that partnership." The partnership agreement may be written or oral. The partnership statutes enacted in virtually every state serve two basic functions: They provide certain outside parameters or rules that may not be altered by agreement, and they provide a set of default principles that are applicable to the extent the partnership agreement does not deal expressly with some facet of the specific partnership relation. An example of an outside parameter that may not be varied by agreement among the partners is that all partners are liable to third parties for partnership obligations. An example of a default rule that may be varied by agreement is the rule that partners share equally in the profits of the partnership.

2. Each partner is an agent of the partnership with power to bind the partnership to obligations within the scope of the business of the partnership.

3. Each partner owes fiduciary duties to each other partner. A partnership involves a relationship of trust and confidence among partners, and courts do not hesitate to enforce duties arising from this relationship when the parties have a falling out.

4. A person cannot be compelled to remain a partner against his will. Each partner has an inherent power at any time to dissolve the partnership and to have his or her interest be valued and be paid that amount by the partnership. Exercise of this inherent power, however, may be a breach of the partnership agreement, possibly leading to liability for damages.

5. A person cannot be admitted as a partner in a partnership without the consent of the other partners. The power of partners to choose who may participate with them in the partnership is sometimes described by the Latin phrase, *delectus personae*. To some extent, the principle of delectus personae may be modified by express partnership agreements. In large partnerships, for example, the partnership agreement may provide that persons may be admitted as partners by the vote of some stated percentage of the partners. The objection of a minority of the partners may not be sufficient under such a provision to block the entry of the new partner, however; an existing partner strongly opposed to the entry of a specific new partner may exercise his or her inherent power to leave the partnership.

6. A partner may assign his financial interest in the partnership to a third person. That person does not become a partner, but merely becomes entitled to whatever financial rights the former partner had.

§4.3 SOURCES OF PARTNERSHIP LAW

The partnership is an ancient form of doing business, traceable back to prehistoric times. For most of history, the rights and duties of partners were not defined by statute but by common law, and in England, by the special rules applicable to commercial enterprises developed during the medieval period, commonly known as law merchants. Partnership law primarily deals with the rights and duties of partners among themselves and only secondarily with the relationship of the partners and the partnership to the outside world. While the roots of partnership law are basically common law in origin, most of the law of partnership that is discussed in law school courses today (and in this chapter) is statutory in origin. These statutes are based on the well-established common law of partnership, though they modify the common law in specific respects.

The law of partnership was largely codified in the United States by the 1914 Uniform Partnership Act, though some areas of partnership law are still governed by common law principles. The 1914 Uniform Partnership Act achieved almost total acceptance and was enacted in virtually every state.[7] Beginning in about 1980, the limitations of that ancient and venerable statute became recognized, and several states amended their statutes to depart from the UPA in significant respects.

In 1994, the National Conference of Commissioners on Uniform State Laws (NCCUSL), after considerable effort and controversy, approved a new Uniform Partnership Act designed to "modernize" the 1914 version of that statute. The old UPA is referred to hereafter as "UPA (1914)" and the new statute as "UPA (1994)."

UPA (1994) unquestionably modernizes the law of partnership in significant respects, and may well gain gradual ascendancy as states amend their partnership statutes. However, it has been criticized on a number of relatively technical matters, and some scholars have recommended that it not be adopted by states in the form it was approved. Much of the criticism has come from an ad hoc committee of the Business Law Section of the American Bar Association that monitored the process of the NCCUSL committee charged with drafting the new statute. This criticism should not be dismissed lightly, since the ABA committee consisted of attorneys with extensive experience in partnership law while the NCCUSL committee was drawn from a diverse constituency, more versed perhaps in the general pro-

---

[7] The only state that did not adopt the UPA (1914) was Louisiana. Illustrative of the complete acceptance of this statute is the fact that there is virtually no case law on the "choice of law" question in partnership litigation. A partnership originally formed in New York, for example, that opened offices in Dallas, Phoenix, and Chicago would find the partnership law in each state to be essentially identical and there was no need to determine the law of which specific state governed issues arising in that partnership.

cess of drafting uniform legislation than in the intricacies and complexities of partnership law.[8] It is doubtful that UPA (1994) will ever receive the same degree of virtually unanimous acceptance that UPA (1914) received. In the discussion that follows, the principal emphasis is on UPA (1914), since that is "the law" in the overwhelming majority of states,[9] but the innovations of UPA (1994) are described where appropriate.

§4.4 WHAT IS A PARTNERSHIP?

The UPA (1914) defines a partnership to be the relationship that exists among persons who are "co-owners of a business for profit."[10] It is important to recognize that the "co-ownership" requirement relates to the "business" and not to specific property. Under this broad definition, many very informal arrangements are partnerships. A partnership may be formed simply by an oral agreement that may or may not be formalized with a handshake without any discussion of the details of the relationship or the rights and obligations of the various participants. There is generally no need for a written agreement and no public filing of any document (other than an assumed name certificate that may be required if the business is conducted under a trade name rather than in the names of the partners). Under UPA (1994), however, some public filings are authorized and may be desirable to make in certain circumstances.[11] With respect to local permits and qualifi-

---

[8]On the other hand, NCCUSL members involved in the revision process complained that the personnel of the ad hoc ABA committee changed frequently and new problems were often raised about sections that had previously been discussed and modifications agreed upon.

[9]Several states, including California and Georgia, made significant amendments to UPA (1914). Texas adopted its own version of a partnership statute in 1993 that has some similarities to UPA (1994) but also a substantial number of differences. As of 1996, about a dozen states have enacted new partnership statutes closely following UPA (1994).

[10]UPA (1914) §6(1). UPA (1994) §201(a) restates this definition and adds a statement that a specific intention to form a partnership is not necessary for a partnership to exist.

[11]For example, UPA (1994) §303 authorizes a partnership to file a statement of partnership authority, apparently designed primarily to simplify transfers of real estate owned by the partnership. These provisions, however, become complicated since a number of additional issues then must be dealt with. For example, the effect of restrictions on authority in the statement, the position of a third party who deals with a partner in ignorance of a filed statement that restricts the authority of the partner, and the position of a person who is named as a partner in a statement of authority but who denies that he or she is in fact a partner. UPA (1994) §304 permits a person to file a disclaimer with respect to statements that appear in a statement of authority filed under §303.

In addition, §704 of UPA (1994) authorizes the filing of a "statement of dissociation"

cations, interstate operations, and the like, generally the same rules are applicable to partnerships as to proprietorships.

Many cooperative, profit-seeking arrangements are entered into by individuals without a clear understanding of the legal consequences. Both UPA (1914) and UPA (1994) take the position that if profits are being shared there is a presumption that the arrangement is a partnership. This is based on the definition of a partnership — the participants are "co-owners" of the business if they share in the profit. In this sense, the partnership is the default form of business for persons who cooperatively own a commercial enterprise.

The issue whether a partnership or some other legal relationship was created usually arises in the context of a failed venture, where creditors seek to hold the "deepest pocket" liable on unpaid business obligations, while the deepest pocket strenuously argues that she was not a partner at all, but only a creditor, a landlord, or an employee whose compensation was based on the profits of the business. These are fact-sensitive cases. UPA (1914)[12] and UPA (1994)[13] both contain very similar provisions that set forth useful guidelines: The sharing of profits gives rise to a presumption of partnership, but the sharing of "gross returns" does not. Hence, a commercial lease that requires the tenant to pay a specified percentage of its gross revenue to the landlord as additional rent (a very common kind of lease provision) does not lead to a presumption that a partnership exists between landlord and tenant. Even the sharing of profits does not give rise to a presumption of partnership where the profits are received in payment of or for:

1. a debt, whether by installments or otherwise;
2. services as an independent contractor (see Chapter 2);
3. rent;
4. an annuity or other retirement or health benefit;
5. interest on a loan; or
6. the sale of the goodwill of a business or other property.

This list is taken from UPA (1994); UPA (1914) is similar but omits items 2, 4, and 6. In addition, the sharing of profits "does not of itself"

---

and §805 authorizes the filing of a "statement of dissolution." Section 907 permits the filing of a "statement of merger."

These various filings may create problems for filing authorities, since there is no registration of partnerships, and it is quite possible for several different partnerships to have the identical name. UPA (1994) §105 permits statements to be filed with the Secretary of State or in the office for recording transfers of real property. There has been only limited experience with public filings by partnerships, and it is uncertain whether these provisions will be widely used.

[12]UPA (1914) §7.
[13]UPA (1994) §202(c).

establish a presumption of partnership between joint owners of property as joint tenants, tenants in common, etc. These provisions may give useful guidance as to when a partnership should be found to exist.

While the sharing of profits in one of these listed relationships does not of itself create a presumption that a partnership exists, a conclusion that a partnership nevertheless exists is justified if, in addition to the sharing of profits, the terms of the actual relationship are inconsistent with the listed relationship. For example, if a person provides capital to another person to open a business but does not wish to be a partner, it is important that the transaction be expressly designated as a loan, that a repayment date be specified, and that the transaction be reflected by a promissory note or other traditional loan document. Open-ended arrangements may readily be viewed as the creation of a partnership. For example, "leasing" certain fixtures and personal property to a business indefinitely in exchange for a percentage of the profits of the business may make the lender a partner rather than a lessor.

Perhaps the most dangerous situation from the standpoint of the putative partner is where a profitsharing interest is combined with a power to participate in business decisions that involve issues not related to protection of that putative partner's relationship with the business. For example, a landlord with a percentage rent lease may readily be found to be a partner if she participates in decisions as to which lines of product to carry or which bank to patronize.

The definition of a partnership is limited to businesses organized "for profit." Many common kinds of nonprofit endeavors are not partnerships precisely because they are not for profit. Unincorporated church congregations or Masonic lodges are good examples.[14]

§4.5 "HANDSHAKE" PARTNERSHIPS

A partnership is essentially a consensual arrangement but it may be extremely informal, tacit, and unstructured. Two or more persons may decide to open a lemonade stand; they may open the stand without any express understanding about any of the basic terms of their relationship. Yet they clearly are "co-owners" of the business and have created a partnership. Both partnership statutes[15] provide a kind of default agreement to determine the

---

[14] If one or more members of a church or lodge sign a contract on behalf of the church or lodge, they are likely to be held personally liable on the contract. Since no partnership exists, however, it is unlikely that other members will also be held liable, though they may be held liable on pledges or promises they made with respect to the contract. In 1992, NCCUSL approved the Uniform Unincorporated Nonprofit Association Act that treats nonprofit membership associations as entities and eliminates all personal liability of members for transactions entered into in the name of the association.

[15] UPA (1914) §18; UPA (1994) §401.

rights and duties of partners in these totally informal arrangements which are usually referred to as *handshake partnerships*. In the absence of express agreement, each partner shares equally in profits and losses. Each has an equal voice in management and decision-making, which may be conducted with whatever degree of informality the partners desire. Each has an equal right to use or possess partnership property on behalf of the partnership. If a vote is taken on specific matters, each partner has one vote and the majority decision controls. The default agreement assumes that each partner will perform services on behalf of the partnership and provides that no partner is entitled to remuneration for those services while the partnership is continuing in business.

Further, within the context of a handshake partnership, an express agreement may be informally reached on certain matters with the remainder of the relation left implicit, to be defined by the default provisions of the statutes. For example, in a handshake partnership between two persons, the parties may agree only that the profitsharing relationship shall be 75/25 rather than 50/50; that agreement overrides the equal sharing rule established by the default provisions of the UPA. Interestingly, the default provisions of both statutes assume that loss sharing should be in the same proportion as profit sharing unless there is a different agreement about the sharing of losses.[16] Hence, if the two partners agree that profits are to be shared 75/25 but make no agreement with respect to losses, losses will also be shared on a 75/25 basis. Of course, this is only a default rule, and the partners could agree, if they wished, that they will share in profits on a 75/25 basis and share in losses on a 50/50 basis.

If the partners are aware of the default provisions, they almost certainly will wish to modify some of them, even in an informal partnership. For example, where financial contributions are unequal, the normal assumption by businessmen is that votes should be weighted in accordance with relative financial interests rather than on a per capita basis, but this is not the case unless the partners so agree. Similarly, in a law partnership, lawyers assume that senior partners will receive a larger share of the earnings than junior partners; again this is not the case unless the partners so agree. Of course, in a handshake law partnership the partners may agree after the year has closed how profits should be allocated, and as a practical matter it is doubtful that a junior partner would have the temerity to suggest, much less insist upon, an equal division.

Abstractly, it seems obviously desirable not only to have an agreement dealing with the various aspects of a partnership relation but also to have the agreement reduced to writing so that rights and duties are explicitly defined and known not only to the partners themselves but also to their heirs, successors, and assigns. However, a surprisingly large number of part-

---

[16]UPA (1914) §18(a); UPA (1994) §401(b).

nerships, including some large New York City law partnerships, have operated successfully for many years without a written partnership agreement. The partnership relationship generally involves mutual trust and confidence; if the partners can work issues out as they arise without friction or bitterness, considerable saving of time and energy will result where the details of a written partnership agreement need not be hammered out in advance. Of course, the partners may well have verbal or implicit understandings as to certain aspects of their relationship. The major problems likely unaddressed in these situations lacking a written partnership agreement arise from either a major falling out that may occur between partners or the unexpected death of an important partner. At that point, the partnership discovers that it is dealing with persons unwilling to cooperate with each other or an executor or administrator of an estate who has no knowledge of prior informal agreements and who may well challenge them if they have unfavorable consequences for the estate.

Written partnership agreements are discussed in section 4.10.

§4.6 PURPORTED PARTNERS

For a partnership to exist, there must be an explicit or implicit agreement among the partners to share profits or be co-owners of the business. There exist situations, however, where partnership-type relationships exist even though there is in fact no agreement either to be co-owners or to share profits. These are situations in which a person represents either that he is a partner with another person or that he is a member of an existing partnership when in fact that is not the case. If another person relies on the representation, partnership-type liabilities may be imposed on the purported partner. A purported partner may also have the authority to bind other purported partners to the extent of the representation and thus one can envision a "purported partnership" as well. The same result follows if a person consents to a partnership representation being made by a third person. Under section 16 of UPA (1914) such a person is called a *partner by estoppel*; under section 308 of UPA (1994) he is called a *purported partner,* a term that is somewhat more accurate since no partnership in fact exists.

If a representation is made in a public fashion, a purported partner may become liable to persons who rely on the representation even if the purported partner is unaware either that such reliance has occurred or that the person who is relying knew that a partnership representation had been made.

Since the reason for imposing liability or creating authority in these situations is to protect reliance by third parties, the rights and duties of purported partners should be limited to situations involving actual reliance. Thus, there should be no basis for imposing purported partner liability for tortious conduct not involving reliance on the existence of a partnership by third parties. And there is no basis for imposing the rights and duties that exist in an ordinary partnership to purported partners except to the extent necessary to protect the reliance of innocent persons. A purported partnership, in other words, is not a real partnership and the persons involved are normally not partners with respect to each other.

§4.7 JOINT VENTURES

Many cases involving partnership-like relations describe the relationship as a "joint venture" rather than as a partnership. If there is any difference, it is that a joint venture involves a more limited and narrower business purpose than a partnership — perhaps a partnership that plans to engage in a single transaction such as the purchase and resale of a specific piece of real estate. Partnership rules are generally applicable to joint ventures, the major difference being in the scope of the actual and apparent authority that each joint venturer possesses to bind the venture.[17]

There is some tendency for courts to accept the categorization of the agreement itself, e.g., an arrangement that is created pursuant to a joint venture agreement is likely to be referred to as a joint venture rather than a partnership by the courts. However, there appear to be relatively few practical differences in the legal principles applicable to a partnership and to a joint venture.

§4.8 THE PARTNERSHIP AS AN ENTITY

A long and rather sterile debate existed under UPA (1914) and the even earlier case law as to whether a partnership should be viewed as a separate legal entity or whether it was, like a proprietorship, simply a legal extension

---

[17]Some states may have created special rules with respect to joint ventures. Texas, for example, has judicially created a rule that for a joint venture to exist there must be an express agreement to share losses as well as profits. See Coastal Plains Dev. Corp. v. Micrea, Inc., 572 S.W.2d 285 (Tex. 1978). This result is not consistent with UPA (1914), since under that statute the sharing of losses is the consequence of a partnership relation, not a part of its definition. If there is no agreement as to the sharing of losses, the default rule is that each partner "must contribute toward the losses, whether of capital or otherwise, sustained by the partnership according to his share of the profits." UPA (1914) §18(a). In an effort to overrule these joint venture cases and return joint ventures to the partnership category, the Texas partnership statute enacted in 1993 states expressly that an association called a joint venture is a partnership and that an express agreement to share losses is not necessary for the existence of a partnership. Vernons Ann. Civ. Stat. art. 6132b — 2.02(a), 2.03(c).

of the individual owners without a separate legal status of its own. This debate was usually phrased in terms of whether a partnership was an "entity" or an "aggregate of the partners." Much of the early case law adopted the aggregate theory, but almost all modern cases treat the partnership as a separate legal entity. UPA (1914) itself contains internal evidence that could be cited to support either theory,[18] but section 201 of UPA (1994) squarely adopts the modern entity view by simply stating that "a partnership is an entity" independent of its partners. This characterization greatly simplifies the issue of who owns partnership property (the partners or the partnership) and also becomes important when analyzing issues not specifically addressed in the UPA. Obviously, the basic rule that each partner may be held personally liable for partnership obligations is not directly affected by the characterization of a partnership as an entity or an aggregate.

§4.9 WHO MAY BE A PARTNER?

One usually intuitively assumes that partners are individual, flesh-and-blood persons. Historically, that was probably always the case. Indeed, until the middle of the twentieth century, the rule was universally accepted that a corporation could not be a general partner in a partnership since the power of other partners to bind the partnership (and thereby the corporation) was inconsistant with the role of the board of directors of the corporation as the sole managers of the corporation. Statements to this effect may still appear in some treatises and in occasional cases, but the modern view, accepted today in apparently all states, is now precisely the opposite: Corporations (as well as other legal entities such as trusts, estates, general partnerships, limited partnerships, or limited liability companies) may act as general partners to the same extent that individuals can. In the modern commercial world, in other words, a partnership may be formed in which one or more of the partners are corporations, trusts, estates of deceased individuals, limited partnerships, or other general partnerships.

UPA (1994) Section 101(8) makes this explicit. It defines *person* to mean "an individual, corporation, business trust, estate, trust, partnership,

---

[18]The history of UPA (1914) largely explains this internal inconsistency. The first drafts of that statute were prepared by Dean Ames, as reporter, who was strongly wedded to the entity theory and was directed to draft a statute on that theory. While this draft was under consideration, Dean Ames died. Thereafter, NCCUSL decided to return the draft to a reorganized committee with Dean Lewis as reporter; the instruction to proceed on the entity theory was eliminated. Under Dean Lewis, a number of entity provisions were deleted (e.g., the power of a partnership to sue or be sued in its own name). However, much of the language drafted by Dean Ames remained so that a number of provisions based on the entity theory uneasily coexist in the statute along with provisions based on the aggregate theory.

association, joint venture, government, governmental subdivision, agency, or instrumentality, or any other legal or commercial entity." The statute then consistently uses the word person throughout the remainder of its text. In connection with termination of partnership interests, UPA (1994) makes specific provision for the termination or dissolution of artificial entities that are partners.[19]

It is possible, in other words, for a partnership or a corporation to be a partner in another partnership. Sophisticated business planners often use combinations of business forms to reach a desired result. For example, the Internal Revenue Code provides that a corporation with a nonresident alien as a shareholder is not eligible for a desirable tax election, the S corporation election discussed in section 9.6. Much the same result may be achieved by forming the corporation without the resident alien as a shareholder, making the S corporation election, and then having the S corporation become a member of an LLC with the resident alien. An arrangement such as this must be carefully reviewed to assure that a court or administrative agency (such as the Internal Revenue Service) will not view it as a subterfuge or as being in violation of some fundamental public policy.

Many law firms today are partnerships composed of professional corporations as well as individuals. This structure permits a lawyer to form his own professional corporation, which becomes a partner in the law firm, while the lawyer becomes an employee of the professional corporation. This device permits the lawyer to develop a pension plan for himself exclusively, and it hopefully limits his liability for the malpractice of his co-partners to the assets in the professional corporation.

B. INTERNAL MANAGEMENT

§4.10 WRITTEN PARTNERSHIP AGREEMENTS

While doubtless many thousands of handshake partnerships are created and dissolved each year, lawyers are much more likely to be involved with partnerships that are formed through formal partnership agreements. Most law firms today have written partnership agreements. Further, handshake partnerships are likely to be marginally financed and therefore not able to afford the luxury of legal advice. Typically, a written partnership agreement is the culmination of a negotiation process among the participants which would normally be expected to lead to a formal written document.

Since a partnership is a consensual arrangement, the formal partner-

---

[19]UPA (1994) §601(8) et seq.

ship agreement controls most aspects of the partnership relationship. It is the "law" for that partnership. Hence, as a practical matter, whenever a legal or economic issue arises within a partnership, the two most basic questions are: Was there a written partnership agreement, and, if so, what does the agreement say about the matter in question? If the answer to the first question is "no," then one must inquire about any oral understandings that existed and, if none are controlling, then, and only then, must one look at the default provisions of the UPA.

One important function of written partnership agreements is that they enable large partnerships with many partners to adopt procedures that permit decisions that normally would be made only by all the partners to be made by a committee of partners or by some fractional vote that may be less than a majority. In a large law firm, for example, many basic decisions such as the admission of new partners, the expulsion of nonperforming partners, or the allocation of profits may be delegated to an executive committee. Individual partners in the firm's New York office may have no information about whether an associate in the firm's St. Louis office should be made a partner, and it would be expensive and time-wasting to require each partner to become familiar with the performance of that associate. Decision by a small executive committee, based in part on the recommendation of the partners in the St. Louis office, may be an efficient and acceptable manner of making such decisions (which sometimes may be difficult and controversial).

Partnership agreements are enforceable as contracts to the same extent as contracts generally. Thus, an agreement providing that a partner who withdraws receives only a specified sum of money (even though the partner's interest is clearly worth much more) is presumptively enforceable like any contract. Specific provisions in a written partnership agreement may be attacked on contractual grounds such as fraud, duress, unconscionability, incapacity, breach of fiduciary duty, or mistake. They may not generally be attacked on the ground that the provision is "unfair" or because it is inconsistent with some default provision of the partnership statutes. Basically, the assumption is that partners are competent adults, free to structure their relationship as they wish, and competent to enter into binding contractual arrangements.[20]

The phrase *partnership agreement* usually is a reference to a formal written agreement among the partners defining their relationship. These agreements are usually complex and formal documents prepared by lawyers, but that is not an essential aspect of partnership agreements. A partnership

---

[20]Of course, the reality may be quite different. An associate in a large law firm who is offered a partnership in that firm, for example, is usually provided a copy of the written partnership agreement. It is highly unlikely that the associate will be in a position to object to specific provisions in that agreement; it is offered to her on a "take it or leave it" basis.

agreement may be written on a restaurant napkin over a pitcher of beer. Of course, a lawyer-prepared partnership agreement increases the cost of formation, but that is usually a minor consideration, and the benefits of clarity and careful treatment of certain issues (such as the rights of a former partner upon his withdrawal from the partnership) may be substantial.

The partnership agreement may contain provisions for internal governance of the partnership, establish profitsharing ratios, and determine how partnership assets are to be divided upon termination of the firm's business. Since partnership law is basically contractual in nature, these agreements define most of the rules which govern the partners' relations with each other, supplanting the default provisions set forth in the UPA. The partnership agreement is called the "law of that partnership," because it sets forth the basic rules about how the partnership is to be governed and the financial and other rights and obligations of each partner.

The partnership agreement may create classes of partners with different voting and financial rights. For example, classes of "junior" or "senior" partners may be created, or a "managing partner" or "managing committee" with designated rights and responsibilities may be established. Many law firms utilize classes of partners in this fashion to ensure that the senior partners have power to govern the affairs of the partnership. In the 1990s, many law firms have created a class of "equity partners" and a class of "contract partners," with the latter having only limited participation rights in profits and no obligation to contribute toward losses.[21] Where classes of partners are created, the importance of having a written partnership agreement is increased, because of the possibility of misunderstanding over the rights and obligations of the classes as among themselves. Some state statutes require partnership agreements establishing different classes of partners to be in writing.

The partnership agreement establishes what each partner is to contribute to the partnership. The simplest situation is where each partner contributes cash in equal amounts and each shares equally in the fruits of the

---

[21] The partnership agreement establishing equity and income partners may be silent on the responsibility of income partners for partnership liabilities, or may provide that the partnership agrees to indemnify income partners against liabilities or losses. An income partner presumably is a partner and not an employee and therefore has the same responsibility for liabilities or losses as an equity partner. See §4.14. However, if an income partner is compensated solely on a salary basis (or on the basis of salary plus year-end bonus of a defined amount), she may be able to argue that she is not truly a partner because she is not sharing in profits. An agreement by the partnership to indemnify income partners against claims by third parties or the obligation to contribute toward losses gives considerable protection, as a practical matter. However, if a disastrous liability is imposed on the partnership, exceeding the total net worth of all equity partners, the promise to indemnify income partners does not provide protection for them. This issue of the responsibility of an income partner for losses is usually academic since income partners rarely have substantial outside assets, and therefore are not pursued by partnership creditors.

partnership. However, the partnership relation is one of complete flexibility. The contributions of one partner to a partnership may differ from the contributions of other partners either in amount or in kind. For example, it is very common for one partner to contribute his or her services, primarily or exclusively, while one or more other partners contribute capital or property, primarily or exclusively. In effect, the service partners are involved in managing and owning a business primarily financed by the capital-contributing partners. Another very common variation is that some capital contributions are to be in the form of cash while other partners are to contribute real or personal property, tangible or intangible.

Elements of bargaining and negotiation are inevitably involved in the formation of partnerships with dissimilar contributions by the partners. In negotiating such a partnership agreement, interests may conflict. A lawyer therefore should be very cautious about agreeing to represent different interests simultaneously in such a situation since the applicable canons of ethics with respect to representation of conflicting interests may impose formal disclosure and written consent requirements. Each partner should be encouraged to obtain individual legal representation.

Where one partner is contributing services over a period of time for a partnership interest, and another partner is contributing capital immediately, difficult issues may arise upon the premature termination and liquidation of the partnership. Consider, for example, the simple situation where one partner contributes money or property and the other contributes services on the understanding that they will share profits equally. What should the service partner receive on the liquidation of the partnership? If the assets owned by the partnership have increased, should the service partner share in the gain reflected by the increase in value of the property contributed by the capital partner? If there are losses, should the service partner be required to contribute cash to the partnership to cover her share of those losses? If so, is the claim of the capital partner to a return of his capital a "loss"? If the property contributed by the capital partner has been lost or destroyed, should the service partner be required to contribute toward that loss? If so, should the value of her services be viewed as a capital contribution to the partnership? The default rules of both UPA (1914) and UPA (1994) protect the capital partner in these situations at the expense of the service partner.[22]

[22]The default provisions of both statutes provide that in the absence of agreement, (a) partners are not entitled to compensation for services rendered by them on behalf of the partnership, (b) as among themselves, each partner must contribute toward losses in accordance with his or her share of the profits, and (c) on dissolution of the partnership each partner is entitled to a return of his capital, and this obligation is a liability of the partnership. Thus, the default rule is that the value of services performed by the service partner do not constitute a contribution of capital (and thus do not enter into the calculation of the service partner's capital investment in the partnership), while the service partner must con-

Partnerships have virtually complete flexibility with respect to agreements about financial interests and their right to distributions. Partners may share profits and losses in any way they agree; they may agree to share losses in a different way than they share profits. Profits may be shared on a flat percentage basis, in proportion to the relative financial investments in the partnership, on a sliding scale based on receipts attributable to each partner's efforts, or on some other basis. Profit sharing ratios may be determined by agreement after the close of the accounting period. One or more partners may be paid a fixed "salary," called *guaranteed payments*. The agreement may require a guaranteed payment to be viewed as an expense of the business (i.e., deducted from revenues before calculating profits), or as an advance against that year's profits, to be charged against the partner's distributive share of profits for that year.

Certain aspects of the partnership relationship, however, cannot be varied by agreement. For example, third persons dealing with the partnership are entitled to hold the individual partners as well as the partnership liable for partnership obligations; the partnership agreement cannot immunize specific partners from liability for partnership obligations without the express consent of the creditors. Under UPA (1914) there was some uncertainty as to which provisions could be modified by agreement and which could not. Section 103(b) of UPA (1994) sets forth a list of nine provisions or rights which cannot be modified by a partnership agreement, the last of which is to "restrict rights of third parties under this [Act]." Other provisions that cannot be modified by agreement include a partner's access to books and records of the partnership, reducing the duty of care or eliminating the obligation of good faith and fair dealing, and restricting the power of a partner to withdraw from the partnership. All other rights or duties within the partnership relationship not included in this list presumably may be defined or established by the partnership agreement.[23]

---

tribute capital to cover her share of the capital losses. Upon dissolution the partnership is obligated to return the capital contributed by each partner (reduced by that partner's share of any losses) and this obligation is a liability of the partnership to which all partners may have to contribute. The result of these various rules is that the service partner may be called upon to make a capital contribution in order to permit the capital partner to recover a portion of his investment without getting any credit at all for the services she provided. In many situations, it may be sensible to change this default rule in the partnership agreement so as to avoid unexpected distortions in ultimate responsibility for losses. This distortion arises because the service partner risks the loss of her services without compensation while being required to make a contribution to restore a portion of the loss incurred by the capital partner.

[23]The list of provisions in §103(b) purports to be exclusive. There is always some risk in creating an exclusive list. For example, UPA (1994) §104(a) states that "unless displaced by particular provisions of this [Act], the principles of law and equity supplement this [Act]." Section 104(a) is not one of the provisions listed in §103(b). Does that mean that a partnership agreement may provide that the principles of law and equity are not to be looked to supplement the UPA (1994)?

Modern partnership agreements are complex documents not so much because of management or liability issues (though such issues certainly may lead to complex provisions) but because of federal income tax considerations. The manner of taxation of partnerships and individual partners is generally discussed in Part C of this chapter; suffice it to say that in many partnership agreements, the tax consequences are the primary concern and objective of the partners. The provisions respecting partnership taxation, and the regulations issued under those sections, are among the most complex provisions in the entire Internal Revenue Code. The following is the first part of a provision from a model form of partnership agreement that was presented to a continuing legal education program in 1994 . It is presented here not so much because of its substance (though that is important and is discussed subsequently) but to demonstrate that the source of complexity of partnership agreements is largely not the substantive law of partnership.

> **Capital Accounts.** A capital account shall be established and maintained for each Partner. Each Partner's capital account (a) shall be increased by (i) the amount of money contributed by that Partner to the Partnership, (ii) the fair market value of property contributed by that Partner to the Partnership (net of liabilities secured by contributed property that the Partnership is considered to assume or take subject to under section 752 of the [Internal Revenue Code of 1986, as amended]), and (iii) allocations to that Partner of Partnership income and gain (or items thereof), including income and gain exempt from tax and income and gain described in Treas. Reg. §1.704-1(b)(2)(iv)(g), but excluding income and gain described in Treas. Reg. §1.704-1(b)(4)(i), and (b) shall be decreased by (i) the amount of money distributed to that Partner by the Partnership, (ii) the fair market value of property distributed to that Partner by the Partership (net of liabilities secured by the distributed property that the Partner is considered to assume or take subject to under section 752 of the Code), (iii) allocations to that Partner of expenditures of the Partnership described in section 705(a)(2)B) of the Code, and (iv) allocations of Partnership loss and deduction (or items thereof), including loss and deduction described in Treas. Reg. §1.704-1(b)(2)(iv)(g), but excluding items described in clause (b)(iii) above and loss or deduction described in Treas. Reg. §1.704-1(b)(4)(i) or §1.704-1(b)(4)(iii).

The "capital accounts" of a partnership are discussed further in section 4.23.

§4.11 THE PARTNER AS AN AGENT OF THE BUSINESS

One basic aspect of the partnership relation is that each partner is an agent of the partnership for the purpose of its business. Thus, each partner has actual authority to bind the partnership to obligations within the scope of its business. Each partner also has apparent authority to bind the partnership to obligations that are "apparently for carrying on in the usual way the business of the partnership" or a business of the same kind as the partnership business.[24] The difference between actual authority and apparent authority is discussed in Chapter 2.

The actual authority of a partner may be limited or restricted by the partnership agreement or by a partnership decision. An example of a restriction in a partnership agreement is a provision that makes one partner the "managing partner" or which defines precisely which decisions a specific partner or committee of partners is entitled to make. A negative implication of such provisions is that other partners do not have authority to make decisions in those areas. An example of a restriction by partnership decision is a determination by a majority of the partners not to purchase a new truck at this time. However, in the absence of knowledge by the third party, a partner may bind the partnership under the principle of apparent authority to obligations he or she was not authorized by the partnership to create. Thus, a partner may have apparent authority to purchase the truck despite a partnership decision not to do so. The partner so acting is presumably in breach of his or her obligations to the partnership and the other partners, but the partnership is nevertheless bound by the commitment entered into by the partner.

If a specific action is authorized by the partners, the partnership is of course bound without regard to whether or not the action is within the apparent authority of a partner.

The scope of actual and apparent authority is determined by the scope of the partnership's business (in the case of actual authority) or of similar businesses in the same locality (in the case of apparent authority). The scope of the partnership's business is presumably a factual question to be resolved like any other factual question. However, in resolving this question considerable weight is likely to be given to the description of the business in the partnership agreement. Hence, in the case of a written partnership agreement, some attention should be paid to how the business is described or defined.

Section 9(3) of UPA (1914) lists certain kinds of actions for which partners do not have authority, except with the authorization of "the other partners." Included are assignments of partnership property in trust for creditors, disposition of the goodwill of a business, actions that would make it impossible to carry on the business of the partnership, confessions of a judgment, and the submission of a claim to arbitration. UPA (1994) omits this provision, presumably because the general rules about authority adequately cover these actions.

[24]UPA (1914) §9(a). UPA (1994) §301(1) changes this language slightly. It refers to actions "for apparently carrying on in the ordinary course the partnership business or business of the kind carried on by the partnership."

§4.12 PARTNERSHIP DECISION-MAKING

The default rule is that "all partners have equal rights in the management and conduct of the partnership business."[25] Thus, in the absence of an agreement, votes on partnership matters are on a per capita basis. Where contributions of capital and services are roughly the same, this method of voting is doubtless appropriate. However, where the contributions are not equal, a more suitable method of voting may be on a weighted basis, though that is somewhat more complicated. In a three-person partnership, where A has contributed 60 percent of the capital and B and C have each contributed 20 percent, it is unlikely that A would be happy if he is outvoted by B and C. A probably believes that because he has made 60 percent of the financial contributions his vote should also count 60 percent also. Similarly, in a law partnership where a single "rainmaker" provides virtually all of the work performed by two junior partners, the rainmaker would doubtless expect to have greater voting power than the two partners combined. An agreement as to the manner of voting, whether oral or incorporated in a written partnership agreement, ensures the desired method of voting, in effect opting out of the default provision.

Because each partner has participatory rights in management, general partnership interests are usually not "securities" for purposes of the federal and state securities law. However, the leading case of *Williamson v. Tucker*,[26] holds that a general partnership interest may be a security if the investor has virtually no power in fact to participate in the management of the enterprise. The court based this conclusion on the broad definition of "investment contract" in the federal securities acts and the need to interpret flexibly the coverage of those statutes.

§4.13 FIDUCIARY DUTIES OF PARTNERS

The relation between partners is one of trust and confidence. This follows necessarily from at least two basic concepts: first, the agency powers that each partner has to bind the partnership and the other partners to unauthorized as well as authorized obligations and, second, the concept of cooperative enterprise that is inherent in the partnership relation. The relation of trust and confidence is enforced judicially through the recognition of a broad fiduciary duty that each partner owes to the other partners in connection with all matters relating to the partnership. The breadth of this fiduciary duty was articulated in the great case of *Meinhard v. Salmon*,[27] where Justice Cardozo stated that co-partners

---

[25] UPA (1914) §18(e); UPA (1994) §401(f).
[26] 645 F.2d 404 (5th Cir. 1981).
[27] 249 N.Y. 458, 164 N.E. 545 (1928).

owe to one another, while the enterprise continues, the duty of the finest loyalty. Many forms of conduct permissible in a workaday world for those acting at arms' length, are forbidden to those bound by fiduciary ties. A trustee is held to something stricter than the morals of the market place. Not honesty alone, but the punctilio of an honor the most sensitive, is then the standard of behavior.

Many cases quote this famous language and apply it broadly.

The fiduciary duty set forth in *Meinhard v. Salmon* may require voluntary disclosure of relevant information. It continues to exist even though the partners are antagonistic to each other and are in the process of dissolving their relationship. It has been held to apply to negotiations leading to the formation of a partnership as well as covering all activities relating to the use and distribution of partnership property. Section 21(1) of UPA (1914) in effect codifies this duty. It provides simply that "every partner must account to the partnership for any benefit, and hold as trustee for it any profits, derived by him without the consent of the other partners from any transaction connected with the formation, conduct, or liquidation of the partnership or from any use by him of its property."

By and large, the case law involving fiduciary duties of partners under UPA (1914) accepts and applies a very broad concept of those duties. Cases talk of the existence of a partnership fiduciary duty similar to that imposed on a trustee of an express trust.[28] Provisions in a partnership agreement permitting a partner to compete freely with his partnership may be construed as being limited to transactions that are "entirely fair" to the partnership.[29]

Some courts have expressed skepticism about the desirability of a broad fiduciary duty in situations where the relationship has become adversarial and any relationship of trust and confidence has in fact disappeared.[30] However, this position seems clearly to represent the minority view.[31] This fiduciary duty extends to a partner negotiating a buyout of the interest of other partners,[32] but not to transactions outside the scope of the venture itself.[33]

During the development of UPA (1994), these broad fiduciary obliga-

[28]See, e.g., Gum v. Schaefer, 683 S.W.2d 803, 805 (Tex. Ct. App. 1984).
[29]See, e.g., Wartski v. Bedford, 926 F.2d 11 (1st Cir. 1991). The court added that such provisions should not be construed as a "license to steal." Id. at 20. See also Loft v. Lapidus, 936 F.2d 633 (1st Cir. 1991).
[30]See, e.g., Fravega v. Security S&L Assn., 469 A.2d 531, 536 (N.J. Ch. 1983). See also Ong Intl. (U.S.A.), Inc. v. 11th Ave. Corp., 850 P.2d 447, 454 (Utah 1993).
[31]See Walter v. Holiday Inns, Inc., 985 F.2d 1232, 1238 (3d Cir. 1993), where the court stated "the existence of persuasive authority supporting the application of fiduciary principles even when partners act as adversaries makes it likely that *Fravega* was too slender a reed to decide this case."
[32]Heller v. Hartz Mountain Indus., Inc., 636 A.2d 599 (N.J. Super. Ct. 1993).
[33]Sind v. Pollen, 356 A.2d 653, 655 (D.C. 1976).

72

tions of partners to each other became the subject of considerable debate. The committee that drafted UPA (1994) clearly attempted to narrow and restrict the scope of these obligations. Section 404 of UPA (1994) states that "the *only* fiduciary duties to the partnership and the other partners are the duty of loyalty and the duty of care." (Whether or not the duty of care is really a "fiduciary" duty is perhaps debatable.) Further, section 404(b) provides that the duty of loyalty "is *limited to*" three areas — accounting for benefits derived by a partner in the conduct and winding up (but not the formation) of the business, refraining from dealing with the partnership as or on behalf of a party having an interest adverse to the partnership, and refraining from competing with the partnership in the conduct of its business before its dissolution. The duty of care in turn is defined in section 404(c) to be "*limited to* refraining from engaging in grossly negligent or reckless conduct, intentional misconduct, or a knowing violation of law." In addition to these "fiduciary" duties, section 404(d) provides that there is a general obligation of "good faith and fair dealing" with respect to partnership matters. Section 404 also carves out two potentially controversial areas as not necessarily involving breaches of duty. Section 404(e) provides that a partner does not violate a duty "*merely* because the partner's conduct furthers the partner's own interest." And section 404(e) adds that if a partner lends money to or transacts business with his partnership, "the rights and obligations of the partner are the same as those of a person who is not a partner, subject to other applicable law."

Under section 105(b) of UPA (1994), the duties of care, loyalty, and fair dealing may not be eliminated by agreement, but the partnership agreement "may identify specific types or categories of activities that do not violate the duty of loyalty, if not manifestly unreasonable," may restrict the duty of care so long as the restriction is not "unreasonable," and, in connection with the duty of good faith and fair dealing, "may determine the standards by which the performance of the obligation is to be measured, if the standards are not manifestly unreasonable."

Also worthy of comment is the decision by NCCUSL to exclude fiduciary duties in connection with the formation of the partnership. Prior to the time the partnership is created, the parties are dealing at arm's length and exclusion of fiduciary duties at this stage of the transaction seems plausible. Further, there is some logical difficulty in finding that a fiduciary duty exists prior to the creation of the partnership which itself creates the duty. Still, there may be a considerable degree of trust in the formation process. One can readily imagine situations in which fiduciary duties should exist.

The intent of the draftsmen of UPA (1994) to limit and narrow the broad fiduciary duty set forth in *Meinhard* seems clear. Only time will tell whether this articulation of duties provides greater guidance to courts in real-life situations than the more general phrasing of the old UPA.

C.   LIABILITIES AND PROPERTY RIGHTS

§4.14 THE LIABILITY OF PARTNERS FOR PARTNERSHIP DEBTS

One of the fundamental aspects of the partnership relation is that each partner has personal responsibility for the obligations of the partnership. Some states take the position that the liability of partners for all types of partnership obligations is "joint and several," which means that suit may be brought against one or more partners without necessarily bringing suit against all of them. UPA (1914) and the statutes of a majority of states, however, provide that with respect to contract claims, the liability of partners is "joint" only, while with respect to other kinds of claims — tort claims, breach of fiduciary duty claims, suits for penalties, etc. — liability is joint and several. *Joint liability* means that all the partners must be named as defendants and served with process if the claim is to be pursued. The existence of joint liability for contract claims appears to be a carry-over from the early days of partnership law when aggregate theories of partnership were generally accepted. However, in large partnerships and those with partners located in different states or countries, joint liability becomes unwieldy and impractical. As large partnerships become more common, states increasingly have adopted joint and several liability as the standard for all classes of liabilities.

Where liability is joint and several, procedural litigation rules often build in some entity characteristics (though again rules differ from state to state). In many states, for example, it is possible to sue a partnership without suing individually any of the partners, and partners may be held individually liable only if the complaint or other process names them as defendants and expressly states that recovery is being sought from them personally. Such defendants must also be served with process. In these states, if a lawsuit names only the partnership without naming any of the individual partners as defendants, the plaintiff may recover only from partnership assets.[34] These principles seem clearly to be based on an entity theory.

In most states, it is possible today to sue any partner individually on a partnership obligation without first suing the partnership. That seems to be an aggregate concept. If a partner discharges a partnership obligation, he then has a right of indemnification from the partnership so that the partnership obligation is ultimately paid from partnership assets and allocated among the partners in the appropriate way for that partnership.

The Uniform Partnership Act of 1994 makes important changes in

---

[34]It may be possible, however, thereafter to bring an independent lawsuit against the partners individually to collect upon the partnership liability.

partnership liability. Section 306 makes all liability joint and several (except with respect to newly admitted partners). Further, section 307 increases the entity characteristics of a partnership. It provides: that a partnership may sue and be sued in the name of the partnership, that an action may be brought against the partnership and any or all of the partners in the same action or in separate actions, that a judgment against the partnership is not a judgment against any specific partner, that a partnership claim cannot be satisfied from a partner's individual assets unless a judgment is obtained against that partner, and that in any event a creditor of the partnership must first proceed against and exhaust the partnership assets before proceeding against the personal assets of the individual partners. (An exception is made for burdensome situations, such as where the partnership has small amounts of property in different states, and the cost of seizing such property is excessive in comparison to the value of the property involved.) The exhaustion requirement virtually makes the partners sureties for the partnership and is clearly based on an entity concept.

These rules about procedure and civil process, of course, do not affect the ultimate responsibility of each partner for the debts of the partnership if they are made defendants in the litigation on an individual basis, though in some states today a failure to exhaust partnership assets, when that is required, or a failure to name a partner as a party in litigation against the partnership, may discharge the partner entirely from personal liability. And, of course, individual partners who have not been named as defendants will normally have a duty to contribute toward partnership losses, including those arising from the indemnification of partners who were named as defendants in the litigation and who actually satisfied the judgment obtained against them.

Because of these various procedural rules (and also the priority rules discussed in section 4.19) it is a relatively common practice today for partnership creditors to require individual partners to enter into personal guarantees of the performance of partnership obligations. Such a guarantee provides a creditor significantly greater rights against the partner than is now provided by the law of partnership in many states. In addition, it is not uncommon for a partnership creditor to require the spouse of each partner also to guarantee the performance of the partnership obligation. If UPA (1994) becomes widely adopted, this trend toward requiring personal guarantees by partners of partnership liabilities will probably accelerate. Indeed, it is likely that sophisticated creditors will change their forms so as to routinely require that all partners personally guarantee all loans and other significant contractual obligations of partnerships.

§4.15 PROPERTY RIGHTS OF A PARTNER — UPA (1914)

One of the major reasons for the development of UPA (1914) was dissatisfaction over the common law's handling of partnership property. Following the aggregate theory, the common law viewed partnership property as being held by the partners as joint tenants, with all the rules and restrictions of that common law property concept being applied to partnership property. This led to undesirable consequences, and the 1914 Act made a radical change in approach by conceptualizing the ownership interests of a partner in a novel but rather complex fashion. Section 24 of UPA (1914) creates three different categories or levels of ownership. The first level consists of the rights of a partner with respect to tangible assets of the partnership: cash in the bank, real or personal property used in the business, inventory, accounts receivable, and the like. The second level consists of the partner's "interest in the partnership," an ownership interest in the business as a whole distinct from the ownership of any specific partnership asset. The third level is the partner's right to participate in management of the partnership. Each of these levels of ownership merits a brief discussion.

1. A Partner's Interest in Specific Partnership Property. Section 25 of UPA (1914) creates a new type of tenancy for property owned by a partnership. It states that partners hold partnership assets as *tenants in partnership*. The elements of this tenancy are defined in such a way as to limit the use of partnership property exclusively to partnership purposes. A partner may not dispose of property held as tenants in partnership except for partnership purposes, and then only by a transaction that disposes of the partnership's entire interest in the property. Further, individual creditors of a partner may not levy upon or seize the partner's interest in such property to satisfy nonpartnership claims against an individual partner. Property held as tenancy in partnership is not subject to claims of dower, curtesy, or community property.

Property held as tenants in partnership is usually referred to as *specific partnership property*, the assets that form the pool of property owned by the partnership. The theory is that the partnership should have the control and use of partnership property for its communal good, not to be disposed of by a partner to satisfy his or her personal obligations or to be seized by persons who are creditors of an individual partner but not creditors of the partnership. The concept of holding property as tenants in partnership is simply a way of effectuating this desired goal.

For example, assume that your client has a judgment against a partner based on nonpartnership claims. Perhaps it is a child support obligation or a claim arising out of an automobile accident not involving the partnership business. Can you collect on the judgment by levying against property owned by the partnership, e.g., by seizing tangible partnership assets or garnishing the partnership's bank account? In a word, the answer is "no." This makes sense when one reflects on it. The other partners in the business have rights of at least equal dignity as the rights of the defendant; seizure of specific partnership property might result in significant disruption of the partnership business, perhaps making it impossible for the partnership to continue in business at all. What is needed is a collection device that is limited to the defendant's interest in the partnership rather than one that affects innocent partners as much as it affects the defendant.

On the death of a partner, his interest in specific partnership property vests in the remaining partners who continue to hold the property as tenants in partnership. If the sole remaining partner dies, the partnership property vests in his or her legal representative, the partnership clearly having ended.

2. The Partner's Interest in the Partnership. The second level of property ownership created by the Uniform Partnership Act of 1914 is the partner's *interest in the partnership*. This interest consists of the right each partner has to receive distributions when and as they are made; it bears roughly the same relationship between a partner and the partnership as the right a holder of stock has against the issuing corporation. It reflects the partner's ownership in the business in general and not the ownership of any specific asset. The partner's interest in the partnership — unlike her interest in specific partnership property — is subject to being seized by individual creditors by the process of a "charging order," described below in section 4.17.

A partner's interest in a partnership is declared to be personal property for all purposes, and may be subject to marital or other claims or rights. In other words, even if the sole asset of a partnership consists of real estate, the interests in that partnership are personal property.

3. The Right to Participate in Management. The third level of ownership under UPA (1914) is the partner's right to participate in the management of the partnership. This may not be a property interest in the true sense of the term, but it is defined to be a property interest in UPA (1914). To the extent it is a property interest, it is immune from seizure by an individual creditor and may not be assigned except to a person who is accepted by the remaining partners as a partner in the partnership.

The assignment of an interest in the partnership assigns neither the partner's right to possess specific partnership property nor her right to participate in management. Indeed, even an express attempt to assign these rights is ineffective unless the partnership agrees to admit the assignee as a partner.

§4.16 PROPERTY RIGHTS OF A PARTNER — UPA (1994)

UPA (1994) basically follows the principles created by the 1914 Act but with material simplification in the structure. While UPA (1914) contains elaborate provisions defining tenancy in partnership, UPA (1994) reaches the same result simply by stating that "a partner is not a co-owner of partnership property and has no interest in partnership property which can be transferred, either voluntarily or involuntarily."[35] This simplification ultimately rests on the complete acceptance of the entity notion of partnership set forth in UPA (1994) section 201: "The partnership is an entity distinct from its partners." If the partnership owns the partnership property there is no room for an argument that the partners own the property.

UPA (1994) substitutes a *partner's transferable interest in the partnership* for the concept of the partner's "interest in the partnership" in the 1914 Act. Section 502 of UPA (1994) defines this interest to be "the partner's share of the profits and losses of the partnership and the partner's right to receive distributions" and states that this interest is the "only transferable interest" of a partner in the partnership. As under the 1914 Act, the partners' transferable interest in the partnership is personal property without regard to the types of property owned by the partnership. While the language is changed somewhat, the legal pattern created by UPA (1994) is very similar to the pattern of UPA (1914).

Thus, under the 1994 Act, like under the 1914 Act, a personal creditor of a partner cannot simply go in and attach or seize partnership assets to satisfy a claim against a specific partner. An attachment of partnership property by such a creditor under these circumstances is simply not permitted since the partnership is an entity separate from the partners. Rather, a personal creditor must proceed against the partner's transferable interest in the partnership through the same device as in the UPA (1914) — a charging order discussed immediately below.

Finally, the enigmatic power to participate in management as a property interest in the 1914 Act is not mentioned in the 1994 Act.

§4.17 CHARGING ORDERS

The *charging order* is the device by which an individual creditor of a partner levies upon the partner's interest in the partnership.[36] Apparently, in 1914 many states did not have a procedure by which a creditor could levy against an intangible interest that consisted of possible future distributions of funds, and hence a special procedure to obtain satisfaction from interests in a partnership was created.

---

[35]UPA (1994) §501.
[36]UPA (1914) §28; UPA (1994) §504.

Section 28 of UPA (1914) provides that only judgment creditors are entitled to seek a charging order, and that the effect of such an order is to "charge the interest of the debtor partner with payment of the unsatisfied amount of such judgment debt with interest thereon." A charging order in effect requires the partnership to distribute the stream of cash otherwise flowing to the partner to the judgment creditor. However, the statute does not give much guidance as to the details and the mechanics of a charging order. It is unclear under the 1914 Act, for example, what should happen if other creditors also lay claim to the stream of cash or what should be done if the stream is not large enough to pay off the judgment within a reasonable period of time. And the case law on charging orders is very sparse.

A partner whose interest in the partnership is subject to a charging order remains a partner in the partnership. For example, he continues to have management rights even though someone else is receiving the distributions from the partnership.

Article 9 of the Uniform Commercial Code, adopted in all states, provides that security interests may be created in intangible property simply by filing a financing statement. Presumably, a lien on a partnership interest may be created voluntarily by following the normal Article 9 process. It is unclear whether the lien so created, if prior in time to the charging order, is superior to the lien of the charging order or vice versa.

Section 504 of UPA (1994) retains the provisions of UPA (1914) section 28 with some minor improvements and clarification. It states, for example, that a charging order constitutes a "lien on the judgment debtor's transferable interest,"[37] and that a court may order a foreclosure of the interest upon conditions the court considers appropriate. Case law under the more skeletal provisions of UPA (1914) reached the same results. The 1994 provision also makes it clear that the judgment debtor may redeem a charged interest, presumably by using personal assets that are not subject to direct seizure by the creditor.

§4.18 RIGHTS OF CREDITORS OF PARTNERS AND OF PARTNERSHIPS

Partnership law classifies obligations on the basis of a sharp distinction between partnership obligations on the one hand and personal obligations of individual partners on the other. The distinction is basically between business debts of the partnership and personal or individual debts of an individual who happens to be a partner. The rights of creditors with respect to the

---

[37] There is no provision for filing notice of this lien other than in the judicial records of the charging order proceeding itself. It is unclear whether creditors and others will have notice in fact that the partner's interest in the partnership has been subjected to a lien that effectively destroys most of the current value of that interest.

individual property of the partners and the property owned by the partner-ship depend on the classification of the creditor, i.e., whether he is a creditor of the partnership or a personal creditor of the individual partner. Thus, a matrix may be created describing the rights of individual and partnership creditors. The matrix might look like this:

Table 4.1

Nature of Creditor	Partnership Property	Individual Property
Individual	Charging order	Direct levy and attachment
Partnership	Direct levy and attachment	Direct levy and attachment but only after exhaustion of partnerhsip assets[38]

Thus, an individual creditor may proceed against individual assets through regular judicial process; against partnership assets, such a creditor must first obtain a charging order. A partnership creditor might proceed directly against partnership assets, but may proceed against individual assets only after partnership assets are exhausted.

§4.19 PRIORITIES OF CREDITORS

Priorities of creditors relate to the order of payment of competing debts when the available assets are limited. Priorities are usually established by whether or not a creditor has a security interest in or lien upon specific assets. Similar issues arise, however, with respect to priorities among unsecured creditors. The federal Bankruptcy Act of 1969 contains detailed provisions establishing priorities among various classes of unsecured creditors.

UPA (1914) set forth priorities as between unsecured partnership creditors and unsecured individual creditors with respect to partnership property and the separate property of the partner. Section 40(i) provides that partnership creditors have priority over individual creditors with respect to partnership property and individual creditors have priority over partnership creditors with respect to individual property. These priorities created under UPA (1914) are usually described as the *jingle rule*. The jingle rule provides a nice degree of symmetry, but is unrealistic in an economic sense, since a partnership creditor might well extend credit only after evaluating both partnership assets and the personal assets of individual partners.

The Bankruptcy Act creates a different set of priorities in bankruptcy

---

[38] As provided by UPA (1994). Under UPA (1914) a partnership creditor could apparently proceed directly against an individual partner without exhaustion of partnership assets.

proceedings. Under that Act, partnership creditors continue to have priority over individual creditors with respect to partnership assets, but they have parity with individual creditors with respect to individual assets. As a practical matter, the more favorable federal priorities for partnership creditors ensure that virtually all insolvent partnerships are placed into federal bankruptcy proceedings where the federal priorities are controlling. As a result, the UPA (1914) jingle rule has little or no practical applicability. The 1994 Uniform Partnership Act accepts the primacy of the federal system of priorities and does not address the relative priority of partners and individual creditors with respect to the separate property of partners.

§4.20 ASSIGNMENTS AND TRANSFERS OF PARTNERSHIP INTERESTS

The law has long recognized that a partner has power to transfer or assign his financial interest in the partnership. Under the 1914 Act, such transactions were referred to as "assignments" of a partner's "interest in the partnership;" under the 1994 Act, they are referred to as "transfers" of the "partner's transferable interest in the partnership." In the balance of this section, the nomenclature of the 1914 Act is used.

It is important to recognize that an assignment does not affect specific partnership property which remains in partnership solution under both statutes for the reasons set forth in previous sections. Further, an assignee of a partner's interest in a partnership receives only limited rights, principally the right to receive distributions to which the assigning partner is entitled. If the partnership agreement provides for periodic distributions, the assignee is entitled to receive whatever amount that is distributed. If distributions are at the discretion of the partnership, the assignee is probably unable to compel any distribution, so long as the partnership was willing not to make any distributions to its other partners. Presumably, a partnership could not make distributions to other partners but withhold the amount due the assigning partner.

An assignee does not become a partner simply by accepting the assignment, and he does not have a right to participate in management as a result of the assignment. An assignee does not automatically become a partner because of the principal of *delectus personae*, a phrase that is a catchword for the basic proposition that one cannot become a partner without the consent of the other partners. Since an assignee does not automatically become a partner, it follows that he has no personal responsibility for partnership obligations, including both already existing and subsequently arising liabilities. He also does not have a right to inspect partnership records. Of course, if the assignee is accepted as a partner, he incurs the general responsibilities of any new partner and has the inspection rights of a partner.

On the other hand, the partner who assigns his financial interest in the partnership does remain a partner and continues to have the right to participate in management. He also remains liable for partnership obligations including those that arise after the assignment. To put the matter another way, a partner can assign his financial rights but his right to participate in management cannot be assigned to a third person unless the other partners accept the assignee as a new partner. While an assignor remains a partner in the partnership, he usually has little incentive to participate in partnership matters except possibly to limit liabilities incurred by the partnership for which he is liable. Because of this narrow interest, partnership agreements usually provide that a partner who assigns his entire financial interest in the partnership thereafter ceases to be a partner, though of course his responsibility for outstanding partnership obligations is not directly affected.

An assignee of a partnership interest does have some limited rights in addition to the right to receive distributions allocable to the assigning partner. Upon a winding up of the business, he is entitled to payments otherwise due to the assigning partner and is also entitled to an accounting of partnership transactions after the assignment. He also may be able to compel a dissolution and winding up of the business under specified circumstances. Under UPA (1914) section 32(2), an assignee may apply for judicial dissolution of a partnership if the term of the partnership has expired or the partnership is a partnership at will at the time of the assignment.[39] UPA (1994) section 801(6) retains this basic provision but adds the requirement that there be a judicial determination "that it is equitable to wind up the partnership business." Presumably, the same standard was implicit in the 1914 Act's requirement that dissolution be by judicial decree.

Assignments of partnership interests occur frequently in circumstances in which the assigning partner remains actively involved in the business. They may arise, for example, when a partner seeks a personal loan and the lender requires an assignment of his interest in the partnership to secure repayment of the loan. They may also arise in connection with marital property settlements where one spouse is a partner. In community property states, an interest in a partnership may itself be community property, and in a sense the nonpartner spouse is a partial owner of the interest of the spouse in the partnership. An assignment of a portion of the partner's interest in the partnership to his spouse may be part of the final allocation of marital property, though it is probably more common, as a practical matter, to allocate the partnership interest entirely to the active partner and assign other marital assets of roughly the same value to the spouse.

---

[39]Partnerships at will and partnerships for a term are discussed in §4.25.

§4.21 ADMISSION OF NEW PARTNERS

When a person is admitted to an existing partnership she joins an ongoing business that has assets and liabilities. The terms of her entry will normally involve a capital contribution roughly equal to the value of the financial interest she is receiving. This payment may be required as a lump sum or it may become payable over a period of time. A determination also must be made of the extent of her voting power which may be per capita or based on her financial interest, or established in some other fashion. However, the scope of her liability for existing partnership obligations is not a matter on which the partnership agreement will necessarily control.[40]

Section 17 of UPA (1914) addresses generally the responsibility of new partners for existing liabilities. That section states that a new partner is liable for partnership liabilities "arising before his admission" as though he had been a partner when such obligations were incurred, "except that this liability shall be satisfied only out of partnership property." Section 306(b) of UPA (1994) expresses the same idea more simply with the use of the entity concept: A person admitted as a partner in an existing partnership "is not personally liable for any partnership obligation incurred before the person's admission as a partner."

One might expect that these provisions set forth a bright line as to the extent of the new partner's liability for existing obligations. In fact, they do not. The interpretation of the words "arising before" and "incurred before" are hardly precise and are subject to considerable uncertainty. Consider, for example, a long-term lease of expensive office space entered into three years before our new partner appears on the scene. Did the monthly rental obligation over the entire term of the lease arise (or is it incurred) at the time the lease was signed, or does it arise (or is it incurred) during the month the space is actually occupied? If it is the former, the new partner has no responsibility for the payment of rent even on the space she occupies within the firm's offices; if it is the latter, she has a personal liability for at least a portion of a lease that was entered into before she became a partner. The case law on this question generally favors the new partner, but it is not uniform.

The cases dealing with when obligations arise in connection with the liability of a new partner reflect the ambiguity in this statutory provision. Compare, for example, the favorable result (for the new partners) reached in *Citizens Bank v. Parham-Woodman Medical Associates*,[41] (partners admit-

---

[40] A partnership agreement may provide that a new partner will be indemnified by the partnership and the existing partners against certain already-existing liabilities. However, that is of scant value to the new partner if she is in fact liable for these liabilities and the partnership and the other partners lack assets sufficient to satisfy those liabilities.

[41] 874 F. Supp. 705 (E.D. Va. 1995).

ted after the partnership entered into a construction loan agreement were not personally liable for advances drawn on the loan after they became partners) with *Barbro Realty Co. v. Newburger*[42] (new partners liable on lease even though premises not used by partnership).

Minnesota has attempted to address the "arise/accrue" issue by enacting a statute that provides that (1) partnership obligations "under or relating to a note, contract or other agreement arise and accrue when the note, contract or other agreement is entered into"[43] and (2) an amendment, modification extension or renewal of a note, contract, or agreement does not affect the time when the obligation arose (even as to a claim involving the subject matter of the modification). The intention was to create a mechanical rule that was easy to apply and would generally conform to the expectation of parties.

D. FINANCIAL AND TAX ASPECTS[44]

§4.22 THE TAX TREATMENT OF A PARTNERSHIP

Even though a modern general partnership has most of the characteristics of a separate legal entity, it is almost never treated as a separate taxable entity under the Internal Revenue Code. Unincorporated businesses may be taxed either as "an association taxable as a corporation" or as "a partnership." The proper tax classification of an unincorporated business is not governed by the classification of the business entity for state law purposes.

It is almost always more desirable from a tax standpoint for an unincorporated business to be taxed as a partnership rather than as an association taxable as corporation. When an association is taxable as a corporation, it and its owners are viewed as different taxable entities and each is separately subject to tax, first at the level of the organization on the income earned by it at corporate tax rates, and second, at the level of the owners on distributions made to them out of the earnings and profits of the business.[45] In most situations, this dual tax treatment is more costly, tax-wise, than the tax

[42]385 N.Y.S.2d 68 (App. Div. 1976).

[43]Minn. Stat. §323.14.

[44] In May 1996, the Internal Revenue Service proposed a considerable simplification of the rules relating to partnership taxation in its so-called check the box regulations. These regulations are discussed below. In addition, a variety of "flat tax" or "alternative tax" proposals are being considered by Congress, which, if enacted, would revolutionize the entire federal tax structure.

[45]The S corporation election, a partial exception to the statement in the text is discussed in §§9.6-9.9

treatment of partnerships discussed below. The corporate tax structure outlined in this paragraph is discussed in greater detail in Chapter 9.

The method of taxation applicable to a partnership is usually referred to as *pass through* (or *conduit*) taxation. A partnership must prepare an information return[46] each year that shows partnership income and expenses, but it does not itself pay any tax. Rather, it then allocates the income or loss of the partnership among the individual partners in accordance with the partnership agreement. Each partner must then include in his or her personal income tax return the amount of each item so allocated.[47]

It is difficult to emphasize sufficiently the importance of the difference in tax treatment described in the previous paragraphs on the development of new business forms and on the adaptation of traditional business forms in modern practice to these tax rules.

The determination of the tax treatment of an unincorporated business entity was traditionally made under Internal Revenue Code regulations usually called the "Kintner" regulations.[48] These regulations, to be superseded by the new *check the box regulations*, list four critical "corporate" characteristics that are to be considered in determining whether an entity should be classified as an association taxable as a corporation — continuity of life, centralization of management, limited liability, and free transferability of interests. An unincorporated business entity that has a preponderance of these corporate characteristics — three out of four — was taxed as a corporation; otherwise, it was taxed as a partnership. A general partnership created under the default rules of partnership law does not have any of these corporate characteristics and thus was taxed as a partnership under the Kintner regulations.[49] It may be helpful to explain briefly why a general partner-

---

[46]This information return is form 1065.

[47]The partnership must send each individual partner a statement on form K-1 as to the amount of each item of income, deduction, or loss allocated to him or her for the year.

[48]Kintner was the name of the taxpayer involved in one of the early cases involving the classification of unincorporated business entities. United States v. Kintner, 216 F.2d 418 (9th Cir. 1954).

The Kintner regulations were modified and liberalized at various times so that the choice of tax regime by an unincorporated firm became virtually elective. See §5.18. The proposed check the box regulations would scrap the Kintner regulations entirely for unincorporated firms, and adopt a simple system by which each new unincorporated entity could elect the tax regime under which it wished to be governed simply by checking the appropriate "box" on a tax return.

[49]In a few rare instances, a general partnership agreement may structure the enterprise so that it has one or more of these characteristics. If it has three of these four characteristics, it will be taxed as a corporation. Detailed regulations have been promulgated defining when each of these characteristics exist. The issue of tax classification is obviously much more difficult in the case of limited partnerships and limited liability companies where most or all of the participants are not personally liable for the obligations of the business. See §§5.15 and 5.18, relating to the tax classification of a limited partnership with a single corporate general partner; §6.9, relating to the tax classification of limited liability companies.

ship normally lacks these characteristics: It does not have limited liability because all partners are jointly and severally liable for business obligations.[50] It does not have continuity of life since a partner may dissolve the partnership at any time by his express will.[51] It does not have centralization of management because each partner has equal management rights in the business.[52] And, it does not have free transferability of interest because assignees of partnership interests do not automatically obtain partnership status.[53] These factors were weighted equally under the Kintner regulations. Under the proposed check the box regulations, the selection of tax treatment is entirely elective. An unincorporated business entity simply "checks" a box to determine the type of tax treatment it prefers.

Tax treatment as a partnership is also attractive for technical reasons unrelated to the double tax issue. These technical benefits include flexibility in allowing special allocations of a partnership's profit and loss to individual partners (so long as the allocations have "substantial economic effect" outside of the tax consequences) and nonrecognition of gain upon the distribution in kind of appreciated property to partners. The detailed tax rules applicable to general partnerships are quite complex and advice by tax counsel is desirable whenever it is desired to obtain these favorable tax results within a partnership.

§4.23 THE CAPITAL ACCOUNTS OF A PARTNER: ALLOCATIONS AND DISTRIBUTIONS

UPA (1914) assumes that some record will be kept of the capital accounts of the partnership, but gives no guidance as to what these accounts should look like. Section 401(a) of UPA (1994) is a much more helpful provision in this regard:

(a) Each partner is deemed to have an account that is:

(1) credited with an amount equal to the money plus the value of any other property, net of the amount of any liabilities, the partner contributes to the partnership and the partner's share of the partnership profits; and

(2) charged with an amount equal to the money plus the value of any other property, net of the amount of any liabilities, distributed by the partnership to the partner and the partner's share of the partnership losses.[54]

[50]See §4.14.
[51]See §4.25.
[52]See §4.11.
[53]See §4.20.
[54]The capital account described in UPA (1994) §401(a) is the minimum accounting requirement for partnerships. In the most informal partnership, no books or records at all

To put this elegant and rather simple definition in ordinary language, a partner's capital account equals his initial capital contribution *plus* additional contributions *plus* allocations of profit to the partner *minus* distributions of cash or property to the partner *minus* allocations of losses to the partner.

The capital amounts determine how the partners will share the ownership interest of the assets and how assets will be distributed upon the liquidation of the partnership.

It is important to recognize that partnership profit or loss (*allocated* to partners) is usually calculated on an accrual basis of accounting and not simply on the basis of cash flow or cash receipts and disbursements. ("Usually" because some partnerships do calculate profit or loss on a cash basis — most law firms, for example.) Some expenses, e.g., depreciation of fixed assets, may be appropriate charges against income even though the partnership's cash account is not reduced by that expense. *Distributions*, on the other hand, are made on an entirely different basis. They involve actual cash payments and decisions whether or not to make distributions must take into account the possibility that anticipated cash flow may not be sufficient to satisfy liabilities as they become due.

Capital accounts may be positive or negative. Negative capital accounts reflect dollars potentially owed by the partner to the partnership. They usually arise after the partnership commences business as a result of a series of losses that exceed the original contributions by the partners. Negative capital accounts may also be created when a partnership is formed or when a person joins an existing partnership. A partner may make a "contribution" in the form of a promise to make one or more payments in the future. Such a person becomes a partner immediately with a negative capital account. Many associates in law firms who "make" partner discover that one of the consequences is that they immediately obtain a negative capital account.

A negative capital account means either that future income will be allocated to eliminate the negative capital balance or that the partner may have to restore capital to the partnership at some later time. Negative capital accounts may continue for extended periods. Upon the dissolution and winding up of the partnership, there is a final allocation of liabilities. Each partner is personally liable on all partnership liabilities; negative capital accounts may have to be raised to zero as part of the final settling up among the partners themselves.

---

may be kept, but the capital account described in that section will nevertheless "be deemed to" exist. Partnerships, like most other businesses, however, in practice must keep separate books to reflect the tax treatment of specific transactions that may bear little direct relationship with the capital accounts of the partnership. Tax accounting differs from general partnership accounting in a variety of areas. There is nothing improper or questionable about maintaining separate tax records in order to determine income and deductions of partners for tax purposes and the partners' capital accounts for tax purposes.

There is a sharp difference between *allocations* of profits or losses for tax purposes and *distributions* of money or property to partners. The partnership agreement determines how profits or losses are to be allocated among the partners. This allocation is referred to as the partner's *distributive share*. Profits or losses are calculated through an accounting system. However, the amount that a partner actually receives from the partnership — distributions — may be greater or less than his distributive share.

In a new business, for example, the partners may agree that they will build up the capital of the partnership by making distributions that are smaller than the profits allocated to them. Thus, a positive allocation of income to a specific partner may occur even though the partnership does not in fact make any distributions of cash or property at all to that partner with respect to the year in question. Similarly, a partnership may have a loss in one or more years even though it makes substantial cash distributions during those years to some or all of the partners. Contributions of property by a partner or the allocation of income to a partner increases a partner's capital account. Losses allocated to the partner and distributions to the partner both reduce the partner's capital account. The relationship between allocations and distributions can be most easily envisioned by comparing an employee's income statement on his W-2 form with his total take-home pay.

Since taxation is determined by the allocation of income to the partners and not by actual distributions to the partner, it is possible that a partner will have to use personal funds to pay additional tax when the allocation exceeds the amount of the actual distribution.[55]

E. DISSOLUTION AND WINDING UP

§4.24 TERMINATION OF PARTNERSHIPS IN GENERAL

A fundamental principle of partnership law is that a person who is a partner cannot be compelled to remain a partner against his or her will. The partnership relation is one of trust and confidence; if that trust and confidence is lost, a partner can terminate his role in the partnership. In this respect, partnerships differ fundamentally from corporations, where termination of the corporation is available only in limited circumstances. This basic difference is usually described as *continuity of life*; a corporation remains in exis-

---

[55]Where accumulations of capital are contemplated, partnership agreements may provide that the partnership must distribute each year an amount equal to the profit allocated to each partner multiplied by the highest federal income tax rate. This assures that the partner will have funds available to pay the tax that is due. These payments are called *tax distributions*.

tence even though the persons who are shareholders may change from time to time, but a partnership is a personal relationship that ends whenever a partner withdraws from the partnership. While this remains true as a general conceptual matter, modern partnerships may in fact have a considerable degree of continuity. Furthermore, provisions in partnership agreements may make withdrawal extremely unattractive as a financial matter.

An important distinction in partnerships is between economic continuity and legal continuity. Where a partner dies, retires, or otherwise withdraws, legal continuity has ended under common law and UPA (1914), but the business may not be affected from an economic standpoint. That depends on how essential the withdrawn partner was in the business of the partnership. A pure capital contributor is unlikely to be essential; a person whose services make the business a success may well be essential if the business is to continue in its present form. The balance of this chapter discusses legal continuity not economic continuity.

§4.25 PARTNERSHIPS AT WILL AND PARTNERSHIPS FOR A TERM

Partnerships may be classified into partnerships at will and partnerships for a term or definite undertaking. If there is no agreement as to how long the partnership is to continue, it is a *partnership at will*. If the partnership is to continue for a specified period or until a specific objective is achieved, it is a *partnership for a term* (or *definite undertaking*). Examples are a partnership that is to continue for one year or a partnership that is to continue until a specific mortgage on a piece of property is paid off. The importance of this distinction lies in the fact that in a partnership for a term, a partner who exercises his power to dissolve the partnership by his express will breaches the partnership agreement. Such a partner has the *power* to dissolve but not the *right* to dissolve.[56] In a partnership at will, on the other hand, any partner has the power to dissolve by his or her express will at any time without any liability to other partners.[57] In a partnership for a term or definite un-

[56]This distinction clearly appears in §31 of UPA (1914). Section 31(1) provides that "dissolution is caused [without violation of the agreement between the partners] . . . (b) by the express will of any partner when no definite term or particular undertaking is specified." Section 31(2) provides "dissolution is caused . . . in contravention of the agreement between the partners, where the circumstances do not permit a dissolution under any other provision of this section, by the express will of any partner at any time."

[57]A few cases have imposed liability on a withdrawing partner in a partnership at will when the withdrawal may constitute a breach of fiduciary duty. The classic example is the partner in a law partnership who has worked full-time on a contingent fee case for several years while being supported by his other partners. Shortly before the successful conclusion of this case he withdraws knowing that the client will wish for him to complete the work on the case and hoping to receive the entire contingent fee to the exclusion of his former law firm.

dertaking, the threat of a claim for damages for breach of contract may be a significant deterrent to exercise of the power to dissolve. As in any other contract, a partnership agreement for a term may contain a liquidated damages clause imposing a significant sanction on the premature or opportunistic withdrawal of a partner.

Where there is a formal partnership agreement, it is relatively easy to arrange a partnership for a term rather than a partnership at will. For example, many of the great law firms that exist in major cities in the United States for decades are partnerships for a term, not partnerships at will. Where an oral agreement is involved, a problem may arise under the statute of frauds if the partnership is to continue for more than one year.

§4.26 DISSOLUTION AND WINDING UP UNDER UPA (1914)

UPA (1914) uses the word "dissolution" in an unusual way. A *dissolution* is defined in section 29 not as the terminal event in a partnership's existence, but rather as the "change in the relation" among the partners when a partner ceases to be a partner. In contrast, a *termination* is the event that marks the end of the partnership's business. Legal continuity thus ends upon the dissolution of the partnership; economic continuity when the business is terminated. Under the 1914 Act, a partnership does not "terminate" upon dissolution but continues in existence to be "wound up." What makes this terminology particularly confusing is that the word "dissolution" in common parlance refers to the termination of a business, not the termination of a legal relationship.

Further, in the real world, dissolution (in the sense used in UPA (1914)) is often not followed by a winding up and a termination of the economic enterprise. As described below, the business of a "dissolved" partnership is usually continued by a new or different partnership composed of some but not all of the former partners and possibly some new partners. Furthermore, this often occurs without the partners really being aware that as a legal matter the old partnership "dissolved" and a "new" partnership took over the business.[58]

One of the principal reasons for the development of UPA (1994) was

---

[58] Indeed, many partnership agreements provide expressly that the withdrawal of a partner does not constitute a dissolution despite the language of the UPA (1914). Some courts have stated that where one partner withdraws but the business is continued by the remaining partners pursuant to the partnership agreement, the partnership is not dissolved at all with respect to the continuing partners but was dissolved with respect to the withdrawn partners. This is intuitively plausible but it seems clearly not to have been the analysis contemplated by the drafters of UPA (1914).

dissatisfaction with the dissolution provisions of the 1914 Act. The confusing terminology was only a small part of the problem. A more serious problem was that the 1914 Act only inferentially recognizes the continuation of the business alternative and does not make adequate provision for the liquidation of the interest of the withdrawing partner. Further, viewing a change in the partners as a "dissolution" sometimes created legal problems under anti-assignment clauses and the like.[59] However, perhaps the greatest cause of dissatisfaction with the 1914 Act was that it gave a former partner (or his legal representative) an absolute right to compel the winding up and termination of a dissolved partnership even though the remaining partners wished for it to continue.[60]

Section 31 of UPA (1914) lists a number of events that automatically cause dissolution of a partnership. These include the death or bankruptcy of a partner, the express will of a partner to withdraw from the partnership, the expulsion of a partner, the termination of the definite term or particular undertaking of the partnership, or an event that makes it unlawful for the partnership business to continue. In addition to the automatic dissolution provisions, section 32 provides for dissolution pursuant to a court order under specified circumstances that largely revolve around the misconduct of a specific partner. Judicial dissolution may also be available for an assignee of a partnership interest in a partnership at will.

Following the dissolution of a partnership, UPA (1914) contemplates that there will be a process of winding up its business and affairs, reducing assets to cash, paying off liabilities, and distributing the balance of the assets to the partners. The partnership is "terminated" only when this process is completed. Each partner must contribute to satisfy all liabilities. Section 40(b) of UPA (1914) provides that liabilities of the partnership rank in the following order of payment: (1) those owing to creditors other than partners, (2) those owing to partners other than for capital and profits (e.g., loans by a partner to her partnership), (3) those owing to partners in respect of capital, and (4) those owing to partners in respect of profits.

---

[59]Consider, for example, a partnership that is the lessee under a lease on favorable economic terms. The lease provides (as leases usually do) that the leasehold may not be assigned without the consent of the lessor. One partner dies and the remaining partners continue the business, making acceptable financial arrangements to pay the deceased partner's estate the value of that partner's interest. The death of the partner is a 1914 Act dissolution of the lessee followed immediately by the creation of a new partnership. May the lessor view this transaction as an attempted assignment of the lease and refuse to grant his assent to the assignment? Probably not, but the issue is troublesome for partnerships because it encourages opportunistic conduct by the landlord.

[60]This power is set forth in §38(1) of UPA (1914). If the dissolution was "wrongful," a concept discussed in §4.31, the withdrawing partner is not entitled to compel a winding up and termination.

Among the assets of the liquidating partnership are the contributions of the partners necessary for the payment of all of these liabilities. Section 18(a) adds that each partner "shall be repaid his contributions, whether by way of capital or advances to the partnership property." The net effect of these provisions is, absent an agreement to the contrary, that in the event the assets of the partnership are not sufficient to discharge all liabilities and repay each partner his contributions to capital and loans to the partnership, each partner may be compelled to make contributions to the partnership to permit the winding up to be completed. If any partner is insolvent or unable to make her necessary contributions, the solvent partners must make them on her behalf.[61] These contributions are allocated among the solvent partners in accordance with their profitsharing ratios.[62]

Among the liabilities to be satisfied in the winding up process is the obligation to return to each partner his capital (reduced by any losses chargeable against that capital account). If the partnership assets are not sufficient to provide for a return of each partner's capital, partners with negative capital accounts may be compelled to contribute additional funds to the partnership to permit each partner to receive a return of his capital, reduced by the contribution required of each partner to make the capital accounts come out right. However, the partnership agreement may eliminate the requirement that these capital-restoring contributions be made.

The statutory winding up process contemplates that assets will be reduced to cash, and the balance after satisfaction of all liabilities distributed to the partner, though the partners may agree upon an in-kind distribution if all liabilities are satisfied. Provisions are also included in UPA (1914) that describe the person or persons who may wind up the business,[63] and authorize partners to seek winding up under judicial supervision.[64]

UPA (1914) recognizes that the partnership business may be continued during the winding up period if appropriate to maximizing the value of the business. Third parties having business dealings with the partnership in ignorance of the dissolution may hold the former partners responsible for post-dissolution liabilities.[65] In this regard, a withdrawn partner continues to be liable on partnership obligations entered into after dissolution unless the third person is aware of the dissolution, or the withdrawn partner has

[61] UPA (1914) §40(d).

[62] For example, if there are one 50 percent partner and two 25 percent partners, one of whom is insolvent, the 50 percent partner must pick up two-thirds of the required contribution of the insolvent partner, and the solvent 25 percent partner must pick up the remaining one-third.

[63] UPA (1914) §37.

[64] Id. last clause. The petition to obtain winding up by the court must be "upon cause shown." Presumably, this means some showing that the partners winding up the business are doing so in an improper or biased manner.

[65] Id. §§33, 35.

caused a notice of the dissolution to be published "in a newspaper of general circulation."[66]

UPA (1914) also contemplates — or rather recognizes by making specific provision for — a "dissolution" that is not followed by a winding up and termination of the business. Even though a withdrawing partner may have a statutory right to compel winding up,[67] that right may not be exercised. Typically what happens is that the remaining partners simply continue the business and the withdrawing partner or his estate does not object. In effect, the continuing partners create a new partnership among themselves (or with additional partners) in order to continue the business in that form and the withdrawing partner does not insist on his statutory right to obtain a winding up. Where this occurs, the UPA (1914) has a valuation provision that is unusually favorable to the withdrawing partners.[68] The amount to be paid to those partners by the partnership is the value of the partnership interest at dissolution (with no guidance as to how that value should be calculated) plus compensation for the partnership's use of the partner's capital, which at the withdrawing partner's election, is equal to either (1) interest on that value from the date of dissolution until the time of payment, or (2) the partner's share of the profits over the same period. The theory is that compensation should be paid to the withdrawing partner for the use of the withdrawn partner's capital for the period the partnership actually has the use of that capital. Furthermore, the case law under UPA (1914) permits this election to be made long after formal dissolution has occurred, indeed, up to the time of final valuation of the withdrawn partner's interest. This permits the withdrawn partner to make this election with the benefit of hindsight as to which alternative is more attractive. Presumably, this after-the-fact election was designed to encourage the partners continuing the business to address promptly after dissolution the amount to be paid to the withdrawing partners. Its effect, however, is to give the withdrawn partner something of an economic windfall. This provision is not carried over into UPA (1994).

§4.27 CONTINUATION AGREEMENTS

It is an observable fact of the business world that most changes in the composition of a partnership that constitute a "dissolution" in the legal sense under UPA (1914) are not followed by a winding up and termination. In

[66]Id. §35(1)(b)(II).

[67]UPA (1914) §38(1). As described in the text, however, this right is available "unless otherwise agreed." Formal partnership agreements usually provide that withdrawing partners do not have this right if the remaining partners wish to continue the business.

[68]UPA (1914) §42.

other words, continuation is the norm and winding up the exception. The reason for this is that it usually makes more economic sense to continue an ongoing business rather than to wind it up, a fact that may be recognized by a withdrawing partner who has the statutory right to compel a winding up and termination. Nevertheless, the power granted to withdrawing partners to compel a winding up by UPA (1914) creates the possibility of opportunistic conduct by those partners who may use the threat of compelling a winding up as a bargaining chip in negotiating the amount to be paid them for their interests in the partnership.

UPA (1914) makes it clear that the right to compel a winding up following dissolution may be eliminated by an express provision to that effect in the partnership agreement. Section 38(1), giving a withdrawing partner the right to compel a winding up and termination of the partnership is qualified by the important phrase "unless otherwise agreed."[69] Provisions eliminating the right of any withdrawing partner to compel winding up and termination are called *continuation agreements*, and their inclusion in formal partnership agreements is virtually routine. Indeed, the need for continuation agreements is so great that they provide a major incentive to have formal written partnership agreements to begin with.

Continuation agreements may specify how the value of the partnership interest is to be calculated and the period over which that amount may be paid. It may provide for interest on the unpaid balance, or provide that no interest should be paid. It may provide that the unpaid amount is secured by a lien on partnership assets, or that it is entirely unsecured. Continuation agreements are binding on the withdrawing partner and his or her estate in accordance with the general principle that the partnership agreement is the law of that partnership. Partnership agreements are often drafted in a way to discourage the withdrawal of partners. The partnership agreement may specify liquidated damages for a withdrawal in contravention of the agreement or contain a covenant not to compete. An agreement may also specify a method of valuation that is so ungenerous as to make withdrawal unattractive. The agreement may provide, for example, that the value of the interest of a withdrawn or deceased partner is limited to the amount of his original capital or some fixed sum, such as $50. Because a partnership is a consensual relationship, it is unlikely that a court will relieve a withdrawing partner from such provisions on the ground of unfairness though it is possible that a court might accept arguments that the provisions are unenforceable penalties, unreasonable restraints of alienation, or are unconscionable.[70]

---

[69] Section 42, creating the one-sided election between interest and a share in post-dissolution profits, is also qualified by the same phrase. In other words, a written partnership agreement may exclude that election if desired.

[70] Usually, it cannot be determined at the time these agreements are entered into who will be the partner who withdraws or dies. As a result, there is an element of Russian Rou-

In short, continuation agreements bind the withdrawing partners as well as the continuing ones to accept a manner of liquidating the interest of the withdrawing partners independent of the provisions of UPA (1914). They provide a method for determining the value of the interest of the withdrawing partners and the terms on which the payment is to be made. In effect, they permit the partnership to establish the basis on which a partner may withdraw from the business.

Many law firm partnership agreements contain covenants not to compete, or may provide that termination payments otherwise payable are reduced if the withdrawing partners thereafter open their own practice in the same city or join a competing law firm within a specified period. The validity of such provisions because of ethical considerations is in some doubt,[71] though similar provisions appear to be routinely enforced in medical and dental partnerships.

§4.28 DISSOCIATION AND DISSOLUTION UNDER UPA (1994)

UPA (1994) substitutes a different legal framework and nomenclature for the dissolution provisions of UPA (1914), and provides considerably more guidance as to how termination issues are to be resolved. While the overall structure is similar to that of the 1914 Act, there are numerous minor differences and some important substantive changes. As indicated above, concern about the dissolution provisions of UPA (1914) was an important factor in the decision to develop a new statute, and probably more attention was paid to these provisions than any other part of the older statute.

Since the 1994 Act provides unambiguously that the partnership is an entity separate from the *persona* of the partners, there is no conceptual problem at all with the view that a partnership continues to exist despite the withdrawal of a partner or the substitution of one partner for another. The UPA (1914), on the other hand, did not unambiguously adopt an entity theory; indeed, the concept in that statute that a "dissolution" involves a change in the relationship among the partners seems clearly to have been based on an aggregate notion.

The 1994 Act introduces new concepts of continuity and a new terminology. The act of withdrawal by a partner leads to what is called a *dissocia-*

---

lette in these clauses. Because of this, and the possibility that an unfair provision will increase the likelihood of post-dissolution litigation, most partnership agreements attempt to treat the withdrawing partner reasonably fairly.

[71] The leading case invalidating penalty provisions on the ground that they deprive the public of free choice of legal advisers is Cohen v. Lord, Day & Lord, 75 N.Y.2d 95, 550 N.E.2d 410 (1989). The leading case rejecting this view is Howard v. Babcock, 6 Cal.4th 409, 863 P.2d 150 (1993).

tion not a "dissolution."[72] Every partner has a power to dissociate at any time, thereby preserving the freedom of a partner to leave a partnership at any time which existed both at common law and UPA (1914). Following a dissociation, one of two different things may happen. Either the partnership will continue and the interest of the withdrawing partner will be purchased,[73] or the partnership will be "dissolved"[74] and its business "wound up."[75] However, the decision as to which is to occur in a partnership for a term is made not by the withdrawing partner but by the remaining partners "by the express will of at least half of the remaining partners."[76] A dissociation in a partnership at will, on the other hand, at the option of the withdrawing partner, leads to a dissolution and winding up.[77]

When a dissociation occurs, the partnership continues if the interest of the dissociated partner is purchased by the partnership. UPA (1994) sets forth in some detail a standard for determining how much should be paid. Section 701(b) provides that the buyout price should be the amount that would have been distributable to the dissociating partner "if, on the date of dissociation, the assets of the partnership were sold at a price equal to the greater of the liquidation value or the value based on a sale of the entire business as a going concern without the dissociated partner and the partnership were wound up as of that date." However, if the dissociation is wrongful, no payment may be due to the dissociating partner until the expiration of the term of the partnership or the completion of the particular undertaking.[78] An earlier payment may be ordered by a court if the partner can establish "that earlier payment will not cause undue hardship to the business of the partnership." The effect of this provision is to make the value of the interest of a wrongfully dissociating partner remain at the risk of the business, though the statute adds that the deferred payment "must be adequately secured and bear interest."

§4.29 ACTIONS FOR AN ACCOUNTING

An action for an *accounting* (or for a *formal account*) is the traditional remedy available to a partner to establish the rights and obligations of the part-

---

[72] UPA (1994) §601.

[73] UPA (1994) §701 et seq.

[74] Early drafts of the statute that became UPA (1994) did not use the "d" word — "dissolution" — at all, but it was added back in relatively late in the revision process to describe the winding up and termination alternative. Given the long history of the use of the "d" word and increasing familiarity with its use in UPA (1914), it is possible that this decision may reintroduce some ambiguity in UPA (1994).

[75] UPA (1994) §801 et seq.

[76] UPA (1994) §801(2).

[77] Id. §801(1).

[78] Id. §701(h).

ners within a partnership. At common law, it was available only after the partnership had been dissolved and the partners were unable to agree upon the appropriate distribution of partnership property.[79] The name of this form of action is somewhat misleading since the action was much broader than simply a judicial review of the accounting records; an inquiry might appropriately be made into breaches of fiduciary duty, transactions affecting partnership property, and so forth. Furthermore, the court might inquire into transactions from the inception of the partnership up to the present, even if the transactions occurred many years earlier, without regard to any statute of limitations. In effect, the entire financial history of the partnership was the subject of judicial review.

Section 22 of UPA (1914) describes this action as a "right to a formal account as to partnership affairs." It apparently relaxed the requirement that it was available only following dissolution by a provision that the right was available "whenever . . . circumstances render it just and equitable." Section 405 of UPA (1994) describes this action as the right of a partner to "maintain an action against the partnership or another partner for legal or equitable relief, with or without an accounting as to partnership business." This provision appears designed to soften the historical limitations of the action for an accounting, and to permit litigation with respect to partnership matters in suits for an injunction or for damages for breach of the partnership agreement. Section 405(c), moreover, limits the claims that may be considered in such an action to claims not barred by an applicable statute of limitations. "The accrual of, and any time limitation on, a right of action for a remedy under this section is governed by other law. A right to an accounting upon a dissolution and winding up does not revive a claim barred by law." Partnership disputes must be litigated reasonably promptly under this provision, or they will be barred.

---

[79]The rule that an action for an account is available only after dissolution was apparently based on the notion that a relationship of trust and confidence necessary for the partnership relation could not exist if the partners were actively litigating claims against each other.

5

Limited Partnerships

§5.1 INTRODUCTION

A limited partnership differs from a general partnership in that there are two classes of partners: (1) One or more *general partners* who have the same rights, obligations, and duties as general partners in a general partnership, and (2) one or more *limited partners*, who are investors in the partnership but who are not personally liable for the debts of the partnership and who are not expected to participate in the day-to-day affairs of the partnership. In effect, limited partners stand to lose what they have invested in the enterprise, but no more. General partners are of course fully liable for the debts of the business to the same extent as partners in a general partnership without limited partners. Because of this basic difference in roles, general partners are traditionally the managers of the business while limited partners are passive investors.

In the 1980s and 1990s, new forms of unincorporated businesses have proliferated with names that are confusingly similar to the traditional limited partnership discussed in this chapter. These new forms of business are called "limited liability partnerships," "limited liability companies," "professional limited liability companies," and, most confusingly, "limited liability limited partnerships."

Despite the similar names, limited liability partnerships, discussed in Chapter 7, are not directly related to the limited partnerships discussed in this chapter. A limited partnership has two classes of partners, denominated as such in the partnership agreement, while limited liability partnerships have only one class of partner, with limited liability being available only with respect to specific kinds or classes of claims, and dependent upon the relationship of the specific partner to that claim.

Limited liability companies combine both partnership and corporate concepts in a different way than limited partnerships. A limited liability company can be most simply described as being similar to a limited partnership composed entirely of limited partners. Limited liability companies are discussed in Chapter 6. Professional limited liability companies are a type of limited liability company analogous to professional corporations. They are discussed in section 8.40.

A *limited liability limited partnership* is a limited partnership in which the general partners have elected among themselves to have the protections provided to general partners by the LLP election.[1]

§5.2 COMPARISON BETWEEN LIMITED AND GENERAL PARTNERSHIPS

The presence of two classes of partners in a limited partnership is a fundamental difference that makes the legal and economic issues in a limited partnership quite different from those in a general partnership discussed in Chapter 4. In a general partnership, the rights and obligations of all partners are substantially the same; in a limited partnership, the general partners necessarily have a different perspective and a different interest from the limited partners. General partners in a limited partnership are exposed to all of the operational risks of the business and it should not be surprising that they therefore have greater control over day-to-day management of the

[1]See §7.1.

business operations than limited partners. Further, because of the differences in the risk assumed, general partners may legitimately demand additional compensation in the form of either smaller capital contributions than required of the limited partners or a greater allocation of profit, or both. On the other hand, both general and limited partnerships are forms of partnership and it should not be surprising that in many areas the rules and practices of general partnerships are applicable to limited partnerships.[2]

It is common in the modern world of limited partnerships for the general partner to be a corporation or limited liability company rather than an individual. Further, one or more of the limited partners may be dominating or controlling shareholders of the corporate general partner. Where limited partnership interests are widely sold to the public by a brokerage firm, the corporate general partner may be controlled by persons associated with the brokerage firm, or by the brokerage firm itself. To some extent at least, these interrelationships between general and limited partners may blunt the simple risk analysis of the previous paragraph.

Limited partnerships, unlike general partnerships, require that a public filing be made as part of their creation. If an attempt is made to create a limited partnership but the filing is not made, a general partnership is created, though some protection may be available for a putative limited partner who erroneously believes that a proper filing has been made.[3] It is therefore not possible to have an oral or "handshake" limited partnership.

§5.3 THE IMPORTANCE OF FEDERAL INCOME TAXATION

To a significant extent, the limited partnership is a tax-driven form of business. It combines the desirable features of limited liability for some partners with the "conduit" or "pass through" tax treatment characteristic of general partnerships. Section 4.22 describes the general federal income tax treatment of partnerships and briefly compares that treatment with the income tax treatment of corporations. Since 1986, the corporate and individual tax rates, and other tax rules as well, have made it advantageous for businesses

[2]Limited partnerships also have similarities to corporations discussed in Chapters 8–10. One therefore finds that some areas of limited partnership law and practice are based on the corporate model rather than the general partnership model.

[3]This protection is available only to a person who "makes a contribution to a business enterprise and erroneously but in good faith believes that he has become a limited partner in the enterprise." RULPA §304. Such a person must then either cause an appropriate certificate of limited partnership to be executed and filed or "withdraw[ ] from future equity participation in the enterprise by executing and filing . . . a certificate declaring withdrawal" from the limited partnership. Presumably, a renunciation of "future equity participation" means that the putative limited partner is entitled only to a return of his contribution with interest.

with few owners to be taxed as a partnership rather than as a corporation, since the tax cost of moving earnings from the business to the owners of the business is usually lowest under the partnership rules.

Since limited partnerships have some of the characteristics of general partnerships and of corporations, their proper tax treatment has been a major tax problem, the resolution of which has significantly shaped practices within limited partnerships. An important — nay, critical — issue for lawyers creating limited partnerships is to ensure that they are structured so as to qualify for partnership taxation.[4]

§5.4 SOURCE OF LAW OF LIMITED PARTNERSHIPS

The cooperative enterprise on which general partnerships are based appears to be a fundamental aspect of cooperative human enterprise and can be traced back to ancient times. The same is not so with respect to limited partnerships. The idea that some persons should be able to contribute capital to an enterprise and share in its profits, but not be responsible for its debts developed comparatively recently. The history of limited partnerships may be traced back to medieval Europe, where a *society comandita* was developed primarily to permit the nobility and the Church to quietly invest their wealth in mercantile enterprises. In England and the United States, limited partnerships were first authorized by statute in the late Nineteenth and early Twentieth Centuries. Today, the limited partnership form of business is exclusively a creature of statute; in the absence of statute (or the failure to comply with the mandatory provisions of an applicable statute), all partners are general partners no matter what their private understanding is or how they are designated in the partnership agreement. Thus, there is no general common law of limited partnerships as there is a common law of general partnerships, and limited partnerships are not a default form of business.

During most of the Twentieth Century the law of limited partnership was based on the Uniform Limited Partnership Act of 1916,[5] which, like the Uniform Partnership Act of 1914, achieved virtually universal acceptance. Dissatisfaction with this statute developed somewhat earlier than with the Uniform Partnership Act, and a revised Uniform Limited Partnership Act was developed and approved in 1976. However, a number of states made modifications to this revised Act, and NCCUSL adopted many of these modifications when it approved significant amendments in 1985. The limited partnership statute in effect in most states today is based on the Uniform Limited Partnership Act (1976) with 1985 Amendments. It is almost universally referred to as RULPA to distinguish it from the 1916 Act. While virtually all states today have enacted some form of RULPA, most states

[4]See §4.22.
[5]The 1916 Act is often abbreviated simply as ULPA or ULPA (1916).

have modified various provisions of the model act, with the result that there is a considerable degree of diversity in limited partnership statutes today.

§5.5 THE 1916 VIEW OF LIMITED PARTNERSHIPS

ULPA (1916) modeled the limited partnership closely after the general partnership but with special provisions defining the rules with respect to limited partners. RULPA follows the same approach but introduces important corporate concepts as well.[6] The corporate analogy is appropriate when the number of limited partners is large and the general partner is itself a corporation. Even though the corporate analogy is therefore appropriate for many limited partnerships, the source of rules for limited partnerships not set forth explicitly in RULPA continues to be the law of general partnerships. This is made explicit by a provision in RULPA that states that "[i]n any case not provided for in this Act the provisions of the Uniform Partnership Act govern."[7]

There are internal indications that ULPA (1916) was prepared on the assumption that the traditional limited partnership was a small local business that desired to raise capital from local risk-adverse investors.[8] What comes to mind is a local hardware store in a small town with two general partners and two or three limited partners, perhaps bankers or other persons of substance in the community, who are willing to invest the necessary capital for the hardware store to operate in exchange for a share of its profits but who are unwilling to assume the risk of personal liability for the hardware store's debts. A major emphasis of ULPA (1916) was to ensure that creditors of the hardware store not be misled as to who was responsible for partnership obligations.[9]

Whether or not that original conception accurately described the use

---

[6]For example, RULPA §901 et seq. provides for the qualification of foreign limited partnerships doing business in a state by a process quite similar to the qualification of foreign corporations. RULPA §1001 et seq. permits limited partners to bring derivative suits on behalf of the limited partnership against the general partner based on the analogy to the power of shareholders of corporations to bring derivative suits. See §5.14.

[7]RULPA §1105.

[8]For example, ULPA makes no reference at all to the possibility that a limited partnership might conduct a business in more than one state.

[9]Provisions included in ULPA (1916) prohibited limited partners from providing services as their capital contribution to the limited partnership, prohibited the limited partnership from adopting a name that included the name of a limited partner, and provided that a limited partner who participated in the conduct of the business became a general partner. Many states adopting this older statute provided that limited partnership certificates had to be filed in the county or city in which the limited partnership conducted its business. Multiple filings in each locality in which the limited partnership conducted business might be required. Also, no provision was made for the possibility that a limited partnership might engage in business in more than one state.

of the limited partnership in the early years of this century, the typical limited partnership today bears little resemblance to that hardware store. The typical modern limited partnership is a federal income-tax-driven business in which there are scores or hundreds of limited partners and one or two general partners that are usually corporations, limited liability companies, or other limited partnerships rather than individuals. The limited partnership form of business in modern business practice, properly structured, combines the partnership form of taxation with limited liability for individual investors who are limited partners or sharholders of the corporate general partner. Viewed in this light, the limited partnership seems economically closer to a corporation than to a general partnership. However, the business form has a most attractive combination of tax and nontax characteristics which explains its continued attractiveness.[10]

§5.6 FORMATION OF A MODERN LIMITED PARTNERSHIP

A limited partnership requires the public filing of a document with a state officer, usually the secretary of state of the state of formation.[11] It is not possible to create a completely oral limited partnership. Unlike a general partnership, a limited partnership cannot be created simply by a handshake.

The formation documents for a limited partnership normally consist of (1) a written limited partnership agreement that sets forth in detail the rights, duties, and limitations placed upon both general and limited partners, and (2) a Certificate of Limited Partnership, the document that is actually filed with the secretary of state. However, two documents are not essential: One may file a copy of the partnership agreement as the Certificate of Limited Partnership (assuming it meets the requirements of the statute), or, in the case of a small and relatively informal limited partnership, there may be an oral agreement among the partners,[12] who create the limited partnership by preparing and filing a Certificate of Limited Partnership

---

[10]This combination of tax and nontax characteristics also explains the attractiveness of limited liability companies discussed in Chapter 6. See §6.3. Because of the flexibility of the limited liability company form, however, it is likely that form will be used increasingly in lieu of the limited partnership.

[11]RULPA §201. If the limited partnership is to conduct business in more than one state, it may also be required to register to transact business in each state other than the state of formation. RULPA §902. Failure to do so may close the courts of the foreign state to suits brought on behalf of the limited partnership. Id., §905.

[12]RULPA §101(9) defines a "partnership agreement" to include oral as well as written agreements.

containing the minimum information required by the statute.[13] However, the risks of following the latter course should be obvious, and the usual practice is to prepare both documents, limiting the Certificate of Limited Partnership to the matters required by statute and having a detailed and complete written limited partnership agreement that is not publicly filed or available to members of the general public.[14]

Most limited partnership agreements are evidenced by elaborate written documents that specify in detail virtually all aspects of the limited partnership relation. The reason that such agreements are the norm is that most limited partnerships have a significant number of limited partners, and it is essential to define clearly the precise role of limited partners in the partnership. Where the number of limited partners is greater than, say, ten individuals, it is also important to describe when limited partners are entitled to vote on specific actions, and whether a unanimous vote or some vote less than unanimity is sufficient.[15] Such a provision obviously should appear in a written agreement.[16] The manner of allocating profits and losses for tax purposes among the limited and general partners similarly is of central importance and should not be the subject only of an oral agreement.

The creation of a limited partnership requires that there be at least one general partner and one limited partner.[17] It is formed at the time of the filing of the Certificate of Limited Partnership or such later time as is

---

[13]It is possible that a limited partner may subsequently contend that the oral agreement was different from the provisions of the certificate. Presumably, in this event the terms of the written Certificate of Limited Partnership will be accepted as controlling, at least in the absence of fraud. More likely, a dispute will arise as to what the oral agreement was with respect to some issue not addressed by the Certificate of Limited Partnership at all.

[14]Investors generally prefer to maintain confidentiality and to limit disclosures to a minimum. RULPA does not require disclosure of the identities of limited partners or the amount of individual contributions. If the limited partnership is to be publicly held, disclosures required by the securities acts will result in more complete disclosure than under the limited partnership statutes.

[15]Unanimity should be avoided where the number of limited partners is large, since there is a risk that a limited partner may withhold his vote opportunistically. For example, if each limited partner must approve the admission of a new general partner, some individual limited partners may withhold their vote of approval seeking to obtain some special payment or benefit from the limited partnership.

[16]Where the statute requires "all" the partners to agree in writing, the limited partnership agreement may appoint the general partner as the "attorney in fact" to execute a writing on behalf of each limited partner if authorized to do so by a majority or some other percentage of the limited partners. Such a provision is presumably binding under general principles of contract law, but should definitely appear in the formal limited partnership agreement if it is to bind all limited partners and their assignees.

[17]RULPA §101(7) defines a "limited partnership" to mean "a partnership formed by 2 or more persons under the laws of this State and having one or more general partners and one or more limited partners."

specified in the certificate.[18] The Certificate of Limited Partnership must be signed by all the general partners but need not be signed by any of the limited partners. The certificate must set forth the name of the limited partnership, the name and address of an agent for service of process, the name and address of each general partner, the latest date on which the partnership is to be dissolved, and such other matters as the general partners determine to place in the certificate.[19]

§5.7 THE NAME OF THE LIMITED PARTNERSHIP

The Revised Uniform Limited Partnership Act contains provisions with respect to the name of the limited partnership that are based on the corporate model rather than on the model of a general partnership. For example, the name must contain the words "limited partnership,"[20] provision is made for the reservation of a limited partnership name,[21] the use of a name that is deceptively similar to the name of an existing corporation or limited partnership is prohibited,[22] and so forth. Further, RULPA contains a provision that prohibits a limited partnership from using a name that contains the name of a limited partner, though exceptions are made if the name is also the name of a general partner or the name was used before the admission of the limited partner with the same name.[23] This provision is a carryover from ULPA (1916), which stated that the use of a limited partner's name in the name of the limited partnership resulted in the loss of limited liability for that limited partner. RULPA does not specify what the consequence is of using a limited partner's name as part of the name of the limited partnership in violation of the statute.

---

[18]RULPA §201(b).

[19]ULPA (1916) required much more extensive disclosures, including both the identities and the amounts of all contributions by all general and limited partners. The admission of new limited partners or the assignment of limited partnership interests required an amendment to the certificate to reflect the changes. These disclosure requirements provided little benefit to creditors of the limited partnership as a practical matter — for one thing, they provided only historical information about the original contributions to the limited partnership and no information about the current economic position of the limited partnership. Further, they created serious practical problems both for investors who desired anonymity and for large, publicly traded limited partnerships with shifting memberships. These detailed disclosure requirements were partially retained in RULPA (1976) but almost totally eliminated when RULPA was amended in 1985.

[20]Id. §102. Many state statutes, however, permit the use of the word "Limited" or the abbreviation "L.P."

[21]Id. §103.

[22]Id. §102(3).

[23]Id. §102(2).

§5.8 RESTRICTIONS ON LIMITED PARTNERS IN ULPA (1916)

ULPA (1916) provided that if a limited partner "takes part in the control of the business" he loses the shield of limited liability and becomes personally liable on partnership obligations.[24] In this early statute, nonparticipation in management in a sense was viewed as the price for limited liability.

A major problem with this Act was that the plain, unadorned language gave no indication of what kinds of management participation by a limited partner would trigger the provision. What if the limited partners retained the power to veto decisions by the general partner? What if the limited partners retained the power to elect a new general partner if the original general partner resigns or goes out of business? Does it matter if such powers were retained but never exercised? What about the limited partner with a large investment in the partnership who was consulted by the general partner about one or more important business decisions? What if the limited partner had power to sign checks but never exercised it or only signed one or two checks over three years when the general partners were unavailable? What if the limited partner was present at the place of business of the limited partnership but there was a large sign stating clearly who the general partner was? What if the sign affirmatively stated that X is only a limited partner and is not liable for the debts of the business? What if the limited partner was a shareholder, officer, or director of the general partner and participated in the control of the business only in the sense that he participated in the management of the general partner itself?

One can spin out questions such as these almost without end, and the 1916 Act gave no clear answer to any of them. Furthermore, there was a split of authority in the cases on two very basic questions. First, was it enough that the power to participate exists or must the power actually be used? Second, must a creditor seeking to hold a limited partner personally liable on partnership obligations establish that he knew of the limited partner's activity, or do all limited partners who take part in control of the business automatically become liable as general partners for all purposes and without regard to knowledge of specific creditors?

Complicating these questions was the fact that limited partners understandably desire at least some participation rights in order to protect their investments. At the very least, they want some voice on who is permitted to become a managing general partner, and may well wish to be able to replace the managing general partner if that partner turns out to be incompetent or dishonest, becomes insolvent, or simply abdicates responsibility to the limited partnership. Therefore, the open-ended and vague prohibi-

[24]UPA (1914) §5.

tion in the 1916 Act against taking part in control was a major deterrent to the widespread use of limited partnerships. Because of uncertainties as to the scope of limited liability provided by ULPA (1916), many advisers counseled against the use of limited partnerships.

§5.9 RESTRICTIONS ON LIMITED PARTNERS IN RULPA

The basic issue about the effect of taking part in the control of the business by limited partners was preliminarily addressed in RULPA (1976), and more completely in the 1985 amendments to that statute. Section 303 of RULPA, as it was amended in 1985, permits significant participation in the management of the business by limited partners without incurring personal liability for business obligations. While the general "taking part in the control of the business" language is retained, it is qualified in two significant respects.

First of all, section 303(b) creates "safe harbors" for numerous kinds of managerial actions by limited partners which by explicit statutory provision do not constitute participating in the control of the business. A *safe harbor* statute or regulation, as its name implies, sets forth a general legal standard but also lists certain specific actions that automatically fall either within or without that general standard. A safe harbor is not exclusive and actions that are not addressed by the safe harbor provision are governed by the general legal standard. Section 303(b) lists nine specific activities that by themselves do not constitute taking part in the control of business. Examples of these protected activities include "being a contractor for or an agent or employee of the limited partnership or of a general partner or being an officer, director, or shareholder of a general partner that is a corporation,"[25] acting as a surety for the limited partnership or "guaranteeing or assuming one or more specific obligations of the limited partnership,"[26] or participating (usually by voting) in a variety of decisions relating to the limited partnership, including the admission or removal of a general partner, a change in the nature of the business, or the dissolution and winding up of the limited partnership.[27] Actions that fall within any of the safe harbors on this list do not create personal liability, but if a limited partner participates in other management activities that do not fall within this list of permitted activities, that partner may still be held not to be participating in control of the business on a case-by-case evaluation of that activity. A safe harbor

[25]RULPA §303(b)(1).
[26]Id. §303(b)(3).
[27]Id. §303(b)(6).

does not create any inference one way or the other about activities not listed.[28]

Second, and probably of greater practical importance, is the following "clarification" of the "taking part in the control of the business" standard itself that appears as the last sentence of section 303(a):

> However, if the limited partner participates in the control of the business, he is liable only to persons who transact business with the limited partnership reasonably believing, based upon the limited partner's conduct, that the limited partner is a general partner.[29]

In effect, under this provision a limited partner who actively participates in the control of the business escapes liability if the creditor is either unaware of the activities of the limited partner or that partner is clearly identified as a limited partner.[30] In a limited partnership of any size, it is not very likely that trade creditors would be aware that one or more limited partners is participating in some way in the management of the business.

§5.10 CONTRACTUAL RESTRICTIONS ON LIMITED PARTNERS

In modern limited partnerships, there are likely to be a substantial number of limited partners, each with a small fractional interest in the limited partnership. In the formal written agreements for such limited partnerships, it is customary to include express restrictions or limitations on what the limited partners may do in terms of participating in the management of the business. In other words, the threat of personal liability under RULPA may not be sufficient to deter unwanted attempts at participation in management by limited partners and limited partnership agreements usually address specifically what limited partners may or may not do.

Contractual provisions dealing with the issue of limited partner participation in management are likely to be carefully negotiated. There are two basic approaches. One is to grant the general partners broad authority to act on behalf of the partnership on a wide variety of matters without consul-

---

[28]That the RULPA §303(b) listing is a safe harbor is made clear by RULPA §303(c), which states that "[t]he enumeration in subsection (b) does not mean that the possession or exercise of any other powers by a limited partner constitutes participation by him in the business of the limited partnership."

[29]RULPA §303(a), second sentence.

[30]This point is sharply made by a hypothetical which assumes that the limited partner wears a tee shirt stating "I am a limited partner" while participating actively in the business.

tation with, review by, or approval of limited partners. In agreements following this approach, the general partner may be authorized to admit additional limited partners, to borrow money, to file or settle law suits, or to merge or consolidate the limited partnership with other limited partnerships, all without the approval or consent of the limited partners or some fraction thereof. The alternative approach is to require some percentage of the limited partners to approve transactions that are not in the ordinary course of business of the limited partnership, including enumerated items such as admitting partners, borrowing money in excess of some specified amount, or entering into transactions that exceed some specified amount. The basic point is that the allocation of power between the classes of general and limited partners in a limited partnership today is more a matter of negotiation and agreement than of interpretation of the liability provisions of the Revised Uniform Limited Partnership Act.

In some situations, limited partners may be willing to accept the risk of unlimited liability under RULPA. This usually occurs where general partners have acted improperly or have disappeared or become insolvent. In these situations, the limited partnership will not have a functioning management and may have suffered substantial losses but itself is not insolvent.[31] Rather than forcing the limited partnership into dissolution, receivership, or bankruptcy, the limited partners may organize among themselves and replace the inactive or nonfunctioning general partner even if there is some risk that their actions may involve participation in the control of the business. The risk that some or all of the limited partners are personally liable for partnership obligations increases substantially when they participate directly in the management of the limited partnership much as though they were general partners. In these situations, even contractual restrictions on the role of limited partners set forth in the limited partnership agreement may be ignored or viewed as abrogated on the theory that the general partner violated express or implied terms of its obligations under the partnership agreement and is therefore unable to insist that other provisions of that agreement be literally enforced.

[31] In these situations, it is possible that the resignation of all general partners, or the last remaining general partner, may constitute a dissolution of the limited partnership. Provision is made in RULPA, however, for the *reconstitution* of a partnership in certain circumstances. RULPA §801(4) permits reconstitution if within 90 days all the partners "agree in writing to continue the business of the limited partnership and to the appointment of one or more additional general partners if necessary or desirable."

§5.11 A PERSON WHO IS BOTH A LIMITED AND A GENERAL PARTNER

A person may be simultaneously a limited partner and a general partner.[32] Such a person has the rights and powers of a general partner, and is liable for all the obligations of the limited partnership as is any general partner. At the same time, the person has the financial and participation rights of a limited partner. If the limited partners are entitled to vote on a matter, for example, the person may vote as a limited partner. A general partner may purchase limited partnership interests at the time of formation of the limited partnership, or may thereafter acquire limited partnership interests from other limited partners. In either event, the general partner thereafter has the right to participate in decision-making and financial benefits as both a limited and a general partner.

§5.12 THE DUTIES OF GENERAL PARTNERS

Section 403(a) of RULPA states that a general partner in a limited partnership has the rights and powers "and is subject to the restrictions of a partner in a partnership without limited partners." However, the last sentence of section 403 permits the duties owed by a general partner to the limited partnership and to the limited partners to be further qualified by the limited partnership agreement.[33] The duties of general partners in a partnership without limited partners are discussed in section 4.13. As discussed in that section, the duties of general partners at common law and under UPA (1914) largely revolved around the broad, classic language of the famous case of *Meinhard v. Salmon*.[34] Dissatisfaction with the open-ended nature of that description of duties led to provisions in limited partnership agreements that narrowed the common law scope of fiduciary duties.[35]

---

[32] RULPA §404, last two sentences.

[33] This sentence states that "[e]xcept as provided in this Act *or in the partnership agreement*, a general partner of a limited partnership has the liabilities of partner in a partnership without limited partners to the partnership and to the other partners" (emphasis added).

[34] 249 N.Y. 458, 164 N.E. 545 (1928).

[35] One such effort is as follows:

> Except as provided otherwise in this Agreement, the General Partner shall conduct the affairs of the Partnership in good faith to further the best interests of the Partnership. The General Partner is liable for errors or omissions in performing its duties with respect to the Partnership only in the case of bad faith, gross negligence, or breach of the provisions of this Agreement, but not otherwise. The General Partner shall devote such time and effort to the Partnership business and operations as is necessary to promote fully the interests of the Partnership; however, the General Partner need not devote full time to the Partnership business.
>
> The General Partner at any time and from time to time may engage in and

In determining the scope of the duties of a general partner in a large limited partnership, courts tend to treat the general partner much as though he were a director of a corporation.[36]

See section 5.15 for a discussion of the duties of directors and officers of a corporate general partner.

In states that adopt UPA (1994) it may be unnecessary to include specific language with respect to the duties of the general partner in the average limited partnership, since that statute significantly narrows the scope of partners' fiduciary and other duties.[37]

§5.13 INDEMNIFICATION OF GENERAL PARTNERS

The limited partnership statutes of several states authorize or direct limited partnerships to indemnify the general partners against loss, judgments, liabilities, and amounts paid in settlement of claims.[38] These statutes are based on the corporate analogy with respect to the indemnification of directors, but are broader than the similar corporate indemnification statute[39] and give deference to the limited partnership agreement in defining the scope of permitted indemnification. Court decisions indicate that indemnification and advancement of expenses agreements in limited partnership agreements will be enforced in accordance with their terms, at least within the broad confines of public policy.[40]

---

possess interests in other business ventures of any and every type and description, independently or with others, including ones in competition with the Partnership, with no obligation to offer to the Partnership or any other Partner the right to participate therein.

The Partnership may transact business with any Partner or Affiliate of a Partner, provided the terms of the transactions with the General Partner or Affiliate are no less favorable than those the partnership could obtain from unrelated third parties.

If all duties are abrogated by the agreement, there is a significant risk that the provision may be invalidated as unreasonable or unconscionable.

[36]Litman v. Prudential-Bache Properties, Inc., 611 A.2d 12, 15 (Del. Ch. 1992). See also Wyler v. Feuer, 149 Cal. Rptr. 626 (Ct. App. 1979) (application of business judgment rule to a general partner.)

[37]See discussion in §4.13.

[38]See, e.g., Del. Code Ann. §17-108: "Subject to such standards and restrictions, if any, as are set forth in its partnership agreement, a limited partnership may, and shall have the power to indemnify and hold harmless any partner or other person from and against any and all claims and demands whatsoever."

[39]Compare Del. G.C.L. §145, which contains significant procedural restrictions on the power to indemnify directors.

[40]In Delphi Ester Partners Limited Partnership v. Spectacular Partners, Inc. 19 Del. J. Corp. L. 722 (1994), the court held that a provision requiring advances for expenses was enforceable in a case involving a claim of breach of fiduciary duty even though the indemnification provision excluded indemnification for "willful misconduct, recklessness, or gross

§5.14 DERIVATIVE SUITS BY LIMITED PARTNERS

There was apparently no way under ULPA (1916) for limited partners to bring suit against the general partner on behalf of the partnership for misconduct or negligence. Corporation law provides precisely such a remedy for shareholders in the form of a derivative suit. A *derivative suit* is a suit brought on behalf of the corporation by one or more shareholders, usually against the directors or officers of the corporation for misconduct or gross negligence.[41] While some courts permitted derivative litigation to be pursued by limited partners against the general partner in the absence of statutory authority, RULPA resolves that problem by expressly authorizing derivative litigation within the limited partnership, closely following the corporate analogy.[42] While experience with derivative actions in limited partnerships is not great, courts appear to rely on the corporate analogy in determining the procedural requirements for such suits. Delaware courts, for example, require pre-suit demand before a limited partner may bring a derivative suit that is similar to the demand requirements applicable to corporations generally.[43]

§5.15 CORPORATE GENERAL PARTNERS

Section 4.9 points out that artificial entities may be general partners in a partnership. Exactly the same thing is true of both general and limited partners in a limited partnership. Because limited partners are predominantly investors, it is not at all noteworthy that a corporation, estate, trust, partnership, or limited partnership may be a limited partner. However, the use of artificial entities as general partners in a limited partnership — particularly as the sole general partner in a limited partnership — makes a genuine change in the dynamics of the traditional limited partnership. For with a corporate general partner, the only assets at risk in the limited partnership are the contributions of the limited partners, the contribution of the general partner (which may be nominal), and the capital of the general partner, which may also be nominal. Further, one or more limited partners may be shareholders, directors, and officers of the general partner, thereby controlling the affairs of the limited partnership to the exclusion of the other limited partners, but apparently without risk of personal liability.

---

negligence . . . or the breach of any fiduciary obligation hereunder or by law on the General Partner." The court pointed out that indemnification and advances for expenses were logically independent of each other and one did not preclude the other. See §8.11 for a discussion of indemnification and advancements.

[41] See the discussion in §8.12.

[42] RULPA §1001 et seq.

[43] Litman v. Prudential-Bache Properties, Inc., 1993 LEXIS 13 (1993).

As discussed in section 4.9, until the middle of the Twentieth Century the rule was universally accepted that a corporation could not be a general partner in a partnership since the power of general partners to bind other partners was viewed as inconsistent with the power of the board of directors to manage the affairs of the corporation. The modern view, accepted today in apparently all states, is precisely the opposite. Indeed, most limited partnerships created today take advantage of this practice and have only a single general partner which is an artificial entity, usually a corporation. The typical modern limited partnership consists of a single general corporate partner and tens or hundreds or thousands of limited partners.

Until about 1975 there was a question about whether a person who was both a limited partner and a shareholder, officer, and director of the general partner would be viewed as taking part in the control of the business and thus liable as a general partner. The limited case law was split on the issue, but RULPA's safe harbor provision answers that question squarely: A limited partner may participate in the management of the limited partnership through being a director or officer of the general partner without fear of becoming liable for the partnership's debts. In this respect, it is important that such a person clearly identify the capacity in which he or she is acting — i.e., as a shareholder, officer, or director of the corporate general partner and not as a limited partner — when participating in the affairs of the limited partnership.

Even though most large publicly held limited partnerships today have a corporation as the sole general partner, there has been surprisingly little litigation over possible problems that may arise particularly with respect to duties owed to the limited partners. In one significant ruling, it was held that the directors of a corporate general partner owe fiduciary duties to the limited partners as well as to the corporate general partner itself.[44] Since a nominally financed corporate general partner in effect means that creditors have no assets to look to other than the assets of the limited partnership itself, there is also a risk that a court may apply a "piercing the shield of the limited partnership" by analogy to the well-accepted principle of piercing the corporate veil.[45] Other problems that may arise include the question whether sales of stock of the corporate general partner to unrelated third parties should be subject to restriction based on the partnership relation, and whether mergers or other fundamental transactions involving the corporate general partner should be viewed as terminating the existence of the corporate general partner and or as assigning the general partners interest without the consent of the limited partners. The limited case law that has

[44]In re USACafes L.P. Litigation, 600 A.2d 43 (Del. Ch. 1991).
[45]See §10.8. Of course, exactly the same issue may arise if a judgment proof individual were named as the sole general partner.

arisen in these areas has involved construction of limited partnership agreements rather than the application of underlying statutory principles.

§5.16 ADMISSION AND WITHDRAWAL OF GENERAL PARTNERS

Under RULPA, the names and addresses of general partners have to appear in the Certificate of Limited Partnership and any admission of a new general partner or the withdrawal of an existing general partner must be recorded in the public records by an amendment to the Certificate within 30 days after the change takes place.[46] The basis on which a new general partner is selected — e.g., by the remaining general partners, or by a vote of the limited partners — may be specified in the partnership agreement. If there is no provision in the agreement, all the partners must consent to the addition of the new general partner.[47]

The withdrawal of a general partner does not necessarily dissolve a limited partnership. If there are other general partners, the partnership agreement may provide that the limited partnership is not dissolved by the withdrawal of a general partner. There also is provision for "reconstitution" of a limited partnership when the withdrawing general partner is the sole remaining general partner. RULPA section 801(4) provides that even where there is no general partner, the limited partnership is not dissolved if within 90 days all the partners agree in writing to continue the business of the limited partnership and to the appointment of one or more additional general partners. Since, as a practical matter, the approval of all the limited partners may not be possible to obtain, limited partnership agreements usually provide that if a specified percentage of all interests in the partnership approve the appointment of an additional general partner, all the remaining partners, both general and limited, agree to vote to reconstitute the partnership with the new general partner, and they appoint a single person as their attorney in fact to execute an appropriate amendment to the certificate of limited partnership.

The *events of withdrawal* of a general partner are similar to the corresponding dissolution provisions with respect to general partnerships.[48] A general partner may withdraw by its express will at any time, but such a withdrawal is wrongful if it constitutes a breach of the limited partnership agreement.[49] The assignment of a general partner's interest constitutes a

---

[46]RULPA §202(b).
[47]Id. §401.
[48]Id. §402. See §§4.26, 4.28.
[49]Id. §602.

withdrawal by the general partner unless the limited partnership agreement provides to the contrary.[50] The bankruptcy of a general partner constitutes a withdrawal, as does the termination of existence of the general partner, by death of a natural person or termination of existence of an artificial entity.

§5.17 ADMISSION AND WITHDRAWAL OF LIMITED PARTNERS

The admission or withdrawal of limited partners does not affect the legal existence of a limited partnership.

ULPA (1914) required that the identities and contributions of each limited partner be set forth in the Certificate of Limited Partnership. Any change in the identity of limited partners required an amendment of the public filing. This requirement created problems for limited partnerships with a large number of limited partners and also may have deterred investments by persons who did not wish their identities or the amounts of their contributions be made a matter of public record. RULPA eliminates these requirements: Neither the identities nor the contributions of limited partners need be set forth at all in the Certificate of Limited Partnership. As a result, the admission or withdrawal of limited partners is entirely an internal matter within the limited partnership.

RULPA does contain default provisions with respect to the identification of limited partners that is applicable in the absence of provisions in the limited partnership agreement. The limited partnership must keep a current list of the name and business of each partner, separately identifying the general partners and limited partners.[51]

The admissibility and withdrawal of limited partners was an important matter under the Kintner rules since it directly affects whether the limited partnership had the corporate characteristic of free transferability of interest, a question that could be of critical importance in determining whether the limited partnership will be treated as a partnership for tax purposes.[52] Hence, provisions relating to changes in the composition of the limited partners were carefully drafted in light of the applicable tax regulations and rulings thereunder.[53]

[50]Id. §702. In this respect, the limited partnership rule differs from the rule for general partnerships. See §4.20.

[51]Id. §105(a)(1). The list of both general and limited partners must be kept in alphabetical order.

[52]Control over entry and withdrawal of limited partners may also be necessary to assure the availability of exemptions from registration for the initial sales of limited partner interests under the Securities Act of 1933 and state blue sky laws. See §5.19.

[53]See §5.18 for a discussion of the application of the "Kintner rules" to limited partnerships. The problem was most acute when the sole general partner was a corporation with

RULPA provides that if the limited partnership agreement does not specify the time or the events upon the happening of which a limited partner may withdraw, a limited partner may withdraw upon six months' prior written notice to each general partner.[54] Typically, limited partnerships do not wish to grant limited partners the power to withdraw on six months' notice; this is one reason why it is customary to include express provisions dealing with withdrawal of limited partners in the limited partnership agreement. The most common provision is that there is no right to withdraw (and receive back the value of one's interest in the limited partnership) until the completion of the venture. In short, agreements usually provide that the limited partner is in for the long haul, having made essentially a permanent capital investment in the limited partnership.

Even though a limited partner has no power to withdraw from the limited partnership, her interest may be assignable with the consent of the partnership. RULPA provides that limited partnership interests are personal property and are assignable.[55] An assignee of a limited partnership interest obtains the financial interest of the limited partner, but becomes a limited partner only to the extent the limited partnership agreement provides (or all partners agree). As is the case with assignments of general partnership interests, a distinction should be drawn between assignments of the *financial* interest and assignments of the *entire* interest. An assignment of the financial interest does not make the assignee a limited partner.[56] Limited partnership agreements typically provide that the assignee of the financial interest of a limited partner becomes a limited partner only upon receiving the consent of the limited partnership itself, as contemplated by RULPA.[57] This consent requires the approval of the general partner and, often, also the approval of some percentage of the limited partners as well. Such a clause assured that the corporate characteristic of free transferability of interest did not exist in the limited partnership.

In the case of limited partnerships that have made a public offering of limited partnership interests, assignments of the financial interest of limited

---

limited assets, since such an entity would have the corporate characteristics of limited liability and centralization of management.

[54]Id. §603.

[55]RULPA §§701, 702. These provisions are analogous to assignments of interests in general partnerships. See §4.20.

[56]Id. §704. See §4.20. However, for federal income tax purposes, an assignee who receives only the financial interests of an assigning limited partner is nevertheless treated as a limited partner, i.e., the assignee is taxed on the limited partner's distributive share even though he has not been admitted as a limited partner.

[57]RULPA §704 contemplates that an assigning limited partner may grant the assignee the status of limited partner pursuant to authority to that effect in the partnership agreement. Limited partnership agreements usually deny to limited partners the power to grant such status.

partners may be on such a scale that a market of sorts, or an information exchange service, may be maintained by the general partner to match persons interested in investing in the limited partnership with limited partners interested in selling their interest. However, the track record of limited partnership interests as investments has been so bad that there are relatively few persons interested in acquiring such interests.[58]

RULPA provides that a partnership interest in a limited partnership may be subjected to a charging order by a creditor in the same way as in a general partnership,[59] and that in the event of death of a limited partner who is an individual (or the dissolution or termination of other limited partners) the legal representative of the limited partner may exercise the rights of the limited partner.[60]

§5.18 THE TAXATION OF LIMITED PARTNERSHIPS

The limited partnership raises the issue of proper income tax classification in its starkest form. *Tax classification* refers to the question whether an unincorporated entity such as a limited partnership should be taxed as an "association taxable as a corporation" under the Internal Revenue Code or whether it is a "partnership" for tax purposes. This tax issue is discussed in section 4.22 in connection with the taxation of general partnerships. Under the Kintner regulations, the proper classification of a limited partnership was much more difficult than it was in connection with general partnerships, since limited partnerships have more corporate characteristics than general partnerships. The issue, furthermore, was a fundamental one since under the 1996 tax rates the limited partnership is an attractive business form only if it is taxed as a partnership.

Under the proposed "check the box" regulations, the classification will become moot since any limited partnership may elect favorable partnership-type taxation simply by checking the appropriate box on tax forms. The consequences of this change will be profound, since many substantive provisions appearing in modern limited partnership agreements are dictated solely by the requirements of the Kintner regulations. These provisions become optional under the check the box regulations, and will be included only if desired for business reasons.

The prior history is interesting. For many years, the Internal Revenue Service issued private rulings on the question whether a specific limited

---

[58] This situation may encourage investment by so-called bottom fishers seeking to acquire the underlying assets of the limited partnership at bargain prices.

[59] RULPA §703.

[60] Id. §705.

partnership met, or did not meet, the requirements for classification as a partnership for tax purposes under the Kintner regulations. By 1992, however, the Internal Revenue Service was handling such a large volume of requests for rulings that it issued Rev. Proc. 92-88[61] which set forth detailed guidelines for determining when a limited partnership would be treated as lacking the corporate characteristics of continuity of life and limited liability. A limited partnership that met these guidelines was treated as a partnership for federal income tax purposes and did not need to obtain a tax ruling. These guidelines made it relatively easy to qualify for partnership taxation if certain very specific provisions relating to the "corporate characteristics" were included, and limited partnerships were routinely structured so as to fall within these guidelines. The result was that tax considerations determined many substantive aspects of the limited partnership relation.

Rev. Proc. 92-88 generally liberalized the detailed Kintner rules to such an extent that virtually all limited partnerships could virtually elect whether to be taxed as a corporation or as a partnership by minor modifications to provisions relating to continuity of life, centralization of management, and free transferability of interest. Hence, the check the box regulations should not cause a significant change in revenue received by the United States.

However, from the standpoint of the Internal Revenue Service, this change promises considerable internal savings in costs as staff time devoted to the continued refinement of the Kintner regulations may be repositioned elsewhere.[62]

§5.19 LIMITED PARTNERSHIPS AND THE SECURITIES LAWS

Whenever a limited partnership is created, consideration must be given to the question whether the limited partnership interests (and possibly the general partnership interests as well)[63] constitute securities that require registration under the federal Securities Act of 1933 and the state blue sky laws. The definition of a *security* for purposes of these statutes generally is that it is a financial interest "in a common enterprise with profits to come

---

[61] 1992-C.B. 496.

[62] It also will require the retooling of lawyers whose specialty was the application of the Kintner regulations.

[63] Since general partners have management powers and duties, general partnership interests are usually not classified as securities. However, it is possible to have general partners who do not participate in the business affairs and who are exclusively financial investors; general partnership interests sold to such investors may be securities, and registration, or the availability of an exemption from registration, may therefore be necessary for some general partnership interests.

solely from the efforts of others."[64] Typical limited partnership interests clearly are securities under this definition, and registration will be required unless an exemption from registration is available for the specific sale of limited partnership interests. The issuance of limited partnership interests are subject to essentially the same securities acts rules as are the issuance of shares of stock by a corporation or debt securities by any type of business.

If the limited partnership interests are originally issued pursuant to an exemption from registration,[65] steps must be taken to prevent subsequent transfers of such interests to cause the loss or destruction of whatever exemption from registration is being relied upon. Control over subsequent transfers may be important for tax purposes, but it usually is absolutely essential to preserve exemptions from registration under federal and state securities law. The following notation should appear on the first page of all limited partnership agreements that involve reliance on exemptions from securities registration to warn all investors that the economic interests in the limited partnership may not be freely transferred, and that approval by the limited partnership is required:

THE SECURITIES REPRESENTED BY THIS DOCUMENT HAVE BEEN ACQUIRED FOR INVESTMENT AND HAVE NOT BEEN REGISTERED UNDER THE SECURITIES ACT OF 1933, AS AMENDED, OR UNDER THE SECURITIES LAWS OF ANY STATES. WITHOUT SUCH REGISTRATION, SUCH SECURITIES MAY NOT BE SOLD, PLEDGED, HYPOTHECATED OR OTHERWISE TRANSFERRED, EXCEPT UPON AN OPINION OF COUNSEL SATISFACTORY TO THE GENERAL PARTNER OF THIS LIMITED PARTNERSHIP THAT REGISTRATION IS NOT REQUIRED FOR SUCH TRANSFER OR THE SUBMISSION TO THE GENERAL PARTNER OF THIS LIMITED PARTNERSHIP OF SUCH OTHER EVIDENCE AS MAY BE SATISFACTORY TO THE GENERAL PARTNER OF THIS LIMITED PARTNERSHIP TO THE EFFECT THAT ANY SUCH TRANSFER SHALL NOT BE IN VIOLATION OF THE SECURITIES ACT OF 1933, AS AMENDED, OR APPLICABLE STATE SECURITIES LAWS OR ANY RULE OR REGULATION PROMULGATED THEREUNDER. ADDITIONALLY, ANY SALE OR OTHER TRANSFER OF THESE SECURITIES IS SUBJECT TO CERTAIN RESTRICTIONS THAT ARE SET FORTH IN THIS AGREEMENT OF LIMITED PARTNERSHIP.

[64]SEC v. W. J. Howey Co., 328 U.S. 293, 301 (1946).

[65]Limited partnerships may take advantage of any of the general exemptions provided by the Securities Act of 1933, and the regulations promulgated by the SEC. These include the nonpublic offering exemption, the intrastate activities exemption, the Regulation A exemption, the exemption for sales to accredited investors, and the three Regulation D exemptions created by Rules 504, 505, and 506 of Regulation D. These exemptions all contain technical and detailed requirements.

The "securities" referred to in this notice are of course the limited partnership interests themselves.

§5.20 MASTER LIMITED PARTNERSHIPS

In 1981, a new type of limited partnership was created. Called a *master limited partnership*, its unique characteristic is that the limited partnership interests are publicly traded on the public securities markets.[66] The units of public trading are technically depository receipts for limited partnership interests rather than the limited partnership interests themselves. Hence, the conduit treatment for tax purposes was not affected by the trading in depository receipts, since they were at most transfers of the economic interest in the limited partnership interests. These receipts are readily marketable and trade over the counter or on securities exchanges much as though they were common shares issued by corporations.

Master limited partnerships owe their creation entirely to tax considerations. The original master limited partnerships were more attractive from a tax standpoint than corporations because investors could benefit directly from a "pass through" of tax deductions in extractive industries, particularly deductions for intangible drilling costs and depletion. The same was also true to a lesser extent of depreciation deductions available to companies involved in the development of real estate. When the business was conducted in corporate form, available deductions exceeded taxable income; however, when conducted in master limited partnership form, the deductions could be fully utilized by the individual investors, in many cases sheltering other income from taxation.

With the enactment of the 1986 Tax Act, the tax rates for individuals and corporations were changed so that it became extremely attractive for a business to be taxed as a partnership rather than as an association taxable as a corporation. The shareholders of virtually every publicly held corporation thus would have benefited from a reconstitution of that corporation as a limited partnership. A substantial number of publicly held corporations announced that they planned to do precisely that for the benefit of shareholders.

Congress put a stop to this burgeoning trend in the Revenue Act of 1987. With certain exceptions, "publicly traded partnerships" are in effect

---

[66]The first master limited partnership was created by an independent oil company that consolidated ("rolled up") 30 pre-existing drilling and exploration limited partnerships into one "master" limited partnership. (Such a transaction is called a *roll-up* and is now governed by federal statute.) The phrase master limited partnership expanded over the years to refer to any limited partnership whose limited partnership interests are listed for trading on public securities exchanges.

characterized as corporations for tax purposes without regard to their business form under state law. Certain master limited partnerships already in existence were granted a ten-year reprieve from this recharacterization; the ten-year period ends with taxable years beginning after December 31, 1985. Oil and gas and real estate master limited partnerships already in existence were exempted from recharacterization indefinitely. Since somewhere between one-third and one-half of all master limited partnerships are involved in oil and gas and real estate, a significant number of master limited partnerships will be around for the indefinite future.

6

Limited Liability Companies

§6.1 INTRODUCTION

The most astonishing development in the area of business forms in the 1990s has been the growth and spread of a novel business form, the *limited liability company* or "LLC" (as it is usually called). The attractiveness of this hybrid business form basically arises from its combination of desirable tax and business features: almost complete internal flexibility coupled with limited liability for all of its owners and the pass through tax treatment of a partnership. An LLC is free to develop its own organizational and management structure, and, at least to some extent, its own governing rules and principles. The default rules for LLCs are drawn in part from corporation law, from general partnership law, and from limited partnership law. In short, the LLC is an eclectic mixture of features drawn from several different traditional business forms that create an attractive package for many enterprises.

Limited liability companies bear a close resemblance to corporations in many aspects since they have more traditionally "corporate" characteristics than either partnerships or limited partnerships. However, they lack the fundamental corporate characteristic of receiving a "franchise" or "charter" from the state of incorporation. An LLC may also be analogized to a limited partnership that is composed only of limited partners. However, neither comparison is entirely apt; an LLC is a novel business form that is neither a corporation nor a partnership.[1]

Because LLCs have been in existence for only a brief period and they draw rules from varied sources, a considerable degree of variation and diversity exists among the state LLC statutes. These variations are much greater than those that exist among state statutes relating to the traditional corporation, general partnership, and limited partnership. As a result, the specific state statute must be consulted whenever formation of an LLC is contemplated or whenever an LLC formed under the laws of one state plans to do business in another state.[2]

As with most modern business forms, the limited liability company is tax driven. LLC statutes have historically been drafted with one eye focused on the Kintner regulations relating to the classification of businesses for income tax purposes,[3] and lawyers involved in the formation of LLCs routinely included substantive provsions designed to ensure that the LLC was to be taxed as a partnership rather than as a corporation.[4] The proposed "check the box" regulations will have a major impact on limited liability companies since substantive provisions in governing documents will then be based on business considerations rather than potential tax consequences.[5]

LLCs are used primarily or exclusively for closely held enterprises. There is no inherent reason why an LLC could not have hundreds or thousands of members. However, once ownership interests become publicly traded, the entity becomes subject to C corporation tax treatment under the "master limited partnership" provisions of the Internal Revenue Code.[6]

[1] Section 6.3 discusses the very limited case law dealing with the categorization of LLCs under state law.

[2] Section 6.7 discusses the prototype and uniform LLC statutes that have been, or are being, developed.

[3] The Kintner rules are described briefly in §4.22.

[4] The current "bible" for the tax classification of LLCs is Rev. Proc. 95-10, discussed in §6.9.

[5] The "check the box" proposal set forth in Rev. Notice 95-14 is briefly discussed in §5.18.

[6] See §5.20.

§6.2 THE HISTORY OF LIMITED LIABILITY COMPANIES

Business entities similar to LLCs exist in many countries. Examples include the German GmbH, the *limitadas* that exist in Latin American countries (including the *sociedad de responsabilidad limitada* (S.de R.L.) of Mexico), and the Portuguese *sociedate por quotas responsibilitidade limitada*. Similar entities also exist in countries in the common law tradition. Perhaps the closest ancestor in the English tradition is the unincorporated joint stock company that developed in England as a commercial substitute for the royal corporate charters that created the City of London and the great universities of Oxford and Cambridge. The American colonies were well acquainted with these joint stock companies and by and large detested them because they had been given monopolies to trade with major portions of the New World.

The LLC also bears resemblance to the partnership associations or limited partnership associations created in Pennsylvania, Michigan, New Jersey, Ohio, and Virginia in the late 1870s.[7] These variant partnership forms, however, have apparently been rarely used during the Twentieth Century, though a modern resurgence in their use appears possible.[8]

Whatever its origins, the LLC is a distinctly modern creation in the United States. It can be directly traced back to the attempt by the Hamilton Brothers Oil Company of Denver in the 1970s to form an entity in the United States similar to the *limitada* it was familiar with in Central America. For some reason, it chose Wyoming as the focus of its legislative effort. According to Professor Carney, the Wyoming legislature "apparently passed [the statute] without much publicity or controversy, on the assumption that it was supported by a major state business seeking an alternative form of business entity for oil and gas development activities."[9]

The Hamilton Brothers company eventually obtained a tax ruling that it should be classified as a partnership for tax purposes. However, at about the same time in 1980 the Internal Revenue Service proposed new classification regulations that took the uncompromising position that an entity should be classified as a corporation if no investor is personally liable for its obligations.[10] These proposed regulations were highly controversial and

---

[7]Keatinge et al., The Limited Liability Company: A Study of the Emerging Entity, 47 Bus. Law. 375, 381 (1992).

[8]In 1995, Colorado authorized the creation of a limited partnership association based on these Nineteenth Century statutes.

[9]Carney, Limited Liability Companies: Origins and Antecedents, 66 Colo. L. Rev. 855 (1995).

[10]Proposed Treasury Regulation §301.7701-2, 45 Fed. Reg. 75709 (Nov. 17, 1980), flatly stated that organizations in which no member had personal liability for the organization's debts would be taxable as a corporation and not as a partnership.

were ultimately withdrawn without ever having been promulgated, when the Service announced it was opening a study project to reconsider the proper classification of unincorporated organizations that provide limited liability for its members.

After six years of study, the IRS study project concluded that limited liability, in and of itself, should not be the determinative classification factor for tax purposes. In Revenue Ruling 88-76,[11] the breakthrough ruling that signified a major change in IRS policy toward LLCs, the IRS publicly announced that a specific Wyoming LLC was to be treated as a partnership for tax purposes under the Kintner regulations. Today, LLCs are clearly subject to the proposed check the box regulations, and hence have the same flexibility in terms of tax classifications as partnerships and limited partnerships.

Florida adopted an LLC statute in 1982, long before the tax issue was resolved. No other state enacted an LLC statute until shortly after Revenue Ruling 88-76 was released in 1988. Then the flood gates opened. Within eight years, all states had adopted limited liability company statutes.

§6.3 COMPARISON WITH OTHER BUSINESS FORMS

As described above, a limited liability company has organizational features that are in part partnership in nature and in part corporate in nature. A general description of the corporate and noncorporate features of the LLC statutes is useful in giving a sense of what this new business form is and where it comes from.

1. *Comparison with a Corporation.* An LLC is superficially more similar to a corporation than to a partnership. An LLC is a separate legal entity that is formed by filing "articles of organization" with the Secretary of State (or other designated state official) and paying a filing fee. It may be formed for "any lawful purpose," subject to exceptions for certain kinds of business such as banking and insurance.[12]

The relationship between the corporate statutes and LLC statutes is made vivid by a comparison of language. One speaks of "articles of incorporation" in a corporation and "articles of organization" in an LLC. Rather than having "bylaws," an LLC will have "regulations" or an "operating agreement." The owners are called "members" rather than "shareholders."

---

[11] 1988-2 Cum. Bull. 360. The Service later stated in G.C. Mem. 39,798 that limited liability was only one factor to be considered in the classification of business enterprises.

[12] Most state statutes do not require that an LLC be formed as a "business for profit." There seems to be no inherent reason why an LLC could not be used, for example, by a chamber of commerce or tenants' association for a condominium development.

Rather than having "directors," LLCs may have "managers."[13] The managers may be chosen by the members in a manner similar to the way directors are chosen by shareholders in a corporation. An LLC may have "officers" selected by the board of managers. Managers and officers need not be members unless the operative documents provide otherwise. LLC statutory provisions relating to purposes and powers are also closely modeled after similar provisions in state corporation statutes.

Many provisions of LLC statutes draw directly from the corporate model. For example, some states provide expressly that a "piercing the corporate veil" principle is applicable to LLCs. The duties of managers of an LLC may be described by language taken directly from the corporation statutes relating to the duties of directors. California provides for dissenters' rights in LLCs analogous to such rights in corporations, not only for California LLCs but also for foreign LLCs transacting business in California if California residents own "more than 50 percent of the voting interests of the foreign limited liability company." This provision is based on a similar quasi-foreign corporation provision that has long been part of the unique California corporate jurisprudence.

As LLCs have proliferated, courts have been compelled to consider whether corporate or partnership principles should be applied when the LLC statute is silent. The limited number of reported cases indicates that courts will turn to the corporate analogy for guidance. *Poore v. Fox Hollow Enterprises*,[14] for example, involved the question whether an LLC, like a corporation, may only appear in court through an attorney, or whether an officer or manager of the LLC who is not a lawyer may appear on behalf of the entity much the way a partner may appear and represent a partnership in court. Without finding any governing or even relevant authority one way or the other, the court concluded that the corporate analogy should be applied since "the underlying purpose of the rule prohibiting the appearance of a corporation by anyone other than a member of the Delaware Bar also applied to the representation of limited liability companies."

Similarly, in *Meyer v. Oklahoma Beverage Laws Enforcement Commission*,[15] the court held that a limited liability company was prohibited by the Oklahoma Constitution from holding a retail package store liquor license. There were two relevant sections: First, "[n]o more than one retail package license shall be issued *to any person or general or limited partnership*," and second, "[n]o retail package store . . . license shall be issued to: (a) *A corporation, business trust or secret partnership*."[16] While these provisions obviously

---

[13]However, an LLC need not have managers; it may be "member-managed," a form of management similar to traditional general partnerships. See §6.4.

[14]1994 WL 150872 (Del. Super. Ct. 1994).

[15]890 P.2d 1361 (Okla. App. 1995).

[16]Oklahoma Constitution, art. 28, §§4, 10 (emphasis added).

long antedate the invention of the LLC, the court concluded that the essence of these provisions was to assign "personal responsibility for compliance with the liquor laws" and that the limitation of liability provided by the LLC was a "shield from the very responsibility and accountability that the constitutional provisions regarding alcoholic beverage laws and enforcement sought to impose." Therefore, an LLC cannot hold a retail package store liquor license in Oklahoma. This kind of reasoning will doubtless be followed in the future as courts fill in the gaps necessarily left unfilled in the jurisprudence of limited liability companies, and is likely to lead to general acceptance of the corporation as the appropriate analogy for most LLC rules.

In some respects, of course, the LLC does not resemble a corporation. As indicated earlier, an LLC lacks one essential corporate characteristic that may be determinative of the tax classification of an entity as a corporation under check the box rules. Unlike a corporation, an LLC does not receive a franchise or charter from the organizing state. But there are also other important differences between LLCs and corporations. The LLC statutes of most states provide extreme flexibility with respect to all aspects of internal organization of an LLC;[17] there are few mandatory statutory requirements, and internal relationships are largely governed by contract rather than by mandatory statutory provision. In contrast, corporation statutes are notoriously specific. They provide detailed rules for the financing and management of corporations, rules which may be binding on all corporations.[18] For example, many state corporation statutes have complex provisions respecting the issuance of securities and legal capital; while LLCs may adopt similar financial structures if they wish, they are free to adopt simpler structures, such as those that typically appear in partnerships. Another difference is that in a corporation the articles of incorporation control over bylaws in case of a conflict; an LLC is based strongly on the theory that it is a contract among the members, and the rule adopted in most statutes is that the operating agreement controls over the articles of organization in case of conflict.

---

[17]LLC statutes were originally classified as "flexible" or "bulletproof." Early statutes in several states were *bulletproof* in the sense that they provided mandatory rules in areas that were sensitive to the Kintner tax classification issue, e.g., (i) unanimous consent for admission of a transferee as a new member was required, and (ii) consent by a majority in interest was necessary to continue the LLC's existence after the withdrawal of a member. Rev. Proc. 95-10 significantly relaxed the tax rules that originally led to these inflexible bulletproof provisions, and more recent statutes are *flexible* in the sense that these tax-sensitive rules are default rules which may be modified as desired by the LLC to meet the needs of a specific enterprise. Under check the box rules, these mandates will probably disappear.

[18]As discussed in Chapter 8, a number of states have adopted special close corporation statutes or §7.32 of the Model Business Corporation Act which permit shareholders to modify the standard management structure for corporations. In these states, the difference between corporations and LLCs in this respect are minimized.

Even though an LLC is not a corporation, it is subject to corporate tax treatment in some states. This is true, for example, in Florida, Pennsylvania, and Texas. The reasons that states may insist that LLCs be taxed as corporations is based not so much on the "corporate" characteristics of an LLC as fear that otherwise state revenues will decline as firms change their business form to LLCs, and as new businesses elect to be LLCs from the outset.

2. *Comparison with a Partnership.* LLCs also have strong antecedents in the law of partnership. An LLC may elect to assume a management structure that is virtually identical to that of a general partnership (with the sole exception of avoidance of unlimited liability). The operating agreement in many LLCs more closely approximates a partnership agreement than corporate bylaws. Many states permit LLC operating agreements to be oral rather than written, an option not available for corporate bylaws. Membership interests in an LLC may have significant partnership characteristics. In some statutes, for example, transferees of membership interests may be admitted only with the unanimous consent of the members, and the death, bankruptcy, or retirement of a member constitutes a dissolution (or "dissociation") of the LLC unless a majority in interest of the remaining members vote to continue the LLC. These partnership rules are usually default rules for LLCs, applicable unless the operating agreement provides to the contrary. Voting in an LLC may be on a per capita basis (though the default rule for voting in LLCs is usually the corporate default rule of voting by percentage of interest). An LLC, in short, is, or may elect to become, quite "partnership-like" without sacrificing the benefit of limited liability.

Some partnership-type liability provisions may appear in LLC statutes or operating agreements despite the fact that members have limited liability. In a general partnership, individual partners have an obligation to contribute to the partnership to cover losses and to indemnify partners who personally discharge partnership obligations. Even though neither type of obligation exists in an LLC, one sometimes finds provisions that the LLC itself must indemnify members for obligations incurred in carrying on the business of the LLC.

An LLC may also provide that some or all of the members will have personal responsibility for the LLC's obligations. Such provisions are not very common.[19] If an LLC elects to retain limited liability only for some members, some partnership rules obviously should become inapplicable. For

---

[19] Individual guarantees of individual obligations are much more common than general guarantees of all obligations of the business. An LLC applying for a bank loan, for example, may discover that personal guarantees of some of its members are a condition for the bank agreeing to make the loan. Of course, the same thing regularly occurs in closely held corporations as well. In HUD Notice H 95-66 (1995), the Department of Housing and Urban Development permitted LLCs to be mortgagors of HUD-financed developments only if all

example, unlike partners in a general partnership, individual members of an LLC without personal responsibility for debts should have no obligation to indemnify either the LLC or other members against losses incurred or payments made by them when acting on behalf of the limited liability company.

3. *Comparison with a limited partnership.* The LLC differs from a limited partnership in that all participants may actively take part in control of the business without restriction and without fear of personal liability for the business obligations. In addition, there does not need to be a general partner, a participant who is personally liable for the business obligations.

The source of the limited liability provided by an LLC is analogous to that provided by the limited partnership statutes for limited partners. A limited partnership files a certificate with the designated state official and the limited partners thereby obtain the shield of limited liability because the statute so provides. Similarly, an LLC files articles of organization with a designated state official and the members of the LLC thereby obtain the shield of limited liability because the LLC statute so provides. In this respect, an LLC resembles a limited partnership more than a corporation, which obtains limited liability through the fiction that a charter has been issued so that a separate legal entity has been created.[20] However, the analogy between an LLC and a limited partnership in which there are no general partners is itself incomplete, since there are no restrictions on the powers of limited partners to participate in the general management of the enterprise.

§6.4. MANAGEMENT STRUCTURE OF LLCS

One important aspect of the flexibility provided by limited liability company statutes is that each LLC has the option of electing to be managed either by managers, in much the way a corporation is managed, or by members, in much the way a partnership is managed. The law and commentary relating to LLCs refer, rather confusingly, either to "*manager*-managed limited liability companies" or to "*member*-managed limited liability companies," phrases that sound and look similar but refer to diametrically different management structures.

Management of a *member*-managed limited liability company is similar

---

LLC members execute a rider to the HUD note making each of them individually liable to HUD as guarantors.

[20] A formal difference of this nature obviously should make no practical difference. The fact that obtaining limited liability by incorporating leads immediately to classification as a corporation for income tax purposes under check the box simply illustrates the formalistic character of the Internal Revenue Code in this respect.

or identical to that of a partnership. Statutes defining member-managed limited liability companies provide that each member is an agent of the limited liability company for the purpose of its business, that each member has the right to possess LLC property for business purposes, and so forth. These statutes may also provide for partnership-type duties of care and loyalty.

Management of a *manager*-managed limited liability company is based on the corporate analogy. Managers are similar to directors of a corporation and have similar powers and duties. Inactive members of a manager-managed limited liability company are roughly analogous to shareholders, or to limited partners in a limited partnership, except that they are without power to participate in management at all (except to the extent permitted by the formation documents of the LLC).[21] Presumably, each LLC is free to tailor either member-management or manager-management provisions to the particular needs of that particular LLC, thereby possibly creating mixed forms of management.

Some state statutes provide that the default rule for an LLC is member-management rather than manager-management. Other statutes adopt the opposite default rule, presuming that all LLCs will be manager-managed unless specific provision to the contrary is made in the controlling documents. Pennsylvania adopts yet another approach, applying the management provisions of its limited partnership statute to manager-managed limited liability companies.

This flexibility in management structure may create practical problems for LLCs when they enter into transactions with third persons who may not be familiar with the limited liability company concept. To take a simple example, when an LLC wishes to open a bank account, the bank officer must decide whether to use standard partnership or corporation forms, whether to require a resolution of the managers of the LLC, and whether to rely on the authority of officers designated by the LLC who represent that they are authorized to act on behalf of the LLC. The answers to these questions may not be self-evident. Similarly, when an LLC wishes to borrow money, the lender may be faced with the question whether to require personal guarantees of all members in order to replicate partnership liability for such obligations, or whether to follow the corporate model and require only a limited number of sureties. Presumably, issues of these types will gradually be worked out with increased experience and familiarity with the LLC form of business.

---

[21] In a limited partnership, if a limited partner takes part in control of the business, she may lose the shield of limited liability. An inactive member of a manager-managed LLC simply has no power to participate in control of the business unless permitted to do so by the operating agreement.

§6.5 LLC DEFAULT RULE PROBLEMS

The limited liability company draws rules from two different sources: close corporation law and partnership law. Each of these two sources of law have their own set of default rules, which are often inconsistent with each other. Individual state LLC statutes may provide for one type of default rule or another, but unfortunately some statutes are entirely silent as to which default rule should be applicable in the event the LLC itself has not made a choice in its articles of organization or operating agreement. Great care must be taken in the drafting of LLC documents to make sure that rules are provided for unanticipated issues that might arise. It is undesirable to remain silent in LLC documents on basic operational questions. The default rule provided by the state statute should be specifically incorporated (if that is what is desired) and governing rules should be established to the extent no default rule is specified by statute, since otherwise it may not be clear which rule will be applicable. Two examples:

> *Example:* First, assume that A, a member of an LLC, assigns his entire interest to X. What does X have? In the absence of specific provision dealing with assignments, either the partnership or the corporate analogy may be applicable. If the partnership analogy is applied, X has all of A's financial interest but no right to participate in management. In the absence of specific provision to the contrary, A retains his management rights even though he has no financial interest in the enterprise.[22] On the other hand, if the corporate analogy is followed, X has all of A's rights, financial and managerial, and is entitled to participate in management to the same extent as the provisions of the operating agreement permit all members to participate.

> *Example:* To complicate matters somewhat, assume that the LLC has three members, A with 30 percent, B with 30 percent, and C with 40 percent financial interests. The agreement is silent not only with respect to the effect of assignments but also whether management participation rights are to be based on a per capita basis or on the basis of financial interests. C purchases B's 30 percent interest, thereby owning a 70 percent financial interest. Does C now have a 70 percent interest in the entire LLC or a 40 percent original interest and a 30 percent assignee's interest? Does C have a 70 percent voting interest (the corporate default rule), a 50 percent per capita voting power (the partnership de-

---

[22]See §4.20.

fault rule), or a right to cast two votes per capita, one for the original interest and one for the assigned interest?

The choice of which rule should be applicable in these instances is perhaps not as important as having rules that are readily ascertainable by members or managers who may themselves not be lawyers.

§6.6 THE TERM OF EXISTENCE OF LLCS

Limited Liability Company statutes make the period of existence of LLCs a matter for determination by the individual LLC. Many of the earlier statutes, however, provided an outside term of 30 years. Some statutes provide for "perpetual" existence, as in modern corporation statutes. Rather curiously, in such states some LLC operating agreements add language such as "except that the term shall not extend beyond a life in being plus 21 years." Such language, of course, is customary in wills and trusts, but the reason for including it in an LLC operating agreement is unclear. As in the case of a corporation, "perpetual" existence really means "indefinite" existence, not existence "for all eternity."

§6.7 PROTOTYPE AND UNIFORM STATUTES

In the initial rush of states to enact LLC statutes, there was no model or uniform statute that could be looked to for guidance. Statutes were loosely modeled after the Wyoming and Florida statutes, but states freely made innovations or changes in their own statutes.

Because of concern that diversity in state laws might create serious problems, particularly for interstate LLCs, attempts began almost immediately after the LLC's tax status was recognized to develop prototype or uniform state LLC statutes. However, the rush of states to enact LLC statutes was underway, and most states enacted LLC statutes before these efforts to develop standardized statutes came to fruition. The first such product was a Prototype Limited Liability Company Act, proposed in 1992 by a committee of the American Bar Association. This statute is clearly a "model" statute to be used as the basis of state enactment, since it is expressly open to variations by individual states. Concepts developed in this prototype statute have been incorporated in many state statutes.

At about the same time the prototype was released, NCCUSL instituted a project to develop a comprehensive Uniform Limited Liability Company Act (ULLCA), intended for enactment *in haec verba* by each state. This project has been controversial and was not completed until 1996. In one sense, the Uniform Act may already be too late in the day, since all but a handful of states have already enacted LLC statutes. Uniform statutes, of course, are designed for enactment by states without amendment or modification. The expectation apparently is that individual states will unify their varying LLCs statutes by repealing their existing statutes and enacting ULLCA. Bills based on ULLCA have been introduced in several states that already have LLC statutes. Whether enactment will in fact occur is doubtful.

There are significant substantive differences between ULLCA and the ABA prototype statute and between ULLCA and the statutes enacted by most states. It is true that the existence of 50 states as laboratories for statutory experimentation has led to innovative and efficient solutions in the corporate and other areas. ULLCA, however, does not build directly upon the experience of the states with these statutes in some respects, but rather substitutes novel and sometimes controversial experimental provisions. The reasons for this development lie within the process followed by NCCUSL in developing uniform legislation. Many participants in the drafting committee process are familiar with general principles of drafting uniform legislation but have little direct experience with LLCs. Others are persons with distinct perspectives on the issues involved with LLCs because they represent interests, such as real estate and similar interests, but are not directly involved in the creation of LLCs.

In any event, for whatever reasons, ULLCA goes much further in incorporating partnership default provisions from the Revised Uniform Partnership Act and the Revised Uniform Limited Partnership Act than does any state-approved limited liability company statute. ULLCA adopts partnership statutory provisions on a variety of topics, creating "at will" LLCs and "term" LLCs, and providing that members have the inherent power to withdraw from an LLC similar to that possessed by partners in a general partnership. These provisions were introduced apparently to implement a substantive decision that it is desirable in LLCs to provide partnership-type rights, including the options to individual members to have a right of "exit" and the further right to have their interests purchased by the LLC when they elect to withdraw — a right to "put" their interests similar to that enjoyed by partners in a general partnership. While these are default provisions and may be negotiated around by provisions in an LLC's operating agreement (in much the same way the partnership provisions themselves may be negotiated around in general partnership agreements), their desirability as default provisions is questionable since they are likely to be used by relatively unsophisticated persons. However, lawyers and business persons generally appear to prefer, given a choice, the stability of the corporate model in which there is no automatic right of withdrawal and no power on the part of a shareholder to compel the corporation to purchase the shares at a time chosen by the shareholder.

134

Other partnership provisions that ULLCA makes directly applicable to LLCs include the effect of knowledge and notice, nonwaivable provisions, the application of "supplemental principles of law and equity," the explication of the duties of care and loyalty of members in partnership terms, broad agency principles making each member a general agent of the LLC, the charging order as the device by which individual creditors of a member obtains satisfaction from the limited liability company, principles of dissociation, expulsion, and winding up, and so forth.[23] Indeed, the heavy emphasis on partnership default provisions in this statute may limit its attractiveness as the standard for state limited liability company statutes.

§6.8 IMPLICIT AND EXPRESS DUTIES IN AN LLC

State statutes vary widely in their descriptions of the duties owed by members and managers of LLCs. Many state statutes define statutory duties in terms similar to the duties imposed on directors in corporation statutes. A few states and ULLCA define the statutory duties in terms similar to the duties imposed on partners by the Uniform Partnership Act (1994). One would normally expect that corporate-type duties would be found to be applicable to managers in a manager-managed LLC and partnership type duties to members of member-managed LLCs. However, the problem is more complicated than that.

A number of states allow the operating agreement to modify or define the rights and duties of managers or members of LLCs without restriction or limitation. If read literally, these provisions may permit the members to draft their own contractual relationships free from all express or implied duties found in corporation law decisions and from the fiduciary duties applicable to partners in a partnership. Provisions authorizing self-dealing transactions without any review by disinterested persons or personal use of business assets by managers would appear to be valid if included in the operating agreement. All lawyers must feel a bit uneasy about opining that managers or members of LLCs have no duty to other members simply because the operating agreement contains language exonerating them from all consequences of their actions. Because the LLC is a new form of business entity, there is no definitive holding one way or the other as to how much reliance may be placed upon exonerating provisions. Also, since many corporate and partnership duties are to some extent implicit in the business form itself, it is likely that courts will imply corporate-like or partnership-like duties in specific cases involving LLCs where necessary to prevent significant injustice despite broad language to the contrary in an operating agreement.

[23]These various provisions appearing in UPA (1994) are discussed in §§4.13, 4.17-4.21, and 4.24-4.28

Thus, one should probably assume that managers in a manager-managed LLC owe duties of care and loyalty[24] similar to the duties owed by directors of a corporation, and members in a member-managed LLC owe duties analagous to those owed by partners in a general partnership.[25] Managers presumably should have the benefit of the business judgment rule applicable to directors in connection with claims of negligence or failure to make an adequate investigation.

A related question that also awaits future resolution is the extent to which courts will apply common law corporate principles to LLCs, such as piercing the corporate veil,[26] restrictions on distributions, fiduciary duties of directors, and equitable principles applied by courts to avoid oppressive conduct. The creation of a doctrine of "piercing the limited liability company veil," analogous to the famous "piercing the corporate veil" doctrine discussed in Chapter 10,[27] seems likely. Similarly, members of LLCs may be required to restore funds to the LLC that were distributed shortly before the LLC becomes insolvent. Judicial intervention compelling a buyout of a member's interest when that member has been the victim of conduct by managing members which the court deems "oppressive" also is plausible. Courts may also invalidate secret voting agreements among members that would be viewed as being against public policy in a corporate context.

Some persons strongly supporting the LLC movement have argued that LLCs will be popular precisely because they do not incorporate these various implied principles that courts have imposed on partnerships and corporations. In their eyes, the LLC should be a "clean" contract-based organization in which courts should enforce literally whatever terms appear in the operating agreement. They argue that the "do-goodism" of these implied principles are undesirable from an economic standpoint because they are doctrines that freely contracting parties would not themselves agree to. It is doubtful that this vision will be (or should be) fulfilled. The equitable partnership and corporate doctrines developed by courts have been in response to specific situations in which courts have concluded that certain participants have been mistreated or abused in violation of their reasonable expectations. When similar abuse or mistreatment appears in the LLC con-

---

[24]These duties should include, at a minimum, prohibitions against unfair self-dealing, the appropriation of LLP property for personal use, and the personal usurpation of business opportunities.

[25]Partners, of course, are personally liable for the obligations of the partnership while members of an LLC are not. It is possible that this difference in liability may justify a more relaxed standard for members of a member-managed limited liability company than should be applicable to partners in a general partnership.

[26]See Comment, Piercing the Veil of Limited Liability Companies, 62 Geo. Wash. L. Rev. 1143 (1994).

[27]The LLC statute of at least one state specifically incorporates a piercing doctrine for LLCs by reference to the corporate doctrine.

text, it is likely that courts will have exactly the same reaction and will devise similar remedies, no matter what the general language of the operating agreement says.[28]

§6.9 TAX CLASSIFICATION RULES FOR LLCs

Because an LLC is not a corporation, its tax characterization is governed by the Kintner rules and the proposed check the box regulations. This is a basic difference in conception from corporate tax treatment. It means that the LLC is not compelled to choose between S and C corporation taxation; rather, it may choose between corporate and partnership taxation, and only if it elects to be governed by corporate-type taxation does it then choose between C and S treatment.[29]

One unique aspect of the tax treatment of limited liability companies under the check the box regulations is that there is special treatment of one-member LLCs. An LLC with only one member is not recognized as a separate taxable entity, and its income or loss must be reported on the owner's personal tax return. As discussed below in section 6.13, many state LLC statutes appear to permit the formation of limited liability companies with a single member, though some apparently do not.

§6.10 ACTUAL AND POTENTIAL USES OF LLCs

The limited liability company is popular because it is the most flexible of business form yet created that is recognized as eligible for conduit tax treatment. It permits the owners of a closely held business simultaneously to participate fully in the management of the affairs of the business, have the limited liability protection available in corporations, and the tax treatment available to general partnerships.

The LLC has the capacity to displace all other business forms for the closely held business. In other words, in ten years or so the LLC easily could

---

[28]To carry this point a bit further, the argument by the pro-contract theorists assumes that people generally negotiate at arms' length on a rational basis, with equal access to information. An allocation of business risks arrived at through such a negotiation process obviously should not be disturbed by judicial intervention based on *ex post* notions of "fairness."

Unfortunately, in the real world many closely held business relationships are created without any negotiation at all, and where negotiation does occur, there may be significant information and sophistication gaps among the various parties. It is doubtful that the "clean contract" argument should be routinely applied in such situations.

[29]See §9.6 for a discussion of conduit taxation and the difference in treatment between S corporations and enterprises taxed as partnerships.

become the standard business form for all businesses in which there are a few owners. Whether or not this will actually occur, however, is another question. In part, this is because of the conservatism of attorneys, who are reluctant to propose untried business forms in place of well-accepted business forms that clearly "work."[30] In part, it depends on possible changes to federal tax law. Radical "flat tax" and other proposals would completely integrate business forms for tax treatment; enactment of such proposals probably would end the growth of LLCs, since the more familiar corporate form could always be used. However, even if the present tax structure is retained, numerous technical issues may restrain the growth of LLCs. These include application of securities laws to LLCs, state tax treatment of different business forms, federal tax rules relating to varying cash and accrual accounting methods, application of the self-employment tax, the passive loss rules, and similar matters. Federal tax regulations written before 1990 often refer to "limited partners" and "general partners," and it is usually unclear how these regulations should be applied to membership interests in LLCs. As a result, uncertainty may persist about facets of the tax treatment of LLCs.

Information about the actual use of limited liability companies in real life in the relatively brief period since they were developed is fragmentary. Partially anecdotal studies reveal that apparently their predominant use is in the businesses of holding and developing real estate and managing or operating shopping centers, hotels, and other real estate projects into which the public is invited.[31] This should not be surprising because the potential for ownership liability in both contract and tort in real estate ventures is substantial,[32] and the tax advantages of conduit-type taxation are often essential if the enterprise is to be viable to begin with. A second major category is farming (though at least two states prohibit LLCs from owning farming lands). A third major use is in professional service businesses — law firms, medical "partnerships," and the like. Many state statutes specifically permit LLCs to engage in professional service businesses, though a number of these statutes follow the peculiar pattern of professional corporation stat-

[30]Statistics indicate that in Texas and Missouri corporations are still formed much more frequently than LLCs even though most incorporations in those states involve small businesses that presumably could readily operate in the form of LLCs. In Texas, for example, more than 35,400 corporations but fewer than 5,600 LLCs were formed in 1996.

[31]Indicative of this area of use of LLCs is the HUD notice providing that LLCs may be mortgagors of HUD financed projects only if all LLC members personally guarantee the payment of the HUD note. See note 19, supra.

[32]Limited liability is particularly important in these areas because some courts have held landowners personally liable for criminal attacks by unknown third persons where such an occurrence is foreseeable, or where the landowner has assumed the responsibility of protecting members of the public from such attacks. See, e.g., Madden v. C & K Barbecue Carryout, Inc., 758 S.W.3d 59, 62 (Mo. 1988); Keenan v. Miriam Foundation, 784 S.W.2d 298, 302-305 (Mo. Ct. App. 1990).

utes[33] and limit an LLC to a single specific professional service. A handful of states flatly prohibit LLCs from engaging in specific professional service businesses, such as the practice of law.

Relatively few LLCs appear to involve manufacturing or retailing. This is surprising, since these businesses would appear to combine the liability risks and tax benefits of a conduit tax treatment that makes the LLC essentially an attractive business form.

There are signs that the use of limited liability companies is gradually broadening. Some state banking commissions have received inquiries whether there are any legal prohibitions against a bank being organized in the form of a limited liability company. At least one attempt was made to acquire a radio station through an LLC vehicle. LLCs have appeared as the bidder for real property in HUD foreclosure sales. As indicated above, one Oklahoma entrepreneur failed in an effort to have an LLC own a retail liquor package store.

Another indication of the type of business favored by LLCs is the datum that apparently more than two-thirds of all LLCs are member-managed rather than manager-managed. In other words, LLCs appear to be involved in businesses in which some form of partnership probably would have been selected for the business if the issue of limited liability were not present.

An LLC also may be used when other forms of business entities are to be members of the LLC. For example, one may use a limited liability company instead of a corporation when one of the investors is a nonresident alien, disqualifying the corporation from S corporation treatment. Similarly, an LLC may be a partner in an operating general partnership, thereby assuring limited liability for the LLC members in a conduit tax structure, and unlimited liability for the remaining general partners. Indeed, this flexibility should permit LLCs to be used in increasingly varied combinations of business enterprises.

An LLC may also be used in a variety of ventures involving a small number of investors which traditionally have been incorporated. For example, an LLC would appear to be a plausible substitute for the joint venture corporation, where two or more entities enter cooperatively into a new business. Rather than operating a subsidiary as a separate corporation, a parent entity may consider using an LLC to achieve cost savings. Venture capital projects also would appear to be logical candidates for LLC use. A leveraged buyout of an operating corporation might be achieved through the conversion of the target corporation into an LLC with the members being the purchasers. Doubtless other ingenious uses of the LLC device will be devised by enterprising attorneys.

A great deal of interest has been expressed in utilizing LLCs (and other forms of unincorporated businesses for that matter) in connection with fam-

---

[33]See §8.39.

ily estate planning. Family limited partnerships are widely used for this purpose. Certainly, an LLC may be used in many situations for estate and tax planning, e.g., to hold life insurance policies. The more difficult question is whether they may be used to avoid the "estate tax freeze" provisions of the Internal Revenue Code enacted in 1990.[34] The flexibility of the LLC permits a wide variety of transactions that have the effect of transferring the value of future income-producing property to the younger generation; the issue is whether devices to restrict the value of the conveyed interests will "work" under sections 2701 through 2704 of the Internal Revenue Code, because voluntary restrictions on transfer must be ignored for purposes of valuation under those sections.

§6.11 APPLICATION OF SECURITIES LAWS TO LLCs

The federal and state securities laws apply to transactions involving "securities." Securities in turn are defined to include "investment contracts." The leading United States Supreme Court case defining the phrase *investment contract* states that it is "a contract, transaction or scheme whereby a person invests his money in a common enterprise and is led to expect profits solely from the efforts of the promoter or a third party."[35] A member's interest in an LLC clearly involves an investment of money in a common enterprise with an expectation of profit. The critical question is whether the profits are expected to be derived from the efforts of a "promoter or a third party."

In a member-managed LLC the members usually participate actively in the business and the interests should not be treated as securities. In a manager-managed LLC the converse is likely to be true. However, this rather simplistic test is incomplete. It is quite possible that individual members of a member-managed LLC may be completely inactive, while it is equally possible that individual members of a manager-managed LLC may participate actively in the business. The difficult cases arise when the LLC is manager-managed, but the members retain significant voting or veto powers. Perhaps the test in these cases will be analogized to the tests applicable for partnership interests in general partnerships.

Under most state securities statutes, general partnership interests are not classed as securities under the principles set forth in the well-known partnership case of *Williamson v. Tucker*,[36] and these holdings are arguably

---

[34]See §9.22.

[35]SEC v. W.J. Howey Co., 328 U.S. 293, 298-299 (1946).

[36]645 F.2d 404 (5th Cir.), *cert. denied*, 454 U.S. 897, 102 S. Ct. 396 (1981). This case sets forth the principle that general partnership interests usually involve direct participation in the management of the business and therefore are not securities for Securities Act purposes, but that registration may be required if the general partnership interests do not in fact involve participation in management.

equally applicable to LLC interests.[37] On the other hand, membership interests in manager-managed LLCs usually closely resemble corporate securities or at least limited partnership interests that are registrable as securities. As a result, compliance with the requirements of federal and state securities statutes when raising capital is probably required.[38]

To complicate matters further, at least eight states have statutes that expressly characterize interests in LLCs as securities. However, various nuances in these statutes illustrate the diversity in treatment of LLC interests in state blue sky laws.[39] For example, some of these statutes expressly provide exemptions for interests in LLCs where, generally, all the members are actively engaged in management. In addition, the securities acts of at least 11 states include LLCs within the definition of "persons," thereby subjecting LLCs to registration requirements for brokers, dealers, or investment advisers, even where the statutes are silent as to whether LLC interests themselves are "securities."

State regulators in at least a dozen states have promulgated exemptions or simplified registration options for LLC interests or transactions even in the absence of specific statutory references to LLCs. A typical exemption excludes sales of LLC interests if the LLC has a limited number of investors who purchase solely for investment purposes and no advertising or general solication is involved and no remuneration is received by anyone in connection with the solicitation. No-action letters have been issued in at least six states on the basis of this test, which is similar to that applied to investment contracts and general partnerships. These letters reflect a case-by-case approach to the question whether LLC interests should be treated as securities. Thus, even while a theoretical debate exists over whether LLC interests should generally be classified as securities, states have quietly applied these statutes to limited liability companies.

§6.12 LLC MEMBERS AS EMPLOYEES AND SELF-EMPLOYED

One question that has received relatively little attention is whether members of an LLC may be viewed as employees (in much the way shareholders

---

[37]However, the general liability of partners for partnership obligations gives each partner a strong incentive to be informed about partnership transactions. The same incentive may be lacking in LLCs in which there is no personal liability, and it may therefore be argued that the analogy with partnerships is not appropriate.

[38]For a general discussion concluding that presumptively LLC interests should not be securities, see Ribstein, Form and Substance in the Definition of a "Security": The Case of Limited Liability Companies, 51 Wash. & Lee L. Rev. 807 (1994).

[39]A majority of these state statutes contain language such as "unless the context requires otherwise," thus permitting state regulators to exempt LLC interests where appropriate.

of a corporation may be employees to the extent they work for it), or whether, like partners, they are to be viewed as owners rather than employees.[40] Some firms have decided not to use the LLC because of concern that the enterprise may become subject to employment discrimination laws with respect to members who work for the LLC. This question is largely unresolved.

One important practical question is whether members of LLCs will also be subject to the federal Self Employment Contributions Act (SECA), which imposes a tax of 12.4 percent of earnings up to $61,000 for old-age survivors and disability insurance,[41] plus an uncapped tax of 2.3 percent on all earnings for the Medicare program. Avoidance of this tax is obviously desirable, but its application to LLCs is uncertain. The closest analogies are to general partners in general and limited partnerships, who are viewed as self-employed, and limited partners in limited partnerships who are viewed as passive investors and not self-employed.

On December 29, 1994, the Internal Revenue Service issued proposed regulations under section 1402 of the Internal Revenue Code, dealing with the application of the self-employment tax to LLCs. These proposed regulations[42] set forth fairly simple and direct rules: In a manager-managed LLC, members who are managers are viewed as self-employed and members who are not managers are viewed as passive investors. In a member-managed LLC, all members are viewed as self-employed (following the partnership analogy for general partners). However, if the business is one that cannot be operated as a limited partnership, nonmanager members cannot be viewed as limited partners and members who would not be limited partners under state law cannot be viewed as limited partners for SECA purposes under this proposed regulation. This regulation seems logical, but flat rules of this character may easily be subject to manipulation. It also may be possible to avoid the SECA tax by using a combination of business forms. For example, creating an LLC to manage the business of another LLC and have the participants receive distributions from the operating LLC and participate in management only through the managing LLC. It is far from certain, however, that such a transparent strategy will succeed.

[40]Employment law protection, however, may apply to partners in partnerships to a limited extent. See Wheeler v. Hurdman, 825 F.2d 257 (10th Cir. 1987) (A "bona fide" general partner is not an employee for employment discrimination purposes). See also Ehrlich v. Howe, 848 F. Supp. 482 (S.D.N.Y. 1994).

[41]If the member is an employee of another business with a salary in excess of $61,200, this portion of the SECA tax is inapplicable.

[42]Prop. Reg. §1.402(a)(18). This regulation is based on id. §1402(1)(13), which states that limited partners are generally not subject to SECA taxation.

§6.13 ONE-PERSON LIMITED LIABILITY COMPANIES

Finally, one should consider briefly the uncertain status of one-person LLCs. The statutes of at least eight states now specifically authorize one-person LLCs, though the details of this business form are not articulated. There is, of course, a direct analogy with one-person corporations, which are widely accepted and recognized for tax and liability purposes. However, the tax status of one-person LLCs is quite uncertain. The Internal Revenue Service's check the box regulations suggest that

> an entity with a single owner cannot conduct business as a partnership. However, the proposed regulations permit a business entity with a single owner that is not required to be classified as a corporation to elect to be classified as an association or to have the organization disregarded as an entity separate from its owner (in which case the business activity is treated for federal tax purposes in the same manner as if it were conducted as a sole proprietorship, branch, or division of the organization's owner).

In other words, it is likely that a one-person LLC will be taxed as though it were a proprietorship. The IRS bases its conclusion that a one-person LLC cannot be a partnership on the theory that a partnership inherently must involve two persons. It is not clear, for example, how an LLC consisting of one individual and a corporation wholly owned by that individual would be taxed.

Another serious question is whether a one-person LLC will provide limited liability for the proprietor. However, if it is felt necessary to have an LLC in a sole proprietor situation, it may be possible to form an LLC with husband and wife being the sole members. As suggested above, it may also be possible to use a "straw" or nominal LLC member, for example a corporation owned or controlled by the proprietor as a second member. Until the status of one person LLCs is clarified, however, it may be sensible to incorporate the one-person business and elect S corporation tax treatment, thereby avoiding a potentially costly reclassification as a corporation.

7

Limited Liability Partnerships[1]

[1]Portions of this chapter are based on a paper presented at a symposium at the University of Colorado Law School in February 1995. See R. Hamilton, Limited Liability Partnerships: Present at the Birth (Nearly), 66 U. Colo. L. Rev. 1065 (1995).

§7.1 INTRODUCTION

The registered limited liability partnership, also known as a "limited liability partnership," or, more colloquially, as an LLP (the abbreviation used throughout this chapter), is a new form of modern business enterprise. A *limited liability partnership* is for most purposes a general partnership.[2] It differs from a general partnership only in that some or all partners are by statute not personally responsible for certain partnership liabilities. The LLP is a new and potentially useful business form that is particularly attractive for professionals such as lawyers and accountants doing business in partnership form,[3] but may also be available to other types of partnerships. It appears likely that this new business form will follow the LLC path and ultimately become available in virtually all states.

The birthdate of the LLP can be precisely identified as August 26, 1991, when Texas House Bill 278 became effective without Governor Ann Richards' signature.[4] The popularity of the Texas version of the LLP is evident from the fact that more than 1,200 law firms in Texas, including virtually all of the state's largest firms, elected to become LLPs within one year after its enactment.[5]

§7.2 TYPES OF LIMITED LIABILITY PARTNERSHIPS

There are two quite different variations or types of LLP statutes:

1. *Narrow Non-liability Statutes.* The original version, adopted in

---

[2]Provisions authorizing LLPs constitute amendments to the state's general partnership statute.

[3]However, there is no inherent reason why the limited liability partnership should be limited to professional partnerships, and under most LLP statutes, partnerships engaged in ordinary business activities may become limited liability partnerships. See §7.7.

[4]Texas Acts 1991, 72d Leg., ch. 901, §84. This original enactment is now codified at Vernon's Ann. Civ. St. (1996 Supp.) art. 6132b, §15.

[5]Statistics collected by the Texas Secretary of State indicate that as of 1996 over 1,600 partnerships have elected LLP status under the Texas statute. While data as to the number of law firms in this group is apparently not separately collected, the impression of persons in the Secretary of State's office is that most of the filings were by law firms. In Texas, a law firm may also elect to do business as a professional corporation or as a limited liability company (LLC) (after a ruling to that effect in 1994; see Texas Ethics Opinion 486 (1994)). Even though a professional corporation or an LLC provides a wider scope of protection against liability than an LLP in Texas, they both suffer from the major disadvantage of being subject to the Texas franchise tax, a tax measured by the income of the entity. A Texas LLP is not subject to this tax.

Texas, Delaware, and about a dozen other states, protects "innocent" partners from personal responsibility for liabilities created by errors, omissions, negligence, incompetence, or malpractice committed by other partners or by employees supervised by other partners. Innocent partners have no responsibility for such liabilities, but the responsible partners and the partnership itself continue to have full responsibility for those liabilities. In other respects, all partners in a limited liability partnership have the same rights, duties, and responsibility for other types of liabilities as partners in a general partnership. The definition of "innocent" varies from state to state, but it usually includes all partners who (1) did not themselves commit the act of malpractice, (2) did not have the responsibility of overseeing the persons who committed the act of malpractice, or (3) were aware of the act of malpractice and did not take reasonable steps to correct it.

The protection provided by this type of LLP might be described as pure "peace of mind" insurance for innocent partners, since it is designed to avoid the fear by a partner that her personal assets may be at risk because of negligence or malpractice by a partner over whom she has no control and quite possibly whom she has never met.[6] On the other hand, the partners that committed the acts of malpractice (or failed to oversee properly those partners) remain personally liable for all partnership obligations.

The original LLP statutes therefore modify in a limited manner the basic principle of general partnership law that each individual partner is personally liable for all partnership obligations to the extent they exceed the assets of the partnership. In this form of LLP, all partners have the benefits, responsibilities, and potential liability of general partners except for malpractice claims or for liabilities arising from other negligence or misconduct in which they were not personally involved.

2. Broad Non-liability Statutes. The second type of LLP statute was first adopted in Minnesota in 1994,[7] and has since been adopted in more than a dozen other states since then. It adopts the general approach of the Texas and Delaware statutes with respect to liability for malpractice, but in addition protects all innocent partners from personal responsibility for most other liabilities. The partnership of course remains personally liable for all its liabilities, so that partnership creditors generally may look only to partnership assets for recourse. Clients injured by malpractice may look to both the partnership assets and the guilty partners for recourse. This type of LLP

[6]In addition, such a partner may be concerned that she might be compelled to go through an ignominious chapter 7 bankruptcy proceeding to be totally shed of liability arising from such risks.
[7]1994 Minn. Laws, ch. 539, §12.

provides protection from liability very similar to that of a limited liability company,[8] though it lacks the continuity and certainty of existence that an LLC provides.[9]

This version of the LLP proceeds on quite a different theory than the narrow non-liability statutes. If the change made by the narrow non-liability statutes is viewed as an "important" qualification to the general conception of partnership law, the change made by the broad non-liability statutes may fairly be described as "revolutionary." They basically insert the word "not" in old section 15 of the Uniform Partnership Act with respect to all electing LLPs:

> All partners are [not] liable
>   (a) Jointly and severally for everything chargeable to the partnership under sections 13 and 14.
>   (b) Jointly for all other debts and obligations of the partnership; . . .[10]

The liability provisions of the Minnesota statute are typical of the broad non-liability type of LLP. Partners in an LLP are not "merely on account of this status, personally liable for anything chargeable to the partnership . . . or for any other debts or obligations" of the LLP if the "charge, debt, or obligation arose or occurred" while the LLP was qualified as such.[11] However, a partner is liable "to the partnership or its partners" if the particular partner has "breached a duty to the partnership or to the other partners" and this liability may be in the form of direct liability to the partners or contribution to the partnership.[12] The application of this last sentence to malpractice liabilities seems reasonably clear, but its application to a variety of other liabilities may be open to question, since liability is imposed for "breaches of duty owed to the partnership or to the other partners" apparently without regard to what duties to third persons may also have been breached. Further, since the grant of the shield of limited liability is constrained by the phrase "*merely* on account of this status," i.e., the status of being a partner in an LLP, a partner may become liable by his own action (e.g., by guarantying a partnership obligation).

Both the ABA's "prototype" LLP statute and the optional amendments to UPA (1994) approved by NCCUSL in 1996 following this approach.

The protection provided innocent partners against personal liability

---

[8]In an LLC, members who actually participate in tortious conduct will be personally liable because of their participation.

[9]See the discussion of dissolution problems of LLPs in §7.12.

[10]UPA (1914) §15.

[11]1994 Minn. Laws, §323.14, subd. 2.

[12]Id.

under statutes of both types is usually referred to as "the shield of limited liability" provided by the LLP, and this terminology is used hereafter.

§7.3 COMPARISON OF LLPs AND LIMITED PARTNERSHIPS

Even though an LLP sounds as though it is similar to or related to a limited partnership (LP), it is in fact quite a different animal. A limited partnership has two classes of partners — general partners and limited partners — with quite different management responsibilities and liability for partnership obligations. In a limited partnership, the limited partners are passive investors with virtually no powers of management and no personal liability at all for partnership obligations; a limited partner's risk of loss may not exceed his contributions of capital to the firm. In a limited liability partnership, on the other hand, all partners have the management responsibilities of partners in a general partnership.

Under the narrow non-liability statutes, partners in an LLP all have unlimited personal liability for all partnership liabilities except for the malpractice liabilities covered by the shield of limited liability for that particular statute.[13] In states with malpractice only statutes, all partners in a registered limited liability partnership remain fully liable, in other words, on office leases, Xerox machine contracts, purchases of CAT scan equipment, salaries of employees, pension plan payments for employees, and so forth. Limited partners in a limited partnership have no personal responsibility for any liabilities of this nature unless they voluntarily elect to become liable.

In states with broad non-liability statutes, the protection of general partners in an LLP and limited partners in a general partnership is virtually the same; presumably, limited partnerships will continue to be used in these states when there is concern on the part of capital-contributing partners that the protection against limited liability provided by the LLP statute may not be in fact as secure as the protection provided limited partners by modern limited partnership statutes.[14]

---

[13]The statement in the text assumes that it is a general partnership that qualifies as an LLP. It is possible, under the statutes of Texas, Delaware, and several other states, for a limited partnership to qualify as an LLP in order to protect its general partners from liability for malpractice or negligence of other general partners. Vernon's Ann. Civ. Stat. art. 6132b-3.08(e); 6 Del. Code, §1553. See §7.21. In such an entity, the rights and duties of limited partners are unaffected by the LLP election, but the general partners' obligations for negligence or malpractice by other partners or employees are determined as set forth in the LLP statute. There apparently is no special name for a limited partnership that has qualified as an LLP under these statutes; they are usually referred to as "LLLPs."

[14]Compare §5.8, §5.9, and §7.12. In particular, as discussed in §7.12, there may be concern about the fragility of LLPs when there are changes in the membership of the partnership.

§7.4 COMPARISON OF LLPs AND LLCs

There is substantial confusion between limited liability companies, on the one hand, and LLPs, on the other. This confusion is clearly based on the similarity of the names and not on a similarity of the two forms of business. The statutes under which limited liability companies are created are quite different from the statutes under which LLPs are created. As described in Chapter 6, LLC statutes embody numerous corporate concepts and provide numerous options and default regulations that give stability and flexibility to the LLC form of business. For example, limited liability company statutes permit an LLC to elect between management by the members and management by managers who have roles analogous to directors in a corporation.[15] If management by managers is authorized, the members have only limited rights to participate in management. In contrast, the LLP statutes are part of the partnership statutes of the state and no analogous flexibility exists; management of an LLP must be on a partnership basis.[16] In short, a registered limited liability partnership is quite unlike an LLC in terms of management and control.

With respect to the scope of limited liability, an LLC gives greater protection than an LLP in states with narrow non-liability statutes. In states with broad non-liability statutes, the scope of coverage appears to be virtually the same, though again there may be concern that the shield of limited liability in an LLP may not be as secure as the protection provided members of an LLC under modern LLC statutes.

§7.5 DEVELOPMENT OF THE LLP CONCEPT IN TEXAS

The narrow non-liability LLP concept was a direct outgrowth of the collapse of real estate and energy prices in the late 1980s, and the concomitant disaster that befell Texas' banks and savings and loan associations. Texas led the nation in bank and savings and loan failures during the 1980s. More than one-third of all the bank failures in the United States occurred in Texas.

Following the collapse of these financial institutions across the state, the Federal Deposit Insurance Corporation (FDIC) and the Resolution Trust Corporation (RTC) and its predecessor, the Federal Savings & Loan Insurance Corporation (FSLIC) devoted a significant part of their total resources to the recovery of funds lost in the collapse of Texas institutions. Suit was brought against hundreds of shareholders, directors, and officers

[15]See §6.4.
[16]However, some centralization of management in a general partnership may be created by provisions in the partnership agreement itself.

of failed financial institutions. However, the amounts recovered from the principal wrongdoers were only a tiny fraction of total losses and attention quickly turned to the roles of the lawyers and accountants who had represented the failed financial institutions before their collapse. "Where were the lawyers?" and "Where were the public accountants?" were cries figuratively heard across the state. Claims against lawyers and accountants for malpractice and breach of duty were attractive because the individual professionals sometimes had been deeply involved in the affairs of their clients. Also, these lawyers and accountants were usually associated with partnerships that had substantial malpractice insurance and numerous wealthy partners. As a result, several highly reputable law firms in Texas found themselves in deep trouble because of their bank and thrift work during the salad days of the 1980s.

The most vivid example is provided by a major Dallas law firm (hereafter referred to as the Dallas Law Firm).[17] Long recognized as one of the leading corporate law firms in the state, the Dallas Law Firm in the early 1980s was a traditional general partnership.[18] One Dallas Law Firm partner, Laurence Vineyard, along with four associates, did legal work for three savings and loan associations.[19] Vineyard severed his relationship with the Dallas Law Firm in 1983 and formed his own firm with his associates; this new firm continued to do work for the S&Ls. In addition to providing legal services, it turned out that Vineyard sat on the board of directors of at least one of the S&Ls and had profitable financial arrangements with the others. These three S&Ls were among the more flagrant "high fliers" which paid little attention to principles of sound financial management and provided lavish benefits and large unsecured loans for their owners. Losses from the collapse of these three S&Ls ran over one billion dollars. Vineyard was deeply involved. He was criminally prosecuted, convicted, sentenced to two five-year prison terms, and disbarred.[20] His personal assets were insubstantial in light of the losses incurred by the S&Ls, and FSLIC and FDIC turned their attention to the malpractice insurer for the Dallas Law Firm and to all persons who were partners during the period the firm represented the

---

[17]The firm continues in business today under its original name and has requested that it not be specifically identified.

[18]The present Dallas Law Firm is a professional corporation.

[19]The records of the Dallas Law Firm indicate that Vineyard did substantial transactional work for Vernon and represented the parties in the acquisition of Brownfield.

[20]Vineyard was actually convicted in connection with transactions involving a Colorado S&L that occurred after he left the Dallas Law Firm. He was also convicted for diverting loan proceeds from an approved S&L project to the purchase of his personal residence, a transaction that also occurred after he had left the Dallas Law Firm. However, the government cited and relied upon these criminal convictions when raising questions about the validity of transactions he performed for the S&Ls while a partner with the Dallas Law Firm. While in prison, Vineyard learned to be an electrician and he practiced this trade following his release from prison.

S&Ls. Caught within the FSLIC/FDIC net were retired partners, partners that had since left the Dallas Law Firm to join other firms,[21] partners that had been promoted from associate to partner, persons who had become "of counsel" to the Dallas Law Firm, and the forty-some partners who had nothing at all to do with representation of the various thrift institutions. The total claims asserted by FSLIC greatly exceeded the liability insurance available to the firm and the assets of the firm itself. To emphasize this point, in one particularly chilling meeting, FSLIC personnel used an overhead projector to show a slide listing the names of each Dallas Law Firm defendant with estimates of total net worth and the amount likely to be available from each of them to satisfy the government's claims.

Needless to say, the Dallas Law Firm litigation caught the attention of the hundreds of law firms that had represented banks or thrifts during the 1980s. Thousands of lawyers in hundreds of Texas law firms watched this litigation closely as it unfolded in the late 1980s with a "There but for the grace of God go I" reaction. The law suit against the Dallas Law Firm was ultimately settled for approximately the amount of malpractice insurance carried by the firm.

The idea of limiting the personal liability of innocent partners in Texas law firms originated in SB 302, a bill introduced by a state senator from Lubbock, Texas during the 1991 legislative session. This bill provided limited liability from malpractice claims exclusively for certain named classes of professionals: lawyers, accountants, doctors, engineers, architects, and real estate brokers. The idea had been developed by a twenty-odd person Lubbock law firm. This bill was immediately and enthusiastically endorsed by the lawyers involved with the legislative process. "A great idea" was the first comment; "Why didn't we think of that?" was another. This was true even though the bill only applied prospectively and could not help those lawyers and accountants that, like the Dallas Law Firm, were enmeshed with the Texas financial institution disaster.

At its first legislative hearing, SB 302 received a very negative initial reception before a house committee. The idea of limiting liability within partnerships generally was received with great skepticism. Representative Steven Wolens, a Democrat from Dallas (and a lawyer with Baron & Budd, a litigation firm that conducted business as a professional corporation) viewed any change in the long-accepted characteristics of a general partner-

---

[21]FSLIC made a major effort to recover a portion of the losses from the malpractice insurers of the firms to which former Dallas Law Firm partners had moved. Malpractice insurance is written on a "claims made" basis, and notice was given after these lawyers had joined their new firms. Some of these firms had independent potential exposure to S&L liability because of their own representation of S&Ls as well as derivative exposure arising from the claims being asserted against former partners of the Dallas Law Firm. Global settlements were negotiated with some of these firms, involving substantial payments to the federal agencies.

ship to be a radical and undesirable proposal. Two other legislators argued to lawyer witnesses, "You want your cake and yet you want to eat it too," and "If you want to swim with the sharks, you should recognize that you might get eaten by them." Further, the argument was strongly made that the bill was not needed, since law firms could become professional corporations and thereby limit their liability.[22] Finally, the bill was objected to because it discriminated in favor of professionals and was, in the final analysis, a "help-a-lawyer bill."

Nevertheless, the pressure for enactment was substantial. After substantial revisions, the LLP provision was quietly attached to an omnibus bill that authorized limited liability companies in Texas and included significant amendments to existing corporation and partnership statutes.[23] Governor Ann Richards allowed this bill to become effective without her signature.

§7.6 MAJOR ACCOUNTING FIRMS ELECT TO BECOME LLPS

On August 1, 1994, three of the nation's "Big Six" accounting firms — Coopers & Lybrand, Ernst & Young, and Price Waterhouse — all simultaneously announced that they had decided to become registered limited liability partnerships under the Delaware LLP statute, a narrow non-liability statute. The three other Big Six accounting firms — Arthur Anderson & Company, Deloitte & Touche, and KPMG Peat Marwick — at the same time each indicated that they were also considering seriously changing their business structure to this new type of business form.[24]

---

[22]Legislators did not appear to be impressed with the argument that incorporation of an ongoing law partnership was impractical because of the bunching of income for tax purposes. In their eyes, that should be the cost of obtaining the benefit of limited liability. At this time, Texas had not enacted an LLC statute.

[23]This initial version of the LLP statute was added as an amendment to §15 of the Texas Uniform Partnership Act, Vernon's Ann. Civ. St. art. 6132b, §15(2).

[24]The reason given was the enactment by New York of a statute recognizing the limited liability created for LLPs formed under the laws of other states. The effective date of this legislation was October 1, 1994 and the changeover to LLP status for the accounting firms became effective on that date.

The New York LLP statute is a broad non-liability type of statute. The statute also permits the creation in New York of both domestic LLPs and domestic limited liability companies. McKinney's Cons. Laws §121-1500 et seq. It is interesting that these major accounting firms preferred the narrow protection provided by the Delaware statute to the much broader non-liability protection provided by these alternatives in the New York statute. I have been informally advised that the decision to become a Delaware LLP and qualify to transact business in New York was based on a preference for the Delaware judicial system over the New York system. The difference in the scope of the limited liability shield was not mentioned.

The major accounting firms made no secret of their reasons for desiring to become LLPs. Like law firms, they have traditionally been required by state law to conduct their business in the form of general partnerships. The Big Six accounting firms are among the largest partnerships in the world, consisting of hundreds or thousands of general partners.[25] Because of the liability rules applicable to general partnerships discussed in sections 4.14 and 4.18, each partner in a Big Six accounting firm that is a general partnership is personally liable, at least theoretically, for all the obligations and liabilities of the firm without regard to his or her own fault or involvement. Thus, it is quite possible that individual partners might be held liable for negligence committed by partners in distant cities whom they had never met and who may not even be named as defendants in the law suit.[26] While personal liability apparently has never been actually imposed on individual partners of a Big Six Accounting firm, the liquidation of Laventhol & Horwath in 1990 showed that the possible imposition of such liability was more than theoretical. Laventhol was the seventh largest accounting firm in the United States at the time of its liquidation, but assets of the firm were insufficient to cover all claims, and the individual partners (including retired partners) were required to come up with $47 million from their personal assets to satisfy those claims.[27]

§7.7 ELECTION OF LLP STATUS

To become an LLP, a general partnership must file a simple registration statement with the appropriate state official and adopt a name that includes a reference to being an LLP. In addition, in many states the partnership must also keep a specified amount of liquid assets on hand or maintain malpractice insurance in a specified amount, or both to assure possible claimants that the firm will be able to reasonably respond to claims covered by the statute.[28]

The registration process involves the payment of a fee usually based on

[25]The Big Six accounting firms operate on a worldwide basis. However, for many years foreign operations have been conducted by separate legal entities to the extent permitted by the laws of each country. The office of a Big Six firm operating in the Bahamas, for example, may be a Bahamian partnership, but it will be a partnership that is separately organized from the United States partnership. See Young v. Jones, 816 F. Supp. 1070 (D.S.C. 1992) (Price Waterhouse, Chartered Accountants a Bahamian general partnership is independent of Price Waterhouse — United States, an American general partnership).

[26]This is true under both UPA (1914) and UPA (1994). See §4.14.

[27]For a discussion of partnership bankruptcy cases involving law firms and accounting firms in which general partners were forced to contribute toward partnership liabilities, see Macey & Kennedy, Partnership Bankruptcy and Reorganization: Proposals for Reform, 50 Bus. Law. 879 (1995).

[28]These provisions are discussed in more detail in §7.8.

154

the number of partners. Registration and the payment of the fee is required annually. Since the fee may be $200 per partner or more each year, LLP registration is a source of revenue of some significance for many states.[29]

Most state statutes authorizing LLPs impose no restrictions at all on the types of general partnerships that are eligible to become registered limited liability partnerships. Any general partnership may become a registered limited liability partnership simply by filing the required certificate. One can envision a partnership composed of three plumbers doing business as a partnership in part to provide economies in purchasing, billing, record-keeping, handling requests for services, and so forth, and deciding to elect to become a limited liability partnership. This election is particularly attractive if each plumber works independently with little or no oversight by the other partners. However, in the relatively brief period since this new form of business was invented, law and accounting firms appear to have been the principal firms to take advantage of it and it seems likely that this form of business will continue to be most attractive to professional partnerships.

New York has adopted a different approach. It limits the LLP form of business to "professional" partnerships. It defines a registered limited liability partnership as "a partnership without limited partners *each of whose partners is a professional authorized by law to render a professional service* within this state."[30] So long as a New York LLP meets the professional partnership requirement it may also engage in other businesses, apparently without limitation.

§7.8 MINIMUM CAPITAL REQUIREMENTS

The Texas LLP statute requires an LLP to either (a) "carry at least $100,000 of liability insurance of a kind that is designed to cover the kinds of errors,

---

[29]In Texas, the filing fee is $200 per partner while in Delaware the fee is $100 per partner up to an amount equal to the maximum annual corporate franchise tax in that state — $150,000 in 1994; there is no cap on the Texas registration fee. Annual reregistration and the payment of another fee appears to be a standard requirement for LLPs. In Texas, at least, the LLP is a significant source of continuing revenue to the state, particularly from the numerous law firms that have elected to become LLPs.

[30]N.Y. Partnership Law, §121-1500 (emphasis added). A "profession" is defined in turn to include not only practice as "an attorney and counselor-at-law or as a licensed physician," but also practice in any of those professions "designated in title eight of the Education Law." Title eight of the Education Law, in turn regulates some 27 different professions, including such diverse occupations as chiropractic, engineering, social work, massage, occupational therapy, midwifery, acupuncture, athletic trainers, and respiratory therapists. N.Y. Partnership Law, §121-1500(m). The reason for limiting registered limited liability partnerships to professional groups is not apparent. The list of professions is so broad that whatever arguments are made for limiting liability for partners in these professions would seem to be equally applicable to businesses generally.

omissions, negligence, incompetence or malfeasance for which liability is limited," as described above, or (b) "provide $100,000 of funds specifically designated and segregated for the satisfaction of judgments against the partnership based on the kinds of errors, omissions, negligence, incompetence, or malfeasance" for which liability is limited. The $100,000 may be in the form of cash deposited in trust or escrow, certificates of deposit, U.S. Treasury obligations, a bank letter of credit, or an insurance company bond.[31] The Delaware statute is quite similar to this basic construct except that the insurance/cash deposit requirement is $1,000,000 rather than $100,000.[32] While many states do not impose a minimum capital requirement on LLPs, several statutes of both the limited and broad non-liability types do follow the Texas/Delaware approach in this regard.

These minimum capital requirements seem somewhat anomalous today because minimum capital requirements have been virtually eliminated for other forms of limited liability entities. In most states today, there is no minimum capital requirement for corporations[33] or LLCs. It seems odd, to say the least, that entities providing virtually complete shields against personal liability (corporations and LLCs) can be created with only nominal capital (or with zero capital) while a narrow non-liability LLP which provides only a partial or less secure shield must maintain a significant capital base. This requirement, however, reflects the force of the political sentiment in Texas and elsewhere that limiting traditional general partnership liability was a radical change taking something of importance away from tort claimants.

As a practical matter, law and accounting firms are likely to have substantial amounts of malpractice insurance — as much as $20 or $30 million in the case of the very large law firms and hundreds of millions of dollars in the case of major accounting firms — so that a minimum capital requirement is probably irrelevant for most professional firms. However, it may create problems for small professional firms composed of two or three partners who desire to obtain LLP status.

The Delaware and Texas provisions[34] that permit financial responsibility to be evidenced by a liability insurance policy "of a kind that is designed to cover the kinds of negligence, wrongful acts, and misconduct for which liability is limited" by the LLP statute create constructional problems. If a liability insurance policy excludes from coverage some specific action that is within the shield of limited liability, does that mean the insurance policy

---

[31] Vernon's Ann. Civ. Stat. art. 6132b-3.08 (1995 Supp.). An earlier version of this statute appears as, id. art. 6132b, §15(2) (1995 Supp.).

[32] 6 Del. Code Ann. §1546.

[33] Texas continues to require a new corporation to have $1,000 of capital before commencing business. Most states have eliminated all minimum capital requirements, which were almost universal 40 years ago.

[34] Del. Code Ann., §1546(a); Vernon's Ann. Civ. Stat., art. 6132(b)-3.08(d)(A).

is disqualified and the shield of limited liability lost entirely? If not, what happens if an act of negligence or malpractice is covered by the shield of limited liability under the statute but is excluded from coverage by a restriction or exception in the particular liability insurance policy? Since the insurance proceeds are not available to the plaintiff in that case, may she ignore the shield of limited liability and go after the innocent partners? The language "of a kind that is designed to cover the kinds of negligence, wrongful acts, and misconduct for which liability is limited" indicates that a complete overlap between coverage and the shield of limited liability is not required, but no one really knows.

The broad non-liability LLP statutes create different problems for partnership creditors. In a general partnership, distributions to partners may be recovered by partnership creditors since they are personally liable to make necessary contributions to permit the satisfaction of partnership liabilities. However, in a broad non-liability LLP, all distributions of partnership assets to non-negligent partners presumptively appears to be beyond the reach of creditors.[35] Of course, much the same thing is true of other non-liability incorporated or unincorporated business forms as well. The Minnesota statute addresses this issue in a section that makes applicable to LLPs a corporate law concept: the legal capital rules for distributions. The Minnesota corporation statute adopts a straight equity insolvency standard for distributions that does not require any specific minimum quantity of capital to be retained by the corporation. Most statutes, however, are silent on this issue.

It seems clear that some restrictions must be placed on distribution policies of LLPs under broad non-liability liability statutes to prevent irresponsibility and actual fraud. The equity insolvency test, requiring partnerships to make a reasonable estimate of the ability of the firm to meet its obligations as they mature before making a distribution, seems plausible. In the absence of an express statutory restriction on distributions on LLPs, courts may also rely on principles of fraudulent transfer or fraud on creditors to give creditors of an LLP some protection against inappropriate distributions.

Unfortunately, the application of a corporate equity insolvency test to LLP distributions may itself create serious problems where malpractice or other major claims are being asserted against an LLP of either the narrow or broad non-liability type. In particular, it is likely that distribution policies used by law firms prior to their qualification as LLPs will have to be significantly modified. Many firms distribute essentially all their earnings each year, planning to borrow if necessary to maintain the necessary cash flow in the early months of the next fiscal year. In the past, it has not been necessary to be very concerned about the impact of distribution policies of law partnerships on creditors, since all partners were personally liable on partnership

---

[35]See §§7.14, 7.15.

obligations. After the LLP election, however, each distribution must be separately evaluated and approved under the equity insolvency test if the distribution is not to be voidable. It may be difficult for a firm to satisfy the equity insolvency test if a major malpractice claim has been made against the firm and is unresolved. Indeed, it may be difficult in this situation to justify any distribution to the partners, even routine monthly draws.

Finally, not all states have modern legal capital statutes such as Minnesota's. Many have older statutes that require stated capital and capital surplus accounts that are not available for distribution to shareholders at all or are distributable only upon a vote of certain classes of shareholders. In these states, a special rule for when distributions by LLPs are permitted may have to be developed.[36]

§7.9 PIERCING THE LLP VEIL

The concept of piercing the corporate veil may be applied by analogy to partnerships that have elected to become LLPs under broad non-liability statutes. The Minnesota LLP statute specifically incorporates the state's case law on piercing the corporate veil, but it is likely that courts will ultimately apply this concept both to LLCs and LLPs formed under broad non-liability statutes. This, by itself, creates significant uncertainty whether the shield of limited liability will be available in specific situations. The tests for piercing the corporate veil are notoriously vague and amorphous; piercing claims are easy to bring and complaints are hard to get dismissed on motions for summary judgment. As a result, a high proportion of piercing cases settle.

Furthermore, it is doubtful that the corporate veil-piercing concepts, at least as usually articulated in the corporate context, are readily transferable to the LLP context, which builds from the partnership model of procedural informality. For example, one of the tests usually mentioned and relied upon by courts is "failure to follow corporate formalities."[37] The LLP does not have formalities by definition. Another test is "inadequacy of capital." Again, it is unclear how this test will be applied in the LLP context.

Despite these uncertainties and the amorphous nature of the piercing the corporate veil doctrine, it seems clear that a similar concept must be found to be applicable to LLPs formed under broad non-liability statutes to prevent irresponsibility and actual fraud on creditors. The narrow non-lia-

---

[36]The distribution rules applicable to LLCs may be a more appropriate reference point in these states.

[37]I should perhaps add that I have never understood why this factor is given the prominence that it has. The Texas piercing the corporate veil statute now states expressly that this test is not to be a factor in piercing the corporate veil in contracts cases. V.A.T.S. Bus. Corp. Act, art. 2.21 A(3). It remains to be seen, however, whether Texas courts will ignore scores of cases in which this factor is given central prominence and enforce this statutory command.

bility LLP statutes presumably avoid this issue by limiting the scope of the shield of limited liability to tort claims and by imposing a minimum capital requirement on LLPs.[38]

§7.10 CONTRIBUTION AND INDEMNIFICATION

The original LLP statutes were concerned with only one avenue by which a partner may be held liable for a partnership malpractice obligation. That avenue is the worst-case Dallas Law Firm scenario, where a substantial malpractice judgment is entered against a partnership and its individual partners and the firm is unable to fully satisfy the judgment from its liability insurance and partnership assets. Absent the LLP election, each partner is then jointly and severally liable on the unsatisfied portion of the judgment and may be sued on this liability; the personal assets of each partner may also be levied upon to satisfy this judgment. Indeed, one newspaper story written at the time the major accounting firms became LLPs stated that the LLP device provides only a limited type of insurance, which might be described as "death insurance" for the innocent partners because it comes into play to protect partners' personal wealth only upon the collapse of a firm when it is unable to satisfy a malpractice claim.[39]

This obvious scenario was quickly recognized to be incomplete. Partners may be held liable for partnership malpractice and similar claims under other scenarios as well. If the partnership itself satisfies a malpractice liability out of its own assets, the payment will be reflected as reductions of the capital accounts of all the individual partners. Negative capital accounts for some or all of the partners are likely to result. Individual partners may be compelled by the partnership or the other partners to make contributions to the partnership restoring capital accounts to at least zero to permit satisfaction of all liabilities upon winding up. Such contributions, if required of innocent partners, are directly traceable to the malpractice or negligence claim, but the payments are technically "contributions" to the "partnership," not a payment to the holder of a claim or to satisfy a liability of the partnership. Thus, they may not be covered by the shield of limited liability since the payments are not made to satisfy the malpractice claim itself.[40]

---

[38]The Texas statute cited above provides that "actual fraud" should be the test of holding corporate shareholders personally liable in contract cases. The statute does not address tort cases at all, since these cases usually present complex questions of the adequacy of contributed capital, distribution policies, and the use of funds for insurance or other purposes. Of course, the Texas/Delaware LLP statutes apply only to tort cases.

[39]Ziegler, Top Accountants to Shield Partners from Lawsuits, Wall St. J., July 29, 1994, at C15.

[40]It is possible that the partnership agreement may permit the capital reductions arising from the satisfaction of a malpractice liability to be allocated to the "guilty" parties rather than to all partners. However, this requires nice exercises of judgment by someone (who

Another possibility is that an individual partner, who is personally liable for an LLP claim, may satisfy the liability out of his personal assets and then seek indemnification from the partnership and the other partners, as the Uniform Partnership Act contemplates.[41] Again, essentially the same argument may be made that the obligation to indemnify the partner arises from the partnership relation and is not a liability arising from the claim or partnership liability itself.

As these possibilities became clear, LLP statutes have been been revised to provide that the shield of limited liability covers responsibility for claims made by the partnership or by individual partners for contribution or indemnification. In 1994, for example, section 1515 of the Delaware statute was amended to provide that innocent partners were not liable "either directly or indirectly, by way of indemnification, contribution, assessment or otherwise, for debts, obligations and liabilities of or chargeable to the partnership."[42] Other states quickly followed suit.

§7.11 INTERPRETATION OF THE SCOPE OF THE SHIELD

The shield of limited liability is easy to describe in abstract terms. But serious issues of interpretation arise at the margin, particularly under the narrow non-liability LLP statutes (though similar problems may arise under the broad non-liability statutes as well). Under the narrow non-liability LLP statutes, joint and several liability for acts of negligence or malpractice continues to exist for (1) the partners actually committing the negligence or malpractice, (2) other partners who had "direct supervision and control" over the partners that were negligent or committed malpractice, and (3) partners who supervised employees who committed the acts of negligence or malpractice. Furthermore, Texas adds (4) partners who were aware of the negligence or malpractice and failed to take reasonable steps to prevent its occurrence.[43]

---

almost certainly has a personal financial interest) within the partnership as to which individual partners were involved in the transaction giving rise to the liability.

[41] UPA (1914) §18(b): "The partnership must indemnify every partner in respect of payments made and personal liabilities reasonably incurred by him in the ordinary and proper conduct of its business, or for the preservation of its business or property."

[42] 1994 Del. Laws, ch. 259, §2.

[43] There is no indication of how this exception to the limited liability shield should be construed. In contrast, the District of Columbia statute imposes liability on partners that had "written notice or knowledge" of the negligence or malpractice without regard to whether the particular partner made efforts to prevent the negligence or malpractice. D.C. Code (1981), §41-146(a)(2). The District of Columbia statute obviously creates far fewer problems of interpretation than the Texas provision, but it hardly improves fairness or pro-

What does "direct supervision and control" mean? How close does supervision have to be to constitute "direct" supervision? Does it cover the ultimate responsibility that a senior partner or rainmaker in a law firm has for "his" client? Is it limited to the mid-level partner who actually does the work or who supervises associates and more junior partners when they do the work? Does it extend to members of the opinion committee of a law firm who review all formal legal opinions before they are released? Very similar issues also arise in accounting firms. Typically, financial audits are performed by employees of an accounting firm subject to the general oversight of the "responsible" partner who actually signs the audit letter. The "responsible" partner may be indirectly involved in a dozen or more audits at the same time. Does he have "direct" supervision? Probably so, even though as a practical matter there is no way he could directly supervise all the people involved in "his" audits. On the other hand, the chairperson of a practice area in an accounting or law firm who sets general policy and who may be consulted on difficult questions arising in areas of specialization arguably does not have direct supervision or control over anyone, and should not be responsible for the negligence or malpractice of persons actually working on the question. These are presumably fact-specific questions on which there is little statutory guidance and virtually no precedents.

The scope of malpractice or negligence that is covered by the shield of limited liability in narrow non-liability statutes also creates difficulty. The scope of acts for which protection is provided to innocent partners is defined in different ways in the state statutes. The Delaware statute, as originally enacted, referred to obligations arising from "negligence, wrongful acts, or misconduct."[44] The original Texas statute referred to "errors, omissions, negligence, incompetence, or malfeasance."[45] Louisiana added to the Texas statute the words "willful or intentional misconduct."[46] Other states adopt different phrases. Despite these variations in language, it seems reasonably clear that the coverage of all these statutes goes beyond traditional negligence or malpractice claims and covers automobile accidents, fraud claims, thefts, and over-billing claims as well as intentional tortious acts such as false imprisonment or assault. However, serious problems of scope nevertheless exist.

Another gray area is whether a plaintiff who phrases her malpractice claim as a breach of an implied warranty that is part of her contract with the law firm is subject to the shield of limited liability in a narrow non-liability LLP. If a client frames her pleading as a contract claim does that

---

vides much protection for otherwise innocent partners, since it is to the interest of guilty partners to give notice to all innocent partners.

[44]6 Del. Code Ann. §1515(b).
[45]Vernon's Ann. Civ. Stat. art. 6132b, 15(2).
[46]La. Rev. Stat. Ann. §9:3431.

mean that all partners, innocent and not so innocent, are personally responsible? If so, the shield of limited liability may easily be avoided by artful pleading. In 1994, the Delaware LLP statute was amended by adding the phrase "whether characterized as tort, contract or otherwise,"[47] and other states have generally followed suit.

A final major gray area involves claims based on statutory provisions, e.g., discrimination on the basis of age, sex, or race. If, for example, a partner intentionally discriminates against a person because she is over 50, can that person hold all the general partners liable? The answer is not clear, but the issue is hardly theoretical.[48]

§7.12 THE DISSOLUTION PROBLEM

The registration requirement for LLPs of all types creates a serious practical problem. What happens to the shield of limited liability if an electing LLP is dissolved during the course of the year in which it is registered as an LLP? This is a potentially serious problem since general partnerships have traditionally been viewed as ephemeral in nature and a technical dissolution of a partnership occurs whenever a partner dies or withdraws from the firm.[49] Of course, in most situations the remaining partners continue the business much as before, but that is technically a new partnership. The dissolution of the old partnership and creation of the new may be completely seamless, and the participants may not be fully aware that from a strictly legal standpoint a new partnership has been created. If the registration is valid only for the partnership that exists at the time the registration is filed, the shield of limited liability may disappear when that partnership dissolves and may not reappear to protect a new and different partnership

---

[47]The precise language of the Delaware statute covers "debts, obligations and liabilities of or chargeable to the partnership arising from negligence, wrongful acts or misconduct, whether characterized as tort, contract or otherwise, . . ."

[48]The law firm of Baker & McKenzie was held liable for a $6.9 million punitive damage award in 1994 based on a claim that a senior partner and "rainmaker" in the intellectual property section of the firm had sexually harassed a legal secretary by, among other things, dropping candies in the pocket of her blouse and pulling back her arms to see which of her breasts was bigger. That is certainly intentional conduct. Woo, The Business of Law, Wall St. J., Sept. 2, 1994 at B3. If Baker & McKenzie were an LLP, would the other partners be protected from personal responsibility for this conduct?

[49]This is certainly true under UPA §29. RUPA (1994) §601 substitutes the word "dissociation" for the word dissolution. This newer version of the uniform act appears to assume (but nowhere states explicitly) that a partnership continues despite the dissociation of a partner. It uses the word "dissolution" in several sections in the context of a "dissolution and winding up." See, e.g., RUPA §603(a). The addition of a new partner to a partnership without more may not be a "dissolution" or "dissociation" under either statute. See UPA §17.

even though it contains many of the same partners as the dissolved partnership. This creates a potential trap for the unwary partnership and could lead to the imposition of liability on partners despite the shield of limited liability.

The Minnesota statute was the first statute to address this issue. The earlier Texas and Delaware statutes do not.[50] The Minnesota statute has made two attempts to resolve this problem. The first attempt provided, first, that the shield of limited liability "continues in full force for the dissolved partnership regardless of any dissolution, winding up, and termination of a limited liability," and, second, if the business is continued "by a successor general partnership . . . then the limited liability . . . also applies to that successor partnership until the expiration of the registration that the dissolved partnership had in effect. . . ."[51] The term "successor general partnership" was not defined, but its ordinary meaning probably encompassed the partnership that continues with most of the same personnel using the same name as the LLP but without one or more of the former partners. It may also cover the same situation with a change in the firm name to reflect the addition or departure of a named partner.

This was not a completely satisfactory solution. While it probably covers the most common situations where some partners withdraw, it does not address, for example, the truly fractured partnership, for instance, where there are four partners and they split into two new firms with two partners each, or where 19 partners remain and 27 leave but the remaining partners continue to use the same name as the former, much larger partnership. Nor does it unambiguously address situations where new names are adopted for both partnership entities resulting from the fracture. Indeed, it may not address the situation where a new name is adopted by a small partnership when it adds one or more new partners but no partners leave.

There are several plausible solutions to this problem. One might consider changing the definition of dissolution so as to refer only to a process of winding up and termination. One might then make the shield of limited liability personal to each partner in an LLP rather than to the partnership itself, and allow each partner to carry that shield with her when she changes firms. This, however, might create problems when a covered partner decides to go into sole practice, when a covered partner moves to a general partnership that has not registered as an LLP, or when an uncovered partner moves to a partnership that has elected LLP status. Even more radical solutions, such as automatically providing limited liability for all professionals, might also be suggested.

---

[50] A possible explanation may be that the issue will arise regularly under the Minnesota statute but much less frequently under statutes that provide a shield of limited liability only for negligence and malpractice claims.

[51] 1994 Minn. Stat. §323.14, subd. 4.

§7.13 WHEN DO CLAIMS ARISE?

LLP statutes provide for protection against liabilities or obligations only if they arise during the period an LLP registration is in effect. In this respect, the shield of limited liability for partners in LLPs differs from the protection accorded investors in limited liability companies or shareholders in corporations.

The first LLP statutes used standard language. The original Minnesota statute provided that the shield of limited liability applied if the "charge, debt or obligation *arose or accrued*" while a registration was in effect.[52] The Texas statute uses different language. It refers to "debts and obligations . . . *arising from* errors, omissions, negligence, incompetence or malfeasance *committed while*" the partnership was registered.[53] These phrases mask considerable uncertainty when applied to both contractual and tort claims. For example, consider a ten-year lease of office space. Did the entire rental obligation "arise or accrue" when the lease was signed, or does the obligation "arise" and "accrue" each month during the lease term, or does the obligation arise on the due date of each rent check? In the case of a malpractice liability, does the obligation "arise" when the representation was agreed to, or when the negligent or wrongful act was committed, or when the act was discovered, or when injury to the client occurs? Perhaps this issue may be resolved by analogy to the extensive case law deciding when statutes of limitation begin to run.

A couple of states have attempted to address the arise/accrue issue by legislation. In 1995, Minnesota added a provision stating that partnership obligations "under or relating to a note, contract or other agreement *arise and accrue when the note, contract or other agreement is entered into*"[54] and, further, that an amendment, modification, extension or renewal of a note, contract, or agreement does not affect the time when the obligation arose (even as to a claim involving the subject matter of the modification). The intention obviously was to create a mechanical rule that was easy to apply and would generally conform to the expectation of parties. While this is a helpful provision so far as it goes, it does not address all questions as to when other types of liabilities arise or accrue. For example, it is unclear whether a "renewal" of a lease at a higher rental and possibly containing some other modifications is sufficiently different that it should be viewed as a new lease. Maryland added a provision to its LLP statute that provides that the LLP liability provision does not affect "the liability of a partner for the debts and obligations of the partnership, whether in contract or in tort,

[52]Minn. stat. §323.14, subd. 2 (emphasis added).
[53]Vernon's Ann. Civ. Stat. art. 6132b-3.08(a)(1) (emphasis added).
[54]Minn. Stat. §323.14 (emphasis added). This section also applies to the Minnesota equivalent of UPA(1914) §17. See §6.21.

that arise from or relate to a contract made by the partnership prior to its registration as a limited liability partnership" unless consented to by the creditor.[55] This provision, added by a creditor's lobbyist, may broaden liability and narrow the scope of the shield of limited liability.

§7.14 OPPORTUNISTIC CONDUCT IN NARROW NON-LIABILITY LLPs

In LLPs formed in states with narrow non-liability statutes, a confluence of interrelated legal principles seems inevitably to lead to a considerable amount of jockeying and opportunistic conduct whenever an LLP is faced with both a major malpractice claim and ordinary business liabilities that together exceed, or may exceed, the available partnership assets and liability insurance.

It is helpful to first summarize the various principles applicable in this situation.

(1) The LLP itself is liable for both the ordinary business obligations and the malpractice claim.

(2) Innocent partners are personally liable only for the ordinary business obligations and they may be compelled to contribute to the LLP to permit it to discharge those obligations.

(3) Innocent partners are not liable for the malpractice claim and cannot be compelled to contribute to the LLP to permit it to discharge that obligation.

(4) The guilty partners are personally liable for both the malpractice claim and the ordinary business obligations and may be compelled to contribute to the LLP to permit it to discharge both types of obligations.

The interaction of these principles inevitably leads to opportunistic conduct as partners seek to minimize their personal exposure to liability. The complicating factor is that all assets of the LLP may be used in an undifferentiated way to satisfy either general trade liabilities or the malpractice liabilities, or both, but the innocent partners may be compelled to contribute only to the satisfaction of the ordinary business obligations. Thus, the way the LLP's assets are used to satisfy its liabilities will inevitably affect the relative wealth of the innocent and guilty parties.[56] A law firm facing a

---

[55]Md. Corporations and Associations Code, §9-307(c)(4).

[56]In these hypotheticals, it is possible that at some point principles of fraudulent transfer, preferences in bankruptcy, or breach of fiduciary duty may come into play to limit opportunistic conduct by one group or the other.

significant malpractice claim that threatens to exceed the LLP's assets is used as an example of how these conflicts arise.

Consider first the incentives of the guilty partners. They will obviously desire that the partnership expend the LLP's assets while they are held by the LLP to satisfy the malpractice claim. This may increase the amount of the ordinary business obligations left unpaid when the LLP's assets are exhausted, but the innocent partners will have to contribute to satisfy these obligations since the shield of limited liability does not protect them against such obligations.[57] Thus, to the extent the LLP's assets are used to satisfy the malpractice claim, the wealth of the innocent partners is reduced.

The innocent partners, however, have a quite different incentive. First of all, they would prefer to use available assets to satisfy or minimize the LLP's obligations other than the malpractice claim. The innocent partners, for example, would be delighted to use the LLP's assets to prepay rental obligations on a lease rather than to use the assets to settle the malpractice claim. Then, if there is a deficiency toward which partners must contribute, it would predominantly be based on the malpractice claim for which the innocent partners have no responsibility. Thus, the use of partnership assets to satisfy ordinary business obligations increases the liabilities imposed on the guilty partners and reduces the liabilities imposed on the innocent partners.

The innocent partners also would prefer that distributions of LLP assets be made to the partners individually rather than being retained by the LLP, since the assets distributed are removed from the LLP and cannot be used thereafter to satisfy any part of the malpractice claim.[58] This strategy is attractive to the innocent partners because it prevents the LLP from using the distributed assets to satisfy the malpractice claim, and the malpractice creditor may not recover them from the innocent partners if the remaining assets prove insufficient to satisfy the malpractice claim.[59]

Indeed, whenever an LLP has assets that are clearly insufficient to satisfy both malpractice and ordinary business claims and is in the process of winding up, direct conflicts of interest are created. There appears to be no rational way to resolve these conflicts. The innocent partners may argue that all available assets should be first applied to general trade liabilities on the theory that those payments benefit all partners in the LLP. The partners

[57]If the partnership assets are insufficient to satisfy the malpractice claim, the guilty partners will also have to contribute to discharge the balance of this claim.

[58]It is possible that the innocent partners may be required to return the amounts distributed to them in the face of a major malpractice claim on a theory of fraudulent transfer or breach of fiduciary duty. These payments also may be recoverable in a federal bankruptcy proceeding.

[59]If the remaining assets are insufficient to satisfy the ordinary business obligations (as well as the malpractice liabilities), the innocent partners will be required to contribute toward them.

with malpractice exposure may argue that a pro rata application of the LLP's assets across all liabilities is fairest.[60] Judicial intervention to ensure an evenhanded use of LLP assets in these situations would seem probable, but it is not at all clear just what evenhanded means in this situation.

One basic feature of LLPs based on narrow non-liability statutes is that innocent partners suffer losses (either a reduction in the amounts otherwise available to be distributed to them or an increase in the amount they must contribute to satisfy ordinary business obligations) to the extent that the LLP uses its assets to pay down the malpractice claim before all ordinary business obligations have been satisfied. For this reason, these LLPs have a strong incentive to obtain liability insurance in amounts sufficient to cover all malpractice claims, if that is possible.

§7.15 OPPORTUNISTIC CONDUCT IN BROAD NON-LIABILITY LLPS

One justification for the decision to broaden the shield of limited liability in the broad non-liability statutes is to avoid the gaps in the shield that may exist under the traditional LLP statutes. Gaps nevertheless exist in new and different areas under the broad statutes, and they also do not avoid the problems of conflict and opportunistic discussed earlier.[61] Since these statutes provide a limited liability shield for both contract and tort claims, it is necessary to consider not only traditional malpractice claims but also contract claims (e.g., the execution of a long-term lease on office space in an area in which real estate values have declined substantially) and the possibility that individual partners may be personally liable on such claims, either because of a personal guarantee or by entering into the contract in violation of a duty owed to the partnership.

In a broad non-liability LLP, conflicts between classes of partners will occur whenever one or more partners are personally liable for contributions to the LLP (because they were guilty of malpractice or negligence) and the LLP's assets and liability insurance are, or may be, insufficient to cover both the ordinary business obligations and the tort liabilities of the LLP. Conflict will also arise in the absence of malpractice claims where partnership assets are inadequate to cover all ordinary business liabilities and one or more partners (but not all of them) have personal responsibility for specific contract claims through personal guarantees.

These conflicts have a different twist than the conflicts arising under

---

[60]These partners may also urge that the LLP's assets be used to negotiate a settlement of the malpractice liability on the theory that that is the most efficient use of the LLP's assets to reduce aggregate partnership liabilities.

[61]See §7.14.

the narrow non-liability LLP statutes. Innocent partners under the broad type of statute have no responsibility to contribute toward ordinary business obligations. However, they would certainly prefer that the LLP make distributions rather than retaining assets to settle its obligations, since, once distributed, they cannot be recovered by creditors if the assets of the partnership are insufficient to pay all creditors.[62] This version of LLP statute therefore provides a strong incentive to keep the capital in the firm as small as possible.

A conflict among partners arises if distributions are not made and capital is retained. Innocent partners are indifferent as to whether the LLP's assets are applied against the ordinary business liabilities or against malpractice liabilities. However, the partners who have personal responsibility for certain claims have a strong interest in applying as many assets as possible against the claims for which they have personal responsibility rather than against the ordinary business obligations for which they do not have personal responsibility.

The likely outcomes under the broad non-liability type statute are, first, that LLPs will be minimally capitalized, and, second, to the extent the LLP has assets, they will be used to satisfy malpractice liabilities while the ordinary business creditors who have small claims or are unsophisticated get stiffed.

§7.16 WAIVER OF THE SHIELD OF LIMITED LIABILITY

It is not clear whether the shield of limited liability in broad non-liability states such as Minnesota is personal to each partner or whether it may be waived for all partners by a single partner, acting within the scope of his actual or apparent authority. A request to waive the protection of the non-liability statute may be made in the course of negotiating long-term contractual commitments such as a lease. The shield extends to liabilities arising "merely" from partnership status and therefore certainly seems to be something that the LLP may waive. If it can be waived only by the individual decision of each partner,[63] it obviously will be very difficult if not impossible to obtain waivers from all partners in a large national law or accounting firm.

Under ordinary agency principles applicable to partners, however, it would appear likely that the shield of limited liability may be waived by a

---

[62]Distributions once made to the innocent partners can be recovered if the distributions violate an equity insolvency test or under principles of fraudulent transfer and the like.

[63]Such an agreement arguably may be within the suretyship provision of the statute of frauds.

single partner when in negotiation with a creditor, even though that action may exceed his actual authority. If this is true, partners in Minnesota LLPs may readily lose their shield of limited liability without their knowledge or personal consent.

The New York statute provides specifically that the shield of limited liability may be waived by a majority vote of the partners, though it is unclear whether a majority is to be determined on a per capita basis or on the basis of weighted financial interests. Presumably, a majority of the partners may waive the shield of limited liability without the prior consent of, or over the specific objection of, the remaining partners. Again, the shield of limited liability for specific partners may disappear without the knowledge or consent of the partners themselves.[64]

§7.17 EVALUATION OF THE ALTERNATIVE LLP FORMS

On balance, is the narrow non-liability LLP a good idea? Is the broad non-liability form more desirable? These are the questions discussed in this section.

1. Narrow Non-liability Statutes. The argument in favor of the narrow non-liability is relatively simple. Given the extreme stress on the legal and accounting professions in the early 1990s from malpractice and S&L litigation, the desire of innocent partners for some protection against catastrophic claims in which they were not personally involved seems understandable. Since malpractice insurance covers the great bulk of these claims, and there is no indication that the LLP election affects the overall amount of insurance purchased,[65] the cost to plaintiffs of providing this limited liability appears to be relatively small.

The principal argument against providing protection for malpractice claims is a fairly abstract argument: It is generally undesirable to provide immunity from tort liability, since such liability encourages better monitoring and distributes the loss among persons who benefit from the activity.[66]

---

[64] Indeed, the possibility of waiver power seems so unpredictable that it is likely that all LLP partnership agreements will routinely withhold this power from the LLP except with the consent of the partnership and all partners. Of course, a partner's apparent authority may continue to exist, despite such provisions.

[65] See §7.18.

[66] Law and economics scholars have suggested that unlimited tort liability is a desirable policy because the firm is compelled to bear the full social cost of its activities. It also encourages careful monitoring of agents by partners and the purchase of an optional amount of liability insurance. For the reasons set forth in the following section, I doubt that the

It is difficult to question the general correctness of this proposition, but its force is mitigated considerably in the narrow non-liability statutes by provisions that impose liability on supervisors and other partners who are aware of the potential tortious conduct.

It is also true that the LLP creates some potentially troublesome anomalies and potential problems for the partnership form of business. However, this does not appear to be an insuperable objection. For one thing, these problems are unlikely to arise regularly. The great beauty of the narrow non-liability statutes is that they provide "peace of mind" assurance without changing the basic partnership rules, except in the case of firms actually facing substantial malpractice claims in excess of their malpractice insurance.[67] Of all the millions or billions of partnership transactions that occur each year in the United States, the limited liability feature of the narrow non-liability statutes will be irrelevant in the overwhelming bulk of them, since very few partnerships in fact ever face malpractice claims of this magnitude. In other words, it provides peace of mind, but actually has application in few real-life situations.

2. Broad Non-liability Statutes. Unlike the narrow statutes, the broad non-liability statutes will primarily affect the liability of partners in cases where there is no malpractice or tort claim at all. Most partnerships that collapse, leaving creditors unpaid, do not do so because of malpractice but because of bad business judgments about leases, the marketability of products, store location, computer equipment, and future growth or prospects in general. Consider law firms, for example. What percentage of law firms collapse leaving a mix of unsatisfied malpractice claims and ordinary business liabilities after exhaustion of partnership assets and liability insurance? Certainly less than 1 percent. Most law firms collapse because (1) they are not able to attract sufficient business to meet their overhead and justify their continued existence, (2) they previously entered into disastrous leases, (3) there are irresolvable personal disagreements among the partners, or (4) rainmakers decide they can do better either by setting up their own firm or by joining another firm. Yet the broad non-liability statute gives all partners, in every collapsed law partnership, protection from disastrous leases, from the consequences of hiring too many support personnel or adopting an inef-

---

narrow non-liability LLPs will affect either the amount of liability insurance maintained by LLPs or the extent of monitoring of agents that will incur in these businesses. This is a result, basically, of the fact that the shield of limited liability is not entirely impenetrable, so that all partners have an incentive to monitor agents and assure there is adequate insurance coverage.

[67] If the firm has malpractice insurance sufficient to cover the entire exposure, the LLP will have no impact on partnership rules.

fective business plan, or from relying upon a hoped-for rainmaker who in fact did not make very much rain. This result is difficult to accept as a matter of simple common sense, given the long history of the principle that partners are personally responsible for partnership obligations.

One argument made for the broad non-liability statute is that it is necessary to make the shield of limited liability against malpractice claims "more perfect."[68] It is true that there are gaps in the coverage of the narrow non-liability statutes, but the proposed cure is so much broader than the evil involved that it seems clearly to be a pretext for quietly obtaining limited liability for all partners in general partnerships without telling the world about it.

Some legal theorists have advanced a normative argument that limited liability is the preferred policy for business entities generally and therefore the broad non-liability statute "gets it right." Limited liability is preferable, it is argued, because it encourages passive investments in firms and protects inadvertent or unwary partners from unexpected and crushing liabilities. Major lenders always may obtain personal liability by contract. A variation of this argument is that it is not very important which rule is adopted with respect to contract claims because parties may negotiate, either for nonrecourse liability in the case of an unlimited liability rule, or for personal guarantees by owners in the case of a limited liability rule. Yet another argument is that smaller creditors with little incentive to determine who is liable on an obligation assume, or are satisfied with a rule, that only the entity with which they deal is responsible for the obligations. In either event, the broader non-liability statute is viewed as a desirable improvement over the much more narrow non-liability versions of LLP statutes.

The law and economics scholarship is based on the assumption that the world consists of persons who act rationally and that alternative choices are available. The real world doubtless has many such people and these people will adjust their behavior to either default rule without difficulty. For example, the practice has developed in some contracts with law and

---

[68]The shield provided by the narrow non-liability type of statute is not fully bulletproof, especially in the situation where a partnership is facing both ordinary business liabilities and malpractice claims that, in combination, exceed the available insurance and the available assets of the partnership. This argument assumes that the property rights of innocent partners should be determined as though no malpractice had ever occurred, or phrased another way, that innocent partners should suffer no ill financial effects from malpractice liabilities incurred by other partners. I see no inherent reason why this principle should be the one adopted. In any event, if this result is desired in the narrow non-liability statutes it could easily be handled by the establishment of special priority rules when a partnership is faced with both ordinary business and malpractice liabilities. It seems inappropriate to solve such a problem by modifying a long-standing liability rule in situations where the problem does not exist.

accounting partnerships of providing limited liability for innocent partners by agreement.[69] There is also a practice among sophisticated creditors of partnerships—particularly commercial lenders and banks—of demanding personal guarantees from individual partners (despite the default rule of personal liability) to avoid procedural obstacles to a direct suit against the partner in question to recover on partnership obligations. Persons with sufficient sophistication to demand guarantees of this type obviously do not rely on default rules. And there may be many other persons of sufficient sophistication to adjust their behavior to this new default rule without difficulty.

However, the real world also contains a tremendous number of people who lack basic sophistication. There are about one and a half million partnerships in the United States; most of them are very small and deal primarily with relatively unsophisticated people. Consider, for example, a small law firm. Its principal contracts will be with its clients, including persons charged with crimes, those pursuing workers' compensation claims, injury claims, tort claims, social security eligibility claims, employment discrimination claims, and on and on. Its principal creditors will be the local bank, which is presumably a sophisticated creditor, a landlord who may or may not be, suppliers of goods, secretarial employees and paralegals, perhaps an associate or two, local firms supplying computer equipment and supplies, and so forth.

Most of the partnerships are like this; they are farm partnerships, small service businesses, small retailers, and the like. Indeed, when one thinks about the population of persons who contract with partnerships, the number of unsophisticated people far, far exceeds the number of sophisticated ones. And, it is the population of persons who contract with partnerships that are adversely affected as a group by the quiet reversal of the default rule of liability in the broad non-liability statutes.

In the real world, most individuals lack any degree of sophistication about the niceties of partnership law or what the innocuous acronym LLP may mean. Most may not even know what a default rule is, much less that it might be in their interest to seek to negotiate a special deal to change it in the unlikely event that something unexpected happens. Many may not know that partners in general partnerships are personally responsible for partnership obligations. The great bulk of society relies, without realizing it, on whatever default rule the legal system provides.

---

[69] Independently of LLPs, a practice has developed in many professional partnerships of negotiating contractual limitations on responsibility of innocent partners for the negligence or malpractice of other partners. Such language sometimes appears in engagement letters that reflect the contract between a client and a law or accounting firm. Such contractual restrictions on liability may be part of a bargain with the client in return for a price concession by the partnership.

The broad non-liability statutes change a basic default rule of personal liability for partnership law that has existed for centuries. How many people are dimly aware that when they deal with a partnership that the personal credit of each partner stands behind the firm? Probably a great many. How many will understand that the little letters LLP on the door means that the rule of personal liability has been changed for that partnership? Not very many, probably.[70]

§7.18 EFFECT ON MALPRACTICE INSURANCE

Assume that a general partnership — a law firm, say — purchases x million dollars of malpractice insurance. If the firm elects to become an LLP of either type, will that partnership then reduce the amount of malpractice insurance it will carry? One might expect that it would reduce its insurance coverage by the amount of the partners' outside wealth. While only experience can tell for sure, it is doubtful that this law firm would reduce the amount of insurance it carries. Each partner's investment in the firm is subject to reduction or elimination as a result of another partner's malpractice liabilities. Hence, liability insurance will be retained. But more basically, there is always a possibility that any partner in the partnership will commit an act of malpractice with uncertain consequences and damages. Hence, it seems likely that the amount of malpractice insurance purchased will not be affected by the decision to become an LLP.

§7.19 EFFECT ON CLAIMS SETTLEMENT

The LLP election apparently changes dramatically the willingness of partnerships to settle negligence or malpractice claims. Several law and accounting firms have settled negligence or malpractice claims arising out of the collapse of banks or thrifts by negotiating a global settlement, payable in part immediately from malpractice insurance and the balance payable by the partnership over a period of several years, presumably to permit the

[70]One argument that has been made is that a limited liability default rule for partnerships is desirable because it is "consistent with the concern for the generally weaker and less aware party." Kindness suggests that the source of this comment be left anonymous. It is of course true that there are cases in which persons inadvertently create a general partnership without appreciating the liability implications of this action. There are also doubtless some unsophisticated persons who knowingly become partners in a partnership without appreciating the implications. However, if one considers the population of unsophisticated persons who deal with partnerships and the population of unsophisticated persons who become partners, it is clear that protection of the "weaker and less aware party" is served by retaining the current default rule, not by reversing it.

payments to be made from future cash flow.[71] These settlements have been negotiated by both kinds of professional firms with FDIC and RTC.

It is unlikely that either type of LLP would ever agree to such a proposal, at least in the form such proposals have taken in the past. In the narrow non-liability LLP, the innocent partners are not liable for the malpractice claim; why should they ever accept a settlement that in effect directs a portion of future earnings to satisfy that claim? Presumably, the subsequent payments with respect to the malpractice liability will be charged directly against the capital accounts of the guilty partners in their entirety. However, that does not provide complete protection either, since, for the reasons described earlier, LLP funds used to pay malpractice liabilities inevitably increase the future risk to innocent partners that the LLP will be unable to satisfy all of its normal business obligations in the event of liquidation. In the broad non-liability LLP, there is little incentive to settle any liability that compels payments from personal funds of partners. Even if such payments are solely the responsibility of partners who are personally liable, the interest of the innocent partners in the partnership assets remains at risk.

Rather than accept a workout type of settlement, it would be more sensible for the innocent partners to leave the firm entirely and join another, since remaining in the firm unnecessarily exposes their future earnings to direct or indirect satisfaction of the malpractice liability for which they are not directly liable. Alternatively, the innocent partners might withdraw from the firm and form a new partnership composed entirely of innocent partners. There would then be no claim against the future income of that firm, and the entire malpractice liability would rest with the old firm to be satisfied by that firm from malpractice insurance plus contributions from the guilty partners. Any innocent partners not invited to join this new firm should certainly sever their relationship with the old firm.

---

[71]Several nationally known law firms have settled malpractice or negligence claims arising out of their involvement in the collapse of the thrift industry. In several cases, settlements exceeded the available malpractice insurance and firm assets. In 1992, the New York firm of Kaye, Scholer, Fierman, Hays and Handler settled claims based on its representation of Lincoln Savings & Loan Association for a payment of $41 million dollars; available insurance covered only $21.5 million dollars. The settlement was structured so as to spread out payments over four years.

Similarly, in 1993, the Cleveland firm of Jones Day Reavis & Pogue settled claims also arising out of the collapse of Lincoln Savings for $51 million; of this amount, $19.5 million was not covered by insurance. These law firm settlements did not cause the liquidation of the firms involved, and since the shortfall was to be paid in installments, presumably the personal liabilities so created were covered by a reduction in future "draws" of all partners.

§7.20 EFFECT ON PARTNERSHIP ALLOCATIONS

As one reflects on the peculiar consequences of creating two classes of partners for liability purposes depending on the nature of the claim asserted, it seems possible that the LLP may affect allocations of partnership interests and partnership decisions in unpredictable ways.

For simplicity, consider a two-person firm with each partner having quite different practices with different risks. Partner A works in corporate mergers and acquisitions, a highly remunerative practice that is both cyclical and carries a high risk of liability. Partner B has a trusts and estates practice that is considerably less risky and more stable, but also less remunerative. In a traditional partnership, there is a kind of synergy, with partner B's stable practice compensating for A's cyclical one in bad years, and with B assuming part of the risk of liability arising out of A's practice. B should obviously expect to be compensated for these contributions to the partnership by receiving a portion of the excess income generated by A. The allocation of partnership interests is, of course, a matter of negotiation. Let us assume that a 50/50 division of profit and loss is negotiated, even though A's practice produces 70 percent of the revenues on the average. Once the AB firm becomes an LLP of either type, however, the allocation should shift. B is no longer assuming the risk of liability for A's practice; A has 100 percent of that risk. Instead of a 50/50 sharing of profits and losses, there is now a 50/50 sharing of profits and a 0/100 percent sharing of the principal malpractice risks in the firm. A should insist that his percentage interest in the firm be increased. And, it is quite possible that A might conclude that if he must bear all the risk of his practice, there is little reason to share a portion of his income from that practice with B, and that he should "go it alone."[72]

§7.21 LIMITED LIABILITY LIMITED PARTNERSHIPS (LLLPs)

Several states authorize a combination of limited partnerships (discussed in chapter 5) and the registered limited liability partnership discussed in this chapter.

A *limited liability limited partnership* (LLLP) is a limited partnership in which the general partners have elected to become an LLP. In such an organization, the limited partners have no liability for the firm's obligations

---

[72]A partnership may continue to be attractive, in A's eyes, because B's more stable practice may provide income in years in which A's practice is at the bottom of its cycle.

under the limited partnership statute, and the general partners have personal liability only to the extent provided by the applicable LLP statute.

While the LLLP is a logical extension of the limited partnership and LLP statutes, it seems unlikely that many entities will avail themselves of this option. It is a complex arrangement when more simple arrangements will work as well. In addition, there is no reason to adopt this more complex form when a corporation is the sole general partner of a limited partnership, a very common arrangement.

§7.22 ONE-PERSON LLPs?

The broad non-liability LLP statutes raise an interesting problem. In a sense, they discriminate against sole proprietors because the shield of limited liability is available only to businesses having two or more owners. The usual view is that there is no legal separation between a proprietor and the business she owns, with the result that the proprietor is personally liable for all obligations of the business. However, presumably a proprietor may obtain the broad non-liability protection of an LLP by entering into a partnership with a straw party and then registering as an LLP. For example, a proprietor may elect to become an LLP with a nominal partner controlled by the proprietor, e.g., a trust for one's children. Why not?

This is not likely to be a problem under the narrow non-liability statutes because the shield of limited liability only protects innocent partners from malpractice or negligence liabilities, and it is difficult to see how a sole proprietorship could commit malpractice or negligence and yet the proprietor be entirely innocent of that malpractice or negligence either as a direct participant or under the control provisions of those statutes. However, the broad non-liability statutes cover contract claims as well as tort claims, and there may be a strong incentive on the part of an individual proprietor to seek the benefits of LLP status so as to avoid personal responsibility for contractual obligations she enters into as agent for her nominal LLP. Such a proprietor might also consider forming a limited liability company, but as described in Chapter 6, a similar problem arises under that business form for a business with only a single owner. A proprietor, of course, may form a one-person corporation and obtain at least some of the benefits of limited liability.

§7.23 WHAT LIES AHEAD?

The limited liability partnership concept was developed less than a decade ago, yet already there have been two competing types of LLP statutes created. Which one will ultimately become the dominant form? While it is too early to tell for sure, all indications are that the broad non-liability type will ultimately become the more popular. The prototype LLP statute developed by the ABA and the optional amendments to RUPA approved by NCCUSL are broad non-liability statutes; a majority of the recent states to have enacted LLP statutes also follow this approach. The attactiveness of the broad non-liability statute is not a result of the fact that it is preferable as an abstract or policy matter. Rather, it appears to be more popular because lawyers are the major participants in the ABA and NCCUSL and they are the principal developers of partnership legislation in the states. Lawyers influential in the development process believe, perhaps with some justification, that increased limitation of liability may at some time be of direct personal benefit both to them and to members of the legal profession generally. Regrettably, self-interest appears to be an important factor in the development of this business form.

PART II

THE CORPORATION

8

Organization and Management of Close Corporations

§8.1 INTRODUCTION

A corporation is a complex form of business that plays a vital role in modern American society. Virtually all large firms are conducted in corporate form, as are millions of closely held businesses. Chapter 1 points out that the 500 largest American firms alone — all corporations — control about 75 percent of the nation's business receipts, while corporations as a group account for about 93 percent of business receipts. Numerically, the number of corporations are far fewer than proprietorships and partnerships. However, in terms of business receipts, corporations dominate. In terms of economic impact, the role of corporations in the American economy dwarfs the cumulative roles of all other types of business forms discussed in earlier chapters.

It is unlikely that the development of new business forms in the 1980s and 1990s described in Part I of this book have affected significantly the gross data described above. For one thing, the economic importance of the corporation is based primarily on the very large corporations for which the limited liability company simply does not appear to be a substitute.[1] For another, data collected by state filing authorities indicate that the number of new incorporations has not been significantly affected by the development of new unincorporated business forms. Most of these new incorporations involve closely held businesses, and the number of new incorporations each year greatly exceeds the total number of unincorporated business forms providing limited liability.

This and the following two chapters consider the corporation as a form for closely held businesses. In these chapters, emphasis is placed on the use of corporations in small and medium-sized businesses. A discussion of the corporation as a business form for the very large business such as Exxon,

[1]The tax laws provide that any business which has a public market for its ownership interests must be taxed as a corporation. See §5.20. The corporate form of business is familiar to investors generally. The more flexible LLC form is not.

General Motors and the like, would take a volume at least the size of the present one.

The present chapter deals with history, formation, and management issues that arise in closely held corporations. Chapter 9 deals with financial issues relating to such corporations. Chapter 10 deals with the extent to which the fiction that a corporation is a separate legal person is recognized in real life.

These chapters describe the use of the corporate form for businesses of roughly the size and complexity of those discussed in the previous chapters relating to proprietorships, partnerships, limited partnerships, limited liability companies, and limited liability partnerships.

A. CORPORATIONS IN GENERAL

§8.2 THE DEFAULT RULES FOR CORPORATIONS

A corporation is formed by filing a document, usually called *articles of incorporation,* with the state filing authority — usually the secretary of state — which must contain specific information about the corporation, its name, its purpose, its duration, the number of shares it may issue, and so forth. The articles of incorporation may also provide rules of governance for the corporation. Following this filing, a corporation usually adopts *bylaws* that provide detailed rules governing its internal operations. This section discusses the principal economic consequences of forming a corporation that meets the various rules and requirements for incorporation but the articles of incorporation and bylaws set forth no special terms or contracts designed to govern the relationships among the shareholders — the owners of the business.

Many of the characteristics described below may be modified by special terms or contracts, and it is usually desirable that modifications be made whenever a new corporation is formed. If no planning occurs, and a "plain vanilla" corporation is formed with average or normal provisions, its essential characteristics are as follows:

1. By definition, there is no external market for the corporation's shares.
2. There is centralization of management in the board of directors, and the majority shareholders may name all or a majority of the board.
3. The duration of the corporation is perpetual, which in fact means that it exists so long as the holders of the majority of the shares

     desire that it continue. Dissolution requires the approval of the holders of at least a majority of the outstanding shares.

4.   Voting for election of directors is by share ownership and is not per capita.

5.   A shareholder who is dissatisfied or who otherwise wishes to dispose of his interest in the corporation does not have the power to compel the corporation or any shareholder to purchase his shares. There is no right of "exit" in the plain vanilla corporation as there is in the general partnership.

6.   Officers and directors of the corporation owe fiduciary and other duties to the corporation, but only limited fiduciary duties to shareholders.

It should be apparent that these rules ought to be softened by special terms or contracts in most situations. Persons who plan to make investments in a corporation but who are not majority shareholders should negotiate more favorable terms than provided by this standard form before they make the investment. The fact that litigation continues to arise in close corporations in which no such provisions were made probably indicates that not all corporations were formed on a completely rational basis.

In addition to these characteristics, there is a standard form of governance for corporations. For many years, this form was viewed as absolutely mandated by the corporation statutes and therefore not subject to significant variation by agreement. In recent years, however, many states have enacted statutes that permit shareholders by contract to modify drastically this standard form of governance.[2]

The standard form of governance assumes that shareholders are the ultimate owners of the enterprise but have limited powers of management. They elect the board of directors and may vote on certain fundamental changes, but basically they have no right to manage the business and affairs of the corporation.

The board of directors elected by the shareholders has general power to manage the business and affairs of the corporation. This power is almost plenary, extending to all facets of the business of the corporation, including decisions as to the payment of dividends to the shareholders, the election of officers to manage the day-to-day business of the corporation, and so forth. The board of directors is where the decision-making power within a corporation lies.

The officers of the corporation[3] have duties that are in part inherent

---

[2] These statutes are discussed in §8.37 and §8.38.

[3] Traditional corporation statutes require that every corporation have a president, a secretary, a treasurer, and possibly other officers as well. More modern statutes leave the question of titles of officers to the discretion of the board of directors.

in the nature of the offices they hold, but their principal function is to implement the decisions of the board of directors. The president may have power to manage the day-to-day affairs of the corporation, but he is subordinate and responsible to the board of directors.

This general description of the roles of shareholders, directors, and officers is applicable specifically to closely held corporations. The relationships are quite different in most publicly held corporations, in which management is entrusted to professional managers and the board of directors oversees the management of the corporation, but does not itself manage.

Closely held corporations are polar opposites to publicly held corporations in several ways. The use of professional managers, common in publicly held corporations, rarely appears in closely held corporations. Typically, in a closely held corporation one majority shareholder (or a group of shareholders who cooperatively form the majority) is actively involved in the management of the business. The majority shareholder dominates the board of directors — indeed, he alone may *be* the board of directors. As such, he oversees the operation of the business in much the way that a proprietor does.

Another difference is in the nature of the shareholders themselves. Shareholders in publicly held corporations view their investments primarily in financial terms; they may purchase or sell shares based on their financial performance without ever knowing what businesses the corporation is in. They usually seek to maintain diversified portfolios so that the collapse of one investment does not significantly affect their wealth. Further, since their investments are publicly traded, there are current market quotations for the value of their portfolio; they may determine the net value of their investments on a daily or weekly basis if they wish.

In contrast, the shareholders of a closely held corporation rarely own diversified portfolios of securities; most of their eggs are usually in the one basket that is the shares of the closely held corporation. Because there is by definition no public market for closely held shares, there is no extrinsic market to determine how much such shares are worth and no immediate way to dispose of such shares if a shareholder wishes to "cash out" her holding.

Finally, in a publicly held corporation, participants typically act as "economically rational" individuals, trying to maximize their personal wealth and usually not concerned with the individual identity of the persons with whom they are dealing. The same is true to some extent in close corporations as well, but often highly personal and family relationships have an influence upon corporate decisions. The shareholders and the managers of a closely held corporation usually deal with each other outside the business and these external dealings may influence how they handle business transactions. The economist would describe decisions made on these bases as "non-economic," or "irrational," since they may not be in the direction of maximizing wealth. These generalizations, of course, are not universally true in every instance.

The great genius of the corporation as a business form is that it is able to provide a single framework for businesses that can range from a one-person candlestick maker to General Motors Corporation.

§8.3 A BRIEF HISTORY OF CORPORATIONS AND CORPORATION LAW

The history of corporations can be traced back to Roman law and early canon law. In England, the monarch was viewed as a "corporation sole" from the earliest period as were bishops and other ecclesiastical leaders. At a very early period, England recognized the creation of corporations for eleemosynary and charitable purposes, as well as for the great universities of Oxford and Cambridge, and the City of London. Some corporations were chartered for business purposes, usually to develop newly discovered or newly conquered lands. By the Sixteenth and Seventeenth Centuries, numerous overseas trading companies and joint stock companies had been chartered, and these became the prototype of the modern business corporation.

In early England, the business corporation was closely associated with monopoly grants. At the earliest stage, the Crown, acting alone, had power to issue corporate charters and grant the entities so created monopoly powers in specific areas. In later years, Parliament assumed this function.

The corporation was well known and established by 1765, the time that Sir William Blackstone published his famous *Commentaries on the Law of England*. His discussion of corporations is interesting because it addresses directly the question of what a corporation is. This discussion appears as part of a broader discussion of "persons." A corporation, according to Blackstone, "must always appear by attorney, for it cannot appear in person, being, as Sir Edward Coke says, invisible and existing only in intendment and consideration of law." While a corporation was a "person," it was not a natural person. A corporation has power to "sue or be sued, implead or be impleaded, grant or receive, by its corporate name, and do all other acts as natural persons may." However, it cannot be excommunicated, "for it has no soul." Nor does it have a body. "It can neither maintain, or be made defendant to, an action of battery or such like personal injuries; for a corporation can neither beat, nor be beaten, in its body politic." Nor did it have the capacity to think or commit crimes of intent. "A corporation cannot commit treason, or felony, or other crime, in its corporate capacity; though

186

its members may, in their distinct individual capacities." Nor could it be subject to punishment in a personal sense. "Neither is it capable of suffering a traitor's or felon's punishment, for it is not liable to corporal penalties, or to attainder, forfeiture, or corruption of blood."

Chief Justice Marshall, paraphrased Blackstone in a famous comment in *Dartmouth College v. Woodward*,[4] when he defined a corporation as an "artificial being, invisible, intangible, and existing only in contemplation of law." This comment itself was quoted by a Justice of the United States Supreme Court as late as 1989.[5]

In this discussion by Blackstone, perhaps the most visible aspect of the modern corporation — the limited liability of shareholders — was not mentioned, though it would seem to follow naturally from Blackstone's conceptualism of the corporation as a "person." The reason for this was that apparently corporations had power to make calls upon shareholders when they were unable to meet their obligations. This power existed until the middle of the Nineteenth Century. Thus, there was in fact no limited liability for shareholders in England until the Industrial Revolution was well underway. Limited liability was specifically recognized in England only by a statute enacted in the 1850s.

In the United States, the power to grant corporate charters is lodged in the state legislatures. Originally, they were granted sparingly and only by special legislative act. Corporations were viewed with suspicion and mistrust because of their close association with monopoly powers granted to English companies during the colonial era — for example, the Hudson Bay Company, The Virginia Company, and the Massachusetts Bay Company.

With the gradual growth of commercial and industrial activity in the early Nineteenth Century, the number of corporations formed by state legislative action slowly increased. However, incorporation by special legislative enactment invited lobbying, bribery, and outright corruption. Over time, both the process of incorporation by legislative grant and the provisions included in legislation creating corporations became increasingly standardized, though problems of corruption and bribery still made the incorporation process haphazard.

The first statutes substituting an administrative process for legislative grants of corporate charters were enacted in about 1800. The beginning of the modern era in corporation law, however, can probably be most accurately traced back to a Connecticut statute enacted in 1837 that not only provided for an administrative process for obtaining corporate charters, but also made that process available for corporations planning to engage in any

---

[4] 4 Wheat. 518, 636, 4 L. Ed. 629 (1819).

[5] Browning Ferris Industries v. Kelco Disposal, Inc., 492 U.S. 257, 284, 109 S. Ct. 2909, 2925, 106 L. Ed. 2d 219, 244 (1989) (O'Connor, J.).

lawful activity.[6] Massachusetts followed in 1851 and New York in 1866. The advantages of the administrative process of incorporation became clear and accepted in all states, though legislative approval of corporate charters continued in some states well into the second half of the Nineteenth Century.

Throughout the Nineteenth and early Twentieth Centuries, suspicion and fear of the corporation continued to exist in some degree in many states, particularly in the primarily agricultural states of the Midwest. This fear was fueled by abuses in the capitalization of railroads and by the Panic of 1871. During this period, many states enacted statutory and constitutional provisions circumscribing the privilege of incorporation, and limiting the powers of corporations. Limitations and restrictions were enacted relating to such matters as permissible purposes, maximum permitted capital, maximum permitted indebtedness, maximum permitted duration of the corporation, restrictions on powers, and residential requirements for directors and officers. Most restrictions imposed during this period proved to be basically ineffectual and have largely disappeared. Today, the statutes of all states are modern enabling statutes that impose relatively few restrictions on what a corporation may do and how it must be governed.

The major factor that caused corporation statutes to take their present form has been the competition that rapidly grew up among states to attract the increasingly lucrative incorporation business. Corporations with their principal business activities in New York, for example, reincorporated first in New Jersey in the Nineteenth Century and then in Delaware in the Twentieth[7] in order to take advantage of liberal incorporation rules, freedom from arbitrary restrictions on corporate activities, and savings in fees and taxes. In order to preserve whatever incorporation business they had, states such as New York with restrictions on corporate activities found it necessary to amend their corporation statutes to remove restrictions and to add provisions that were in the New Jersey or Delaware statutes. Many restrictions, however, were not fully eliminated until after World War II. Texas, for example, did not provide for perpetual existence of corporations until it enacted its first modern corporation statute in 1955.[8] This competition for state incorporation business has been felt to a greater or lesser degree in every state.

___

[6] The first statutes providing for an administrative incorporation process were enacted in North Carolina (1795), Massachusetts (1799), and New York (1811). However, these statutes permitted incorporation only for corporations with narrowly defined purposes.

[7] The migration from New Jersey to Delaware occurred beginning in the early Twentieth Century when New Jersey adopted a more aggressive regulatory posture under the governorship of Woodrow Wilson.

[8] Prior to that time, Texas corporations had a maximum duration of 50 years, a provision that created no end of problems since many corporations forgot to renew their existence shortly before the 50-year period expired.

In the case of partnerships and limited partnerships, there have long existed uniform statutes that were enacted in practically every state.[9] The same pattern of uniform legislation never developed in the corporate area.[10] Each state today has a general corporation statute with at least some unique provisions. Nevertheless, there is today a considerable degree of conformity in important respects in the corporation statutes of all states. The variations that do exist by and large are relatively minor and do not go to the basic nature of corporateness. One predominant force and factor in this area has been the leadership of the small state of Delaware; most publicly held corporations are incorporated in Delaware,[11] and the Delaware General Corporation Law is unquestionably a very influential state statute. Many innovations first adopted in Delaware have found their way into statutes of other states which have adopted the substance, if not the precise language, of the Delaware statute. A second important factor is the Model Business Corporation Act, a product of the Committee on Corporate Laws of the American Bar Association. The Model Act was first published in 1950, important amendments were made in 1969, and a major revision and recodification was completed in 1984.[12] (All references to the "Model Act" or the "MBCA" in this book are references to the 1984 version.) The Model Act has been substantially adopted in about 20 states, and has had influence in the revision of corporation statutes in several other states.

While the Model Act itself reflects the influence of Delaware law in many areas, it contains many unique provisions which have been adopted by states. Together, these two statutes are the predominant sources of corporation statutory law in the United States today.

The process by which the small state of Delaware became the winner of the competition for the nation's incorporation business and the preferred state of incorporation for America's largest businesses has been said by some to reflect the "liberalization" and "modernization" of corporation statutes; by others it has been called "a race . . . not of diligence but of laxity"[13] and a "race for the bottom." However one views these developments, it is clear that the competition among states has affected the statutes of all

---

[9]See §4.3 and §5.4.

[10]The National Conference of Commissioners on Uniform State Laws did promulgate a Uniform Corporation Act in 1929, presumably because of its success with uniform statutes for partnerships and limited partnerships. However, this statute was adopted only by a few states and never came close to having the same impact on corporation law that, for example, the Uniform Partnership Act had on partnership law. This statute was formally withdrawn in 1957.

[11]Even though most publicly held corporations are incorporated in Delaware, very few have their home offices or significant manufacturing facilities located in that state.

[12]The author was the Reporter for the 1984 revision of the Model Act.

[13]Mr. Justice Brandeis, dissenting in Louis K. Ligget Co. v. Lee, 288 U.S. 517, 53 S. Ct. 481 (1933).

states, and has been healthy in the sense that onerous and restrictive provisions that serve no significant public purpose have largely been eliminated in all states. Corporations in the United States may structure their business and affairs with a freedom that does not exist in many other countries.

§8.4 WHAT IS A CORPORATION: THE TRADITIONAL ENTITY VIEW

Following roughly the analysis of Blackstone, a corporation is traditionally viewed as a fictitious legal entity separate from its owners, the shareholders. This fictitious entity is created by a grant of a *charter* or a *franchise* by the state of incorporation. However, as a practical matter, today the role of the state is largely a formality. The secretary of state receives a document called articles of incorporation or a certificate of incorporation, along with a filing fee from a person who desires to form a corporation. The document is filed in the public records of the filing office after a more-or-less cursory review by a state employee. Statutes in every state provide that the separate existence of a corporation begins when the state official accepts the document for filing.[14] Even though the corporate existence begins with the filing of this document, a number of steps remain to be undertaken before the corporation can actually commence business.[15]

A corporation so formed has basic characteristics that are clearly distinguishable from the business forms discussed in earlier chapters:

First and foremost, a corporation is clearly a legal entity in its own right separate from its owners. It has essentially the same power as an individual to conduct business in its own name; it is entitled to many of the federal and state constitutional protections that are available to individuals, and, unlike the conceptual view of Blackstone, is responsible for its actions, both in civil and criminal proceedings.

Second, a corporation provides limited liability to its shareholders. In a sense, this conclusion flows naturally from the notion that a corporation is a separate entity able to enter into obligations in its own name. However, partnerships also are treated as entities for most purposes, and yet there is a residuum of personal liability of partners for partnership obligations. Chapter 10 describes in greater detail the legal and practical limitations of the concept of limited liability in the corporation.

Third, the shares of a corporation are transferable without affecting

---

[14]Some states permit a corporation to use a deferred formation date later than the date of filing. The predominant practice is to treat the date the office in question receives the document as the filing date and the date of incorporation will be shown as that date. In other words, in most filing offices, the processing time is ignored.

[15]See §8.14.

the existence of the organization. While they are freely transferable in theory, there is no guarantee that there will be persons willing to buy shares that a shareholder wishes to sell. The existence of a market for shares depends on economic and legal factors that are not really related to the corporate business form. Section 8.24 discusses the practical effect of limited markets for shares of closely held corporations. Furthermore, corporations may limit the free transferability of shares, and many do so for a variety of valid reasons.[16]

Fourth, the corporation has centralized management. A corporation in theory is managed by a board of directors elected by the shareholders but independent of them. Directors need not be shareholders and most business decisions by directors are not subject to review and approval by the shareholders.

Fifth, the corporation has perpetual existence, which means that the corporation is not affected by the death or withdrawal of shareholders. A corporation is "forever"; its duration is perpetual as a matter of legal theory, though typically finite as a practical matter. "Perpetual existence" really means indefinite existence so long as a majority of the shareholders wish it to continue.

While it is easy to describe in outline form the essential characteristics of a corporation and the advantages of conducting business in corporate form, the nature of the fictitious entity that is a corporation is itself never precisely defined. Is it a person, a process, a thing, a conception, or what?

While a corporation can be envisioned, as Blackstone did, as an artificial person having most of the same powers, rights, and duties of an individual, it is manifestly not a person in the ordinary sense of you or I. It is a reification of something that is not a person. This artificial person is an imaginary person, or a figment of the genius of the legal mind; it has no flesh, no blood, no eyes, or mouth but it may nevertheless do many things that real people do: it may sue and be sued, enter into contracts, purchase property, run a business, commit crimes, libel a person or another corporation, make gifts to charities, and so forth.

A corporation may also be readily envisioned as a process rather than a person. A corporation acts through agents, and works to benefit shareholders who may or may not be involved in the management of the corporation, and who may or may not be agents of the corporation. Real people must always act on behalf of the corporation, real people must make decisions for the corporation, and at the other end, real people profit or lose from the corporate activities. The corporation may be viewed as a sort of meat grinder into which the input from real people is placed in the form of raw materials, efforts, and skills, and out of which at the other end other people obtain profits or incur losses. This analogy views the corporation as

---

[16]See §8.27.

a process, not a person. By a somewhat similar process of analysis, a corporation may also be viewed as a fund of property, a band of investors, a crew of workers, or merely as an entry in official records.[17]

§8.5 WHAT IS A CORPORATION: CONTRACT THEORIES

Modern corporate theorists tend to view the corporation as a contract, or rather a combination of several or many contracts. In one sense, the idea of viewing a corporation as a contract is not new. Indeed, that approach goes back at least as far as the famous case of *Dartmouth College v. Woodward*[18] in 1819. The English Crown had granted a charter to Dartmouth College in 1769; in 1816, the New Hampshire legislature passed a statute amending that charter in certain respects in order to reduce the independence of the College trustees. The Supreme Court first held that the Dartmouth College charter was itself a contract:

> An application is made to the crown for a charter to incorporate a religious and literary institution. In the application, it is stated that large contributions have been made for the object, which will be conferred on the corporation, as soon as it shall be created. The charter is granted, and on its faith the property is conveyed. Surely in this transaction every ingredient of a complete and legitimate contract is to be found.

The court then concluded that the 1816 amendments violated the Contract Clause of article I, section 10 of the United States Constitution prohibiting states from enacting legislation that impairs the obligation of contracts.

The contract envisioned by the Supreme Court was between the English Crown — the Government, since assumed by the state of New Hampshire — and the College. The charter embodied the contract, a grant of authority on the basis of which contributions were made by many persons to the College. The closest analogy is to the grant of land or property by the Crown; once granted it was gone and no longer the property of the Government, and thus no longer subject to the control of the Government. Mr. Justice Story suggested, however, that a contract consisting of the grant of a corporate franchise might itself be subject to subsequent legislative control if a reservation of such a power was included in the grant; based on this early Nineteenth Century case, every state incorporation statute now includes such a reservation in its corporation statute.[19]

---

[17]See A. Conard, Corporations In Perspective 416 (1976).

[18]17 U.S. (4 Wheat.) 518, 624 (1819).

[19]The Delaware "reservation of power" statute (Del. GCL §394) states "This chapter may be amended or repealed, at the pleasure of the General Assembly. . . . This chapter

A different kind of contract analysis appears in a smattering of cases that argue that the corporation's articles of incorporation are essentially a contract between the corporation and its shareholders, or among the shareholders themselves. These statements usually arise in cases involving the relative rights of different classes of shareholders. It is accepted today that the defining provisions of rights of classes of shares in the articles of incorporation are binding upon the corporation and the holders of shares of various classes; hence the contract analogy.

§8.6 THE NEXUS OF CONTRACTS THEORY

An entirely different and quite novel contract theory of the corporation has recently been developed by law and economics theorists.[20] Usually known as the *nexus of contracts*, this theory develops a model of the corporation as a bundle of contracts entered into by the managers of the enterprise with providers of labor, services, raw materials, capital, and contractual commitments of various types.[21] In this model, the managers are viewed as the essential glue that fits together all the various contributors to the firm in the most efficient way. The shareholders are viewed as contractual suppliers of residual capital, the group whose contract entitles it to the residual profits of the business and requires it to assume the primary risk of loss since all other providers to the corporation have priority in payment over them. Shareholders are not viewed as "owners" of the corporation. Rather, common shareholders who are passive investors are only one of several contractual suppliers of debt capital, labor, and services to the corporation.

A corporation is viewed entirely as a set of consensual relationships established by the managers of that corporation to best fit (i.e., to make

---

and all amendments thereof shall be a part of the charter or certificate of incorporation of every corporation except so far as the same is inapplicable and inappropriate to the objects of the corporation."

There may continue to exist in a few states corporations formed a century or more ago under statutes that did not contain this reservation of power. The contract analogy presumably continues to apply to these corporations and the state of incorporation lacks power to amend the rules under which these corporations operate.

[20]This theory is expressly addressed to publicly held corporations. The contractual aspects of closely held corporations are even clearer and are generally viewed as involving an a fortiori application of this novel contracts approach. See §8.27, §8.37, and §8.38.

[21]There is a burgeoning literature on the nexus of contracts theory. Perhaps the most interesting and useful discussion of this theory is the symposium entitled Contractual Freedom in Corporate Law, 89 Colum. L. Rev. 1395 (1989). For a supplemental debate arising from this symposium, see Eisenberg, Contractarianism Without Contracts: A Response to Professor McChesney, 90 Colum. L. Rev. 1321 (1990); McChesney, Contractarianism without Contracts? Yet Another Critique of Eisenberg, 90 Colum. L. Rev. 1332 (1990).

most profitable and efficient) that particular business. In this model, there is no room for mandatory rules defining intracorporate relationships; all such relationships are created by contract, either express or implicit. The role of corporation statutes therefore becomes very limited; they provide an "off the rack" standard set of intracorporate relationships that many individual corporations might find to be suitable, but every corporation should be free to accept or to modify this set of intracorporate relationships as they think appropriate. Since many corporations will find that their nexus of contracts are quite consistent with this off the rack standard form, the corporation statute avoids the costs involved were many different corporations to "reinvent the wheel" and develop similar intracorporate relationships from scratch.

What is one to make of this theory? The first point is that this is an economic model, a theoretical construct of the corporation, not necessarily a description of the reality of what a corporation is. It was, furthermore, developed with the large publicly held corporation in mind, though there is no inherent reason why it should be limited to such corporations.

Normative models do not necessarily describe what reality is but what it ought to be. Descriptive models explain what reality is: With the use of such a model, one can discover internal relationships that may not be visible in the real world. Professor McChesney has neatly encapsulated this distinction when he distinguishes *positive economics* — attempts to understand the world the way it is — from *normative economics* — a study of the way the world ought to be.[22] It is not clear in which category the nexus of contracts theory fits. There is some dispute among law and economics scholars as to whether the nexus of contracts should be viewed as essentially normative, or as descriptive, or as both.

It seems clear that the nexus of contracts is not entirely descriptive of today's real world, even though many corporate relationships are clearly based on contract concepts. For example, it is simply not true today that modern corporation statutes provide off the rack models which participants in the corporation are free to amend or modify as they wish. As described in the following sections, modern corporation statutes, while permitting corporations considerable freedom to establish internal rules as they see fit, also contain a large number of mandatory requirements that corporations have no power to waive or modify.

The most controversial aspect of the nexus of contracts theory has been its attempted application to publicly held corporations. So far as closely held corporations are concerned, it is generally agreed that many aspects of this relationship are in fact contractual, and therefore the nexus

---

[22]See McChesney, Positive Economics and All That — A Review of the Economic Structure of Corporate Law by Frank H. Easterbrook and Daniel R. Fischel, 61 Geo. Wash. L. Rev. 272 (1992).

of contracts "fits" rather neatly. However, there is at least one area of major controversy: Should courts infer fiduciary or other duties on the part of controlling shareholders when they are dealing with minority shareholders,[23] or should the courts simply enforce whatever express agreements exist, and then in the absence of agreement, the principles the statutes literally make applicable as part of the nexus of contracts?

There are, of course, dangers in the activism of courts when they infer fiduciary duties in order to protect unsophisticated or minority shareholders. It is problematic to assume that many persons are, or a specific person is, ignorant or unsophisticated. Many persons enter into transactions knowing that some risk is involved and they are being compensated for that risk. When the risk actually occurs and the person suffers a loss, it is tempting for that person to claim ignorance or lack of sophistication in order to avoid precisely the risk knowingly undertaken. Courts, when they establish implied rights, may do more harm and cause more injustice than they prevent.

Also, concern about unsophisticated persons has social consequences. It tends to reward naiveté and penalize diligence in protecting one's own rights. These arguments tend in the direction of enforcing whatever "contract" is involved without regard to how one-sided the transaction appears *ex post*. On the other hand, it should not be surprising that many courts have intervened to protect minority shareholders from oppressive conduct that is literally not prohibited by agreement or by statute.

Evaluation of these arguments is inevitably going to be inconclusive because there is no data on relative frequency of events. Theorists tend to support the nexus of contracts rule, while judges who sit on real life cases are often more willing to imply duties to achieve basic justice in the case before them. And, as a result, the normative arguments about the nexus of contracts theory also are inconclusive.

This is not to suggest that the nexus of contracts model is without value or insight. Its adherents have pointed out forcefully that many aspects of corporations do closely approximate the nexus of contracts model. Certainly, this is usually true of the initial formation of a corporation if the parties are independent of each other, reasonably sophisticated, and dealing at arms' length. An investor who "cuts a deal" with a promoter or controlling shareholder of the corporation should normally expect that the deal he cuts will define his relationship with the corporation. As described in a later section, there has been a strong movement, particularly in the close corporation area, to recognize as entirely valid the agreements reached by the parties even though they may not be consistent with the default provisions of the state's corporation statute.[24] However, many transactions involv-

---

[23]See §8.25, §8.26, and §8.35.
[24]See, e.g., §8.26, §8.37 and §8.38.

ing new corporations may occur between family members or may involve unsophisticated persons. While courts have increasingly been willing to accept the contract model for closely held corporations, at the same time they have retained principles of fiduciary duty and contractual obligations of good faith and fair dealing in order to prevent fraud or injustice in appropriate cases.

§8.7 SOURCES OF CORPORATION LAW

In the United States there is no general federal or national corporation statute.[25] Every domestic business corporation, no matter how small or large, is incorporated under the statute of some state. The major source of corporation law is therefore the state corporation statutes, the provisions of which vary to some extent from state to state. These statutes largely deal with the internal relationships within a corporation, but they also may affect important external aspects of corporation behavior. As indicated earlier, while there are numerous variations in these statutes, there is also a very large core of uniformity in them. There is virtually unanimous agreement on the basic structure of the corporation, the roles of shareholders and directors, the nature of shares, the duties directors owe to the corporation, the power of corporations to amend their articles of incorporation, the procedures that must be followed to merge with other corporations or to dissolve, the terms on which foreign corporations may qualify to transact business in various states, and so forth.

Furthermore, there is a common core of uniformity on many mundane matters that may be important in a particular case but can hardly be described as fundamental: voting procedures for shareholders, shareholder inspection rights, the power of the board of directors to delegate functions to committees of the board, restrictions on dividends and distributions, the right of different classes of shareholders to vote separately on certain proposals without regard to their voting rights generally, and so forth. Doubtless, much of this uniformity may be traced to the influence of the 1984 Model Business Corporation Act and the Delaware General Corporation Law. However, it may also be traced to natural selection and the advantage of having 50 different states experimenting with various provisions and arrangements. If one state comes up with an improvement — a better mouse trap, so to speak — the natural tendency of other states is to adopt the innovation in their own statutes.

---

[25] Federal incorporation is available for banks and a few other types of commercial and financial institutions. Most federally chartered corporations, however, have been created to administer specific governmental programs and the process of federal incorporation is not generally available to businesses.

One should not overestimate the amount of uniformity, however. There are many variations of provisions major and minor. Some thirty-odd states, for example, continue to have arcane and obsolete statutes dealing with par value of shares and eligible consideration for shares; the remaining states have followed the lead of the Model Act and swept away these provisions.[26]

Another area in which diversity continues to exist is the vote required to approve so-called *fundamental transactions*: amendments to articles of incorporation, mergers, consolidations, sale of substantially all the assets of the corporation, and so forth. Many states now require that such transactions be approved by a majority of all the outstanding voting shares. Other states require a two-thirds vote of *all* shares, voting and nonvoting alike. Still others dispense with a shareholders' vote entirely for sales of substantially all the corporate assets not in the ordinary course of business.[27] A few states require cumulative voting by shareholders in elections for directors; most states make such voting permissive.[28] About 17 states provide special statutory treatment for closely held corporations that elect to take advantage of those statutes;[29] the balance of the states may permit closely held corporations analogous freedom to a limited extent or not at all.

Numerous other examples may be cited. Thus, even though it is accurate to say that there is a great deal of uniformity in state corporation statutes, it is equally fair to state that there are many variations in individual states, and the selection of the state of incorporation often does matter.

The legislative enactment process for state corporation statutes is interesting. Such statutes are largely technical in nature and generally not the subject of extensive debate in state legislatures. Routine changes in corporation statutes are usually developed by committees of the state bar association, though these provisions of course must run the same legislative gauntlet as any other proposed legislation. Some states have legislative drafting commissions that prepare drafts of bills with the assistance of interested groups. These commissions may have skill in drafting legislation gen-

---

[26]These statutes are discussed in §9.25 and §9.38.

[27]The concern about such sales is that they enable the corporation to reduce all its assets to cash and then to redeploy that cash in entirely new and different lines of business. States disagree on whether such a major change in corporate activity requires shareholder approval or whether the decision should be left entirely up to the board of directors.

[28]*Cumulative voting* permits a minority shareholder to concentrate her voting power so as to enable her in some instances to elect one or more directors even though holding a minority interest in the corporation. In cumulative voting to elect five directors, for example, each shareholder is entitled to cast votes equal to five times the number of shares she owns, for a single candidate or to spread them over two or more candidates. In a straight election, a shareholder may cast only one vote for each share she owns for a single candidate. The cumulative voting concept is relatively easy to state, though the problems created in specific situations may be complex.

[29]These statutes are discussed briefly in §8.37 and §8.38.

erally, but usually have limited experience with corporations and business law. In a few instances, individual legislators may have practiced corporation law before being elected to the legislature, and may develop amendments to the corporation statutes on their own. But that is definitely the exception, not the rule.

Much more likely is that a specific corporation with economic importance to the state may propose legislation it desires, either directly or through a lawyer involved with bar activities in the business area. Implicit or explicit may be the threat that the corporation will migrate to a more hospitable state if the statutory change is not approved. Not surprisingly, proposals from this source are usually considered carefully and with sympathy by state legislators, though opposition from other powerful groups in the state may prevent their enactment.

There are many federal and state statutes in addition to the general corporation statutes that impact corporations to a greater or lesser degree. The most important of these are the federal securities statutes and their state analogues, the *blue sky laws*. These statutes regulate, among other things,[30] the public sale of securities by closely held businesses. The federal and state securities laws are of particular importance in close corporate practice because they may apply to innocent capital-raising transactions by closely held corporations. The federal securities laws potentially apply to all businesses in the United States that raise capital from the public through the use of mail or facilities in interstate commerce, from practically everyone, in other words.

It is generally — and erroneously — believed by many that these statutes are applicable only to public offerings of securities through professional underwriters. In fact, they apply, at least potentially, to every issuance of shares that in any way uses the mails or is in interstate commerce. A "public" offering is defined broadly to include offerings to persons who are unsophisticated and need the protection of these statutes. Hence, raising of capital by even small corporations must be carefully structured to avoid the application of these statutes.[31]

Also applicable to corporations are a variety of substantive federal and state statutes, including the antitrust statutes, workers' compensation, envi-

---

[30]These statutes have their principal impact on publicly held corporations, including many aspects of the governance of large publicly held corporations, e.g., disclosure of information, the regulation of proxy solicitations, the protection of the securities markets against fraud, the regulation of securities exchanges, the regulation of securities brokers and dealers, and the protection of individual investors against financial collapse of brokers. Indeed, most very large corporations have more legal issues arising under the federal securities laws than they do under the state corporation law of the state in which they are incorporated.

[31]The Securities and Exchange Commission has mitigated the effects of these statutes by special rules and exemptions relating to offerings by small businesses.

ronmental laws, statutes regulating the terms of employment, the Uniform Commercial Code, and statutes regulating specific industries, such as insurance and banking.

§8.8 THE INTERNAL STRUCTURE OF A CORPORATION

As described in section 8.2, the internal organization of a traditional corporation consists (at least theoretically) of three levels or tiers: shareholders, directors, and officers. While these levels are often blurred in corporations with a few shareholders, it is nevertheless important to recognize that these levels are defined by the corporation statutes, and affairs of a corporation should be conducted consistently with this theoretical structure if the protection of limited liability is to be ensured.

Shareholders in the traditional structure are the residual claimants to the assets and income of the corporation but they have limited management participation rights. As a result, shareholders generally may act in their own self-interest and owe no fiduciary duties to the other shareholders or to the corporation. However, controlling shareholders have been held to owe fiduciary duties to the corporation and to other shareholders in certain limited circumstances.[32]

Historically, the board of directors was viewed as a body essentially independent of the control of the shareholders who elected them; the board was charged with the duty of acting in the best interests of the entire corporation and not solely in the best interest of specific shareholders. As a result, directors do have significant fiduciary duties with respect to the corporation and its shareholders. Shareholders of course have the power to elect different directors at the next annual meeting of shareholders if the actions of the directors dissatisfy the holders of a majority of the shares. A variety of other rules were established to ensure directoral independence: Contracts among shareholders that attempted to make business decisions falling within the discretion of the board of directors were void as against public policy; directions by a controlling shareholder to the board of directors as to specific business decisions were not binding on the board and could be ignored; directors could not be removed by the shareholders during their term except for cause; and so forth. Many of these rules have been softened,

---

[32] The duties of controlling shareholders are necessary to protect the corporation from self-dealing transactions which may injure the corporation, and to protect minority shareholders from sales of controlling shares to thieves or others that the selling shareholders have reason to believe will loot the corporation. A fiduciary duty has also been imposed when the controlling shareholder seeks to purchase the shares of minority shareholders on the basis of information not available to the minority shareholders, or when the controlling shareholder acts through intermediaries, hiding the identity of the purchaser of the shares.

or have disappeared entirely in closely held corporations. However, the basic notion is still accepted that the board of directors has the final authority to make business decisions in a corporation in light of the best interests of the corporation as a whole. This power is clearly lodged in the board of directors as a group and not in a controlling shareholder or the person who holds the position of chairman of the board of directors, or president or chief executive officer of the corporation.

Directors must be individuals. There is a limited practice in some European countries of permitting corporations or legal entities to serve as directors, but there is apparently no similar practice anywhere in the United States. Until relatively recently, most statutes also required a board of directors to consist of three or more persons; apparently the view was that three minds were better than one. Today, a board of directors may usually consist of a single director, though in some states the privilege of having a board of one or two members is limited to corporations with one or two shareholders. In the few states where three directors are still required, a sole proprietor planning to incorporate his business must find two loyal persons to serve as directors with him.[33]

Officers of the corporation are selected by the board of directors and their functions are to execute and carry out the decisions of the board as well as conducting the business on a day-to-day basis. Corporate officers, like directors, must be individuals rather than artificial entities. Traditional officers are a president, one or more vice presidents, a secretary, and a treasurer, though the 1984 Model Act and many modern statutes do not require designated offices. The popular understanding of corporate management and control is that the president of the corporation is its principal policy-maker and controlling force. That may be true in practice, but it is important to recognize that the theory is to the contrary. The president of a corporation has only limited power under corporation law with respect to corporate matters. She may have authority to bind the corporation with respect to ordinary business matters, but the locus of discretionary power in corporations is in the board of directors, not in the executive officers. The reality may be different because if there is a controlling shareholder of a corporation, she will most likely hold the position of president as well as being a director and the controlling shareholder. The power that person wields in fact flows from her position of dominance on the board of direc-

---

[33]One can envision situations in which the two "loyal" directors may turn out to be disloyal and attempt to run away with the corporation. This possibility is usually made moot by the provision in modern statutes that permits removal of directors without cause. At an earlier time, this problem was usually handled by the sole shareholder insisting that the other directors sign undated letters of resignation before they were elected directors. In the rare case today where there is no power to remove directors without cause, the sole shareholder should adopt a similar procedure.

tors, not her position as president of the corporation, though many of her actions may be taken in the name of and as president of the corporation.

Older corporation statutes prohibit a single person from holding simultaneously the offices of corporate president and secretary. The justification for this requirement was that execution of formal documents by a corporation usually required the certificate of the secretary that the action being taken by the president had been duly authorized by the board of directors, and it was inappropriate for the same individual both to execute the document and to certify its authorization. Of course, there is no inherent reason that this should be so, and modern statutes generally permit any or all offices within a corporation to be held by a single person.

It is often convenient for the board of directors to elect or appoint one or more vice presidents, assistant secretaries, and assistant treasurers to make sure that someone is always available to execute corporate documents, sign checks, and so forth. The governing corporate documents, or the board of directors, may also authorize corporate officers to appoint additional assistant officers and employees.

There is no statutory requirement that officers be directors or shareholders, though such a requirement may be imposed voluntarily by appropriate provisions in the governing documents of the corporation. Such provisions are fairly common.

Until the middle of the Twentieth Century, all corporations were expected to fit this common mold of internal governance. Beginning in about 1965, however, the rules about internal governance gradually began to be relaxed for closely held corporations. Many state statutes have been amended to permit closely held corporations to adopt nontraditional, even radical, forms of management. Judicial decisions have also become increasingly liberal in terms of recognizing and enforcing nontraditional management devices.[34]

§8.9 DUTY OF CARE

Unlike shareholders who are viewed as passive investors with minimal management functions, directors and officers owe significant legal duties to the corporation correlative with their power to participate in the management of the business and affairs of the corporation. These duties shape and describe the roles of directors, and to a lesser extent, the roles of officers as well.

Directors owe a *duty of care* to the corporation when exercising their managerial powers. In some states, the duty of care is not defined by statute.

[34]See §8.27, §8.37 and §8.38.

But many states follow the approach of the Model Business Corporation Act (1984) and define this duty in traditional due care terms: A director must perform his duties —

1. In "good faith,"
2. "With the care an ordinarily prudent person in a like position would exercise under similar circumstances," and,
3. "in a manner he reasonably believes to be in the best interest of the corporation."[35]

This articulation of the duty of care, however, is potentially quite misleading. It is an aspirational standard of conduct toward which directors should strive. It is qualified by an important, largely nonstatutory principle known as the business judgment rule, which establishes the standard for imposing liability on directors for failing to exercise due care. The articulation of this "rule" was quite controversial both during the development of the 1984 Model Act and in the floor debates on American Law Institute's Principles of Corporate Governance. The following is a reasonable approximation:

> Directors are not personally liable for the consequences of decisions they make if the following are true: (1) they have no personal interest in the transaction itself, (2) they make the decision in good faith and on the basis of an investigation or inquiry into the facts and circumstances that they deem to be appropriate under the circumstances, and (3) the decision has some rational relationship to the best interests of the corporation. In addition, in making the inquiry or investigation, they are entitled to rely on other directors, on committees of the board of directors, on officers or employees of the corporation, or on experts (such as lawyers or accountants), if they have confidence in the judgment of those people.

The business judgment rule so articulated makes clear that due care on the part of directors making business decisions is not at all the same as the "due care" involved in other conduct, such as driving an automobile. The corporate law system *expects* the directors to cause the corporation to engage in risky enterprises in an effort to develop profits for shareholders; the system does not expect that people driving cars to take risks but to drive cautiously and carefully.[36]

The business judgment rule is primarily about the process by which directors make a decision rather than about the substance of the decision

[35]Model Business Corporation Act §8.30 (1984).

[36]An additional justification for the business judgment rule is the difficulty the legal system would have in assessing fault when making business decisions. Business decisions must usually be made quickly on the basis of incomplete or fragmentary information.

itself. One looks only to the procedures followed by the directors in making the decision in determining whether due care was observed.

Even as so stated, liability has been imposed on directors for duty of care violations. In the most famous such case, *Smith v. Van Gorkom*,[37] the Delaware Supreme Court held the outside directors of a publicly held corporation personally liable for agreeing to sell the corporation to a purchaser selected by the CEO without investigation as to the market value of the corporation's business. The uproar over this decision was so great that Delaware promptly amended its General Corporation Law to permit corporations to place a provision in its certificate of incorporation "eliminating or limiting the personal liability of a director for breach of fiduciary duty as a director" so long as the action did not violate a "duty of loyalty," was not intentional misconduct "or a knowing violation of law," or involved an unlawful distribution.[38] At least 40 states have enacted similar provisions, and in many states it is now almost routine to place language in articles of incorporation specifically limiting the scope of the directors' duty of care.[39] Such provisions now appear in articles of incorporation of closely held corporations as well as publicly held corporations.

While most of the concern about the duty of care has arisen in the context of a publicly held corporation, that duty is equally applicable to closely held corporations. The duty of care is owed to the corporation and may be asserted by minority shareholders on behalf of the corporation (see section 8.12) or by a trustee or receiver appointed following the financial collapse of the corporation.

§8.10 FIDUCIARY DUTY

Directors also owe fiduciary duties to the corporation in addition to the duty of care. The principal fiduciary duty relates to self-dealing transactions with the corporation. A *self-dealing transaction* is one in which a director personally enters with the corporation into a transaction which is not shared proportionally by all other shareholders. The classic example is a director who sells a piece of land to his corporation at a price that may or not may not be fair. In the close corporation, a more common type of self-dealing transaction may be a claim that the controlling shareholder is being paid unreasonable compensation. However, self-dealing transactions come in many forms and may include, for example, transactions between two corpo-

---

[37]488 A.2d 858 (Del. 1985).

[38]Del. GCL §102(b)(7).

[39]There is a considerable amount of diversity in the language of these statutes. See Hanks, Recent State Legislation on Directors and Officer Liability Limitation and Indemnification, 43 Bus. Law. 1207 (1988).

rations with a common director, between the corporation and a family member of a director, or between the corporation and a business entity owned by such a family member.

The original common law rule was that all self-dealing transactions were voidable by the corporation without regard to the fairness of the transaction. However, many self-dealing transactions are in fact quite beneficial to the corporation, and a rule of automatic voidability undoubtedly deterred such transactions.[40] As a result, all states have adopted statutes providing for a process by which disinterested directors may validate self-dealing transactions by a decision which comports with the business judgment rule. These statutes provide that a transaction that is judicially determined to be fair to the corporation may not be avoided by the corporation whether or not it has been approved by disinterested directors.[41] The process by which disinterested directors act is usually referred to as "sanitizing" a transaction.

Directors owe other fiduciary duties to the corporation. For example, they owe a duty not to take advantage of corporate opportunities that legitimately belong to the corporation or to utilize information about corporate prospects to make a personal profit. Seizure of a corporate opportunity is a type of self-dealing transaction that may be sanitized by disinterested directors. Other transactions, such as the payment of excessive salaries to persons other than major shareholders, may be attacked as "spoilation" or "waste," or as illegal dividends.[42]

In some instances, directors and officers may owe duties directly to shareholders. For example, purchases of shares from minority shareholders may impose special duties of disclosure on the purchasers, either because of the federal securities laws or because of state judicial decisions.

§8.11 INDEMNIFICATION OF DIRECTORS

Indemnification of directors means that the corporation reimburses a defendant/director who has been sued for some action taken while a director of the corporation for her expenses of the litigation, and in some cases amounts paid in settlement of such litigation. Indemnification at first blush may appear to be unnecessary and even against public policy, but the realities in today's litigious society is that most persons would decline to serve as

---

[40]Examples of a self-dealing transaction that are beneficial to the corporation include a director who makes a personal loan to the corporation on favorable terms or a director who permits the corporation to occupy commercial space without the payment of rent.

[41]A judicial determination that a transaction is fair is apt to involve complex issues and consideration of considerable background and expert testimony. This complex litigation may be avoided if disinterested directors approve or ratify the transaction in accordance with the requirements of the business judgment rule.

[42]See §9.30 and §9.38.

directors of a corporation in which they do not have a major financial interest in the absence of some protection against the cost of litigation that they become involved in solely because they agree to be directors.

The statutes of all states authorize corporations to indemnify directors upon a finding by disinterested directors that the action of the director was in good faith and in a manner that the director believed was in or not opposed to the best interests of the corporation. Such indemnification is "permissive" in the sense that the corporation must determine whether it wishes to grant indemnification under the specific circumstances. Further, if a director is entirely successful in the litigation "on the merits or otherwise," the director is entitled to indemnification without further inquiry into the merits of the original claim. Generally, a finding that the defendant violated duties of loyalty or care precludes indemnification of expenses and amounts paid in settlement, but even a guilty director may appeal to a court for a finding that the person is equitably entitled to indemnification despite the finding of breach of duty.

Most state statutes also permit corporations to "advance expenses" to directors or officers who are defendants in corporate litigation. *Advancements of expenses* are related to but independent of the indemnification described in the previous paragraph. Advancements are made as needed to permit the defendant director to make an effective defense, to obtain skilled legal assistance, engage in pretrial discovery, and so forth. Directors with limited personal resources would find it difficult or impossible to mount an effect defense if they were limited to their own personal financial resources. Advancements are somewhat unusual since they must be made long before there is any kind of judicial determination as to the merits of the claim against the defendant director or officer, and often before the corporation itself has investigated the allegations. As a result, complex rules exist about the terms on which advancements are made and the obligation to refund them if the defendant is found to be ineligible for indemnification.

Indemnification and advancement of expenses are partially based on statutory provisions and partially on provisions in the corporation's governing documents. Many corporations undertake in their bylaws to grant a right to indemnification as broad as public policy permits. It is important to recognize that such provisions give legally enforceable rights to directors who may be entitled to indemnification or advancements of expenses even though the corporation no longer wishes to provide such benefits to the specific directors.

In addition to indemnification and advancement of expenses, many corporations provide insurance to protect directors and officers from claims brought by shareholders. This insurance, usually called *D&O insurance*, is widely used as an extra level of protection of officers and directors of both publicly held and closely held corporations. D&O insurance coverage is in many respects similar to the coverage of bylaw provisions mandating indemnification and advancements for expenses. An important aspect of D&O insurance is that it provides a fund from which the corporation may obtain reimbursement for funds paid to directors under indemnification and advancements for expenses obligations; it becomes the only source of funds to protect directors if the corporation has become insolvent. However, D&O insurance may also sometimes protect directors against claims that the corporation cannot indemnify against under the applicable statute, and in some instances indemnification may be available for risks specifically excluded from a D&O policy.

§8.12 DERIVATIVE SUITS

Where a controlling shareholder arguably has violated his duty of care or one of the duties of loyalty, he is not likely to authorize the corporation to bring suit against him for damages. One is not likely to want to authorize potentially embarrassing litigation to be brought against oneself. In this situation, the legal system permits a minority shareholder to bring a so-called *derivative suit* in the name of the corporation to enforce the corporate claims. The corporation is a nominal plaintiff, but is classed as a defendant for procedural purposes. Derivative suits are most common in publicly held corporations, but also may be effectively used in closely held corporations with minority shareholders who have complaints against the action of the majority shareholder.

Delaware courts have pioneered a new approach toward the handling of derivative suits brought against publicly held corporations. This approach involves reliance on litigation committees composed of directors who are not involved in the claims that form the basis for the suit to review and evaluate whether continuation of the suit is in the best interest of the corporation. These rules are themselves quite controversial and complex, but they permit many suits to be disposed of before a trial, though typically the final decision is delayed by one or more appeals.

Most states have statutory provisions that regulate derivative suits. Older statutes required shareholder/plaintiffs who had small financial stakes in the outcomes to file a bond as "security for expenses." More modern statutes regulate the litigation committee device pioneered in Delaware in various ways. Both the Delaware litigation committee device and these state statutes have potential application in close corporation as well as public corporation litigation.

Several states recognize that derivative claims brought in the close corporation context usually involve controlling/non-controlling shareholder disputes. Most close corporations, furthermore, do not have independent directors. Rather than applying the complex rules developed in the public corporation context to decide those controversies, these states simply permit such suits to be brought as direct claims rather than as derivative ones, thereby avoiding the complex rules that have been developed in the public corporation context.

B. FORMATION OF CORPORATIONS

§8.13 DOCUMENTS GOVERNING INTERNAL CORPORATE MATTERS

As described earlier, the two basic documents that define the corporation and set forth internal rules for corporate governance are the articles of incorporation, the document filed with the appropriate state agency to form the corporation, and an internal document, the bylaws of the corporation, adopted by the board of directors after it is formed. The state filing agency is usually the office of the secretary of state, but the name of this office varies in some states.

Terminology with respect to the basic document filed with the secretary of state is not uniform from one state to another. In the Model Act, and the statutes of most states, the basic document filed with the appropriate state agency is called the *articles of incorporation*. In many states with older statutes, the filing office issues a formal document called a *certificate of incorporation* when it accepts the document for filing. The existence of the corporation begins upon the issuance of this certificate. In some states, including Delaware, the basic document filed with the state is called the *certificate of incorporation*.[43] In still other states, it may be called the *charter* of the corporation, or possibly by other names as well. In the balance of this chapter, the phrase articles of incorporation is used to describe the basic document filed with the secretary of state.[44]

The provisions of both the articles of incorporation and the bylaws are of course equally binding on the corporation, and on its directors, officers

---

[43]In Delaware, a duplicate or conformed copy must accompany the original. The Secretary of State endorses on the original the term "Filed" and the date and hour of filing. The same information is then endorsed on the copy which is then delivered to the Recorder of the county where the corporation's registered office is located, and the Recorder is required to record and index the instrument. In practice, this delivery for recordation is handled by the attorney preparing the certificate of incorporation or by the corporation service company.

[44]The Model Act originally provided that the secretary of state or other filing agency must issue a "certificate of incorporation" after approving the articles of incorporation for filing. In 1984, however, the Model Act was amended to provide that the filing agency simply stamps "filed" on a copy of the articles of incorporation and returns it along with a fee receipt to the incorporator.

and shareholders. One difference is that amendment of the articles of incorporation is more difficult than amendment of bylaws; amendments to the articles of incorporation generally require approval by a specified vote of the shareholders following a favorable recommendation by the board of directors. The bylaws, on the other hand, may be amended either by the board of directors, acting alone, or by the shareholders.[45]

Articles of incorporation have generally become shorter and simpler over the years. They have changed from complex, multi-page documents containing a great deal of legal language to simple documents that easily fit on one average sized piece of paper. Formal requirements that the document be executed under oath or be verified by outside witnesses have disappeared in many states. Under the Model Act, the minimum document meeting the requirements of that Act looks something like this:

ARTICLES OF INCORPORATION

1. The name of the corporation is ABC Corporation.
2. The corporation is authorized to issue 1,000 shares of stock.
3. The street address of the corporation's registered office is 125 Main Street, Austin, Texas, and the name of the corporation's registered agent at that address is Robert W. Hamilton.
4. The name and address of the incorporator is Robert W. Hamilton, 125 Main Street, Austin, Texas.

/s/ *Robert W. Hamilton, Incorporator.*[46]

Under the Model Act, a corporation formed with this absolutely bare-bones articles of incorporation would (1) have perpetual existence,[47] the purpose of engaging in any lawful business,[48] and the same power as an individual to "do all things necessary or convenient to carry out its business and affairs."[49]

---

[45]See Model Business Corporation Act §10.20. This section permits amendments or repeal of bylaws either by the board of directors or by the shareholders, but the articles of incorporation may provide that this power is expressly reserved to the shareholders. The shareholders may also provide, when amending a bylaw, that its future amendment is reserved to the shareholders. Special provisions are also included for amending bylaws that increase quorum or voting requirements for meetings of the board of directors or the shareholders.

[46]The role of the *incorporator* today is largely formal. There must be a signature on the articles of incorporation and someone to whom the filing authority returns the filed document. Historically, the role of incorporators may have been more substantial; at least older statutes required three incorporators who were individuals, were residents, were above a certain age, and so forth. The incorporator in some states may complete the formation of the corporation. See §8.14.

[47]Model Business Corporation Act §3.02, introductory clause.

[48]Id. §3.01.

[49]Id. §3.02.

Furthermore, it has the power to issue up to the specified maximum number of shares of stock for whatever money or property it decides to be appropriate.[50]

Of course, many corporations may wish to include additional provisions in its articles of incorporation. For example, if it decides to have two or more classes of shares, a much fuller explication of those shares will be necessary.[51] It may also wish to put provisions relating to internal governance in the articles of incorporation on the theory that they become part of the basic constitution of the corporation, and therefore are more difficult to amend.

The bylaws of a corporation constitute an internal set of rules for the governance of the corporation. They are usually not a publicly filed document. They deal in some detail with such matters as elections, notices, size of board of directors, restrictions on the transfer of shares, and a host of similar matters. Bylaws may be as short as one or two pages, but ten or so typed pages are a more common length.

Many provisions relating to the internal affairs of the corporation may be placed either in the articles of incorporation or the bylaws, at the option of the management of the corporation. Provisions placed in the articles of incorporation become a matter of public record. Where the number of shareholders is large, articles of incorporation may be considerably more difficult to amend than the bylaws, a factor that may be either desirable or undesirable. Many lawyers prefer that important and unusual governance provisions appear in the articles of incorporation rather than in the bylaws because the provisions are then a matter of public record. On the other hand, corporate officers and directors are more likely to be familiar with the bylaws than with the articles of incorporation, and therefore lawyers also suggest that governance provisions that appear in the articles of incorporation be repeated in the bylaws.

In the present-day litigious society, most corporations include complex provisions in their articles of incorporation or bylaws relating to the indemnification of directors and officers of the corporation against the expenses of defending against claims made by shareholders against them.[52] It is customary to place indemnification provisions in the bylaws of the corporation, but they also may be placed in the articles of incorporation.

Forms for articles of incorporation and bylaws are widely available through form books, computer programs, and corporation service companies. Law firms with an active incorporation business usually have a standard set of articles of incorporation and bylaws stored on their computers, which can be called up and modified as appropriate when a new corporation is to be formed.

[50]Id. §6.21.
[51]Id. §6.01.
[52]See §8.11.

§8.14 THE FORMATION OF A TURNKEY CORPORATION

Turnkey is a slang term (originally arising in the real estate construction business) roughly meaning that something is ready to be put to use immediately without further work. In the sense used here, the term means a corporation that is fully formed and ready to commence business. A corporation is formed as a legal matter simply by filing articles of incorporation with the appropriate state filing authority. However, a number of additional steps must be taken before the corporation can actually conduct business — for example, it must have capital, officers, directors, a bank account, and all of the normal accouterments of a functioning corporation.

While the steps necessary to create a turnkey corporation vary somewhat from state to state and from corporation to corporation, the following are part of the normal checklist:

1. Make sure all **filing and notice requirements** have been met. Delaware, for example, requires a local filing as well as a filing with the state office; some states require that a notice of the formation of a corporation be published in a local newspaper, and so forth.

2. Prepare **bylaws,** making sure that all desired elections have been reviewed by the participants and are lawful under the statutes of the state of incorporation, and that all desired provisions have been included.

3. Prepare **minutes** of the necessary initial meetings, consents to action in lieu of meetings, or waivers of notice to be executed by shareholders and/or directors.

4. Assure that a number of **legal requirements** have been taken in an appropriate manner. These include assuring that sufficient legal capital has been paid in, that the issuance of shares has been properly authorized,[53] that directors and officers have been duly elected, and that necessary contracts between the corporation and various suppliers of goods and services have been entered into by officers who are duly authorized to do so.

5. Obtain necessary **recordation** materials, such as a corporate seal, minute book, and blank share certificates so that shares may be issued and capital received at the organizational meeting.

6. Open a corporate **bank account.**

7. Ensure compliance with all requirements of federal and state **securities laws** with respect to the issuance of shares and the raising of capital by the corporation.

8. Prepare employment contracts, voting trusts, shareholder

---

[53]The requirements of legal capital and the issuance of shares are discussed in §§9.23 through 9.25.

agreements, share certificates, share transfer restrictions, and other **formal documents.**

9. Review available corporate and tax **elections,** advise participants of the available choices, and make sure that desired elections are validly made.

10. Obtain **licensure and identification** like taxpayer identification numbers, certificates of occupancy, and governmental permits or consents necessary for the operation of the business.

Since requirements vary from state to state and from community to community, a more detailed and specific list is usually developed by a law firm that regularly forms corporations; this list (along with the standardized forms) is usually stored in computer memory and used (with appropriate changes) when the firm is requested to form a corporation for a client.

§8.15 CORPORATION SERVICE COMPANIES

Corporation service companies are private companies that provide incorporation services, primarily for lawyers. These companies, for a fee, will prepare and file articles of incorporation and perform most of the additional steps described above that are necessary to permit a new corporation to begin business. While a corporation formed by a corporation service company will be competently prepared, it may lack the individual tailoring that a lawyer practicing in the specific state routinely provides.

Corporation service companies provide many services besides basic incorporation. They may serve as registered agents, providing a statutory registered office for both domestic[54] and foreign corporations. They provide the necessary personnel to maintain in good standing inactive corporations formed, for example, to ensure that a name will be protected from use by other parties. They may provide a search service for UCC-1 filings, which are financing statements required by Article 9 of the Uniform Commercial Code filed publicly to perfect security interests in collateral as security for a loan. They may file limited partnership certificates, limited liability company or limited liability partnership registrations in specific states, or qualify these entities to transact business in foreign states.[55] They may provide

---

[54]Thousands of Delaware corporations with home offices outside of the state of Delaware, for example, use the services of corporation service companies in Delaware to meet the statutory requirement that each domestic corporation have a registered office and registered agent in Delaware.

[55]"Foreign states" in this context refers to American states other than the state of incorporation. Corporation service companies may also provide services in popular foreign countries, particularly the small "offshore" tax havens in the Caribbean and Central America.

meeting rooms for shareholders' meetings, and may conduct such a meeting if necessary. They provide name checks to determine the availability of a specific name in a specific state, and reserve or register that name if requested to do so. In states where local filing or public advertising is necessary for the formation of a corporation, they ensure that all requirements are met and that appropriate certificates evidencing that fact are obtained. They provide certified copies of documents filed publicly in states in which they are active.

As a special service, some corporation service companies maintain an inventory of already formed and fully qualified corporations in Delaware that may be acquired on an overnight basis anywhere in the United States. In other words, from some corporation service companies one can order a fully formed and qualified Delaware corporation for next-day delivery simply by making a telephone call and giving a credit card number, much as though one were buying clothing or electronic equipment. The "corporation package" is received the next day by overnight mail.

If a lawyer is requested to form a corporation in a state in which she does not regularly practice, the simplest (and usually the cheapest) way to do so is to engage the services of a corporation service company.

§8.16 DO IT YOURSELF CORPORATIONS

Under modern statutes, the legal requirements for forming a corporation are relatively simple and the cost involved in most states is not very high. While it is almost always desirable to have legal assistance when forming a corporation, many persons without legal training successfully form corporations on their own, either by "playing lawyer" on a "do it yourself" basis or by using kits advertised in many magazines. Corporate forms may also be available on electronic bulletin boards. Since the paperwork to form the corporation is in fact largely routine, it is not surprising that many corporations formed by a non-lawyer function satisfactorily. Many such corporations involve one-person corporations formed by a person who has read or erroneously been told that corporations are an efficient and tax-saving way to conduct business. In fact, the efficiency and tax saving in the 1995 environment is largely nonexistent for a business owned and operated by a single person. Most such businesses would probably be better off as proprietorships than as corporations.

One problem with do it yourself corporations is that there is always some risk that important or essential matters may be overlooked or unexpected problems may arise which demonstrate the inadequacy as a legal matter of what was done, perhaps to the sorrow of the persons attempting to do business in corporate form. Some important elections within the corporate form are available to newly formed corporations of which a lay person

212

may be ignorant. Examples include: (1) the close corporation election,[56] (2) the S corporation election,[57] (3) shareholders' agreements and restrictions on transfer of shares,[58] and (4) limitations on the liability of directors.[59] It is likely that adequate consideration will not be given to these various matters in a do it yourself corporation, or for that matter, in a corporation service company-created corporation.

§8.17 SELECTION OF THE STATE OF INCORPORATION FOR A CLOSELY HELD CORPORATION

If a small business located in Lincoln, Nebraska, say, is considering incorporation, there are strong justifications for incorporating in Nebraska even if that state's statute may not be viewed as an ideal corporation statute.[60] The reason for this is that the costs of forming a corporation in Delaware or another state and qualifying it to transact business in Nebraska are almost certainly going to outweigh the benefits that the Delaware General Corporation Law or another state's law provides to a small, closely held corporation. These costs include not only the double cost of incorporating and qualifying to transact business but also the possibility that the corporation may be sued in the state of incorporation, and thus be compelled to defend a suit in an unfamiliar state. There must be substantial disadvantages to incorporation in the home state to justify the decision by a closely held corporation to incorporate in Delaware or another state and qualify as a foreign corporation in the home state.

C. MANAGEMENT OF A CLOSE CORPORATION

§8.18 THE INCORPORATED PROPRIETORSHIP

In considering what it really means to conduct a closely held business in the corporate form, it is useful to begin with the one-person corporation in a state that requires compliance with the traditional corporate structure. A

[56]See §8.37.
[57]See §9.6.
[58]See §8.28.
[59]See §8.9.
[60]As of January 1995, the Nebraska Business Corporation Act was based on the 1969 version of the Model Business Corporation Act, but with a number of individualized amendments. A new statute based on the MBCA (1984) went into effect on January 1, 1996.

one-person corporation is simply a corporation in which one single individual owns all the outstanding shares. Such a business is usually called an *incorporated proprietorship*.

A proprietor conducting her own business in her own or under an assumed name, may become increasingly unhappy with the legal consequences of conducting a business as a proprietorship. She may be particularly unhappy with the potential personal liabilities inherent in that form of business, particularly if the business is successful and grows in size so that liabilities involved are large in absolute terms and most business activities are conducted by employees of the proprietor rather than by the proprietor individually. The logical solution is for the proprietor to incorporate the business, or more precisely, to form a corporation and transfer the business to that corporation. It was pointed out earlier that in an unincorporated proprietorship there was usually a fair degree of economic separation between the proprietor's personal assets and the business's assets, but there is no legal separation.[61] The incorporation of the proprietorship creates a legal separation between the proprietor and her business to correspond to the economic separation.

In every state today, a single person may form a corporation and be the sole shareholder. In virtually every state today, one person may also fill all the required roles within a corporation. It is therefore usually unnecessary for a proprietor to involve friends, relatives, nominees, or straw parties in the business or to fill mandatory statutory roles. An incorporated proprietorship today may be operated by the proprietor acting alone with virtually the same privacy and freedom of action as if the business were an unincorporated proprietorship.[62]

Let us assume that our proprietor forms a corporation, transfers the business assets to the corporation, and receives in return all the shares of stock issued by the corporation.[63] Thereafter, all business transactions and

---

[61] See §3.7.

[62] It was not always this way. Forty years ago, corporation statutes required at least three incorporators, three directors, and two different persons to occupy the positions of president and secretary. An incorporated proprietorship therefore required at least the nominal participation of two persons other than the shareholder.

A handful of states still require a board of directors consisting of two or more persons. Somewhat more require the president and secretary be different persons. No statute today requires that a director or officer must be a shareholder, so that the proprietor does not need to issue a qualifying share to these persons.

[63] In this transaction, the proprietor will normally transfer all the operating assets of her proprietorship to the corporation in exchange for the common stock of the corporation. She will also assign all outstanding business liabilities to the corporation and cause the corporation to enter into an agreement to pay them when they come due. This assignment of liabilities does not of itself release the proprietor from pre-incorporation liabilities for which she was personally responsible, but if the corporation is able to discharge them, she is of course relieved from having to do so. Immediately following the creation of the corporation,

business-related obligations are incurred in the name of the corporation, if possible. What difference does the incorporation of the business make? In practical and economic effect, the difference may not be noticeable at all. The shareholder runs the business much as she did before it was incorporated. She decides what business the corporation should be in, whether it should enter into specific contracts, what price to charge for its products, and so forth. The most visible differences are formal ones: Documents are executed in the name of the corporation rather than simply by the proprietor; banks and creditors demand "certified resolutions" of the board of directors that must be prepared in order to open a bank account, enter a lease, or obtain a loan; additional routine documents entitled "minutes of meeting," "waivers of notice," or "consent to action" should be created and the required tax returns are entirely different and more complicated.

The sole shareholder exercises theoretical control over corporate activities not primarily through direct ownership of business assets or shares but by serving the corporation basically as its agent. Manifestly every fictitious entity can only act through agents. The standard model of internal governance of corporations described earlier, is in most states, as applicable to incorporated proprietorships as it is to corporations with hundreds or thousands of shareholders. The shareholder must therefore elect a board of directors (consisting solely of herself) which in turn has theoretically a general power of management and control of the business and affairs of the corporation. The board of directors in turn theoretically elects corporate officers (again consisting solely of herself) who have limited authority to manage the ordinary operations of the business and carry out the directions of the board of directors.

This internal management structure seems unreal in the context of an incorporated proprietorship with a single shareholder, but nevertheless the form usually must be followed. The sole shareholder elects herself as the sole director constituting the board of directors; acting as the board of directors, the sole director appoints herself to various corporate officers, e.g., president, secretary, and treasurer. She then runs the business wearing the hat of "director" in some instances, "president" in others, and "treasurer" or "secretary" in still others. She may decide that the corporation should hire employees or a manager at a specified salary; she may initiate these actions as "president" and approve them as the "board of directors." She may decide for purposes of convenience to have an employee serve as secretary or treasurer. However, the reality is that the economic operation of the incorpo-

---

the proprietor may also lend money to it to improve its probable viability. From an income tax standpoint, as described in Chapter 9, this transaction does not involve the recognition of gain for federal income tax purposes under I.R.C. §351 and the tax basis of the stock in the proprietor's hands becomes the basis of the contributed assets in her hands immediately before the transfer.

rated proprietorship is the same as it would have been if the business was being conducted as an individual proprietorship.

Now assume that the sole shareholder decides she not only wants to be sole shareholder, sole director, and president of the corporation, but also she wants to be employed by the corporation and receive a salary of $10,000 per month. She may decide that she wishes to have the title of "chief executive officer," or less grandly, "general manager." She may wish to have an employment contract, though that seems to be gilding the lily. Acting as the sole director of the corporation she directs herself as president of the corporation, on behalf of the corporation, to offer herself employment in the named position with the corporation at the specified salary. She may also authorize herself to offer herself the security of an employment contract. Then acting as an individual she accepts the corporation's offer. While it may seem astonishing to an uninitiated observer, this is not a sham transaction for most purposes. The IRS, for example, unhesitatingly recognizes the validity of such a transaction if the compensation is reasonable in amount, giving the corporation a deduction for the salary paid, requiring the corporation to withhold for federal income taxes, FICA, and the like, and requiring the shareholder to include in her personal income tax return as wages the amount paid to her under this arrangement.

Even though it is not a sham, it does seem a bit incestuous. There is obviously play-acting in closely held corporations because the formalities that must be followed do not reflect the reality that the business is actually being owned and operated by an individual; the theory assumes that the same individual assumes different roles as shareholder, director, or agent, and acts according to the appropriate role. But there is a serious aspect to these formalities. For, as indicated in Chapter 10, a failure to follow them may result in the court piercing the corporate veil — and holding the shareholder personally liable on corporation obligations.

Of course, in one very basic sense all of the internal corporate formalities in an incorporated proprietorship are meaningless. If the sole shareholder decides she wishes to be an employee, it is a foregone conclusion that she will become that employee since there is no one to complain or object. Because of this, not uncommonly, non-lawyers fail to sense the risk of ignoring formalities. They may pride themselves as being "realists" and view the lawyer's insistence on preparing "meaningless" documents as an effort to run up his fee. However, every corporate lawyer recognizes that this view is mistaken, that it is important to follow corporate formalities even when the outcome of the decisional process is not in doubt.

If one is to rely on a fiction to lead to desirable economic consequences (such as limited liability for the shareholder), one should carefully follow the rules that the fiction imposes; if the shareholder ignores the fiction and simply pays herself a salary without going through the rigmarole of becoming an employee, other people may be able to ignore the fiction as well. Perhaps the "shield" of limited liability will disappear in litigation just when it is needed the most, or the Internal Revenue Service will insist on treating the payments as nondeductible distributions by the corporation rather than as deductible salary payments. While doubtless many, many corporations do not follow formalities the way they should, those corporations and their owners are taking an unnecessary risk.

Since the shareholder owns all the outstanding shares of the corporation, there is no other co-owner to complain about what is done with the business. Total ownership of shares means total control; this often leads the shareholder to believe that she still owns the corporation's business and property much as though the business were conducted in the form of an unincorporated proprietorship. "I own this business," she may proudly say. While in an economic sense this is undoubtedly true, in the legal sense it is not at all true. If a business is incorporated, the assets of the business are legally owned by the corporation, not by the person who owns the shares in the corporation. The shares have value only to the extent the corporation's business and assets have value, but the shares are not the same as the corporate assets.

In recent years, corporation statutes have been amended to simplify internal procedures in closely held corporations, and an incorporated proprietorship is perhaps the most logical candidate to take advantage of these new provisions. For example, rather than giving "notice" of a meeting followed by a "meeting" of one person, statutes permit action by shareholders and by directors by means of unanimous written consent. That is much simpler, but someone must take the time to prepare the written consent and remember to have the shareholder sign it. And, of course, one has not complied with the specific statutory requirement if there is no document labeled "Consent to Action" prepared or, if there is one, it is not signed.

About 18 states have gone much further, as described in section 8.37, and have enacted special close corporation statutes that permit corporations with a limited number of shareholders to dispense with the various levels of corporate governance, and simply permit the shareholders to conduct the business with virtually no formalities at all. These statutes, however, usually require the corporation to make an election in its basic corporate documents to become subject to these statutes. Incorporated proprietorships, of course, may take advantage of these statutes, and doubtless many of them do. It is surprising, however, that the available data indicates that relatively few corporations eligible for special treatment under these statutes actually take advantage of them.[64] In part because these statutes are not widely used in states that have them, there is little incentive for additional states to

---

[64]This phenomenon is discussed further in §8.37.

follow this approach even though the statutes cause no harm and may marginally reduce the cost of operating as a corporation.

In 1993, The Model Business Corporation Act (1984) was amended to permit virtually all kinds of internal procedural modifications within the corporate structure by simple shareholder agreements that do not need to be reflected or referred to in the articles of incorporation.[65] In a state that enacts such a statute, even the board of directors and corporate officers may be dispensed with by contractual provision and the business conducted directly by the shareholder.

§8.19 THE CORPORATION WITH SEVERAL SHAREHOLDERS: INTRODUCTION

A corporation with two or more shareholders is as different from the incorporated proprietorship as a proprietorship differs from a partnership. The presence of two or more shareholders means not only that careful consideration must be given at the outset to the amount and type of capital contribution that is to be made by each participant and the terms on which profits and management are to be shared, but also that problems arising from death, retirement, and future disagreement and discord must be addressed. These problems are more serious in a corporation than in a partnership since the "default" provisions in the corporation statutes provide for complete control over management and distributions by the controlling shareholders, and virtually no protections for minority shareholders. Furthermore, a partner always has the power to "exit" by compelling the dissolution of the partnership;[66] the same is not true in a corporation. Dissolution requires the affirmative approval of at least a majority of the outstanding voting shares.[67] In other words, the default provisions with respect to corporations give virtually no protection to minority participants in the enterprise. Participants in any close corporation should therefore be concerned that special provision be made not only with respect to the right to participate in the financial returns of the business, but also the right to participate in decision-making, and to be able to withdraw from the enterprise on acceptable terms in certain circumstances. These latter concerns are usually described as *voice* and *exit* rights.

An earlier section[68] pointed out that it was not uncommon in one-person corporations for the corporation to be formed on a do it yourself

---

[65]Model Business Corporation Act (1984) §7.32, discussed in §8.38.
[66]See §4.24.
[67]See §8.24 and §8.27.
[68]See §8.16.

basis without legal assistance, usually using a corporation formation package or a commercially available computer software program. It is much more dangerous to attempt to do this with a corporation with several different participants. Indeed, it is equally undesirable to use a corporation service company without legal assistance for this purpose, because the rights of the minority participants may not receive the protection they need.

The services of a lawyer are thus always desirable when several different persons are to be involved in the ownership and management of the corporation and its business. This is certainly true if, as will often be the case, the contributions of different participants will vary, some contributing cash and others property, services, or ideas. However, even in corporations with the simplest capital structures, careful planning is necessary to avoid inadvertent injustice. One must always take into account the possibility of future discord that may arise either from a major disagreement among the original participants or from an unexpected change in the identity of shareholders arising from assignment, gift, or the death or retirement of a participant.

From the standpoint of a lawyer consulted by promoters of a new corporation, an important question is whether the lawyer may act as "attorney for the situation" and give advice to all participants without running afoul of ethical considerations relating to conflicting interests in a multiple representation. Twenty-five years ago, lawyers were rarely concerned about such issues, but in today's litigious society it is a problem that should be addressed. Today, it is recognized that the interests of participants in a closely held corporation may well conflict with each other on a number of important issues. A lawyer who represents all interests in a corporation must view her position as involving potential conflicts of interest. Rule 1.7 of the Model Rules of Professional Conduct permits multiple representation if the lawyer "reasonably believes the representation will not adversely affect the relationship with the other client" and "each client consents after consultation."[69] If multiple representation by a single lawyer is viewed as undesirable, each participant should be urged to get his or her own legal representation, even though this increases the cost of the formation process and may well be viewed as an unnecessary expense by parties who are currently in amity and who believe they will be able to work out future problems on an amicable basis when they arise.

The discussion below first considers the traditional close corporation and then modern developments that have ameliorated, at least to some extent, the problems that may arise in the typical close corporation.

---

[69]This consultation must "include explanation of the implications of the common representation and the advantages and risks involved." Lawyers should obtain this consent in writing from each client before undertaking the multiple representation

§8.20 THE MEANING OF CONTROL IN A CLOSE CORPORATION

Control in a closely held corporation normally resides in the person or group that owns or has the power to vote a majority of the shares entitled to vote for the board of directors of the corporation. The practical importance of the control of a corporation cannot be overstated. Such voting power means that the controlling shareholder has the power to elect the board of directors[70] and thereby control all important aspects of corporate affairs. The board of directors may consist solely of the controlling shareholder or may include his allies. The board of directors has general power to manage the business of the corporation. It may determine what business the corporation should engage in, how it shall be pursued, who will run the day-to-day affairs of the business, who will be employed by the corporation and who will not, how much each employee will be paid, and what his or her responsibilities will be. The board of directors may determine that all shareholders will be employees of the corporation, or that some or all will not be so employed. If a shareholder/employee does something that irritates the controlling shareholders, she may be fired. The board of directors also has discretion to determine whether the corporation should make distributions to shareholders, and if so, how much, and whether the corporation should borrow money or whether it should seek to raise additional capital in some other way.

Clearly, control is virtually everything within the corporation. It is a significant intangible asset owned by the controlling shareholders that makes the value of their shares greater than the value of otherwise indistinguishable shares the owners of which do not share in control.[71] In the law and practice of close corporations, a sharp distinction must be made between "controlling shareholders" and "other" or "non-controlling" shareholders.

One brutal fact is that in the absence of specific, carefully drafted agreements or provisions in the governing documents of the corporation, the controlling shareholders have the power to exclude minority shareholders from any participation in or gain from the corporation. The controlling shareholders may refuse to permit the corporation to employ the minority. They may refuse to pay dividends, taking out the earnings themselves through salary payments, bonuses, or loans from the corporation. As discussed in Chapter 9, closely held corporations that are taxed as C corporations rarely pay dividends, preferring to accumulate surplus or disguise

---

[70] An alternative method of voting, called cumulative voting, permits minority shareholders in some circumstances to obtain representation on the board of directors. The principal method of voting, called straight voting, permits a majority shareholder to elect the entire board of directors. See §8.7 note 28.

[71] See §14.17.

distributions as salary expenses or other payments to shareholders that are deductible by the corporation.[72]

A shareholder who is not employed by a C corporation is unlikely to receive either dividends or any of these informal distributions or benefits. Such a shareholder has an investment that provides a zero return and poor prospects for improvement. In the absence of advance planning, shares of stock owned by a minority shareholder are little more than tickets to enter the lottery of litigation. Colorful language such as "oppression," "freeze outs," or "squeeze outs" is used to describe such exclusionary tactics.

A second brutal fact, discussed at length below, is that a minority shareholder in a closely held corporation has no power of exit in the absence of advance planning. There is by definition no market for the shares and usually no acceptable way to recover his investment in the enterprise.[73] A shareholder who is (or feels) oppressed, frozen out, or squeezed out by actions of the controlling shareholder has no easy way out. He may be able to persuade a court to intervene on his behalf based on judicial doctrines created to protect unsophisticated investors, as discussed in section 8.35. But that requires litigating in circumstances where the size of the investment and the uncertainty of outcome may not justify the cost.

A third brutal fact is that, absent an enforceable agreement, a minority shareholder cannot prevent the sale of a controlling interest to a person or group unacceptable to her.

Potential investors in a closely held corporation must be aware of the need to "cut a deal" before investing.[74] Vague assurances by the controlling shareholder may not be legally enforceable and may not save such an investor from disaster if the need for succor arises. Real, express contracts are required. If the controlling shareholders are unwilling to grant the investor reasonable voice and exit rights, the investor should seriously consider "walking" and finding a suitable investment elsewhere. Of course, if the investor decides to trust the majority shareholders, it is quite possible that things will work out to everyone's satisfaction. On the other hand, the investor is relying on the goodwill and good faith of the controlling shareholders, and if that reliance is misplaced, he is probably out of luck.

---

[72]If distributions cannot be made to the controlling shareholders on a tax deductible basis, the corporation may simply accumulate surplus, refusing to pay dividends in which the minority shareholders would share. Ultimately, the business may be sold on terms that permit capital gain treatment for the portion of the sale proceeds that reflects appreciation in the value of the business. A non-controlling shareholder may sometimes participate in this transaction, but such participation is by no means assured since, in the absence of an enforceable agreement, her shares may be excluded from the sale.

[73]See §8.24.

[74]Contractual provisions designed to protect minority interests in closely held corporations are discussed in §8.27 through §8.32.

§8.21 TRANSFER OF CONTROL

Control of a closely held corporation may exist because a single shareholder owns or controls a majority of the voting shares, or it may exist because two or more shareholders who collectively own or control a majority of the voting shares may agree to vote together. This agreement may be a legally binding contract or it may be a voluntary treaty. The dynamics of the transfer of control may differ in these situations.

Where a single shareholder owns a majority of the voting shares of a corporation, that block will usually be treated as a single economic unit. It represents the power to manage the corporation. If the owner of that block decides to sell out, the block will usually be sold as a unit. It may be sold to an outsider, a third person, or it may be sold to some or all of the current shareholders. The disposition of the control block may be governed by a legally binding share transfer restriction giving the other shareholders or the corporation the duty or option to purchase the control shares, or the sale may be negotiated from scratch through an arms' length negotiation.[75]

If the controlling shareholder gives or bequeaths his controlling block of shares to his children, one child will usually end up in control of the business at least temporarily, whether or not the controlling block is being divided up among several heirs. A controlling block of shares is most likely to be broken up because the shareholder finds that external fairness considerations outweigh the desire to keep controlling shares in single ownership. The founder and sole shareholder of a profitable close corporation, for example, may decide to transfer shares equally among his three children despite the fact that control may be destabilized as a result.[76] Consequently, while control of a successful closely held corporation often passes down through one or more generations of a family, it rarely remains in a single person from one generation to the next. That is simply the result that individuals usually have more than one child and feel that children should be treated equally. It is possible, of course, that the controlling block of voting shares may be left to the grandchild who has worked in the business for ten years and shows managerial aptitude, while other family members receive cash, other property, or non-voting stock. However, it is much more common for controlling shares to be passed down through gift and inheritance in a way that leads to them being divided up among children and grandchildren. This may be because the value of a control block of shares is much more mercurial with a strong upside potential than the value of other property. To assure equity in the younger generation, the controlling block may be divided up.

---

[75]See §8.22.

[76]In this situation, the controlling shareholder may, of course, create a trust and place his shares in that trust. The question then becomes, who should the trustee be? An outsider? One or more of the children? A financial institution?

Where controlling shares are divided among several heirs or donees, control by a single person no longer then exists, but a collective control block often results that may continue for many years. The family as a unit retains control of the business despite possible internal disagreements which must be worked out within the family structure or by appeal to the oldest generation. However, things often do not work out harmoniously. Many of the most bitterly litigated disputes within closely held corporations arise in family corporations where the family is unable to resolve internal disputes peacefully. For example, a situation where two brothers who grew up together in bitter rivalry prove to be unable to leave their childhood competition behind. The treatment of "black sheep" within a family corporation may also cause bitter dispute and a fracturing of a once monolithic family group. In these situations, it makes little sense to talk about parties contracting at arms' length for voice and exit. There is no opportunity to contract. If the former majority shareholder failed to set up a viable structure of control for the next generation, family members who own a minority of the shares may find themselves in the position of any minority shareholder who has failed to obtain by contract needed protection against oppression or freeze-out tactics.

Where control is based on the fact that two or more shareholders collectively own or control a majority of the voting shares but individually each own less than a majority of the shares, the situation is more fluid. In this scenario, there will necessarily be minority shareholders who are not part of the control group. Very commonly, there are legally binding agreements among the controlling shareholders that assure that the control bloc will remain intact. In the absence of binding agreements, however, there is a possibility that whatever informal agreement or treaty exists among the original controlling shareholders may collapse or dissolve in the face of death, retirement, or significant disagreement. In these situations, a new control coalition may be forged, including minority shareholders who formerly had no power to participate in control. Such coalitions may themselves be temporary or fleeting, or they may exist over long periods of time. They may also be solidified by binding agreements among the new control group. Also, minority blocks of stock will have great economic value in this situation if they represent the balance of power between two competing factions.

§8.22 LEGAL RESTRAINTS ON SALES OF CONTROL

A controlling block of shares may be sold to outside interests in the absence of share transfer restrictions in the same way as any other personal property. Since closely held shares by definition have no market, the price is set by negotiation between the potential purchaser and the owners of the control block. Whatever price that is agreed upon will necessarily include or reflect as an element of value the power of control inherent in that block of shares. Valuation principles relating to stock reflect this economic reality. Valuation usually begins by determining the intrinsic value of a share as a fractional interest in an economic enterprise. Then a control premium is added to the value of the controlling block to reflect its true economic value (or, alternatively, a minority discount or lack of marketability discount is subtracted from the non-control shares).[77]

Sales of a controlling block of shares are unlike ordinary personal property sales in one important respect. The control block carries with it the power to affect the wealth of minority shareholders who have no voice in the original sale of control transaction and no right to veto an unacceptable purchaser. Further, the seller of the control block is out of the picture as soon as he receives the purchase price; the other shareholders must deal with the consequences of an incompetent, greedy, or dishonest purchaser. Creditors are in a somewhat analogous situation, but they have legal doctrines that give them at least some protection. Minority shareholders, however, appear to be unable to block transactions that dissipate corporate assets.

Legal restraints on the sale of control grew up as a result of the concern for minority shareholders. A discussion of such restraints is a staple of corporation law courses. There was a series of early cases in which the controlling shareholder of the corporation sold his shares at an inflated price[78] to a third person who turned out to be a looter, taking corporate assets and converting them to his own use. The ultimate losers, of course, were the minority shareholders (and to a lesser extent creditors) who had no power to control the events taking place in the corporation and did not learn about them until after the depredations occurred and the assets dissipated. In several of these cases, the theft from the corporation was substantial and occurred almost immediately after the purchaser obtained control. Further, in some of these cases the selling shareholder made little or no investigation of the background of the purchaser and, in their haste to complete a favorable sale of their shares, ignored indications that the purchaser intended to loot the corporation. The looter had absconded or was judgment proof; the only possible defendant around was the seller of the control shares.

Liability based on a failure to investigate the purchaser's reputation and history before turning the corporation over to him has been imposed

---

[77]See §14.17.

[78]While the value of shares in a closely held corporation cannot be ascertained from market transactions, an approximate value or range of values may be determined from the economic performance of the corporation itself. Prices referred to in the text are based on a comparison with approximate value or range of values.

in several cases. At one time, there was extensive discussion of an "equal opportunity" rule that would require controlling shareholders who plan to sell their control shares to a third party to offer the opportunity proportionately to minority shareholders. This rule would certainly give the selling shareholders a motive to investigate the purchaser carefully, because that shareholder would become a minority shareholder in the corporation following the sale, and would suffer from any depredations by the purchaser. However, one consequence of the equal opportunity rule is that it would deter many sale of control transactions, both desirable and undesirable. If this rule were uniformly applied, it is likely that the controlling shareholder would insist that the potential purchaser acquire all the outstanding shares. This would increase the cost of all sale of control transactions and reduce the potential profitability to legitimate investors.

It is probably true, however, that most sales of control are made to entirely legitimate investors who plan to operate the business for the benefit of all the shareholders and who have no intention of taking personal advantage of the power of control. In other words, the sale of control to looters is probably an atypical transaction. Further, if the sale is to honest and competent investors, the minority shareholders may benefit from the sale of control even if it were made at a premium price. They would get new, more energetic managers who would increase the value of the corporation. In evaluating the equal opportunity rule, one must weigh the losses incurred by deterring desirable transactions against the benefit to minority shareholders that the rule provides in the looting cases. Based largely on armchair analysis, law and economics scholars have concluded that the equal opportunity rule is undesirable and no special rules are needed to govern sale of control transactions.

The American Law Institute's Corporate Governance Project revisited the sale of control issue in the early 1990s and concluded that a desirable rule is that the selling shareholder should have responsibility for the purchaser's misconduct only where "it is apparent from the circumstances that the purchaser is likely to violate the duty of fair dealing . . . in such a way as to obtain a significant financial benefit for the purchaser."[79]

A person who has entered into a contract to purchase the controlling shares of a corporation will also usually offer to acquire the minority, noncontrolling shares as well.[80] However, there is no legal requirement that the

---

[79]American Law Institute, Principles of Corporate Governance: Analysis and Recommendations §5.16.

[80]The purchaser may wish to acquire these shares in order to avoid possible disputes with the minority shareholders in the future. The principles limiting self-dealing by directors are designed to protect minority shareholders. If there are no minority shareholders, the controlling shareholders have much greater freedom to use the assets of the corporation as

purchaser offer the same price per share to the non-controlling shareholders, and normally the price that will be offered to non-controlling shareholders will be significantly below the price offered to the controlling shareholders, the difference in the price representing at least in part the control value of the majority shares and the lack of power inherent in minority shares. The non-controlling shareholders may take it or leave it, but as a legal matter such transactions are presumptively lawful.

An example may help to make the transaction clear. An investor, purchasing control of a corporation offers to buy the shares owned by the controlling shareholders at a negotiated price, say $500 per share. At the same time, the investor also offers to purchase the shares owned by minority shareholders at a much lower price, say $300 per share. In theory, shares are fungible. One share of common stock is no different from any other shares of common stock. As a result, a price differential of $200 per share in favor of the controlling shareholder's stock may be difficult to explain to the minority. Certainly, it may be bitterly resented, but there is really not very much that the minority can do about it. On the other hand, some purchasers may be uncomfortable about a dual purchase price offer and insist that the same price be offered to all shareholders. It is also possible that the selling shareholder may feel uncomfortable about taking a higher price than his fellow shareholders. Of course, the controlling shareholders may insist that the purchaser offer the minority shareholders the same opportunity to sell that they have as a condition to agreeing to the transfer of control. But that decision reduces the controlling shareholders' real wealth arising from the transaction. The basic point is that there is no legal principle that requires equal treatment of controlling and minority shareholders.

§8.23 DEADLOCKS IN CONTROL

In some corporations, control may be evenly balanced between two shareholders or two groups of shareholders. This usually arises when two shareholders own precisely the same number of shares. Equal ownership may be pre-planned, e.g., by two equal partners deciding to incorporate their ongoing business, or by two entrepreneurs deciding they wish to share equally in all aspects of the business. It may also arise from planning decisions by a prior shareholder, as when she gives or bequeaths one half of her holdings to each of two descendants. Corporations with equally divided voting power involve potential deadlocks: Tie votes at the critical level of the election of the board of directors means that no directors may be elected. The rule in

---

they wish. The purchaser also usually wishes to acquire as many shares as possible to increase his percentage interest in the corporation if he can do so at favorable prices.

this situation is quite clear. Directors in office remain in office until their successors are elected and qualify. Thus, a deadlock at the shareholders' level means that persons who are serving as directors continue to serve indefinitely.[81]

Potential deadlocks may also arise from a variety of control patterns other than equal ownership interests in the voting power of the corporation. A super-majority voting requirement — a requirement that the affirmative vote of 80 percent of the shareholders is needed to elect a director — may prevent a majority shareholder from electing any directors without the approval of one or more minority shareholders. An 80 percent super-majority requirement creates a potential deadlock if there are two shareholders or two groups of shareholders, one of which owns more than 20 percent of the voting shares. A 100 percent super-majority requirement means that any one shareholder may deadlock the election of directors, no matter how small his percentage interest. A high quorum requirement for shareholder meetings may also create a deadlock because a shareholder may intentionally stay away from a meeting to prevent a quorum, thereby making it impossible for the shareholders to elect directors at all.

Deadlocks may also occur at the directoral level. A deadlock at this level means that there will be little or no oversight of the actions of the officers and managers of the corporation. Directoral deadlocks regularly arise where there is an even number of directors and the voting structure for directors permits each shareholder or each faction to elect precisely the same number of directors as the other shareholder or faction.

A common example in a two-shareholder corporation is a structure that involves two classes of shares, one class wholly owned by each shareholder, and a board of directors consisting of four directors, two of whom are to be elected by each class of shares, voting separately. A deadlock at the directoral level may also arise from other governance provisions. For example, a provision that requires a unanimous vote of directors for every action creates a potential deadlock whenever there is more than one director. Deadlock may also be created by a high quorum requirement for directors' meetings so that a director may prevent a quorum by staying away from a meeting. Even a normal quorum requirement may be used to deadlock a directors' meeting in some circumstances.[82]

It is often assumed that when a deadlock actually occurs, the corporation is paralyzed and unable to function. That is usually not true. Typically,

---

[81] All state statutes have a fairly boilerplate provision to the effect that directors remain in office despite the expiration of their term until their successors are qualified. Thus, if shareholders become deadlocked on the election of new directors, the directors then in office remain there indefinitely.

[82] For example, in a four-person board with a quorum requirement that three directors be present, if there is one vacancy a single director may prevent a quorum by refusing to attend the meeting.

what happens is that whoever is in control of the corporation when the deadlock occurs remains in control, and the corporation continues to function in a business sense. Production continues, sales are made, checks are written, and so forth.[83]

Most deadlocks are probably resolved pragmatically by the persons involved. They may reach a compromise, and agree to agree in the future. They may agree upon an outside person to act as a tie-breaker. Where the deadlock appears to be irreconcilable, the logical solution may be for one party to buy out the other party. Major issues may be the price and the question of who is to be the buyer and who is to be the seller. Where a buyout cannot be worked out by agreement, the parties may agree that the corporation should be dissolved voluntarily, the assets reduced to cash, and the proceeds be distributed to the shareholders.

If no agreement can be obtained on any solution, the state statutes provide the ultimate solution. The traditional legal remedy is involuntary dissolution if the deadlock continues for more than a specified period. Immediate involuntary dissolution may be available if one shareholder complains of oppression, or the assets of the corporation are being wasted. However, statutes vary widely. Some impose a mandatory period of receivership before authorizing judicially imposed dissolution. Some provide a statutory buyout procedure. Some provide for the appointment of a custodian, an independent director, a temporary director, or a "disinterested person" to participate in corporate management to break the deadlock. However, dissolution or buyouts are the only solutions likely to be successful when the parties are intransigent.

Deadlock situations almost always arise because of the lack of advance planning, or more accurately, the lack of effective advance planning.

§8.24 THE IMPORTANCE OF "EXIT" IN A CLOSE CORPORATION

In theory, the shares of stock of any corporation are freely transferable. Shares of publicly held corporations are of course usually traded in large and active securities markets and therefore are salable simply by a telephone call to one's broker. The reality is far different when one is dealing with shares

---

[83] If the directors themselves are deadlocked because they are evenly divided, the corporate officers then in office (particularly those who have the power to write checks on corporate funds) have complete power over corporate activities since the deadlocked board of directors is unable to remove them or limit their power. Modern corporation statutes provide a variety of remedies for deadlocks so that a corporation in which the directors are deadlocked is unlikely to remain in that status for a long period of time.

of a closely held corporation. In a closely held corporation, by definition there is no active market for shares. The power to sell shares is meaningless if there is practically no one interested in buying them, or if the only person who is interested in them will offer only what is viewed to be a ridiculously low price.

In the absence of a binding option or buy-sell agreement, a minority shareholder has no meaningful power to exit. In the absence of agreement, he cannot compel the corporation or the other shareholders to purchase shares. Further, he cannot compel the corporation to dissolve (in a manner similar to the power of a partner in a partnership). Rather, to exit the shareholder must seek voluntary transactions with the corporation, with one or more other shareholders, or with some outside third party. The corporation is a surrogate for the remaining shareholders in this connection since a purchase by the corporation is the economic equivalent of a proportionate purchase by all the other shareholders.

Neither majority nor minority shareholders have any obligation to pay a generous price for the shares if they decide to purchase at all. On the contrary, they have a strong incentive to offer the selling shareholder a very low price. The majority shareholders by hypothesis already have a controlling position and therefore do not need the additional minority shares to cement or preserve that control. By purchasing minority shares they do not materially improve their control or economic position with the corporation. Rather, they simply reduce the amount of their personal liquid assets. Similarly, minority shareholders also have little incentive to purchase minority shares since the purchase does not generally improve their position significantly vis a vis each other or the majority shareholder. They simply become larger, but still minority shareholders. As is the case with the controlling shareholders, their investment in the corporation increases but their power does not. And, if the shareholders have no incentive to pay a fair price, the corporation does not either.

Controlling shareholders do have an incentive to eliminate minority interests if they can at an acceptably low price. Minority shareholders are of course shareholders, and they do have rights that may prove troublesome to controlling shareholders. These rights limit the power of the majority to treat corporate assets as though they were owned by the controlling shareholders personally. For example, they have the power to inspect corporate books and records and to file direct or derivative lawsuits charging the controlling shareholders with self-dealing or the breach of fiduciary duties. They may claim the directors have refused to pay dividends in good faith. They may become, in short, real nuisances. And, if the corporation is dissolved and its assets distributed, they are entitled to a pro rata portion of the liquidating distribution. As a result, controlling shareholders do have an interest in eliminating minority interests, if the price is right. Thus, a very marginal market may exist for minority shares with the potential buyers being either the controlling shareholders or the corporation itself. From the selfish interest of the controlling shareholders, there is little incentive to offer much more than the nuisance value of the minority interests.

Controlling shareholders may try to "soften up" minority shareholders by depriving them of all return on their shares for an extended period before opening negotiations with them. The controlling shareholders are in no hurry. Time is on their side. Thus, while this may be a "market" for minority shares of sorts, it is not a very attractive one from the standpoint of sellers. It is not at all like a market involving the traditional willing buyer and willing seller contemplated by economic theory.

Sales of minority interests to third parties also are extremely unlikely to occur unless the purchaser is acceptable to the controlling shareholders and is able to negotiate an arrangement with them. Otherwise, the purchaser will be in exactly the same position as the shareholder desiring to sell. Because controlling shareholders have the power to reduce or eliminate the return received by minority shareholders, it is unlikely that an outsider would even consider the purchase of minority shares without some assurances from the controlling shareholders. Before agreeing to do so, the outsider would probably insist on reaching a firm agreement with the controlling shareholders. If an advance agreement with the controlling shareholders cannot be reached, the outsider will most likely look elsewhere for an acceptable investment, or conceivably the outsider might insist upon such a significant further discount in the price of the shares that the minority shareholder may decide he might just as well keep the shares or offer them directly to the controlling shareholder.

Of course, where three or more factions exist, none of which individually has a majority of the outstanding shares, the dynamics may be quite different. If the shares owned by the shareholder who wishes to sell represent the balance of power if they are conveyed to one of the other factions, spirited bidding by the remaining factions may occur as each seeks to obtain the "swing shares" necessary to acquire the controlling interest in the management of the business. The per share value of the swing block may overstate the aggregate per share value of the business in this situation since the owner of the swing shares in effect has captured the value of the control element within the corporation.

§8.25 OPPRESSION AND FREEZE-OUTS

Oppression and freeze-outs are terms with very similar meaning in the close corporation context. They refer to the actual use by controlling shareholders of the power they possess to exclude minority shareholders from participation in the management of the business and to deprive them of significant economic return on their shares. The term *oppression* is a comparative term that assumes a minority shareholder has a certain minimum economic return or right of participation that she is now being deprived of by the controlling shareholders' conduct. This minimum return or right of participation is usually judged, where applicable, by the terms on which the minority shareholder originally invested in the corporation or the promises which induced her to invest.[84] The term *freeze-out* refers to an oppressive tactic in which a controlling shareholder prevents all payments from the corporation to a minority shareholder in an effort to persuade the minority shareholder to sell her shares at an unreasonably low price.

Oppression and freeze-outs are possible because of the combination of the power of controlling shareholders to exclude minority shareholders from participation in the affairs of the corporation and the absence of a meaningful right of exit by minority shareholders from a corporation.

Sections 8.33 and 8.35 discuss legal remedies that are available to protect minority shareholders from oppression and freeze-outs. However, resort to these remedies should be unnecessary because both the power to participate and the power to exit on the part of non-controlling shareholders may readily be negotiated in advance through a variety of devices. Because oppression and freeze-outs may be avoided so easily by rational investors, law and economics scholars tend to view these problems as rare, unusual, and of little practical importance. They view the close corporation, in short, as an example of contract law in action. That is certainly often true, but regrettably every corporation lawyer regularly encounters situations in which for one reason or another minority shareholders did not obtain adequate contractual protection against abusive conduct by controlling shareholders. Thus, courts continue to apply legal remedies to protect minority shareholders from unfair or inequitable conduct.

§8.26 PROTECTION OF "VOICE" AND PARTICIPATION IN CLOSELY HELD CORPORATIONS

This and the following sections consider devices by which a potential investor in a closely held corporation can avoid becoming an oppressed minority shareholder. It assumes that the potential investor plans to participate in the management of the business but owns a minority of the voting shares. In the model of the close corporation favored by law and economics schol-

---

[84]This standard may not be applicable in situations where the minority shareholder obtained her shares by gift or inheritance. In these situations, a court is likely to use as a minimum standard what the court believes to be "decent" conduct by controlling shareholders.

ars, the potential investor has alternative investment opportunities and is therefore free to walk away from the negotiations if a satisfactory deal cannot be agreed upon. Likewise, the corporation is able to attract other similarly situated investors if this specific investor cannot be satisfied. In other words, it assumes the traditional arms' length negotiation in which both parties are adequately informed and under no compulsion to enter into the transactions. These assumptions are usually but by no means always true.[85]

Consider the situation, based on a famous old case,[86] involving an outside investor (McQuade) who was in treaty with the controlling shareholder (Stoneham) of the corporation that owned the New York Giants baseball club. McQuade agreed to buy 70 shares directly from Stoneham for slightly more than $50,000, a large sum in 1919. Stoneham owned over 1,000 shares of the stock, well over 50 percent of the total shares outstanding both before and after the McQuade transaction.[87] Stoneham promised that he would use his "best endeavors" to name McQuade as a director of the corporation, and would also have him named as treasurer of the corporation at a salary of $7,500 per year. Some ten years later, a disagreement arose between Stoneham and McQuade, and McQuade was unceremoniously removed as treasurer of the New York Giants.

There are two basic ways in which an arrangement of this type affecting voice and economic participation in a corporation may be effectuated. The first is for the investor to enter into an employment contract *with the corporation*, presumably for a long period of time to assure he has a contractual right to serve as treasurer of the corporation. The second is for the investor to insist that the structural rules of the corporation be changed in a way that permits the investor to be assured of his remaining as treasurer of the corporation even if the controlling shareholders no longer wish for the investor to do so. One way to do this is to amend the corporation's articles of incorporation to give the investor a special class of common shares and to provide that only a holder of one or more shares of that class may serve as treasurer of the corporation, and that a treasurer may be removed only with the consent of the holders of a majority of the shares of

[85] There are several very common situations in which a person becomes a minority shareholder, usually without any bargaining at all. The first is where a person receives a gift or bequest of shares from a controlling or non-controlling shareholder. The second is where a trusted, long-term employee is given (or permitted to buy) a small number of shares as a reward for long service and to provide additional incentive for the employee. In the latter situation, the shares are usually sold directly by the corporation to the employee. There are also situations where the potential investor so completely trusts the controlling shareholders that she fails to request adequate protection against subsequent disagreement or transfer of control. Finally, there are situations where, because of unsophisticated advice, a plan that is entered into turns out to be legally ineffective.

[86] McQuade v. Stoneham, 263 N.Y. 323, 189 N.E. 234 (1934).

[87] At the same time, Stoneham also sold a small number of shares to McGraw, the legendary manager of the New York Giants.

that class.[88] Obviously, the contract route is much simpler and more direct; it also avoids the problem of requiring amendments to the governing documents of the corporation both when the arrangement begins, and when it ends and McQuade is no longer to be treasurer or to own shares of a class that has special rights with respect to the selection of a corporate treasurer.

It is important to recognize that neither of these techniques (if they had in fact been tried) provides a 100 percent guarantee that McQuade will in fact serve as treasurer of the corporation, as he desires. In the employment contract scenario, the corporation can always fire the investor if it is willing to pay damages for breach of contract. In the structural approach, the corporation may be able to remove the investor if there are grounds — cause — to do so. And, even if not, there is probably nothing that would prevent the controlling shareholders from isolating McQuade from the decisional process and having functions traditionally performed by a treasurer be performed by someone else, titled a "comptroller," or something like that. In this scenario, McQuade would be entitled to his salary for the period of the contract. Of course, both of these alternative ways to avoid the "deal" are expensive from the corporation's standpoint and may give the treasurer a considerable degree of security of tenure, as a practical matter.

Neither of these arrangements raise the specter of potential deadlock. Both the contract and the structural change are focused narrowly on McQuade's relationship with the corporation and does not give him power to veto or block other actions by the corporation. Of course, McQuade could have been given greater rights than suggested above. For example, he could have been given a veto right over all decisions by the board of directors (for example, by putting in the articles of incorporation a provision requiring unanimity by the board to take any action) but there is no real justification for McQuade to request such a power and no incentive on the part of Stoneham to give McQuade such a broad veto power, which might permit McQuade to act opportunistically at some future time.[89]

In the actual case, the arrangement between Stoneham and McQuade was reflected simply as a personal contract between the two individuals. When suit was brought to compel specific performance of this contract, the

---

[88]These kinds of arrangements can be tricky, however. In order for McQuade to be assured of his post, the corporate documents would have to be further modified to make sure that McQuade is able to veto any proposals to issue additional shares of his class of stock.

[89]See Frank H. Easterbrook and Daniel R. Fischel, The Economic Structure of Corporate Law 238 (1991):

> Drafters of the organizing documents of a closely held corporation cannot avoid a trade-off. On the one hand, they must provide some protection to minority investors to ensure that they receive an adequate return on the minority shareholder's investment if the venture succeeds. On the other hand, they cannot give the minority too many rights, for the minority might exercise their rights in an opportunistic fashion to divert returns.

court held the contract to be unenforceable in its entirety, since a controlling shareholder had no power to bind boards of directors to select specific people as officers or to set their compensation. The board of directors, the court strongly suggested, must have power to exercise its unfettered discretion on such matters, discretion that must be exercised to benefit the corporation as such, and not solely the controlling shareholder. As a result, Stoneham was able to breach his agreement with impunity.

Since there were shareholders of the baseball club that were not parties to the Stoneham/McGraw contract, the result reached by the court might be alternatively justified on the theory that these outside shareholders deserve protection against a controlling shareholder's personal contracts. However, since none of those shareholders were complaining, that seems to be less than persuasive to justify an obviously unfair result. It is likely that many courts would refuse to follow the *McQuade* decision today, but that is really very difficult to predict, and it would be silly for any lawyer representing a person in McQuade's position to accept a simple contract with the controlling shareholder. At the very least, that solution requires litigation to enforce the client's rights.

An outside investor typically desires to have a voice in the corporation in the form of representation on the board of directors of the corporation but without necessarily having participation in the management of the enterprise. It is relatively easy to assure such representation through the device of a shareholders' agreement that requires the parties to the agreement to vote for specific persons as directors. Such an agreement does not run afoul of the *McQuade* principle, because that principle only relates to promises by the controlling shareholder that pertain to decisions of the board of directors. Decisions as to *who* should be on the board are quite different than decisions as to *what* the board should do.[90]

§8.27　THE RIGHT TO EXIT: BUY-SELL AGREEMENTS

The most widely used device to provide protection to minority interests in a corporation is a contract that requires the corporation (or the controlling shareholders) to purchase the shares owned by minority interests in specified circumstances. Such contracts are known as *buy-sell agreements*. They are a part of a broader set of agreements called "share transfer restrictions." Buy-sell agreements create a contractual power to exit, and are an essential aspect of sensible planning for all closely held corporations. Enforceable buy-sell agreements also may provide important independent tax and business benefits, including important limitations on estate tax liabilities upon the death of a shareholder. Moreover, they permit shareholders to determine who shall be permitted to participate in the corporation and, depending on

---

[90]See the discussion of traditional roles of directors and shareholders in §8.8.

234

the terms of the agreement, may give each shareholder an opportunity to purchase other shareholders' interests when they wish to sell.

Prior sections have pointed out that there is only a very limited market for non-controlling interests in closely held corporations. Sales of non-controlling stock in the absence of advance agreement will usually be at distressed levels even without oppression or freeze-outs. Further, there is a need for liquidity in many situations not involving oppression or freeze-outs, particularly the death, retirement, or divorce of a participant. A buy-sell agreement provides liquidity that permits smooth changes in ownership in closely held corporations which otherwise might be achieved only through bitter and protracted negotiation. Shares owned by a controlling shareholder may be subject to a buy-sell agreement as well as shares of non-controlling shareholders.

A buy-sell agreement commits either the corporation or the other participants in the venture, to purchase the interest of a shareholder at a fixed or determinable price upon the occurrence of specified events, such as death, retirement, or significant and substantial disagreement. Probably the most common arrangement requires the corporation to purchase the shares if it is able to do so, but if it is not, then the shareholders have the obligation to purchase the shares. The purchase price may be made payable over a period of time, in effect permitting the corporation to purchase the shares partially out of future profits or cash flow of the business. The obligation to buy the interest of a participant in the case of death is usually funded by the business through the purchase of insurance on the life of each shareholder.[91] In a C corporation,[92] funds may also be accumulated at the lower tax rates applicable to corporations for this purpose, but this may itself create tax problems.[93]

Buy-sell agreements may involve cross purchase shareholder agreements[94] rather than an agreement by the corporation to purchase the shares. Cross purchase agreements become more complicated if the number of shareholders is more than two, particularly if the obligation is funded by life insurance policies on the other shareholders. The payment of premiums by individual shareholders may create cash flow problems because corporate funds are not available for this purpose except on an after-tax basis. Cross

[91] This assumes, of course, that the shareholders are insurable. The purchase of insurance by a corporation on the lives of its shareholders has tax implications. The premiums on life insurance policies owned by the corporation are not deductible by the corporation. Internal Revenue Code §264(a)(1). The receipt of the proceeds of life insurance by a corporation may be taxable under the alternative minimum tax.

[92] For a discussion of the tax treatment of C corporations and S corporations, see §9.2 through §9.9.

[93] Such a corporation may run afoul of the accumulated earnings tax, Internal Revenue Code §532, since the accumulation of surplus to meet the obligations of a buy-sell agreement is not viewed as "a reasonable need of the business."

[94] A *cross pruchase shareholder agreement* is made among shareholders along the lines of "If you die first, I will buy your shares; if I die first, you will buy mine."

purchase agreements also must address the issue of what happens if one or more of the potential purchasers refuse, or are unable, to complete the purchase of the shares.

§8.28 SHARE TRANSFER RESTRICTIONS

Buy-sell agreements are the most common type of share transfer restriction, but other types do exist and should be discussed briefly. A share transfer restriction is usually imposed by the corporation on all shares it issues. *Share transfer restrictions* include (1) option arrangements, by which a shareholder who wishes to sell or dispose of her shares must first offer them to the corporation or the other shareholders, (2) rights of first refusal, (3) consent requirements that permit the board of directors of the corporation to reject a potential purchaser, or (4) prohibitions against the transfer of shares to specific classes of persons. Share transfer restrictions permit a closely held corporation to determine who will and who will not be participants in the profits of the enterprise. They create rights analogous to the *delectus personae* concept of a partnership.

Share transfer restrictions constitute restraints on alienation of property and the black letter rule is that unreasonable restraints on alienation are invalid. Consent restrictions and prohibitions against transfer to specific classes of persons are the most likely types of share transfer restrictions to be stricken as unreasonable restraints on alienation.[95] First options to purchase, first refusal rights to meet competing offers to buy, and buy-sell agreements have uniformly been upheld, and it is dangerous to depart into unchartered waters in this area by creating novel types of restrictions, since if a restriction on transfer is found to be unreasonable it is simply invalidated in its entirety and not trimmed back to a reasonable degree.

One consequence of treating share transfer restrictions as restraints on alienation is that they may become subject to a rule of strict construction. For example, a restriction triggered by the proposed sale of shares to a third party may be held not to cover a proposed sale of shares to the corporation or to other shareholders. This is unfortunate, since a narrow reading of a carelessly drafted restriction may defeat the reasonable intentions and expectations of the parties.

Share transfer restrictions may be placed in the articles of incorporation of the corporation, in its bylaws, or in a separate agreement entered into by the shareholders. Buy-sell agreements are usually set forth in separate contracts to avoid overly complicating the basic corporate documents and to avoid placing the details of the arrangement in a public record. State statutes require that the existence of transfer restrictions be noted on the face of share certificates, and may require a detailed description of the re-

[95] A good guide to the reasonableness of restrictions on transfer is provided by §6.27 of the Model Business Corporation Act (1984).

strictions on the back of the certificate. However, these notation requirements are designed to make the restrictions applicable to third-party purchasers. If a person is aware of the restriction when she acquires the shares (or thereafter agrees to be bound by the restrictions), she is bound by the restrictions even if there is no notation on the certificates.

§8.29 BUY-SELL AGREEMENTS AND THE DEATH OF A SHAREHOLDER

A buy-sell agreement triggered upon the death of a shareholder provides immediate benefits to the estate of the deceased shareholder and her family. The shares owned by the decedent are sold at a fair price without negotiation, haggling, or bargaining. The estate has immediate liquidity for the payment of debts, death taxes, and expenses of administration. Further, the agreement may fix the value of the closely held shares for estate tax purposes, thereby avoiding a potentially damaging and costly valuation dispute with the Internal Revenue Service. Finally, if the purchaser is the corporation, the transaction permits the withdrawal of funds from the corporation in a transaction that does not involve the payment of a dividend to the other shareholders (which would be the case if a distribution were made to the other shareholders to permit them to meet their obligations under a cross purchase agreement).

In the absence of a buy-sell agreement, the estate of the deceased shareholder would own closely held shares of stock as an illiquid asset. These illiquid assets not uncommonly represent the great bulk of the decedent's wealth.[96] Almost immediately, the decedent's estate and her family may face a serious cash-flow crisis. The income from the decedent's employment with the corporation normally ceases upon or shortly after death, and it is unlikely that the spouse or heirs of the decedent have the necessary skills to be able to perform services on behalf of the business that would enable the decedent's salary to be continued. There may be death benefits, salary continuation agreements for a brief period, and insurance proceeds. But the support of a spouse and minor children of the decedent may consume these liquid assets in the estate in a relatively short time. A buy-sell agreement minimizes this cash-flow crisis since it permits the estate to receive cash for the illiquid shares shortly after the death of the decedent.

Another major advantage of a buy-sell agreement is that it often avoids a nasty and disagreeable fight with the tax authorities over the appropriate value to be placed on the closely held shares for estate tax purposes. The extent to which buy-sell agreements have been held to control the valuation of closely held shares for estate tax purposes has a long history. A low

---

[96]This is simply a reflection of the fact mentioned at the beginning of this chapter that in most closely held corporations it is not possible for the shareholders to hold a diversified portfolio of investments.

buy-sell price for transfers within a family may readily be used as a device to "freeze" estate tax values. The regulations and the case law developed a number of tests as to when a price set in a buy-sell agreement should be accepted to determine valuation of closely held shares. In the Omnibus Budget Reconciliation Act of 1990, Congress enacted new standards for acceptance of these values in section 2703 of the Internal Revenue Code. The basic tests of that section are that the buy-sell agreement (1) must be "a bona fide business arrangement," it (2) must not be "a device to transfer such property to members of the decedent's family for less than full and adequate consideration in money or money's worth," and (3) its terms must be "comparable to similar arrangements entered into by persons in an arms' length transaction."[97] A right or restriction is considered to meet the three statutory requirements "if more than 50 percent value of the property subject to the right or restriction is owned directly or indirectly . . . by individuals who are not members of the transferor's immediate family."

The corporation and the surviving shareholders also benefit from the use of an enforceable buy-sell agreement. In the first place, it avoids friction between the corporation and the heirs of the deceased shareholder. In the absence of such an agreement, the surviving spouse or children of the decedent may literally appear on the doorstep of the corporation demanding immediate financial assistance or the continuation of salaries and distributions. If there is a buy-sell agreement, an advance usually may be made immediately to be repaid from the proceeds of the stock transaction when details are worked out. Secondly, it assures the corporation and its shareholders that it will not have to deal with a potentially hostile shareholder that may be the estate of the decedent or one or more heirs who have become minority shareholders. In effect, it assures the corporation that control will be unaffected and unfriendly third parties will not become shareholders. It also assures that critical tax elections will not be adversely affected, as may be, for example, if the decedent's will provides that property is to pass to an unqualified testamentary trust.[98] Finally, if the buy-sell arrangements are funded with life insurance owned by the corporation, the insurance proceeds provide the purchase price for at least a substantial portion of the required purchase without draining the corporation of its working capital.

While discussion of buy-sell agreements usually focus around the death of a minority shareholder, the agreements themselves are usually reciprocal, and therefore it is quite possible that the decedent will be the controlling shareholder or one of the controlling shareholders of the corporation. A buy-sell agreement to meet this situation involves the development of a

---

[97]Internal Revenue Code §2703.

[98]The principal election that may be terminated is the S corporation election which requires that shareholders be individuals (with a narrow exception for estates of decedents). See §9.6.

plan of succession for the business; advance planning is certainly to be preferred to planning after the fact, with the likelihood of opportunistic conduct by shareholders.

§8.30 OTHER ROLES FOR BUY-SELL AGREEMENTS

While death of a shareholder is the most common triggering event for buy-sell agreements, such agreements also provide liquidity in connection with other events which lead to a termination of the relationship between the corporation and the shareholder: retirement, withdrawal from employment (either voluntarily or involuntarily), disability, competition with the corporation, divorce, contemplated sale of the shares to a third party, oppression, or deadlock. Triggering events of these types may justify a right of exit provided by buy-sell agreements, but they also raise serious problems of definition, of funding (since life insurance is not payable upon these events),[99] and of additional determinations such as who is to buy and who is to sell, and who was at fault. A particularly important issue concerns who has the power to trigger the transaction. In the case of a buyout on death, the trigger occurs automatically. However, in connection with these alternative triggering events, either the corporation or the shareholder may have power to trigger the buyout to occur.

A useful distinction may be made between "put" and "call" rights. If the shareholder has the power to compel the corporation to buy her shares at a predetermined or determinable price, the buy-sell agreement involves a *put*. If the corporation has the power to compel the shareholder to sell, that is a *call*. In some instances, it may be appropriate to have both put and call rights, depending on the circumstances. Further, the price may vary depending on the basis of the triggering event and whether the employee/shareholder engaged in misconduct while working for the corporation. Brief discussion of the most likely triggering events follows:

1. *Disability.* If a shareholder is clearly totally disabled — no longer able to work — her family may well desire for a buyout to take place promptly in order to provide liquidity for the support needs for the shareholder and her dependents. The other shareholders may equally desire for a buyout to take place to avoid any possible involvement in the business by the disabled shareholder or her family. In other words, both a put and a call might be appropriate. The most serious problems in this area are how to determine whether a specific condition constitutes a disability and who is to make that determination. Alternatives range from examination by a

---

[99]Disability insurance may be available, but typically such insurance is owned by the beneficiary and provides only a fractional income continuation benefit.

group of disinterested professionals to a decision solely in the discretion of the board of directors.

2. Retirement and Change of Employment. When a minority shareholder's employment is discontinued (either voluntarily or involuntarily) the corporation will normally wish to have a call on the employee's shares. If the termination is for cause, the corporation may wish to have a call on the shares at a low price, a so-called bad boy provision. Where, however, the employee is terminated for the convenience of the corporation, i.e., not for improper conduct by the employee, a higher price may be appropriate and either party should be able to compel the transaction to be completed. If the employee leaves voluntarily, the corporation will certainly expect to have a call on the shares; the employee may also seek a put, but the corporation may resist this proposal because the employee may then act opportunistically by demanding a buyout at a time that is inconvenient for the corporation. The corporation may also seek a "noncompetition" clause prohibiting the employee from working for a competitor or opening a competitive personally owned business for a stated period of time. Noncompetition clauses are enforceable in most states if reasonable in duration and geographical scope, and do not deprive the employee of alternative sources of income or support.

3. Divorce. As a general proposition, all buy-sell agreements should provide for the possibility that a shareholder may be involved in a divorce, since the divorced spouse otherwise may have, or receive, property interests in the shares. Typically, neither the corporation nor the shareholder will wish the spouse to become a shareholder in the corporation so that a buyout of any shares transferable to the spouse is usually triggered automatically by the divorce, with the purchaser being either the divorced shareholder or, if the shareholder is unable to purchase the shares, the corporation. In order to assure the spouse is bound, it is customary to require all spouses to execute the buy-sell agreement. This is particularly important in community property states, where the spouse may have a property interest in the shares that is independent of and not derivative from the interest of the shareholder.

4. Voluntary Transfers. Buy-sell agreements may also be triggered by a voluntary transfer of the shares by a shareholder. This may be in the form of an option or a right of first refusal, but the corporation traditionally has a call but the shareholder does not have a put. A transfer of a security interest in the shares — that is, the shareholder pledges the shares as security for a loan — may be exempted from the transfer restriction since otherwise the restriction may prevent a shareholder from realizing upon a potentially important source of collateral. The agreement may provide, however, that an involuntary transfer, such as foreclosure of a pledge of the stock, constitutes a trigger of the buy-sell agreement.

5. Deadlocks. Where a governance structure contains a high probability of potential deadlocks, it is not uncommon to find the parties contracting for a resolution through a buy-sell agreement. Such an agreement must address, in addition to the usual issue of how the price is to be set or determined, two other critical questions: (1) How should a deadlock be defined for purposes of triggering the agreement?; and (2) Who is to stay and who is to be bought out? The nature of the provision that creates a deadlock should affect how these questions are resolved. A deadlock based on two 50 percent shareholders making the same financial contribution and both participating in the management of the business should be handled differently from a deadlock that arises because one participant owning a minority of the shares has been given a veto power through a unanimity requirement. A definition of deadlock may be based on the failure to elect new directors for a stated period or the inability of the board of directors to reach a decision on some contested issue after a specified number of reconsiderations. A decision as to who should be the buyer and who the seller seems to be entirely fact-specific. Normally, the younger would buy out the older, but it may be equally plausible in specific circumstances to have the older buy out the younger. If financial investments are unequal, typically the one with the larger investment would do the buying and the one with the smaller investment do the selling. It may be practical to use a reciprocal option arrangement that involves a setting of the price by one shareholder with the option for the other shareholder either to buy or to sell at that price.[100] Finally, if all else fails, the question may be decided by a coin flip or the drawing of straws.

6. Oppression. Oppression is typically not directly addressed in a negotiated buy-sell agreement except indirectly by terms relating to the termination of employment of the shareholder or his removal from the board of directors. Other objective tests of oppression, such as the discontinuation of dividends to a nonparticipating shareholder, may also be used as a triggering event of a buy-sell agreement, though such provisions do not appear to be very common. A general reference to oppression as the triggering event in a buy-sell agreement should be avoided because of the extreme subjectivity of that word.

As described below,[101] however, many state statutes provide for a judicial remedy upon proof that oppressive conduct occurred. That remedy may

---

[100]See §8.31 part 6.
[101]See §8.33.

involve involuntary dissolution or a mandatory buyout of the shares of the oppressed shareholder at a price determined by the court.[102]

7. Buyout on Demand. In a general partnership, a minority-in-interest partner who claims that he is being oppressed by the other partners has the power to force dissolution of the partnership and compel either a winding up and termination of the business or the payment to him of the present value of his partnership interest.[103] The suggestion is sometimes made that a shareholder in a closely held corporation should have a similar power to compel a buyout on demand. In fact, however, such rights, if included at all in buy-sell agreements are exceedingly uncommon. The reason for this is very simple: A right to a buyout on demand opens up the possibility that the minority shareholder may use this power opportunistically by demanding a buyout when he knows that such a demand will embarrass the corporation and compel it to negotiate from a position of weakness.

§8.31 THE PRICE PROVISION OF BUY-SELL AGREEMENTS

Perhaps the most difficult aspect of both buy-sell agreements and option arrangements in closely held corporations is establishment of the appropriate price term. By hypothesis there is no independent market for shares of a closely held corporation against which a putative price can be measured. In most buyout arrangements, however, at least initially there is a strong incentive for the parties to reach a mutually acceptable and fair price, since there can be no assurance as to which participant will be the first to withdraw, and thus the first to have his or her interest valued and purchased pursuant to the agreement. If appropriately drafted, the price provision may also set the estate tax value of the shareholders' shares upon their deaths.

Chapter 14 of this book discusses valuation of closely held businesses in some detail. Valuation is not a scientific process and is to some extent dependent on the issue under consideration and the identity of the person paying for the appraisal. As indicated above, the price at which shares are to be purchased may depend to some extent on the cause that the triggered the buy-sell obligation. This section discusses the normal situation where fairness of price is the predominant consideration. The following methods of establishing the price for shares may be considered:

---

[102] As described in §8.33, a number of state courts have ordered a buyout as a matter of discretion even though the state statute only provides that involuntary dissolution is the remedy for oppressive conduct.

[103] See §4.24. If the partnership is for a term, a dissolution may be a breach of contract which may lead to the value of the partnership interest being reduced by damages caused by the breach. See §4.25.

1. *Specific Fixed Price*. A price may be set in the buy-sell agreement itself, negotiated as part of the agreement. This has the virtue of simplicity, but is likely to become increasingly unrealistic by the passage of time as the corporation's fortunes wax or wane. A fixed price may be supplemented by an agreement to reset the price periodically, but the valuation of shares is such a difficult issue that it is easy for the shareholders to procrastinate and not reset the price. Also, if there is a wide age disparity among the shareholders and the corporation is profitable, the younger shareholders may be tempted to ignore the revaluation process (if the more senior shareholders fail to bring it up) on the theory they are likely to outlive the older shareholders and therefore will be able to purchase the shares at a price that does not reflect current market value. An automatic adjustment, e.g., the fixed price plus net earnings per share minus net losses per share may provide some desired flexibility, but such arrangements appear not to be widely used.

2. *Book Value*. Book value, discussed in detail in section 14.13, is simply the per share value of shares as reflected in the corporation's financial records normally computed either at the date of withdrawal, the end of the month during which the withdrawal occurs, or at the close of the year prior to, or during which, withdrawal occurs. Book value has the advantages of being easy to calculate and it also fluctuates more or less with the fortunes of the business. However, as discussed in Chapter 12, book value often fails to reflect accurately even the liquidation value of the business.[104] In fact, the market value of a closely held corporation logically should be calculated not on the basis of book value at all but on the basis of future earnings and cash-flow potential. A further complicating factor with book value, as often calculated in closely held corporations, is that accounting principles may be adapted by the specific corporation for the purpose of minimizing annual earnings. Where book value is utilized, the agreement may consider setting forth specific adjustments to be made and specific assets to be reappraised, in an effort to make book value a more realistic estimate of probable resale value. These various factors are discussed in some length in Chapter 14.

3. *Capitalization of Earnings*. A method of valuation which specifically addresses earning power involves the multiplication of average corporate earnings over the recent past by a capitalization factor obtained by analyzing price-earnings ratios of comparable publicly held companies in the same industry. This method of valuation, discussed in section 14.7 and subsequent sections, is not without its problems for a closely held business:

---

[104]The asset values shown in the corporation's books are suspect, particularly in periods of inflation, since they are calculated on the historical costs of assets rather than on current market values.

(1) accounting principles may be skewed in the direction of understating earnings and overstating expenses, (2) the estimate of earnings is usually based on earnings averaged over several years and may not accurately reflect anticipated future earnings, and (3) there may not be a truly analogous publicly held corporation from which a reliable capitalization ratio may be derived.

4. *Appraisal at Time of Triggering Event.* Yet another possibility is not to set the price in the buy-sell agreement, or specify a formula by which it can be calculated, but instead provide for an appraisal of the value of the business at the time the triggering event occurs. This solution has its own difficulties. The appraisal of the value of a closely held business is necessarily subjective to a considerable extent and may lead to widely varying results depending on what assumptions are used and what techniques are followed. The use of outside appraisers to determine the buyout price therefore involves the question, who is to select the appraisers? One possible solution is to have the corporation select one appraiser, the shareholder a second, and the two appraisers to select a third, perhaps from a list of appraisers provided by a third-party organization such as the American Institute of Appraisers.[105] Appraisal draws a third party into the valuation process and may lead to a number that is basically "off the scale" from the expectations of one (or even both) of the parties. Appraisal by three independent persons also strongly tends in the direction of the acceptance of a compromise or average valuation.

5. *Automatic Formulas.* Depending on the nature of the business it may be possible to devise a formula based on actual earnings or asset valuations that provides an automatic valuation of the firm. This method of valuation also may be used when the agreement provides that the purchase price is to be paid in installments depending on actual earnings for several years, though this may lose the benefit of the estate tax valuation that a fixed buy-sell agreement may provide. For example, a formula might be five times average earnings over the last three years plus book value, all divided by two.

6. *Reciprocal Options.* One may recall the story about cutting a cake to be divided among several brothers and sisters, with the one in charge of the cutting getting the last piece. Such a procedure gives a strong incentive to make equal-sized pieces. A somewhat similar device may be used in buy-sell agreements where the parties are alive. Under this type of arrangement, one party may set a price for his shares, and the other shareholders have an

---

[105] If this selection process is adopted, provision should be made for the eventuality that one party may refuse to cooperate in appointing an appraiser.

option either to buy his shares for that price or sell their shares to the offeror for that price. While intuitively appealing, this device tends to favor the party with the superior knowledge about the corporation's affairs and also the party with the greater wealth.

There is no general requirement that the price in a buy-sell agreement be fair or reasonable at the time the obligation to purchase matures. Courts have regularly upheld buy-sell agreements that involve a purchase price set many years earlier which now represents only a small fraction of the current value of the shares.[106] It is important, however, that the price be reasonable at the time it is set to avoid the argument that the provision is an unenforceable penalty rather than an attempt to liquidate the value of the shares in advance in good faith.

§8.32 ASSURING THE PAYMENT OF THE PURCHASE PRICE

In many instances, a shareholder whose shares are subject to purchase by the corporation or other shareholders have little concern about the purchaser's financial ability to complete the purchase. However, even where the transaction appears to be well within the corporation's financial ability at the time the buy-sell agreement is entered into there is always some risk that the corporation may not be able to perform its unsecured obligation when it matures because the corporation's business has suffered reverses. Failure to complete the purchase may be little short of catastrophic from the standpoint of the sellers.

Where the purchase price is to be paid in a lump sum, the ability of the corporation to use its own assets to complete the purchase may be barred by the legal restrictions on distributions and dividends described in Chapter 9.[107] Even where the corporation has adequate surplus to complete the transaction, the use of corporate funds may strip the corporation of working capital needed for the day-to-day business affairs of the corporation. In this situation, a corporation may be able to borrow the necessary funds from a third party on a long-term basis in order to complete the purchase of the shares. However, the redemption of shares constitutes a form of distribution that reduces the net worth of the corporation,[108] and commercial lenders

---

[106] A few courts have relieved the shareholder of her resale obligation in this situation, but these cases are distinctly in the minority. Where a court feels that the buyout price is clearly unfair, it is more likely to avoid the buyout obligation by determining that the shares in question are not subject to the buy-sell restriction because the various statutory requirements to impose such an obligation were not complied with or that for some reason the language of the buy-sell agreement does not cover the particular transaction in question.

[107] See §9.38.

[108] See §9.33 for a discussion of this basic fact.

may decline to make loans to a corporation for this purpose. Where this is the case, the corporation may find it impossible to complete the transaction without causing serious internal cash-flow problems.

There are at least three plausible solutions for these problems. The first is to require the remaining shareholders in the corporation to personally commit to purchase the shares if the corporation is unable or unwilling to do so. This may or may not be acceptable under the specific circumstances, depending in part on the number of remaining shareholders and their financial resources. The second is to provide in the buy-sell agreement that the purchase price is to be paid out in installments over time. In this way, the financial strain on the corporation is greatly reduced because the corporation may meet its obligations under the buy-sell agreement by utilizing future earnings and future cash flows. However, the right of the selling shareholder to receive the entire purchase price then remains dependent on the financial success of the corporation for an extended period into the future. The third possible solution is for the selling shareholder to accept a periodic payment schedule but demand that the corporation reflect its future obligation to make payments by a series of promissory notes and to secure the payments with security interests on corporate assets to assure that the balance of the purchase price will be paid even if the corporation is insolvent or has serious cash-flow problems. In this third scenario, the selling shareholder is in effect making a loan to the corporation by not demanding the purchase price be paid immediately, and these promissory notes and security interests simply reflect that fact. If the corporation does become insolvent, a serious priority issue arises as between the secured selling shareholder and the unpaid trade creditors of the corporation. The Model Business Corporation Act addresses this issue by providing that promissory notes and security interests created to secure the selling shareholder's claim against the corporation are not to be subordinated to the claims of the corporation's trade creditors.[109]

§8.33 STATUTORY REMEDIES FOR OPPRESSION AND DEADLOCK

State corporation statutes recognize the possibility of oppression and deadlock in a closely held corporation. Usually, these terms are not defined.

---

[109]Model Business Corporation Act §6.40(f). The theory underlying this result is that a loan by a selling shareholder should be treated no differently from a loan by an independent third party and the proceeds paid to the selling shareholder. If the transaction were structured in this way, an unsecured commercial lender would clearly be in parity with unsecured trade creditors, and the commercial lender could obtain priority by obtaining a security interest. The intent of §6.40(f) is to make the same rules applicable to the selling shareholder who accepts corporate promissory notes to reflect future payments.

The statute simply provides remedies for "illegal, oppressive, or fraudulent conduct" without more; the statute may define "deadlock" in terms of the shareholders being unable to elect new directors at a specified number of annual meetings. State statutes also include other bases for judicial intervention: the assets of the corporation are being "misapplied or wasted," or "irreparable injury" is being threatened or suffered by the corporation.[110] However, most of the cases arising under these provisions involve either oppression or deadlock.

There is a large amount of case law on the scope of these words, particularly *oppressive*. Courts have given broad definitions to this term. Perhaps the most common definition is conduct that "substantially defeats the expectations that objectively viewed were both reasonable under the circumstances and were central to the minority shareholder's decision to join the venture."[111] Another definition widely quoted is "burdensome, harsh and wrongful conduct," or "a visible departure from the standards of fair dealing, and a violation of fair play on which every shareholder who entrusts his money to a company is entitled to rely."[112]

The traditional remedy granted for oppressive conduct is involuntary dissolution, though case law and statute both recognize that this often-extreme remedy is within the discretion of the court. Because the remedy of involuntary dissolution seems draconian, particularly in the case of a corporation conducting a profitable business, many courts have been reluctant actually to dismember the corporation.[113] Case law has also demonstrated that in some circumstances involuntary dissolution may benefit rather than injure the dominant shareholders since it effectively eliminates unwanted shareholders.[114] Because of the draconian nature of the dissolution remedy, many state statutes provide for interim remedies short of an actual involuntary dissolution. Some statutes provide, for example, that in-

---

[110]Model Business Corporation Act §14.30(2).

[111]In re Weidy's Furniture Clearance Center Co., 487 N.Y.S.2d 901, 903 (App. Div. 1985).

[112]Baker v. Commercial Body Builders, 507 P.2d 387, 393 (Or. 1973).

[113]Two studies document not only that the number of cases in which involuntary dissolution has actually been ordered is small, but also the number of such cases is declining. Compare Hetherington & Dooley, Illiquidity and Exploitation: A Proposed Statutory Solution to the Remaining Close Corporation Problem, 63 Va. L. Rev. 1 (1976) with Haynsworth, The Effectiveness of Involuntary Dissolution Suits as a Remedy for Close Corporation Dissension, 35 Cleve. St. L. Rev. 25 (1987). Even where involuntary dissolution is ordered, the parties may subsequently reach agreement that permits the corporation to continue in existence.

[114]If the business is highly specialized and success is largely due to the personality and skill of the controlling shareholders, they may be able to buy the assets and goodwill of the corporation at a judicial sale at a favorable price. This appears to have been the situation in the leading case of In re Radom & Neidorff, 307 N.Y. 1, 119 N.E.2d 563 (1954), where the controlling shareholder unsuccessfully petitioned for involuntary dissolution.

voluntary dissolution must be preceded by a receivership designed to cure the basis for the claim for involuntary dissolution or authorize the court to appoint a custodian, or a temporary or independent director. The efficacy of these intermediate remedies is doubtful.

By far the most important alternative remedy recognized by some courts is a mandatory buyout: A judicial determination that the controlling shareholders must purchase the shares of the complaining shareholders at a price established by the court. This remedy appears to have increased significantly in popularity in the last 15 years as a significant number of courts have ordered such a buyout even in the absence of specific statutory language authorizing such a remedy.[115] In these cases, the court determines an appropriate value of the shares owned by the minority shareholders; it may then impose a discount for lack of marketability,[116] and then order the corporation or the minority shareholders to purchase at that price. If the purchasers fail to do so, the court may order the corporation to be dissolved.

There is much to be said for a mandatory buyout over involuntary dissolution. Its primary advantage is that it is much less disruptive to a profitable business. In effect, it imposes by judicial order the terms of a buyout agreement that the parties failed to negotiate some time earlier when they were in amity.

§8.34 SECTION 14.34 OF THE MODEL BUSINESS CORPORATION ACT

In 1991, the Committee on Corporate Laws adopted a new section of the Model Business Corporation Act that codifies the buyout remedy courts have devised to resolve oppression cases. However, the rules it imposes are much less flexible than the remedies devised by the courts. A major limitation of section 14.34 is that it is triggered only if a shareholder brings suit for involuntary dissolution under the traditional statute.[117] When such a suit is filed, the corporation or the remaining shareholders may elect to purchase the shares owned by the plaintiff. There is no reciprocity or discretion here; the shareholder who files the suit must be the seller if the corporation or the remaining shareholders make the election to purchase. As a result, a lawsuit to force involuntary dissolution becomes a high-risk enterprise. In the case of a deadlocked corporation with two 50 percent shareholders, it is easy to visualize a situation where neither party is willing to file the suit. In this situation, paradoxically, the effect of MBCA section

[115]This unusual development is discussed in Haynsworth, The Effectiveness of Involuntary Dissolution Suits as a Remedy for Close Corporation Dissension, 35 Cleve. St. L. Rev. 25 (1987).
[116]See §14.17.
[117]In the Model Business Corporation Act that is §14.30.

14.34 may be to chill attempts to obtain judicial assistance in resolving permanent deadlocks.

Section 14.34 gives little guidance as to how fair value should be determined. It is clearly an issue of fact on which expert testimony may be appropriate. The section does authorize the court to order the purchase price be paid in installments, and to allocate or apportion shares among the various shareholders of various classes "to preserve the existing distribution of voting rights among holders of different classes insofar as practicable." If the terms determined by the court are unacceptable to the corporation or its controlling shareholders, the corporation may elect to dissolve rather than complete the purchase.

§8.35 FIDUCIARY DUTIES WITHIN A CLOSE CORPORATION

The black letter rule of corporation law is that while directors owe fiduciary duties to the corporation,[118] shareholders do not owe such duties either to the corporation or to each other. A relatively recent development in corporation law is the recognition in many states that controlling shareholders in a closely held corporation in fact owe a fiduciary duty not to engage in transactions that are oppressive to minority shareholders.[119] In states that recognize this principle, non-controlling shareholders facing oppressive conduct may have a cause of action against the corporation and the controlling shareholders to ensure fair and equal treatment in the absence of statute.

The paradigm situation in which courts have found a fiduciary duty of controlling shareholders is where the controlling shareholders decide to cause the corporation to purchase some of their shares — but not enough shares to effect control — at a favorable price, while refusing to offer the same opportunity to the minority shareholders (or offering to purchase their shares only at a much lower price). Faced with this precise situation, a number of courts have held that a principle of equal opportunity must be applied to protect the minority shareholders. Courts have also applied a fiduciary duty to controlling shareholders who negotiate to purchase shares of minority shareholders without disclosing relevant information to them about the value of their shares or that the controlling shareholder has already obtained a right to resell the shares at a higher price.[120]

Many cases applying this fiduciary duty concept do so in broad terms

[118]See §8.10.

[119]The leading case taking this position is Donahue v. Rodd Electrotype Co., 367 Mass. 578, 328 N.E.2d 505 (1975). This decision has been widely cited and has been approved by courts in more than 20 states.

[120]See, e.g., Van Schaack Holdings, Ltd. v. Schaack, 867 P.2d 902 (Colo. 1994).

that literally may apply to all sorts of business transactions. For example, a minority shareholder who is fired as an employee may argue that such an action violates the fiduciary duty that controlling shareholders owe to minority shareholders. While it may be that injustice in fact occurred in some specific cases, a broad fiduciary duty in the close corporation context has a significant capacity for mischief, since it opens up litigation prospects to test the validity of many business decisions.

When a minority shareholder is fired, it may have been because he regularly drank too much alcohol at lunch and was ineffective for the rest of the day. It may have been because the nature of the corporation's business has changed and the skills of the minority shareholder were no longer needed by the corporation. It may have been because the corporation has hired a younger person who turns out to have superior skills so that the minority shareholder has become superfluous or redundant. Yet these clear business decisions may become litigable issues by a broad application of the fiduciary duty concept.

The fiduciary principle also has a significant capacity for mischief, since it may be utilized by a sophisticated investor to obtain a court order in effect rewriting the original "deal" he cut with the corporation. Law and economics scholars have also criticized the cases creating a special fiduciary duty on the ground that it imposes an *ex post* duty that the parties to the transaction almost certainly would not have selected if they had considered what term to include in their corporate "contract."

In a potentially important decision, the Delaware Supreme Court has rejected the holding of the cases described in the last paragraphs and refused to impose special judicially created duties for closely held corporations.[121]

§8.36 THE POWER TO EXPEL AN UNWANTED SHAREHOLDER

Corporations may use a statutory merger procedure to expel unwanted shareholders, compelling them to accept cash for their shares. At first blush, this power seems to border on the unconstitutional: after all a minority shareholder is in fact a shareholder and has a property interest in his shares. How can he be deprived of his shares without his consent?

A brief excursion into the law of corporate mergers is necessary to explain how this power crept into the modern law of corporations. The layperson's understanding of a merger is the coalescence of two independent corporations into a single corporation under the name of one of the two merging corporations. When Corporation A merges with Corporation B, Corporation B is the surviving corporation and shareholders of Corporation

---

[121]Nixon v. Blackwell, 626 A.2d 1366, 1380–1381 (Del. 1993).

A become shareholders in Corporation B on some predetermined ratio.[122] Many modern merger transactions are of this type, but many are not.

It has long been established that a merger of two corporations does not require the approval of each individual shareholder. For many years, the standard requirement was that persons holding two-thirds of all shares, voting and non-voting alike, of each corporation must approve the merger if it is to proceed. Most states today have reduced the minimum voting requirement to a majority of all the voting shares.[123]

Two new variables in the modern merger scene permit mergers to be used to expel unwanted shareholders: (1) mergers may be effectuated between parent and subsidiary or between corporations with common shareholders, and (2) most importantly, shareholders in any corporation that is a party to a merger may be entitled to receive "shares, obligations, or other securities of the surviving or any other corporation *or . . . cash or other property in whole or in part*."[124] Furthermore, the terms of the merger — including how much "cash or other property in whole or in part" shareholders are to receive in a merger — are to be determined and approved by the board of directors of the corporations planning to merge, and only then are they to be submitted to shareholders for a vote.

Let us consider how these rules might be used to expel an unwanted shareholder. X Corporation has three shareholders: A, B, and C each own 100 shares of common stock and each is a director of X Corporation. There is a falling out, and A and B decide they want to eliminate C as a shareholder. A and B therefore create a new corporation, Y Corporation in which they each own one share and are the sole two directors. C is not a shareholder in Y Corporation. A and B then cause X Corporation and Y Corporation to enter into a plan of merger on the following terms: X Corporation will transfer all its assets to Y Corporation, which is to be the surviving corporation. Shareholders A and B are to exchange their shares in X Corporation for $1 each and C is to exchange his shares in X Corporation for $10,000. Following the closing of the merger, A and B each own one share of Y Corporation (which now owns all the assets of the former X Corporation) while C has received $10,000 in cash from X Corporation but owns no shares in Y Corporation. C has in effect been "cashed out," presumably over his vehement protest and objection. But it happens all the time and is perfectly legal under the language of modern corporation statutes.

---

[122] A *consolidation* of two corporations, recognized in some states, is similar except that a new corporation, Corporation C, automatically springs into existence and is the continuing corporation. Shareholders of both Corporations A and B exchange their shares to become shareholders in Corporation C.

[123] Model Business Corporation Act §11.03(e). This is a higher requirement than for most other shareholder actions. Most shareholder actions must be approved only by a majority of shares present at a meeting at which a quorum is present. To approve a merger a majority of all the voting shareholders must approve the transaction.

[124] Model Business Corporation Act §11.01(a)(3) (emphasis added).

Where did the $10,000 figure come from? In effect, it was set by A and B when they decided to cash C out. They could equally well have chosen $5,000 or, for that matter, $5. If transactions of this type are to be permitted, there obviously has to be some way that the C's of this world can obtain an independent evaluation of the fairness of the transaction. And indeed there is. Corporation statutes provide *dissenters' rights* or "a right of dissent and appraisal" that permits a nonassenting party to a merger to reject the consideration offered for shares and obtain an independent judicial valuation of his or her shares.[125] This right of dissent and appraisal is not an inexpensive remedy from the standpoint of the corporation or the shareholders involved, and is the principal factor that induces A and B to give C fair value for his shares when setting up the terms of the merger.

A few judicial decisions intimate that unfair cash out merger transactions may violate fiduciary or other duties of controlling shareholders. Most states, however, appear to take the position that if the only complaint of the cashed-out shareholder is the adequacy of the price, the statutory appraisal procedure is that shareholder's sole remedy.[126]

§8.37 SPECIAL CLOSE CORPORATION STATUTES

Most states have modified the standard corporation form to some extent to reflect the peculiar problems of the closely held corporation. Provisions allowing action by written consent, increasing quorum and voting requirements, reducing the size of the board of directors, permitting one person to perform all corporate functions, and permitting some traditional directoral functions to be reserved to the shareholders are now very common. About 18 states have gone much further and authorized corporations that meet specific statutory definitions of a close corporation to abandon the traditional corporate structure and adopt quite radical management structures. These statutes also permit corporations to adopt special remedies for deadlock and oppression, such as dissolution on demand or mandatory buyouts.

The genesis of these special close corporation statutes is the famous decision in *Galler v. Galler,*[127] in which the court upheld an highly unorthodox shareholders' agreement in a two-person corporation. The opinion contains a strong plea to state legislatures to consider the unique problems and needs of closely held corporations.

While the special close corporation statutes vary widely from state to state, they have the common characteristic that they are optional and must

---

[125]Id. §13.01 et seq.
[126]The leading case in this respect is Weinberger v. UOP, Inc., 457 A.2d 701 (Del. 1983).
[127]32 Ill.2d 16, 203 N.E.2d 577 (1964).

be specifically elected by an eligible corporation by inclusion of a statement in the articles of incorporation that "this corporation is a statutory close corporation" or some other similar statement. Eligibility is usually defined by the number of shareholders: a maximum number of 25, 30, or 35 are typical.[128] These statutes permit an electing close corporation to dispense entirely with a board of directors and have the business conducted by the shareholders either following the partnership format or by adopting some other system of governance. Bylaws, meetings, and elections of managers may also be dispensed with. Shareholders' agreements are validated even though they interfere with the discretion of boards of directors. A variety of judicial remedies for oppression, dissension, or deadlock, including the appointment of provisional directors, are specifically authorized. Special dissolution provisions also may be included.

These special close corporation statutes have been widely praised by commentators but, rather surprisingly, they do not appear to be widely used "on the ground" by corporate practitioners. Studies in various states indicate that exercise of the close corporation election is relatively uncommon. This may indicate only that old habits of corporate lawyers die hard. It may also indicate, however, that the need for special treatment of close corporations has been overstated. In part because of this lack of widespread use of these special elections, the drafters of the Model Business Corporation Act withdrew a special "close corporation supplement" in 1992 and substituted a much simpler provision broadly validating all shareholder agreements relating to management within closely held corporations.[129]

§8.38 SECTION 7.32 OF THE MODEL BUSINESS CORPORATION ACT

Section 7.32 is a broad provision authorizing shareholders' agreements that depart completely from the traditional statutory scheme. An agreement entered into by all the shareholders at the time of the agreement may, among other things, eliminate the board of directors entirely, authorize distributions not in proportion to share ownership, establish who shall be directors or officers and specify their manner of selection, delegate the authority of the board of directors to one or more shareholders or other persons, require

---

[128]These statutes also usually deal with what happens when the number of shareholders exceed the maximum number set forth in the special statute. Indeed, many statutes have rather elaborate provisions dealing with how the election is to be made, which corporations are eligible for the election, and how the election may be revoked.

[129]Model Business Corporation Act §7.32. At the same time, §14.32 was added, authorizing courts to order buyouts of shares of plaintiffs bringing suit for involuntary dissolution for oppression or deadlock.

dissolution on demand of one or more shareholders or upon the occurrence of a specific contingency, and so forth. The Official Comment states that these provisions are illustrative and not exclusive. A further example given in that Comment approves a system of weighted voting for directors based on shareholdings. However, there are outer limits. The Official Comment suggests that a shareholder agreement that provides that the directors of the corporation have no duties of care or loyalty to the corporation or the shareholders would be beyond the purview of section 7.32. If the powers of directors are vested in persons other than directors, the directoral duties are imposed on those other persons.[130]

Shareholder agreements valid under section 7.32 are not legally binding on the state, on creditors, or on third parties. For example, a shareholders' agreement that provides that only the president has authority to enter into contracts would not preclude third persons from relying on other corporate officers' actions under general principles of agency. Special rules are also provided for persons who subsequently acquire shares in the closely held corporation. A purchaser of shares who is unaware of the existence of the agreement is bound by the agreement, but she is granted an unqualified power to rescind the purchase upon discovering the agreement. However, if the shares are represented by certificates that contain a proper legend, the purchaser is presumed to have knowledge of the existence of the agreement and has no power to rescind. Persons acquiring shares through gift or bequest also are bound by the agreement and have no power to rescind unless the contrary is provided in the agreement itself.

Agreements under this section are valid for ten years unless the agreement provides otherwise. Section 7.32 also provides that the agreement terminates automatically if the corporation makes a public offering of its shares.

PART D. PROFESSIONAL CORPORATIONS

§8.39 PROFESSIONAL CORPORATIONS

Individuals engaged in certain professions — law, medicine, and dentistry, primarily — have historically been prohibited by ethical considerations from conducting business in corporate form. The professional corporation is a specially developed business form that was created during the 1960s to enable professional firms to incorporate within the limits of the ethical proscriptions applicable to those professions. In some states, these entities

[130]Model Business Corporation Act §7.32(e).

may be known as "professional service companies," "professional associations," or by other names. Today, in the 1990s, they seem sort of a historical relic, containing restrictions and limitations that are out of keeping with modern limited liability companies and other business forms, but providing benefits in the form of limited liability to shareholders and some modest fringe tax benefits.

In the modern tax regime, tax rates applicable to individuals and corporations are such that businesses strongly desire to avoid corporate taxation in favor of partnership or conduit taxation. Back in the 1960s, marginal personal income tax rates were at very high levels, and quite the contrary was true: Successful professionals desired corporate taxation for their businesses primarily so they could be "employees" of the business and thereby become eligible to participate in tax-qualified employee retirement plans. The Internal Revenue Service has long taken the position that partners are "owners" of the partnership for tax purposes and therefore cannot be "employees" of the partnership. The professional corporation statutes were enacted by states in order to permit these professionals to become "employees" as well as shareholders.

A modern reader will immediately think that the professional corporation was also created in order to provide limited liability for professionals who often are the target of malpractice suits today. Rather surprisingly, this was not the case. In the 1960s, malpractice claims were not as common as they are today. Indeed, law firms routinely conducted business as general partnerships with little concern about individual liability; many firms during this period did not carry malpractice insurance, even though that insurance was generally available and very inexpensive (at least as compared to current costs of malpractice insurance). Limited liability, to the extent it was a factor at all, was distinctly secondary and subordinate to the desire of partners to become "employees."

The most important tax benefits available to employees in the 1960s (that were not available to business owners, including partners) were qualified pension or profitsharing retirement plans. Under these plans, the employer made tax-deductible contributions each pay period to specially created trusts for the exclusive benefit of permanent employees. The amount of the contribution was based either on a formula usually dependent either on the employer's profits or the employee's salary (a *defined contribution plan*) or on an actuarial computation to provide each employee with a pension of a specified amount upon retirement (a *defined benefit plan*). Such plans might be entirely employer-funded or contributory, with the employer making its own contribution and also withholding some relatively small amount from each employee's salary check. The great beauty of these plans was that each employee-beneficiary was not taxable on the plan benefits until they were actually distributed to her. Further, the employer received an immediate tax deduction for the payment to the plan and the income from the funds invested in the plan was not taxed at all until funds were distributed to the employee. For a law firm, for example, the professional corporation device permitted the partnership to create a huge tax-deferred savings account for each partner (without tax cost to the professional corporation) that grew tax-free and became taxable only when and to the extent of payments to the partner many years later, after retirement.

The first state professional corporation statutes were developed in about 1960 and promptly enacted in virtually all states. Thousands of professional firms have since incorporated under these statutes. These statutes have certain common characteristics.[131] By and large, these characteristics mirror similar rules established by bar associations or state supreme courts, medical and dental licensure boards, and similar governmental regulation of professional firms. These characteristics include:

1. A professional corporation may be formed to engage in only one professional service.[132]
2. All the shareholders of the corporation must be professionals licensed to practice that professional service. Since usually only individuals may be licensed to practice these professions, the practical effect is to limit shareholders to individuals.
3. In the event shares pass by involuntary transfer to a person who is not licensed to practice that professional service, the shares must promptly be sold back to the corporation,[133] or to another licensed professional. Some states specify the price at which the shares are to be sold, usually book value or "fair value." If a transfer cannot be made, the corporation must withdraw from the practice of the profession and be dissolved.
4. If a shareholder is disqualified from professional practice, the shares owned by that shareholder must be sold to the corporation or to another licensed professional.
5. About a dozen states prohibit a licensed professional from simultaneously owning stock in two or more professional corporations.
6. Incorporation does not affect the personal liability of a professional who commits negligence or malpractice while engaged in professional activities. The extent to which incorporation provides limited liability against other types of claims varies from state to state.
7. The name of the corporation must include the initials "P.C." or otherwise identify the corporation as a professional corporation.

[131] There are individual exceptions to virtually all the statements set forth immediately below. This enumeration reflects the positions taken by the majority of state statutes.

[132] A few states permit two different professional services, e.g., architecture and engineering, to be performed by one professional corporation.

[133] This is feasible, of course, only if the professional corporation has qualified shareholders other than the shareholder whose shares are being transferred.

8.   The corporation may not engage in outside business activities other than those incidental to provision of professional services.
9.   To the extent matters are not dealt with specifically in the professional corporation statute, the provisions of the state business corporation statute controls.

In 1982, Congress eliminated the tax advantage that professional corporations had over general partnerships by equalizing the retirement benefits available to professional corporations and those available to partners creating Keogh plans.[134] The Tax Equity and Fiscal Responsibility Act of 1982 (TEFRA) essentially eliminated the federal income tax benefits that had been the subject of the professional corporation battle for 20 years. TEFRA reduced the maximum deductions permitted for defined benefit plans, increased the maximum deductions permitted for Keogh plans created by personal service corporations, and then applied the same maximums consistently to both Keogh plans and qualified retirement plans maintained on behalf of personal service corporation employees. Thus, in a single stroke, the principal benefit of professional incorporation was eliminated, since a profession could conduct business as a proprietorship or partnership and obtain the same retirement income benefits through a Keogh plan that could be obtained through a professional corporation.

At the time, Congress expected that professional corporations would gradually disappear. That expectation has not been not borne out. By the early 1980s, liability concerns for professionals had emerged as a major problem, and the proliferation of malpractice suits in the United States made it clear that limited liability might itself be a sufficient justification for utilizing a professional corporation for a professional practice. Several state statutes were quietly amended in order to make it perfectly clear that shareholders of a professional corporation have the same — but no greater — liability than shareholders in an ordinary business corporation.[135]

[134.] 1962, Congress responded partially to the complaints by professionals that they were being discriminated against by reason of their inability to obtain employee tax benefits by enacting legislation that specifically permitted owners of unincorporated businesses to create personal, limited self-employed qualified retirement plans. These plans are known as "Keogh Plans." A partner or self-employed individual may create a Keogh plan and make contributions to the Plan that are tax deductible. The earnings in the Keogh Plan thereafter grow on a tax-deferred basis until the partner or self-employed individual begins to withdraw the funds after retirement. The initial Keogh plan legislation failed to quell the demand for corporate tax treatment for professionals primarily because maximum tax deductions initially were very low: they were limited to $2,500 per year in 1962 and had increased to only $7,500 per year by 1973.

[135] Some professional corporation statutes made it clear that shareholders in professional corporations were to be treated the same way as shareholders in ordinary business corporations for liability purposes. However, because many statutes were not crystal-clear on the question (and because there is a long history and tradition that professionals have personal

Not only did businesses already formed as professional corporations continue to do business in this form but new firms have elected to become professional corporations. Thus, the professional corporation has remained a permanent part of the business association scene. This can be traced primarily to two factors: fringe tax benefits and limited liability.[136]

In the modern era, there has been a movement away from a single professional corporation for an entire firm. Rather, each partner sets up his or her own professional corporation, and the firm then becomes a partnership of the professional corporations and the individuals who elected not to form professional corporations. The professional corporation that was a partner provides services to the firm through an "employee" who is of course the shareholder of the professional corporation. Many law firms today have this structure. Their letterhead usually identifies themselves as being a "partnership composed of professional corporations and individuals."

There are two major advantages to this structure. First, it permits each professional to tailor his or her own retirement plan to the needs of that individual rather than creating a global retirement plan for all professionals in the firm. For example, a professional in her early 50s might adopt a defined benefit plan while a professional in his early 30s might adopt a defined contribution plan. Second, it avoids problems of discrimination and top-heaviness. Secretaries, messengers, file clerks, data entry employees, and the like are all employees of the partnership, not employees of the individual professional corporations. Whether these lower-paid personnel should have retirement benefits at all, and how generous their plan should be, become issues entirely independent of the question of the generosity of the retirement benefits being provided to the professionals themselves.[137] The

---

liability for their acts and the acts of their partners), the case law has not been uniform. At least two state supreme courts have held that shareholders in a legal professional corporation have personal liability for malpractice committed by other shareholders or professional employees. There is also contrary authority. The decisions imposing partnership-like liability on shareholders in professional corporations seem quite anomalous in light of the widespread acceptance of limited liability today, and it seems likely that cases imposing personal liability upon nonparticipating shareholders will be reconsidered in the future.

[136]An additional problem of converting existing professional corporations to some other business forms is that there may be adverse tax consequences through the "bunching" of income if they elect to be reconstituted as a limited liability company or other unincorporated business form. This "bunching" doubtless deterred some professional corporations converting to other business forms.

[137]Some professionals choose not to form professional corporations and remain as individual partners in the firm itself. Those professionals are not be entitled to participate in the firm's employee retirement plan, if there is one (since they are not employees). Associates, however, presumably would be eligible to participate as employees in the firm's employee retirement plan.

Some partners decline to form professional corporations despite the obvious tax benefits. The reasons vary widely. Some once believed that the whole idea was "gimmicky" and could not last; others simply were satisfied with the status quo.

Internal Revenue Service unsuccessfully attacked this structure on the theory that it served no business purpose except the avoidance of taxes.[138]

Another partial explanation for the continuation of professional corporations is that corporations may provide some minor tax benefits not available to proprietors or partners. The most important benefit today is that employers may provide accident and health insurance plans for employees without having the value of that benefit be included in the employees' taxable income. The cost of such insurance plans is immediately deductible by the employer. As the cost of health insurance has steadily risen, this benefit has increased in importance. A corporation may also provide employees (on a tax-deductible, nonincludible basis) with group life insurance in an amount up to $50,000. A death benefit of up to $5,000 may also be provided. While it is doubtful if these benefits alone are of sufficient importance to justify the use of an otherwise obsolete business form, they do provide some advantages in addition to the principal benefit of limited liability.

The professional corporation continues to be used to a greater or lesser degree today primarily because of the advantage it provides in the form of limited liability. Today, however, the popularity of professional corporations appears to be declining in the states where the listed professions may conduct business in the form of limited liability companies, which are simpler, less expensive, and much more flexible.[139]

---

[138]Keller v. Commissioner, 77 T.C. 1014 (1981).

[139]See Chapter 6. The flexibility of the LLC should be contrasted with the very narrow and detailed rules applicable to most professional corporations. Professional corporations may also be subject to state franchise and other taxes that are not applicable to LLCs.

9

Financial Aspects of Closely Held Corporations

§9.1   INTRODUCTION

This chapter deals with three basic topics. First it deals with the federal law of taxation of incorporated entities, particularly small, closely held corporations. This discussion is of central importance to understanding the reasons for the growth of limited liability companies discussed in Chapter 6.

Second, it provides basic information about how close corporations are financed, including a discussion of traditional (and not so traditional) corporate securities. The basic lore of corporate securities discussed in this chapter is equally applicable to securities issued by publicly held corporations. Perhaps no other area of corporation law is more confusing to persons without prior business backgrounds than corporate securities. The language is new and unfamiliar, the concepts seem mysterious and sometimes illogical, and everything seems to build on historical concepts of dubious relevance today. This chapter should help to dispel this mystery. The rights given to security holders by statute or by contract build on simple principles. Words such as cumulative or convertible may sound difficult and confusing, but the concepts are not.

Third, this chapter deals with the legal rules applicable to the issuance of shares by closely held corporations and to the distribution of assets by closely held corporations, in the form of dividends, and the provision of informal benefits to shareholders. This discussion is predominantly legal in nature.

A. CORPORATE TAXATION

§9.2 TAX TREATMENT OF CORPORATIONS IN GENERAL

The federal income tax treatment of corporations differs significantly from that of the various forms of unincorporated associations or entities discussed in earlier chapters in this volume.[1] In general terms, unincorporated associations or entities are not separate taxable units. Rather, the various tax consequences of their activities are passed through to the owners who must include gains, losses, income, deductions, and so forth on their individual returns. This method of taxation is usually described as conduit or pass through taxation.

The starting point for corporate taxation is this: The corporation is a separate taxable entity independent of its shareholders.[2] Thus, the earnings of a corporation may be subject to federal income taxation at two different levels: at the corporate level on the corporation's "taxable income" (see section 9.5) and a second time, at the shareholders' level when the corporation distributes assets to the shareholders. Of course, a corporation is not required to make distributions to its shareholders, and no tax is due at the shareholders' level until distributions are made. If the corporation is profitable but distributions are not made, the value of the assets of the corporation will increase. Shareholders may be able to capture this increase in value indirectly by selling their shares of stock to a third person. The gain from such a sale will usually be taxed as a long-term capital gain subject to a flat tax rate of 28 percent.

This basic difference in approach toward the tax treatment of business entities may have dramatic impact on the tax liability of an entity and its owners, depending on the way the entity is classified. It therefore places great stress on the rules that determine which entities should be taxed as corporations and which should be taxed as partnerships. It would have been simplest, perhaps, to classify entities on a straight state law test: entities formed under the corporation law statutes of a state must be taxed as corporations while entities formed under other statutes or under common law must be taxed as conduits. However, the federal tax authorities resisted adopting this simple test, apparently because of concern that it would have made the selection of the form of taxation entirely elective, given the interchangeability of the various business forms. The classification test currently

---

[1] Indeed, much of the justification for the development of newer forms of business has been to avoid the corporate income tax.

[2] I.R.C. §11(a) imposes a separate tax on the income of corporations, while §301 imposes a tax on shareholders on distributions to them of property from corporations.

proposed by the Internal Revenue Service, embodied in the so-called check the box regulations described earlier,[3] in fact makes the tax classification for unincorporated business forms entirely elective. Corporations, however, are not eligible for check the box treatment.

To complicate matters even further, federal income taxation of corporations is not monolithic. In 1957, Congress created a special tax election for certain corporations, the S corporation election, that permits most corporations with less than 35 shareholders to elect to be taxed in a manner that generally permits income to be passed through the corporation and be taxed directly to shareholders. Subchapter S tax treatment is similar to (but in some respects significantly different from) the conduit tax treatment applicable to partnerships and other unincorporated entities. A corporation that has elected to be taxed under subchapter S is called, not surprisingly, an *S corporation*.[4] Subchapter S itself is discussed briefly in sections 9.6 and 9.7. A corporation that has not elected to be an S corporation is called a C *corporation* since the corporate income tax is imposed by Subchapter C of the Internal Revenue Code. The discussion that immediately follows deals with the traditional tax treatment of corporations that have not elected S corporation treatment. Since the S corporation election is available only for corporations with fewer than 75 shareholders, all large publicly held corporations have no choice but to be C corporations. In addition, many smaller corporations may be ineligible for S corporation treatment, or may not elect such treatment if it is available, so that C corporations include many small, closely held businesses.

In summary, there are two basic taxation schemes currently applicable to general business entities:[5] "pure" conduit taxation, and C corporation taxation. S corporation taxation is a variant of conduit taxation.

§9.3 C CORPORATIONS AND DOUBLE TAXATION

A C corporation is a separate taxpayer that must pay taxes on its income according to a tax rate schedule set forth in the Internal Revenue Code that is different from the schedules applicable to individuals. As of 1996, the corporate tax schedule begins at 15 percent (on the first $50,000 of income) to a maximum tax of 35 percent applicable to corporate income in

[3]See §4.22 and §5.18.
[4]I.R.C. §1361(a)(2).
[5]To complicate matters even further, there are special tax regimes created for nonprofit entities and for a variety of specialized for-profit entities not subject to general corporate taxation. Perhaps the best known of these specialized tax schemes is the system applicable to mutual funds.

excess of $10 million.[6] C corporation taxation involves double taxation in this sense: The corporation is first taxed directly on its income, calculated using this corporate rate schedule. If it then makes distributions to its shareholders, the amount of those distributions is subject to a second tax at the shareholder level to the extent the distributions reflect corporate earnings and profits.[7] From the prism of a shareholder in a closely held corporation who must have distributions in order to meet ordinary living expenses, this double taxation has long been viewed as unfair, as a needless penalty on the use of the corporate form of business, and as the imposition of an unreasonably high tax on corporate earnings.

The extent of the penalty caused by this double tax depends not only on the tax rates applicable to corporations but also the rates applicable to individual shareholders. The effect of the double tax at 1994 rate levels is a good illustration. If a corporation has exactly $100,000 of taxable income in 1994, it will pay a tax of $22,250, reducing the income available for distribution to $77,750. The tax due on this distribution depends on the shareholder's other income, deductions, and marital status. If we assume that there is only one shareholder, a married person filing a joint return, with precisely $140,000 of taxable income from salaries and other sources, and the couple of which the shareholder is a member is in the 36 percent bracket, the distribution of the extra $77,750 will increase the couple's tax bill by $27,990 ($77,750 × .36 = $27,790). Of the $100,000 of taxable income originally received by the corporation, the shareholder will be able to retain exactly $49,760 ($77,750 − $27,990 = $49,760) after all taxes have been paid. Even though the effective corporate rate was 34 percent and the effective personal rate was 35 percent, the effective tax rate on the corporation and shareholder combined is 50.24 percent.

If the same business had been operated in a form that provided for conduit tax treatment, the shareholder's total income would have been increased from $140,000 to $240,000 by the inclusion of the corporation's income in the shareholder's tax return. The additional income would have

---

[6]The corporate tax schedule is complicated by the fact that special surtaxes are applicable at specified income levels to "recapture" the benefits of the lower marginal rates on corporate income.

[7]The tax treatment of individuals is considerably more complicated than that applicable to C corporations and cannot be summarized simply. Separate rate schedules are applicable to four different classes of taxpayers; there are recapture provisions for certain exemptions and personal deductions at varying levels of income, and there are special schedules for taxpayers with relatively small incomes. For more affluent taxpayers, the lowest tax bracket for a married couple filing a joint return is 15 percent for incomes up to $36,900, followed by a 28 percent bracket for incomes between $36,900 and $89,150, a 31 percent bracket for incomes between $89,150 and $140,000, a 36 percent bracket for incomes between $140,000 and $250,000, and a 39.6 bracket for incomes above $250,000. These are marginal rates applicable to incomes within the designated brackets.

been taxed at the 36 percent rate, and the couple's tax bill would thereby have been increased by exactly $36,000.[8] In this scenario, the couple would have retained $64,000 from the corporation after tax. In other words, permitting the income to be taxed twice in the C corporation creates a minor disaster, costing the shareholder an additional $13,760 ($49,760 - $36,000 = $13,760) in unnecessary taxes in a single year.

Corporate earnings of C corporations are subject to the double tax only to the extent earnings are distributed to the shareholders. If they are retained in the business, they are taxed only once, at the applicable corporate rate. Of course, the shareholders then do not have the direct use of those earnings since they are technically owned by the corporation and not by the shareholders. However, it is usually possible to structure the contractual relationships between the corporation and the shareholder in such a way that most of the distribution to the shareholder is deductible by the corporation as salary, rent, interest, or other deductible payment,[9] rather than as a distribution that is a nondeductible dividend. This reduces the double tax bite by eliminating the tax at the corporate level.

In some situations, it may be attractive not to make distributions and allow the earnings to accumulate in the corporation. Of course, it is expected by the shareholders that earnings will have to be withdrawn at some point and so the second tax at the shareholder level is presumptively deferred but not eliminated. The simplest way of "withdrawing" the earnings is by selling all the shares to some third party. At that point, the shareholders will realize gain equal to the difference between their basis[10] for the shares and the sales price. However, this gain, which presumably incorporates the accumulated earnings, will usually be taxable as a long-term capital gain rather than as ordinary income, which reduces somewhat the second tax "bite."

In an earlier era, the individual income tax rates for ordinary income

---

[8]This additional tax would be due whether or not distributions were made by the entity to its owner. If it is assumed consistent with the textual hypothetical that the entity distributes the entire $100,000 to the owner, the owner's after-tax income would be increased by $64,000.

[9]Other suggestions might include having the corporation lease an automobile for the use of the shareholder that qualifies as an "ordinary and necessary" expense from the standpoint of the corporation, provide a country club membership for the shareholder if business is extensively conducted at that location, and so forth. If these are ordinary and necessary expenses of the corporation, they are deductible by it and are not income taxable to the shareholder. Of course, claiming deductions of this nature, particularly if substantial in amount, might trigger an audit of the corporation's tax returns, and if such amounts are disallowed, the Internal Revenue Service will view the payments to the automobile leasing company or country club as constructive dividends to the shareholder as well as disallowing their deduction by the corporation.

[10]*Basis* in the tax context means essentially the amount invested in the asset being disposed of, i.e., its aggregate costs.

266

were at a very high level (as high as 90 percent immediately after World War II) while capital gains rates were "capped" at 25 percent. Under this tax regime, the strategy of accumulation followed by sale of the stock was so common that it has its own name: the "accumulate and bail out" strategy. Today, the accumulate and bail out strategy is less attractive than it was in the post-World War II era, when the differential between capital gain and ordinary income marginal rates was as large as 65 percentage points. Today, the capital gains tax rate is 28 per cent while the maximum individual income tax rate is 39.6 per cent, still significant but not as massive a difference.[11] For persons in the 39.6 percent bracket, the accumulate and bail out strategy may yield a better tax result than the S corporation election or by a partial "zeroing out" of corporate income by tax-deductible payments to shareholders.

The accumulate and bail out strategy is most attractive for elderly shareholders who do not need current distributions for living expenses. When a shareholder dies owning the appreciated shares, the tax law provides a "stepped up" basis for the deceased's property equal to the fair market value of the property at the date of death, and the increase in basis is never subject to income tax by anyone. This yields the "best" income tax result; however, the fair value of the shares may be subject to estate taxation.

A final alternative is to give shares to children or grandchildren in relatively small amounts that avoid gift taxes.[12] The gift of shares results in a transfer of the donor's tax basis to the donee, so the children or grandchildren would have to pay income tax on the gain from any resale of the shares.[13]

It perhaps bears emphasizing that the double taxation problem is of concern primarily for shareholders who are individuals. It is not generally a problem for shareholders who are corporations since a dividend-received deduction is available for corporate shareholders based on their percentage of ownership.[14] This deduction ranges from a 100 percent deduction for dividends paid to an affiliated corporation that owns 80 percent or more of the voting power and value of the payer's stock to a 70 percent deduction for dividends paid to corporations owning less than 20 percent of the payer's stock.

---

[11]Prior to 1986, the voluntary dissolution of a profitable corporation was attractive because unrealized appreciation of corporate assets escaped income taxation entirely under a principle known as the *General Utilities* doctrine. The 1986 Tax Act repealed this doctrine, thereby greatly complicating conversions of ongoing corporations into other business forms.

[12]Estate planning for a wealthy individual whose major asset consists of a closely held business is a complex subject that is necessarily beyond the scope of this chapter.

[13]The so-called kiddie tax greatly reduces the attractiveness of gifts to children or grandchildren under the age of 14 since it taxes income to the children at the marginal rate applicable to the donor.

[14]I.R.C. §243.

§9.4 ECONOMIC EFFECTS OF THE DOUBLE TAX REGIME

From an economic standpoint, the double tax structure applicable to corporations has serious economic costs. For example, it encourages indirect distributions that are claimed as tax deductions by the corporation. It is common practice for closely held corporations to provide automobiles, country club memberships, and the like for shareholder/employees. The corporate tax treatment also imposes tax at the corporate level without regard to shareholder characteristics, arguably overtaxing low bracket or tax-exempt shareholders. It encourages the excessive use of debt since corporations prefer debt financing rather than equity financing because interest payments are tax deductible while dividend payments are not. It leads corporations to adopt a policy of retaining excess earnings within the corporation rather than distributing them promptly to shareholders who may reinvest them. It therefore encourages overinvestment at the corporate level and a misallocation of limited capital resources. Finally, it deters the use of the corporate form of business for closely held businesses and encourages the development of new business forms whose principal advantage is tax savings. Arguably none of these practices are in the best interest of society generally.[15]

Virtually all industrialized nations do not impose a double tax burden on corporate distributions; the United States is unique in this respect. As a result, there have been numerous proposals to amend the tax structure in some way in order to eliminate the double tax. Tax academics generally support the Haig-Simons view that an individual should be taxed only on her accretion of wealth and no source-based rules should be imposed. While this ideal is easy to state, and there is no shortage of suggestions as to how integration may be achieved, there are serious problems in implementation.

The double taxation problem might be eliminated by the outright repeal of the corporate income tax or by permitting corporations to deduct dividend payments the way they now deduct interest payments. Shareholders might be permitted to exclude all or a substantial portion of dividend distributions from their adjusted gross income[16] or to treat corporate tax payments as a credit against their own tax bill in much the same way an employer creates credits for individual taxpayers by withholding income.

---

[15]The issue of who actually bears the cost of the double taxation imposed on corporations is a difficult one, but there is general agreement by economists that the double taxation environment does not lead to optimal results. See Arlen and Weiss, The Political Economy of Double Corporate Taxation, U. So. Cal. Working Paper No. 94-2 (1994).

[16]At the present time, there is available to individuals a very modest dividend-received exclusion.

Plans to eliminate the double tax are generally referred to as *integration proposals*.

Enactment of an integration proposal requires recognition of certain political realities and numerous conflicting claims of equity. The simple fact is that the present law has developed a morass of tax preferences, rules of deductibility, and special tax rates for certain types of receipts, e.g., capital gains, or for certain types of taxpayers. Integration is difficult because it reopens many controversial and difficult issues over which figurative blood has been shed in the past.[17]

While amendments to the Internal Revenue Code eliminating the double taxation of dividends is possible, as this is written it does not appear to have very high priority. In part, this may be because the development of the limited liability company, discussed in Chapter 6, permits businesses with relatively few owners to obtain the desired limited liability benefits of incorporation combined with true conduit or pass through taxation.

§9.5 TAXATION OF C CORPORATION INCOME

A C corporation calculates its taxable income in a manner that is analogous to the calculation of an individual's taxable income,[18] but there are some important differences. A corporation is not entitled to personal exemptions or standard deductions, which presumably were designed to provide some tax-free income for individuals and families for purposes of support, food, shelter, clothing, education of children, and medical attention. However, corporations are entitled to some deductions not available to individuals, for example the dividend-received deduction for distributions from corporations in which the corporate taxpayer has a specified economic interest. Corporations generally must adopt an accrual method of accounting for tax purposes;[19] unlike individuals, they may not elect a cash basis accounting system.[20] Corporations are entitled to select fiscal years for tax purposes that need not be based on the calendar year ending December 31; individuals and most partnerships do not have this power.

---

[17]It may be noted that tax integration did not even make the grade of the Republican's "Contract with America" in 1995, a grab bag of issues representing dissatisfaction as to the current state of governmental affairs.

[18]That is, in the same manner as a sole proprietor filing a schedule C to her form 1040 (see §3.18) or a partnerhsip filing a form 1065 (see §4.22).

[19]For a discussion of the difference between cash and accrual accounting systems, see §§11.2, 11.7, 12.2, and 12.3.

[20]Exceptions are made for qualified personal service corporations and corporations having average annual gross receipts of $5 million or less. I.R.C. §§482(b)(2), (3).

Shareholders of a C corporation may not take advantage of operating losses incurred by the corporation. Losses may be carried over by the corporation backward or forward to years in which the corporation has taxable income. A major advantage of unincorporated businesses taxable on the conduit basis or the S corporation election is that unlike C corporations, operating losses may be passed through to the owners or shareholders to shield other income from tax.

There are several special tax rules that are applicable only to C corporations and are designed to prevent or limit tax avoidance by the corporation and its owners. Perhaps most important is the alternative minimum tax applicable to corporations that limits the use of a variety of different tax exclusions, deductions, or credits that were created to encourage corporate economic activity.[21] Another important provision is section 531 of the Internal Revenue Code that is designed to limit the use of the accumulate and bail out strategy described in section 9.3. Section 531 imposes a special penalty tax on corporations "formed or availed of for the purpose of avoiding the income tax with respect to its shareholders or the shareholders of any other corporation, by permitting earnings and profits to accumulate [beyond the reasonable needs of the business] instead of being divided or distributed."[22] The possible application of this tax may cause a closely held corporation to declare dividends despite the adverse tax effect of such a distribution.

A second special tax provision that is of direct relevance to lawyers and other professionals is the special flat 35 percent tax rate applicable to *qualified personal service corporations*, which is defined as a corporation substantially all of the activities of which involve the performance of services and substantially all of the stock of which is held by employees or former employees (or estates of any of the foregoing) of the corporation.[23] This special tax eliminates the incentive of persons providing professional services to set up a corporation to take advantage of the 15 and 25 percent corporate brackets in lieu of conducting business as a proprietorship or partnership.

Yet another set of tax provisions are designed to prevent a corporation from taking advantage of tax-oriented strategies that have no significant business purpose. For example, one provision prohibits a single business

---

[21]The *alternative minimum tax*, or AMT as it is usually called, is a tax system largely independent of the regular corporate tax structure. The calculation of this tax is complex. A corporation must calculate its tax liability, first on the basis of the regular tax system, and second on the basis of the alternative minimum tax rules, and then pay whichever tax is higher. Many major corporatios have to pay substantial AMT even though they owe little or no regular corporate tax.

[22]I.R.C. §532.

[23]I.R.C. §448(d)(2).

from breaking itself into several different corporations in order to reduce taxes by permitting each corporation to take advantage of the 15, 25, and 35 percent brackets.[24] Other provisions permit the Internal Revenue Service to attack specific intrafamily corporate transactions that are primarily driven by tax-avoidance goals and to disallow deductions, credits, or allowances arising from acquisitions of businesses the principal purpose of which was avoidance or evasion of income taxes.[25] Yet another section authorizes the Service to allocate items of gross income and deductions among commonly controlled groups of organizations, trades, or businesses to prevent evasion of tax and to clearly reflect the income of any such trade or business.[26] Finally, the case law has developed a doctrine that permits the Service to ignore corporations that are "shams," multiple corporations that "exist in name only, serving no business purpose and in reality performing no business or other functions."[27] However, there is a presumption that a corporation validly created under state law has a legitimate business purpose if the formalities have been observed.

§9.6 THE S CORPORATION ELECTION IN GENERAL

As indicated above, the major alternative to C corporation tax treatment is the S corporation election. The effect of this election is that the corporation has many of the tax characteristics of a conduit entity, with corporate income or loss being allocated to the shareholders. This election is available only if the corporation has fewer than 75 shareholders. Additional prerequisites that must be met before a corporation becomes eligible for this election include: (1) all shareholders must be individuals (with a limited exception for estates of decedents and certain trusts), (2) no shareholder may be a nonresident alien, (3) the corporation must have only one class of stock, and (4) the corporation itself may not have subsidiaries, i.e., it may not be part of an "affiliated group" as defined in the Internal Revenue Code.[28] There is no size limitation on corporations eligible for the S corporation election, though most businesses eligible for that election are relatively

---

[24]Id. §1561.

[25]Id. §269.

[26]Id. §482.

[27]See, for example, Greenberg v. Commission, 62 T.C. 331 (1974), *aff'd per curiam*, 526 F.2d 588 (4th Cir. 1975), *cert. denied*, 423 U.S. 1052 (1976).

[28]In 1996, an amendment to the Internal Revenue Code relaxed these limitations. For example, the maximum number of shareholders was increased to 75 and an S corporation was permitted to have subsidiaries.

small. However, some very large and profitable businesses are eligible for the S corporation election.[29]

The reason why all of these technical requirements were originally imposed, or why they survive today, is in some respects unclear,[30] and the 1996 amendments simplified the S corporation election requirements. However, a recurring problem is whether transactions that involve the issuance of debt might disqualify the corporation from the S corporation election on the theory that the debt might be considered a second class of stock by the Internal Revenue Service.[31]

An S corporation election can be made relatively easily. It requires the written consent of all persons who are shareholders on the day the election is made. Once made, the election continues indefinitely. It may be terminated by a voluntary revocation by more than 50 percent of all the shareholders, by the failure of the corporation to satisfy any of the requirements for qualification (e.g., by having more than 75 shareholders or having an ineligible entity as a shareholder), or in certain other limited instances. Generally, a corporation can move from being an S corporation to a C corporation at any time, but if it does so, it cannot again elect to return to being an S corporation for five years unless the Internal Revenue Service consents.

One undesirable feature of the S corporation election is that technical rules about disqualification make it relatively easy for a single shareholder in an S corporation to commit some act that effectively revokes that election, e.g., by transferring her shares to an ineligible shareholder or to another corporation, or by dividing up her shares so that there are more than 75 shareholders. In some instances in which there is conflict within the corporation, the threat by a minority shareholder to commit such an act carries some weight, even though the consequences probably will be to create financial injury in the form of increased tax liabilities for all sharehold-

---

[29]Following the 1986 tax legislation, it became attractive for profitable corporations to elect S corporation tax treatment. Many highly profitable closely held corporations therefore rearranged their capital structure by eliminating senior classes of stock and by dissolving subsidiaries into the corporation in order to meet the S corporation requirements.

[30]The underlying purpose was to assure that shareholders bearing the tax burden were in fact the true economic beneficiaries of the corporation's activities. However, this justification does not explain all the technical rules.

[31]In 1982, Congress enacted Internal Revenue Code §1361(c)(5) to address the reclassification of debt issue. That section defines *straight debt* to be debt that involves a written unconditional promise to pay a sum certain in money if (a) repayment and interest are not contingent on profits, the borrower's discretion, or similar factors, (b) there is no direct or indirect inconvertibility into shares, and (c) the creditor is eligible to be an S corporation shareholder. Straight debt is a safe harbor, ensuring that such debt will not be classified as a second class of stock for S corporation purposes.

ers. In order to prevent this tactic, share transfer restrictions may be imposed that effectively prohibit the minority shareholder from transferring her shares.[32] In the absence of advance planning, however, the S corporation election itself may well become a bargaining chip in resolving intracorporate conflict.

§9.7 THE S CORPORATION: A LIMITED CONDUIT

S corporation tax treatment is often described as pass through or partnership-type tax treatment. While the S corporation election makes partnership-type taxation generally available to small corporations, there are significant differences in detail between the tax treatment of an S corporation and the tax treatment of a proprietorship or partnership.[33] These differences reduce significantly the attractiveness of the S corporation alternative when contrasted with true partnership type taxation. These technical tax rules, together with the procedural requirements for making and revoking the S corporation election, doubtless have encouraged the development of the limited liability company which combines limited liability with true partnership taxation.

It is important to recognize that a limited liability company, if properly structured, is treated as a true partnership for tax purposes and not as an S corporation. The Internal Revenue Service has under consideration a proposal to recommend modification of the S corporation rules so that they conform generally with the rules applicable to partnerships. Until this is accomplished, however, there are substantial tax costs in electing S corporation tax treatment rather than true partnership type tax treatment.

§9.8 STATE INCOME TAXATION OF S CORPORATION INCOME

The treatment of S corporations under state income tax laws varies widely. Many state income tax statutes are now keyed to the federal system. In other words, individual taxpayers simply report to the state their adjusted

---

[32]See §8.30.

[33]For example, the partnership tax rules give a partnership some discretion as to how income or loss are to be allocated among the participants; the S corporation rules require that all income or loss be allocated strictly in proportion to the relative shareholdings of the participants. The 1996 tax bill pending in Congress (see note 28) does not affect the technical rules described in this section.

gross income as reflected on the federal return, make specified adjustments, and the amount of the state income tax is calculated from the resulting taxable income. Many of these states consistently follow the federal pattern to the extent of making the S corporation itself not subject to tax and taxing the shareholders on the corporate income allocable to them under the federal income tax rules. Not all states follow this pattern, however.

Some states simply treat S corporations as separate taxable entities in the same way as they treat C corporations. New York, for example, imposes a tax on all corporations, including corporations that have made the S corporation election. Other states require the S corporation to make a separate tax election by filing an information return and the consent of all shareholders to report the S corporation income as taxable income of the shareholders for state income tax purposes. A few states impose franchise taxes on corporate income irrespective of the federal tax election; in these states an S corporation is itself subject to the franchise tax.

§9.9 THE S CORPORATION ELECTION AND MINIMIZATION OF TAXES

Corporations that are eligible for the S corporation election determine whether or not to make this election on the basis of what minimizes the overall tax liability of the corporation and its shareholders. The decision whether an eligible corporation should elect S corporation treatment depends on three basic variables: the relative tax rates applicable to corporations and to individual taxpayers, the probable distribution pattern that the corporation will follow in the future, and whether the corporation may have losses for tax purposes in the near future. This section considers the interplay of these factors in deciding whether or not to elect S corporation status.

Before 1980, the individual marginal income tax rates for upper-income taxpayers were considerably higher than marginal rates for corporations. The highest individual marginal rate was over 70 percent, while the maximum corporate rate was 48 percent. In this environment, the pass through feature of the S corporation was usually a detriment rather than a benefit to high-income shareholders. If shareholders were in high tax brackets and the corporation was profitable, the S corporation election was almost never the most tax-efficient solution. During this period, most profitable closely held corporations operated as C corporations, and adopted the accumulate and bail out strategy discussed in section 9.3.[34] Taxable dividends and distributions were minimized, and the ultimate resolution

---

[34]Of course, in this tax environment the C corporation election coupled with a policy of large dividend distributions to the shareholders would be even more costly from a tax standpoint than the accumulate and bail out strategy.

involved either a sale of the stock of the corporation at favorable long-term capital gain rates, a dissolution of the corporation, or the death of shareholders, with a subsequent step-up in basis on death.

In this pre-1980 tax environment, an entirely different set of minimization principles applied to a corporation that expected temporary operating losses. If the corporation had high-bracket shareholders, as was often the case, the S corporation election permitted the shareholders to use the corporate losses to shield other taxable income from rates as high as 75 percent. When the corporation became profitable, the S corporation election was terminated. This sequence was again so common as to be almost routine. During this period, the number of corporations electing S corporation treatment was relatively small, presumably reflecting the fact that this election was attractive only for loss corporations.

The very high individual tax rates of the pre-1980s were steadily reduced during the 1980s. The lowest point of individual tax rates in the modern era were established by the Tax Reform Act of 1986, a statute that made sweeping changes in tax rules. This Act reversed the historic relationship between the maximum personal and corporate tax rates: the maximum individual tax rate was reduced to 28 percent while the maximum corporate rate was reduced only to 34 percent. Further, the special treatment of long-term capital gains was eliminated. These changes in basic structure suddenly made partnership-type taxation much more attractive for all corporations, and the number of S corporation elections soared. Indeed, this was the period during which master limited partnerships were created,[35] and there was concern that the changes in tax rates might lead to the disincorporation of much of corporate America.

Subsequent tax statutes have partially reversed the pattern of tax rates established by the 1986 Act. The maximum individual rate was gradually increased to 39.6 percent, while at the same time the maximum corporate rate was increased to 35 percent.[36] These changes in the relative tax rates applicable to individuals and corporations have caused further changes in the use of the S corporation election and distribution policy by closely held corporations as shareholders have continued to adopt corporate and individual strategies that minimize their total tax bills.

[35] See §5.20.

[36] All rates discussed in this section, it should be emphasized, are the maximum marginal rates applicable to high-income taxpayers. Lower marginal rates are applicable to individuals and corporations with smaller incomes. However, even these statements require further qualification. Both corporate and individual rate schedules have special surtaxes designed to recapture the benefit of lower brackets and a portion of personal deductions so that at specified brackets the marginal tax rates are higher than those described in the text. Further, individual tax rates are affected by the marital status of the taxpayer. However, for purposes of discussion of tax strategy, these complications of the modern tax structure may be ignored. See §3.18 and §9.2.

In today's relatively even tax bracket environment, the choice between C and S corporations depends on specific circumstances. The single tax structure applicable to partnerships or S corporations is certainly to be preferred to a C corporation that distributes most of its income in the form of nondeductible dividends. A partnership or S corporation election is preferable if the business expects to show losses for a period of time. However, there are several situations where C corporation tax treatment may be attractive. Since the maximum corporate rate is somewhat lower than the individual rate, a corporation that plans to reinvest substantially all of its earnings in plant and equipment for an extended period reduces taxes by electing to remain a C corporation. Furthermore, since it is possible to make at least some distributions in a form that is tax deductible by the corporation, a corporation in a strong reinvestment of earnings mode may make substantial distributions to shareholders without incurring the double tax. Another situation in which C corporation tax treatment may be preferred today involves elderly shareholders who expect to retain shares indefinitely, so that it is likely that their shares will receive a tax-free step-up in basis on their death.

B. CORPORATE SECURITIES

§9.10 CORPORATE SECURITIES: DEBT AND EQUITY SECURITIES

The traditional analysis of corporate securities draws a sharp distinction between "equity" securities on the one hand and "debt" securities on the other. *Equity securities* reflect ownership interests in the corporation itself; they include "common" shares and "preferred" shares.[37] *Debt securities*, on the other hand, reflect fixed obligations that must be repaid at some future date. Debt securities include "bonds" and "debentures."[38]

This useful classification is basically followed in the discussion below. It is important to recognize, however, that these are not sharp classifications: their edges are blurred and some types of hybrid securities may arguably be classified in different ways. Modern corporate practice has undoubtedly hastened the blurring of the distinctions between common and preferred shares on the one hand and between preferred shares and debt securities on the other. The fact is that the relations between the corporation and the

[37]Common shares are discussed in §9.13. Preferred shares are discussed in §§9.15-9.22.
[38]The distinction between bonds and debentures is discussed in §9.11.

276

holders of its securities are essentially contractual in nature,[39] and if the parties so desire they may create securities that do not neatly fit into one of these traditional pigeonholes. Illustrative of this fact is that the 1984 Model Business Corporation Act completely avoids the use of words common and preferred in describing equity securities.

The discussion below deals primarily with closely held debt securities. However, it is necessary to talk briefly about publicly held securities in some instances because these transactions regularly serve as a model for similar transactions in closely held corporations.

§9.11 DEBT SECURITIES GENERALLY

There are, of course, all kinds of loans and debts, running from overnight loans, to credit card obligations, to short-term loans with a maturity date of a few months, to multiple-year obligations for automobile loans, to even longer obligations for real estate loans. Most debt incurred by closely held businesses will fall into one or more of these categories.

Debt securities arise from transactions that are somewhat different from ordinary credit transactions. They arise from long-term loan transactions that may involve investments by members of the general public. A corporation that borrows $50 million, for example, may do so through an underwriter who resells bonds to numerous investors scattered around the country. Bonds may be issued in $1,000, $5,000, $10,000, $25,000, $50,000, $100,000, and perhaps even larger units. The obligations so created last for a term of years and are evidenced by certificates (or modern substitutes for certificates) that may be publicly traded. Public markets thus exist for many types of debt securities, and an investor who wishes to dispose of his investment in such a bond simply sells it into the market much the same way as shares of publicly traded stock are sold. A large closely held corporation may issue publicly traded debt securities even though its common stock is held by a few shareholders, though such corporations are relatively rare. Such a corporation, however, must register its debt securities with the SEC and with state agencies before their sale and thereafter comply with the public disclosure requirements of these governmental agencies.

The two types of debt instruments most commonly classed as securities are debentures and bonds. These types of securities have close economic similarities to preferred stock. Both bonds and debentures reflect unconditional obligations by the issuer to pay the face amount of the instrument at a specific date in the future and, in addition, to pay interest in specified

---

[39] These relations are also largely unconstrained by state statute. Some state statutes, however, may appear to prohibit some types of rights being attached to some types of securities. See §9.21 for examples.

amounts at specified times in the interim. Technically a *debenture* is an unsecured corporate obligation while a *bond* is secured by a lien or mortgage on specific corporate property. However, the word bond is often used in a generic sense to refer to both bonds and debentures. The presence or absence of security for these marketable debt interests (that is, the distinction between bonds and debentures) is not nearly as important as might be first supposed, because if a corporation defaults on an obligation and a secured holder seeks to foreclose on corporate property, the corporation will promptly file for bankruptcy reorganization under Chapter 11 of the Bankruptcy Act and obtain protection from property seizures for an extended period from the federal bankruptcy court. Of course, the secured bond holder usually has greater rights in the reorganization proceeding than an unsecured debenture holder does, and that is the real benefit of holding a bond rather than a debenture.

§9.12 CONVERTIBLE DEBT SECURITIES

Debt securities may be made convertible into equity securities, almost always into common shares, on some predetermined ratio. This ratio must be established by the creating documents themselves. The securities into which a convertible security may be converted are called the *conversion securities*. Convertible debt securities are almost always unsecured debentures; in fact the most common name for convertible debt securities is *convertible debentures*. When convertible debentures are "converted," they, and the debt they represent, both disappear and new equity securities (the conversion securities) are issued in their place. Convertible debentures themselves are treated as equity securities for some accounting, economic, and legal purposes.

Convertible debentures may be attractive investment vehicles for venture capital funds or other investors providing capital to promising closely held corporations. Such debentures assure the investor some immediate return on his investment plus the right to share in profits of the enterprise if it is successful and "goes public."[40] Such debentures also commonly have a "put" feature that permits the investor to compel the closely held enterprise to repay the debt at specified times, if called upon to do so by the investor. This "put" may be in the form of a power to accelerate the payment date or an option on the part of the investor to resell the securities back to the enterprise at a specified price.

---

[40]There are other investment vehicles that provide similar rights to investors in closely held enterprises, including convertible preferred shares, debentures with warrants to purchase stock attached, and straight options to purchase shares at bargain prices.

§9.13 COMMON SHARES

Shares of common stock are the fundamental units into which the proprietary interest of the corporation is divided. If a corporation issues only one class of shares, they may be referred to by a variety of similar names: "common shares," "common stock," "capital stock," or possibly simply "shares" or "stock." Whatever the name, they are the basic proprietary units of ownership and are referred to here as *common shares*.

The two fundamental characteristics of common shares are (1) they are entitled to vote for the election of directors and on other matters coming before the shareholders, and (2) they are entitled to the net assets of the corporation (after making allowance for debts and senior securities) when distributions are to be made, either during the course of the life of the corporation or upon its dissolution.

The fundamental incorporating document of every corporation must state the number of shares of common stock the corporation is authorized to issue. This number is known as the corporation's *authorized capital* or *authorized shares*. Corporations usually authorize more common shares than they currently plan to issue. Additional authorized shares may be useful if it is decided, for example, to raise capital in the future by selling additional shares, to provide economic incentives to executives or key employees by granting them options to purchase shares at favorable prices, to create an Employee Share Ownership Plan (ESOP) for all employees, or to issue debt or senior classes of securities that have the privilege of being converted into common shares.

The *capitalization* of a corporation is based on the number of shares actually issued and the capital received therefor, not on the number of authorized shares. Capital received in exchange for shares is usually referred to as the corporation's *invested capital* (or sometimes its "contributed" capital) and from an accounting standpoint (though not necessarily from a legal standpoint) is viewed as being invested in the corporation permanently or indefinitely.

In states with older statutes, the fundamental incorporating document must also set forth the par value of the authorized shares or a statement that the shares are without par value. Par value is an arbitrary number without economic significance that, in older statutes, determines the amount of permanent capital and capital surplus in the original capitalization of the corporation. See section 9.25.

§9.14 CLASSES OF COMMON SHARES

State statutes give corporations broad power to create classes of common shares with different rights or privileges. For example, the rights of two classes of shares may be identical except that one class is entitled to twice the dividend per share of the second class. Or, shares of each class may have identical financial rights per share but each class of common shares (regardless of the number of shares) is entitled to elect one director (thereby assuring equal class representation on the board of directors even though the number of shares in the two classes and the financial interests represented by those shares are unequal). Classes of shares are widely used in closely held corporations to govern the control relationships between two or more shareholders. Such classes are usually designated by alphabetical notations: Class A common, Class B common, and so forth. A corporation with two or more classes of shares that differ *only* with respect to voting rights is eligible for the S corporation election (assuming, of course, that it meets the other requirements for that election). Classified common shares are very common in closely held corporations but are rarely used by publicly held corporations.

§9.15 PREFERRED SHARES: INTRODUCTION

Preferred shares lie somewhere between common shares and debt. They are equity securities created by provisions in the articles of incorporation (or in other publicly filed documents). In effect, preferred shareholders are granted limited economic rights that are carved out of the rights of common shareholders. "Preferred" simply means that some economic right of the preferred shareholders — a right to distributions or a right to share in the surplus on dissolution, or both — must be preferred, i.e., satisfied ahead of, the rights of common shareholders. A dividend preference means that the preferred shares are entitled to receive a specified dividend each year before any dividend may be paid on the common shares; a liquidation preference means that the preferred shares are entitled to receive a specified distribution from corporate assets in liquidation (after provision has been made for corporate debts) before the common shares are entitled to receive anything. Some preferred shares may have only a dividend preference and no liquidation preference, or vice versa, but usually preferred shares have priority both with respect to dividends and with respect to liquidation distributions.

Preferred shareholders are indeed "shareholders," not "creditors." Their dividend right is not guaranteed and remains at the discretion of the board of directors in the same way that dividends on common shares are not guaranteed; traditional legal restraints on distributions to common shareholders (see section 9.38) also may limit the power of a corporation to pay dividends on preferred shares. These legal limitations, of course, do not apply to payments required on debt securities. In the event of liquidation, preferred shares rank behind debt securities in priority of payment.

Dividend rights of preferred shares are traditionally limited to a fixed amount and no more, no matter how profitable the corporation. In this respect, preferred shares are more similar to fixed-income securities than to common shares. From an investment point of view, preferred shares seem to have the worst of both worlds, having the limited upward potential of pure debt securities but without the same assurance of payment that debt securities have. Further, they lack the unlimited claim to all residual gains that common shares have; they are entitled only to a limited financial bene-fit no matter how profitable the corporation.

A closely held corporation that has issued a class of preferred shares with economic rights different from the rights of common shares is ineligi-ble for the S corporation election. This election is discussed in section 9.7.

Preferred shares usually are non-voting shares, though a limited voting right may be granted under specified circumstances, e.g., upon the omission of a preferred dividend for a specified period. And, there is no inherent reason why preferred shares may not be given the right to vote, either on other specific matters or generally on all matters coming before the share-holders, if that is what the parties agree to.

The rights of preferred shareholders are defined in the corporation's articles of incorporation or in directors' resolutions filed with the secretary of state (in the case of certain types of preferred shares discussed below). If an existing corporation wishes to create a new class of preferred shares, it must usually formally amend its articles of incorporation.

Collectively, the provisions relating to preferred shares in basic corpo-rate documents are referred to as the *preferred shareholders' contract* with the corporation. Basically, this usage reflects that rights of preferred shareholders are generally limited to those set forth in this "contract" and that preferred shareholders have relatively few rights outside of those granted expressly to them.

A single corporation may have outstanding several different classes of preferred shares with varying rights and preferences. While a specific class of preferred may have subordinate rights with respect to another class of preferred, both are still preferred shares since they both have preferences over the common shares.

Closely held corporations issue preferred shares more often than they do debt securities. Preferred shares are ideal for planning purposes as they give participants in the business a financial interest while giving them little or no right to participate in management.

§9.16 PREFERRED SHARES: DIVIDEND RIGHTS

Most classes of preferred shares are entitled to a limited preferential divi-dend, and no more. The *dividend preference* may be described either in terms of dollars per share (the "$3.20 preferred") or as a percentage of par or stated value (the "5 percent preferred"). A dividend preference does not mean that the preferred is entitled to the payment in the same way that a creditor is entitled to payment from his or her debtor. A preferred dividend is still a dividend, and may be paid only if the corporation has available surplus from which a dividend may be paid and the board of directors decide to declare a dividend on the preferred shares. The board may decide to omit all dividends, common and preferred. The incentive to pay a preferential dividend comes from the principle that if no dividend is paid on the preferred all dividends on the common shares must also be omitted. The preference feature of preferred shares technically means that they are entitled to the dividend first from any amount set aside by the board of directors for the payment of dividends.

Shares preferred as to dividends may be "cumulative," "noncumulative," or "partially cumulative." If *cumulative dividends* are not paid in some years, they are carried forward and both they and the current year's preferred dividends must be paid in full before any common dividends may be declared. *Noncumulative dividends* disappear each year if they are not paid. *Partially cumulative dividends* are usually cumulative to the extent of earnings, that is, the dividend is cumulative in any year only to the extent of actual earnings during that year. Unpaid cumulative dividends are not debts of the corporation, but a continued right to priority in future earnings.

An example may help to illustrate the concept of cumulative, noncumulative, and partially cumulative dividends. Assume that a preferred stock has a preferential right to a dividend of $5 per share per year, but the directors, as is their right, decide to omit all dividends for two consecutive years. In the third year they conclude that the corporation is able to resume the payment of dividends. If the preferred shares' preferential right is cumulative, the board of directors must pay $15 on each preferred share ($5 per share for each of the two years missed plus $5 per share for the current year) before any dividend may be paid on the common shares in the third year. If the preferred shares' preferential right is noncumulative the preferences for the two omitted years disappear entirely, and a dividend on the common shares may be paid after the $5 preferred dividend for the current year is paid. If the dividend is cumulative to the extent earned, the earnings of the corporation in each of the two years in which dividends were omitted must be examined, and the dividend is cumulative each year only to the extent the earnings cover the $5 preferred dividend: If the corporation had a loss in one of those years, the preferred dividend for that year would be lost much as though the dividend were entirely noncumulative.

In evaluating dividend policies with respect to preferred shares, one starts with the basic principle that distribution rights of most preferred shares are limited to specific preferential amounts set forth in the preferred shareholders' contract. Preferred shareholders are thus entitled to the specified dividend before anything is paid on the common, but they will never be paid anything more than the amount specified in their contract, irrespective of how large the earnings of the corporation become. Indeed, an attempt by directors to pay a dividend to preferred shareholders in excess of their limited dividend right may be enjoined by common shareholders as a violation of their rights.

Preferred shareholders normally work on the assumption that the board of directors is elected by the common shareholders and will therefore maximize the dividends payable on common shares at the expense of preferred shareholders to the extent they lawfully may do so. A board of directors may seek to minimize the preferred shareholders' rights so long as they do so without violating contractual rights. A noncumulative preferential dividend right, in particular, leaves the preferred shareholders quite exposed to strategic maneuvers, because the common shareholders' position is improved in the future whenever a preferred dividend is omitted. Indeed, a policy of paying dividends erratically once every few years materially improves the position of the common with respect to noncumulative preferred. Do you see why? Such a policy, however, may be subject to legal attack as a breach of the directors' fiduciary duty to treat fairly all classes of outstanding shares.

Cumulative dividends provide preferred shareholders considerably greater protection than noncumulative or partially cumulative dividends. But cumulative dividends are not a complete answer either, because the board of directors may defer the payment of all dividends indefinitely in an effort to depress the value of the preferred which may then be acquired by the corporation at attractive prices by direct negotiation with individual preferred shareholders. On the other hand, preferred shares often are given the right to elect a specified number of directors if preferred dividends have been omitted for a specified period, and the presence of one or more directors elected by the preferred shareholders may be unappealing to the incumbent management; such a right therefore tends to minimize the possibility of such overtly unfair strategies.

§9.17 PREFERRED SHARES:
PARTICIPATING PREFERRED

While the foregoing sections may create the impression that there is a sharp line between common and preferred shares, that impression is not really accurate. The rights of preferred and common shareholders are a matter of contract and it is possible to create "in between" shares that have characteristics of both common and preferred shares. A classic example is *participating preferred shares*.

Participating preferred shares are shares that are entitled to an original preferential dividend. In addition, if a specified dividend per share is paid on the common shares, the participating preferred then becomes entitled to share with the common in any additional distributions on some predetermined basis. Such shares are relatively uncommon. Preferred shares are participating shares only if their rights are expressly so defined in the preferred shareholders' contract. Participating preferred shares are sometimes called "class A common shares" because they have the open-ended dividend characteristics of common shares.

§9.18 PREFERRED SHARES: CONVERTIBILITY

Preferred shares may be made convertible at the option of the preferred shareholder into common shares at a specified price or a specified ratio. When convertible shares are converted, the original preferred shares are turned in and canceled, and new common shares are issued. The conversion price or ratio is fixed and defined in the preferred shareholders' contract. The conversion ratio is usually made adjustable for share dividends, share splits, the issuance of additional common shares, and similar transactions affecting the underlying common shares. The provisions requiring such adjustments are called *anti-dilution provisions*.

The security into which the convertible preferred may be converted, typically common stock, is called the *conversion security*. The typical convertible preferred security — by far the most common — involves a "downstream" conversion, that is, the right to convert preferred into common at the option of the holder. In some closely held corporations, however, an "upstream" conversion, that is, the right to convert common into preferred, or preferred into debt, may be authorized as part of an estate plan involving the transfer of the business to the younger generation at minimum tax cost.[41] Many state statutes specifically authorize the common downstream conversion but may not directly authorize an upstream convertible security.[42] The balance of this section deals with the traditional downstream convertible security.

The determination of the conversion ratio, that is, how many shares of common stock a preferred shareholder receives upon the exercise of the conversion privilege, may involve negotiation between the corporation and a potential investor. Convertible preferred shares may be the vehicle desired by a venture capital fund or other investor in a closely held corporation to reflect an equity investment in the enterprise. The theory is that so long as the business is closely held, the venture fund will retain the convertible security, thereby having a prior claim to any distributions but not requiring such distributions if it is inconvenient (or unlawful) for the corporation to

---

[41] These transactions are discussed in §9.22.

[42] Where such a convertible is not authorized, much the same effect may be obtained by a voluntary recapitalization.

make them. Later, if the business is successful and the corporation "goes public" by registering its common shares under the Securities Act of 1933 the venture capital fund may convert its preferred shares into marketable common shares and sell them profitably into the public market.

§9.19 PREFERRED SHARES: REDEEMABILITY

Preferred shares are often made redeemable at the option of the corporation upon the payment of a fixed amount for each share. Such shares are therefore *callable* or *redeemable shares*. The redemption price may be a matter of negotiation between the corporation and an investor at the time the preferred stock is issued. Redemption prices are established in the preferred shareholders' contract; they are usually established at a level somewhat higher than the consideration originally paid by the investor for the preferred shares, but tied to the original issue price. For example, if preferred shares are issued for $100 per share, they may be made redeemable at $105 or $110 per share. The redemption right is of particular importance in connection with convertible preferred shares since its exercise may in effect require holders of these shares to elect to become common shareholders or be cashed out at the redemption price.

  The power to redeem preferred shares is usually applicable only to the entire class or series of preferred as a unit. However, the preferred shareholders' contract sometimes provides that redemptions of a portion of a class or series are permitted; such provisions may also include rules for determining which shares are to be redeemed. If a convertible preferred is called for redemption, the conversion privilege continues after the announcement that the shares will be called for redemption until the shares are actually redeemed.

§9.20 SERIES AND CLASSES OF PREFERRED SHARES

Corporations may issue preferred shares in "series" as well as classes. The difference is solely in the manner of creation. Creation of new "classes" of preferred shares requires an amendment to the articles of incorporation, including a vote by common shareholders, and also by classes of preferred shareholders whose rights may be affected adversely by the new issue of preferred shares.[43] In a large publicly held corporation, particularly, this

---

[43] In the rather arcane language of the Model Business Corporation Act (1984) those classes of preferred shares become separate "voting groups." Model Business Corporation Act (1984) §1.41(26). Each adversely affected class of preferred shares is entitled to vote on the amendment to the articles of incorporation creating the new class, even though the shares are otherwise non-voting, id. §10.04.

process is time-consuming and expensive. To simplify this process, the concept of a series of preferred shares was developed.

Series of preferred shares may be created only if specifically authorized by the state corporation statute and by the corporation's articles of incorporation. Under these statutory provisions, a board of directors may create and authorize the sale of series of preferred shares without shareholder approval if specifically authorized to do so by the articles of incorporation. The articles of incorporation must in effect create a class of shares without any substantive terms and authorize the board of directors to create (or "carve out") series from within that class from time to time and to vary any of the substantive terms of each series at the time it is created. Shares of different series must have identical rights except for the specified business terms which may be varied. Shares of this type (before issuance) are sometimes referred to as "blank shares," because the items are not specified in the articles of incorporation and may be "filled in" by the board of directors.

In economic respects, the concept of a "series" and the concept of a "class" are indistinguishable; both terms describe a group of shares with identical provisions, rights and privileges.

§9.21 PREFERRED SHARES: RECENT DEVELOPMENTS

The high interest rates of the early 1980s led to the development of novel financing devices, many of which involved preferred shares. For example, many corporations issued preferred shares that were redeemable at the option of the holder, or that became redeemable upon the occurrence of some external event, such as a change in interest rates or the lapse of a specified period of time. Still other corporations issued preferred shares with floating or adjustable dividend rates that depended on interest rates or some similar measure.

Most of these novel preferreds were designed to give corporate holders of the preferred shares a dual benefit: the tax benefits of the exclusion for intercorporate dividends plus most of the economic benefits of holders of traditional debt. Indeed, the dividend-received exclusion often makes an investment in preferred stock more attractive to a corporate lender than a straight loan of funds by one corporation to another. In the case of a straight loan, the interest paid by the debtor is a deductible business expense to the debtor and the interest is ordinary income to the creditor. In contrast, distributions upon preferred shares are partially or wholly excludable from income by the recipient (under the dividend-received exclusion) and not deductible by the paying corporation.

A "loan" made pursuant to a preferred stock transaction thus reverses the tax consequences of a true loan. A corporate creditor, desiring to minimize the tax cost of the transaction to it, may insist that "loans" by it to

286

another corporation be cast in the form of a purchase of a special class of preferred stock which may have a variable dividend rate tied to an interest rate index and a contractual obligation on the part of the issuing corporation to redeem the special class of preferred upon demand or upon a specified date. The redemption price may be a matter of negotiation between the corporation and an investor. In other words, the loan transaction is dressed up as a sale of preferred stock with the identical economic terms as the contemplated loan transaction but with entirely different tax consequences.

These novel types of preferred shares in some instances raised questions under older corporation statutes. For example, some corporate statutes expressly authorize downstream conversions but are silent with respect to upstream conversions, arguably thereby prohibiting them. There is no indication that this was done intentionally; presumably, it was done by inadvertence in the drafting of provisions designed to make sure that downstream conversions were expressly authorized. Since a lender who is an individual is not entitled to a dividend-received deduction, there is no incentive to transmute a loan transaction into a preferred stock purchase in the case of individual lenders.

§9.22 PREFERRED SHARES AS ESTATE FREEZES

Consider the situation faced by the owners of a successful family corporation as they age and begin to look toward eventual retirement and passing the business on to the next generation. In creating their estate plan, a major — indeed the predominant — problem will be the valuation of the business on their death, and the estate taxes that will be due when the shares are transferred to the younger generation. Let us assume that the business is now worth several million dollars and is growing rapidly, so that when the shareholders die, the corporation may well be worth tens of millions of dollars. The federal estate tax becomes a major concern in such situations, since it is a transfer tax imposed on estates in excess of $600,000 (adjusted for inflation and with special rules for interspousal transfers) that begins at 35 percent and increases to 55 percent on estates in excess of $3 million. If the shares owned by the deceased shareholder are valued at $25 million when the principal shareholder dies, the estate tax arising from the inclusion of these shares in the estate will be in excess of $10 million. It is unlikely that the estate will be able to pay a tax of this magnitude without selling the business, and there will be no business for the affluent younger generation to own and manage.[44]

---

[44]It might be possible for the older generation to purchase sufficient life insurance to cover the estate tax liability. Such insurance, however, might not be available at all, and if it is, may be prohibitively expensive. The older generation may also make gifts of common

Before 1990, the solution adopted by many shareholders was to recapitalize the corporation before most of the growth in value occurred. The older generation received preferred shares that were voting shares, were redeemable by the corporation, and also carried large dividend preferences that were noncumulative. The gift of the common shares to the younger generation was subject to the gift tax, but the value of the common was relatively low because much of the value was absorbed by the prior claims of the preferred. Each year thereafter the corporation would redeem some preferred shares, thereby providing funds to the older generation for living expenses and indirectly increasing the value of the common shares. On the death of the preferred shareholder, the balance of her shares would be redeemed by the corporation, again increasing indirectly the value of the common shares without involving a transfer from the older generation to the younger. These transactions were sufficiently common that they have a name, corporate *estate tax freezes*.

The secret of the estate tax freeze was the conveyance of the common stock to the younger generation at a time when most of the increase in value was potential and had not yet occurred. Viewed in another way, the estate freeze "worked" because the Internal Revenue Service accepted undervaluations of the common stock in light of the family relationship. The common stock reflected the future potential growth in the business; the older generation continued to work to create this future growth, but the increase in value inured to the benefit of the younger generation without any transfer tax.

A variety of corporate estate freeze strategies were developed. For example, the older generation might impose restrictions on the transfer of their shares in order to be able to argue later that the restrictions should be reflected in a reduction of the value of the shares. Another type of freeze involved the sale of 5 percent, say, of their stock to the younger generation and then causing the corporation to redeem the remaining 95 percent by giving them a promissory note for the balance of the purchase price, payable in installments. Other plans involved the use of puts, calls, redemptions, or conversions of shares.

In 1990, the Internal Revenue Code was amended to limit the use of such transactions as a tax-avoidance device by imposing gift-tax liability on many intrafamily transactions in which the growth potential of a business is transferred to the younger generation while the older generation retains a limited preferential interest that may be eliminated for a fixed amount. Sections 2701 through 2704 of the Internal Revenue Code attacked the

---

stock to the younger generation within the limits of $10,000 per donor per year, that is exempt from gift tax. However, it is unlikely that such gifts would effectively reduce the estate tax liability, particularly if the value of the business itself is growing rapidly.

problem of estate tax freezes by changing the method of valuation. If family members receive a transfer subject to a retained interest, the transaction is viewed as transferring the entire property minus the value of the retained interest calculated as the amount of the consideration actually paid by the recipients. Further, the value of the retained interest — if subject to puts, calls, or conversion rights — is calculated at the lowest possible value that may be obtained by the exercise of such discretionary rights.

Estate tax freezes may also be created though the use of general partnerships, limited partnerships, or limited liability companies. Sections 2701 through 2704 are equally applicable to those business forms if attempts are made to transfer the potential value of the business to the younger generation in a way that does not involve an *inter vivos* gift or transfer or death.

C. FINANCIAL ASPECTS OF CORPORATE FORMATION

§9.23 THE ISSUANCE OF COMMON SHARES IN GENERAL

This part discusses the legal, economic, and tax principles that control the initial capitalization of a newly formed corporation. The legal issues primarily concern obsolete historical rules that require shares of stock to be issued in specified amounts for specified and enumerated types of consideration.[45] The economic issues generally relate to assurance that the participants in the venture are treated in a fair manner, particularly if the venture aborts shortly after its inception. The tax issues consider the extent to which the capitalization of a corporation is itself a taxable event[46] and whether the capital structure selected is consistent with the desired tax treatment of the corporation after its formation, that is, whether the corporation is to be taxed as a C corporation or as an S corporation.[47]

The various factors described in the previous paragraph are interrelated. It is not uncommon for the legal, economic, and tax considerations each to point in different and conflicting directions when considering a specific transaction. Where this occurs, the participants must decide upon the relative priorities that each of them have, and adopt a plan that achieves their most important goals.

Some problems discussed in this part may be avoided by the use of *treasury shares*, shares that were originally lawfully issued under the rules

---

[45] Discussed in §9.25(1).
[46] Discussed in §9.28.
[47] Discussed in §9.6.

discussed in this part and have since been reacquired by the corporation. Such shares under traditional statutes have an intermediate status; they are viewed as being "issued" and held in the corporation's treasury for purposes of the technical rules of issuance discussed in this part, but at the same time they are not eligible to vote or to participate in distributions. Treasury shares are discussed more completely in connection with transactions by which the corporation reacquires the shares.[48]

§9.24 DISSIMILAR CONTRIBUTIONS

It is very common for participants in a new business to make quite dissimilar contributions to the venture. One or more participants may contribute capital to permit the new firm to acquire necessary machinery, equipment, and physical assets, and to provide working capital for the firm after it commences business. Other participants may contribute intangible property, ideas, patents, copyrights, or an attractive design for the storefront. Still others may contribute nothing at the outset but promise to render services for some period of time in exchange for an equity ownership interest in the firm. A trained chef may be an essential participant in a high-end restaurant; her skill and training may justify her becoming a part owner of the restaurant. A skilled programmer may legitimately insist on becoming a part owner of a software start-up enterprise as a condition to working for it. Others may contribute other types of property; a piece of real estate, a lease, a farm, or a valuable software program. Still others may agree that they will guarantee the payment of the corporation's debts to financial institutions within specified limits. Basic business, legal, and tax questions have to be addressed by the participants wherever dissimilar contributions are involved.

It is often difficult afterall to assess accurately at the outset the relative value of contributions being made by persons making dissimilar contributions.

§9.25 PAR VALUE AND WATERED STOCK

The provisions of state statutes relating to the issuance of shares — common or preferred — may be roughly classified into two categories, "modern" statutes and "par value" statutes. Since the technical rules about the issuance of shares are completely different under the two types of statutes (but the words used to describe the types of shares are similar), it is essential to first establish which type of statute one is working under. It is easiest to begin with a discussion of par value.

[48]See §9.33.

1. *Par Value Statutes*. The idea that shares of stock must have a fixed value, called *par* (or *stated*) value, assigned or attributed to them, goes back to ancient times. The par value is an amount selected when the corporation is formed or when articles of incorporation are amended to authorize a new class of shares. The par value is a dollar value that is part of the definition of the security itself. For example, the shares issued are "common shares with a par value of $x." The par value appears prominently on certificates for the shares and remains fixed unless the articles of incorporation are amended to change the par value. Apparently, the original purpose of par value was to define the issuance price of shares in order to guarantee each investor that the other persons who are also acquiring shares are paying the same amount as the investor. In the absence of such a guarantee, investors might find the value of their investment diluted if other investors were permitted to buy identical shares at lower prices or for promises to make future payments.

Of course, placing a dollar amount on the face of a certificate does not guarantee that each investor will in fact pay that amount. During the last half of the Nineteenth Century, promoters and their friends often were permitted to purchase shares for less than par value — indeed, often for nothing at all. Politicians might readily be bribed by being given shares in new ventures for nothing even though the shares recited that they had par value of hundreds or thousands of dollars. Shares issued for less than par value are called *watered stock* and much of the corporate jurisprudence of the last century was devoted to stamping out this perceived evil.

While the most serious problem with watered stock was dilution of the financial interests of outside investors who paid full par value in cash, the watered stock jurisprudence developed along another route. When par value shares are issued, the assets received must be recorded on the books of the corporation as being worth their par value.[49] When watered stock was issued, some assets had to be recorded at more than their actual value or some fictitious assets were created out of whole cloth so that the balance sheet balanced.

The watered stock jurisprudence assumed that the initial capital of a corporation was the source of its credit, that the par values of issued shares was a representation as to how much capital had been invested in the corporation, and that the issuance of watered stock therefore constituted a fraud on subsequent creditors who extended credit to the corporation after the watered stock was issued, presumably in reliance on the representation based on the par values of the issued shares. The usual rule adopted was

---

[49]This proposition may not seem to be self-evident. The reason that it is generally accepted is intimately involved in the basic accounting concepts that underlie balance sheets. For present purposes, it is simplest just to accept the accuracy of the statement in the text at face value.

that persons receiving watered stock might be compelled by subsequent creditors to "squeeze out the water" by contributing to the corporation "real" assets in an amount that made their total contribution at least equal to the par value of the shares issued. Of course, this did not address the problem of dilution of the interests of other investors, and was always somewhat fictional besides, because there was almost no evidence supporting the assumption that creditors in fact relied on the formal accounting records of the corporation in deciding to extend credit.

Certainly, creditors today do not usually rely on the corporate financial records; they rely on credit reports from national credit reporting firms, on the obtaining of security interests in corporate property, and on personal guarantees of individuals who are known to have substantial assets. But this is beside the point; the old rule about liability for watered stock continues in existence today.

Hence, the one basic rule in states that have par value statutes is that shares should never be issued for less than par value. To issue par value shares for less than par simply creates a contingent liability on the part of the acquiring shareholder to pay the difference to the corporation. This contingent liability is not consensual; it is created by operation of law to protect the interest of creditors who are presumed to rely on the stated capital of the corporation when extending credit. Thus, if a par value is assigned to shares, the shares must *always* be issued for assets or cash at least equal to the aggregate par value of the shares being issued to the investor if the creation of liability is to be avoided.

Today, par value is largely irrelevant to the issuance of shares because modern practices have trivialized the concept. Lawyers routinely use either no par shares or nominal par value shares — shares with a par value of one cent, ten cents, one dollar, or ten dollars — when the shares are to be issued for a substantially larger amount. In this way, the problem of watered shares is basically rendered moot in most situations, though cases continue to arise from time to time involving situations where lawyers or others have assigned high par value to shares out of ignorance of the consequences.

To complicate matters, most states that have par value statutes also permit the issuance of shares "without par value" or "no par shares." No par shares do not dispense with the need for the corporation to establish a value to be placed on the shares before they are issued. Before no par shares are issued the board of directors must establish the consideration for which such shares are to be issued, and that determination by the board of directors essentially substitutes for the provision in the articles of incorporation establishing the par value. It is possible, therefore, to have watered stock liability created by the issuance of no par shares.[50]

---

[50]The likelihood that such liability may be imposed, however, is small because statutes provide that the valuation placed on property by the board of directors received by the corporation in exchange for shares is conclusive in the absence of fraud.

Most states that retain par value concepts also have statutory or constitutional provisions that are designed to assure that shares are issued only for
assets that in some sense are tangible and real. The usual provision is that
shares may not be issued for a consideration consisting of future services or
promissory notes. Some states phrase the principal affirmatively: Shares may
be issued only for cash, property actually received, or services actually rendered. These rules about eligible and ineligible consideration are technically
independent of the par value rules; some states have eliminated the mandatory concept of par value but retain the rules about eligible consideration.
A few have retained par value but liberalized the rules about eligible consideration. Most of the states that have either of these sets of principles have
both.

These restrictions limiting the kinds of consideration that may be used
for the payment for shares often create practical problems for lawyers. The
paradigm situation involves a new venture in which one or more of the
investors plan to pay for their shares by rendering future services or
by providing ephemeral consideration, such as an idea or concept. The restaurant example in which the chef agrees to become an employee of the
corporation only if she becomes a shareholder in the business is a good
example.

Assume that A, a wealthy investor, and B, a trained chef, plan to open
an upscale restaurant. A agrees to contribute $250,000 in cash to permit
the restaurant to be fully equipped and open, and B agrees to serve as chef
and manager of the restaurant, having sole responsibility for day-to-day operations. Each is to receive 50 percent of the shares and B, in addition, is
to be an employee and receive a salary of $3,000 per month. Assuming that
the corporation is being formed in a par value state with limitations on the
types of eligible consideration for shares, how should this corporation be
capitalized?

The most direct solution is to issue the same number of shares to A
and to B, and off they go. Assume that the corporation decides to create $1
par value shares, and to issue 250,000 shares to A and 250,000 shares to B.
Why so many shares? No particular reason, except that it looks good. This
direct solution is disastrous from the standpoint of B. First of all, she has
received par value shares for less than par, and so has a contingent liability
to creditors to pay up to $250,000 in cash to the corporation even though
the understanding with A was that she was not to be required to put up any
capital. Further, the consideration for the shares issued to B, her promise to
perform future services is not eligible consideration for the shares she received, and A probably can sue to have B's shares canceled since they were
invalidly issued.

It does help in this example to reduce the number of shares being
issued to A and to B to a small number, say 100 shares to each. Since these
are $1 par value shares the effect of doing this is to reduce B's contingent
liability from $250,000 to $100, and it really does not affect control because

A and B both own exactly the same number of shares. However, that does not solve the eligible consideration problem. B still has been issued shares for an invalid consideration.

Another possible solution is for A to purchase his 100 shares for $250,000 and B to purchase his shares for $100. Since the par value of each block is $100, there is no watered stock liability because all shares have been issued for cash at least equal to the par value of the shares. However, what happens if the business is for some reason closed down within a few weeks of formation — perhaps the corporation is unable to obtain a desired zoning change to permit the restaurant to open? If the corporation is then dissolved, A and B will share equally in the proceeds of the dissolution. In other words, B obtains 50 percent of whatever part of A's original capital investment that is recoverable, a result that is clearly undesirable.

Another possible solution is for A and B each to purchase 100 shares of stock for $100 each, and A to provide the remaining $249,900 either as a loan to the corporation or by purchasing preferred stock. B then signs a three-year employment contract to manage the restaurant and serve as chef. While these proposals may create tax problems and it is unlikely that a court would view B's loan as anything but an equity investment, they do solve the formal problem created by the par value statutes.

Yet another approach is to award B his shares only after the expiration of the three-year employment contract. Since "services actually rendered" satisfy the tangible consideration requirement, stock issued to B after her services have been performed meet the statutory requirement. However, in this scenario, B does not become a 50 percent shareholder for three years, and may be frozen out of the corporation in the same manner as any other minority shareholder. Other possible solutions may revolve around a contract between A and B, not involving an ownership interest in the corporation. A may agree to make payments to B in an amount calculated to be 50 percent of the profits of the restaurant in exchange for B's promise to continue to work for the restaurant for three years. This contract seems clearly to be enforceable, though it substitutes personal liability of A for what otherwise would be a corporate obligation.

2. Statutes Based on the 1984 Model Act. The 1984 Model Business Corporation Act eliminates both par value and the rules about eligible consideration.[51] About 20 states have adopted these provisions from the new Model Act. Under this statute, par value becomes an optional set of provis-

---

[51] The 1969 Model Business Corporation Act has both par value and eligible consideration rules. The par value rules were eliminated by amendments in 1980, and the eligible consideration rules were eliminated in the 1984 revision. States with statutes based on these earlier versions of the Model Act generally therefore continue to recognize these doctrines.

ions,[52] and the board of directors has virtually complete discretion to determine what property should be acquired in exchange for shares: promissory notes of investors or contracts for future services are as eligible as cash or tangible property. Also eligible are other "tangible or intangible benefits" to the corporation. It would be permissible under this statute, for example, to issue A 250,000 shares of stock for $250,000 in cash and to issue B 250,000 shares of stock in exchange for the three-year employment contract. Under the 1984 Model Act, the board of directors has discretion to determine how many shares should be issued for an employment contract; there is no arbitrary rule or standard to be complied with.

Shares issued under statutes similar to the 1984 Model Act do not have a par value, and yet they are not the same as no par shares issued under par value statutes. Similarly, shares issued under the 1984 Model Act statutes may have an optional par value, but the issuance of such shares for less than par value does not create watered-stock liability unless the articles of incorporation so provide. These two types of statutes are basically different regimes, each with their own rules and principles.

§9.26 DEBT AND EQUITY IN INITIAL CORPORATE STRUCTURES

In planning corporate structures, it is customary to include some debt in the capital structure, particularly if the corporation is to be a C corporation. It is relatively easy to even off disparate contributions by giving shareholders who contribute property in excess of the amount of their proportionate contribution a debt instrument that equals the amount of the excess.[53] Furthermore, if the business fails shortly after its creation, the shareholder holding debt claims against the corporation may be able to participate in the insolvency proceeding along with trade creditors, thereby recouping a portion of the initial investment.[54]

Over and above these planning advantages, the tax advantages of maximizing the amount of debt and minimizing the amount of equity capital in

---

[52]Since a number of states continue to impose stock or transfer taxes based on par value, corporations that plan to transact business in several states may elect to have an optional par value, thereby minimizing possible exposure to taxes in the future.

[53]As discussed below, however, organization of a corporation with this type of capitalization may not be entirely tax-free.

[54]The so-called *Deep Rock* doctrine, however, may result in the subordination of such claims to those of general trade creditors in bankruptcy proceedings. If subordination occurs, it is likely that the subordinated creditor will receive nothing since other claims usually exhaust assets available for distribution. A similar doctrine, sometimes called a "subordinating equity" doctrine may be applicable in state insolvency proceedings.

a C corporation may be quite substantial if the corporation is seeking to "zero out" its income. Interest payments are deductible by the corporation while dividends to the shareholders are not. Both types of payments are of course taxable to shareholders who are individuals; structuring the transaction as a loan therefore reduces the aggregate tax bills owed by shareholders and the corporation. Also of importance is the fact that corporate debt may be repaid by the corporation without tax consequences to the creditor/shareholders. This is a return of capital, not a dividend. A pro rata redemption of shares will almost always be treated as a dividend whereas interest on and repayment of debt that is proportionately held will usually be treated as debt; in other words, periodic payments of interest are deductible and ultimate repayment is a tax-free return of capital. Also, accumulation of corporate earnings to repay debt is a valid business purpose for purposes of the penalty tax on unreasonable accumulation of earnings.[55]

These advantages are so substantial that many close corporations are "thinly capitalized," that is, most of the capitalization is in the form of corporate debt and a small portion is in the form of equity capital. One recurring issue in litigation today is whether debt in a corporate capital structure is so "stock-like" that it should be treated as a second class of stock, a kind of preferred stock, rather than as debt. If it is stock, the tax advantages are lost. Essentially the same question arises with respect to loans made by shareholders to the corporation after it has been formed: should they be viewed as loans or as contributions to capital? If they are loans, the interest payments are deductible by the corporation and repayments of principal are tax-free returns of capital. If they are capital contributions, all payments by the corporation are nondeductible distributions and may also be taxable to the shareholders as dividends.

The *debt/equity ratio* of a corporation is the mathematical ratio between a corporation's liabilities to its shareholders and the shareholders' equity. For example, a corporation which is capitalized by its shareholders with $10,000 of common stock and $90,000 of loans from the shareholders to the corporation has a debt/equity ratio of 9:1.[56] At one time, it was thought that a ratio of 4:1 was the boundary line above which debt would be reclassified as equity, but courts now favor a more flexible test. Important considerations in these classification disputes are whether the debt capital is essential for the corporation's business, whether there is a bona fide expectation of

[55]One disadvantage of capitalizing the corporation with excessive debt is that tax-free organization under Internal Revenue Code §351 may be inapplicable.

[56]This ratio is sometimes described as the inside ratio to distinguish the ratio calculated by using all corporate liabilities, including those owed to third persons, as compared to shareholders' equity. For purposes of the thin capitalization doctrine discussed in the text, the inside ratio is typically used. For purposes of financial analysis, the outside ratio is used (and, indeed, loans by shareholders to the corporation may be viewed as a kind of permanent investment in the corporation).

repayment, and whether payments of interest and principal occur on a regular basis or are subject to the vicissitudes of the business.

In an S corporation, income is taxed directly to the shareholders so that the issues of deductibility of interest and capital repayment versus distribution of earnings do not arise. Thin capitalization of an S corporation may permit the Internal Revenue Service to argue that the debt is a separate class of stock that disqualifies the corporation from the S corporation election entirely. In 1982, Congress resolved this issue by creating a class of debt, generally known as *safe harbor debt* or *straight debt* which may not be viewed as a second class of stock.[57]

§9.27 MULTIPLE CLASSES OF STOCK AS A PLANNING DEVICE

The planning advantages of using debt in a corporate structure may be partially replicated by the use of one or more classes of preferred shares. The facts of one classic case[58] make this point sharply. Obre and Nelson formed a new corporation, Annel Corporation, to engage in the dirt-moving and road-building businesses. Obre agreed to contribute to the corporation equipment and cash worth $65,000 while Nelson agreed to contribute $10,000 in cash. However, shares were to be issued on a 50/50 basis. Presumably, Nelson planned to contribute services to even matters up. Based on advice from an accounting firm, the parties capitalized the corporation as follows:

Obre:	$10,000 common stock[59]
	$20,000 preferred stock
	$35,000 unsecured promissory note
Nelson:	$10,000 common stock

The $55,000 additional capital being provided by Obre was allocated entirely to debt and preferred stock, itself a neat solution to problems of dilution and watered stock. When the corporation failed shortly after it commenced business, an additional benefit (at least from Obre's standpoint) became apparent. Obre filed a claim in the insolvency proceeding and was recognized as an unsecured creditor to the extent of the $35,000 promissory note. The court rejected an argument that the corporation was inadequately capitalized and the note should be subordinated to all claims of creditors,

---

[57]See I.R.C. §1361(c)(5).

[58]Obre v. Alban Tractor Co., 228 Md. 291, 179 A.2d 861 (1962).

[59]This $10,000 figure presumably was the par value of the shares issued to Obre and Nelson.

since the total equity capitalization of $40,000 could not be said to be inadequate.

If Obre had taken a promissory note of $55,000, it is quite possible that a court would have concluded that the capitalization of only $20,000 was inadequate, and the note was itself a type of preferred stock that was subordinate to the claims of all creditors. The major disadvantage of the *Obre* plan is that the two classes of stock make the corporation ineligible for the S corporation election.

§9.28 TAX CONSEQUENCES OF FORMATION TRANSACTIONS

The Internal Revenue Code contains detailed rules about the tax consequences of the formation and capitalization of a corporation. Section 351 provides for nonrecognition of gain or loss on pure contributions of property to a corporation solely in exchange for shares if the contributing shareholders own more than 80 percent of the shares of the corporation immediately[60] following the transfers. For example, assume that A contributes $25,000 in cash for 100 shares of a new corporation while B contributes property that has a current market value of $25,000 but a tax basis[61] of $10,000 also for 100 shares. No gain is recognized on the transaction by B; B has a tax basis for his stock of $10,000[62] and the corporation has a tax basis for the property of $10,000.[63] A has a tax basis of $25,000 for his stock. Section 351 reflects a basic policy decision that contributions of appreciated property to a new enterprise should not involve immediate recognition and taxation of the appreciation. In a sense, such transactions constitute a change in form of ownership rather than a realization of the economic gain inherent in the appreciated property.[64] Also, it may reflect concern that recognition of the gain in such situations may deter desirable business formation.

The nonrecognition of gain, however, extends only to exchanges of property. If the chef/general manager of the restaurant receives shares for a

---

[60]Problems have sometimes arisen as to whether the contributing shareholders own the requisite percentage of shares when a pre-existing plan exists to resell or distribute the shares shortly after the contributions to the corporation are made.

[61]Basis as used in tax law means roughly the amount invested by the owner in the property, or in other words its cost to the owner. Gain on a sale of property for tax purposes equals selling price minus basis, though other adjustments may be made as well.

[62]I.R.C. §358(a)(1).

[63]Id. §362(a)(1).

[64]Placing appreciated property in a C corporation means that the basis of both the corporation in the property and the shareholders' stock is set at a low level. Depending on the timing, this decision may create tax costs at a later date. See §9.3 note 10.

contract to perform services, she will be immediately taxed on the fair market value of those shares as compensation for services to be rendered.[65] Furthermore, since the chef/general manager in section 9.25 did not contribute property for her shares, her shares cannot be included within the control group to determine whether the 80 percent requirement is met. Property does include intangible property such as patents, secret processes, etc., but not services.

Section 351 is applicable only to the extent the contributors to the corporation receive "stock." If a contributor receives cash or property in addition to stock, that cash or property is called *boot* (as in, "stock plus cash, to boot") and is subject to tax to the extent of any cash received and the fair market value of other boot received.[66] If a contributor of property receives stock and corporate debt obligations in exchange for stock, the debt is boot.

§9.29 ISSUANCE OF SHARES BY EXISTING CORPORATIONS: PREEMPTIVE RIGHTS

Assume that a corporation that has been in existence for some extended period of time determines that it needs additional equity capital. Should the corporation seek to obtain the additional capital by offering to sell new shares to its present shareholders, or should it try to sell the new shares to third parties? The most basic issue raised by this question is the economic one: Which alternative offers the necessary capital at the best possible price per share? However, other issues also exist. Selling common shares to third parties may create political problems. It will introduce new shareholders into the closely held corporate "family." It may also conceivably affect who has working control of the corporation, since the new shares have general voting power. Further, depending on the price paid by the new shareholders, existing shareholders may complain that their economic interests are being diluted since the new shareholders received a bargain price less than the "true" value of the shares of the corporation.

Many states impose legal restrictions on the issuance of shares by a corporation to outside parties. The doctrine of *preemptive rights* states that the current shareholders have a right to purchase their pro rata portion of new shares proposed to be issued in order to preserve their economic and management position within the corporation. Preemptive rights were originally viewed as an inherent part of the concept of owning shares.[67] Preemp-

---

[65] Id. §351(d)(1).

[66] Id. §351(b)(1).

[67] In other words, all shareholders automatically had a preemptive right to protect their interests in the corporation from dilution.

tive rights are now universally viewed as an optional right that the governing corporate documents may grant or deny, or may grant on a qualified basis. Sophisticated lawyers generally believe that preemptive rights create more problems than they solve, particularly in corporations with publicly traded shares, but they nevertheless continue to exist in many corporations.[68] Where preemptive rights exist, a number of ancillary questions should be addressed, for example what happens with respect to shares subject to the preemptive right that are not purchased by the shareholder.[69]

Preemptive rights may also not provide realistic protection for shareholders of a closely held corporation. The issuance of shares by an ongoing corporation may also be used to oppress minority shareholders. This is most likely to occur where controlling shareholders purchase their proportionate part of the new shares through the cancellation of debts already owed to them by the corporation, while the non-controlling shareholders have the choice between investing additional capital (that is thereafter subject to the management of the controlling shareholders) or seeing their proportionate interest in the corporation being diluted. Preemptive rights provide no protection against this type of transaction, and may even encourage them. However, some courts have evolved a fiduciary duty imposed on the controlling shareholders to prevent the issuance of shares where there appears to be no valid business purpose, i.e., where the transaction appears to be designed solely to dilute the interest of minority shareholders. This duty may also protect minority shareholders from other types of oppressive transactions.[70]

D. DIVIDENDS AND DISTRIBUTIONS

§9.30 DISTRIBUTIONS AND DIVIDENDS IN GENERAL

The word *distribution* in corporation law is a general term referring to any kind of payment (in cash, property, or obligations of indebtedness) by the corporation to one or more shareholders on account of the ownership of shares. The word *dividend* is usually understood to be a narrower term referring to a special type of distribution: a payment to shareholders by the cor-

---

[68] State statutes may make preemptive rights either an "opt in" or an "opt out" election. Where the articles of incorporation are silent on preemptive rights, the state statute must therefore be consulted to determine whether silence means the corporation has, or does not have, preemptive rights.

[69] Model Business Corporation Act §6.30 provides a model form that deals with a number of these questions.

[70] See §8.35.

poration out of its current or retained earnings in proportion to the number of shares owned by the shareholder. An example of a distribution that is not a dividend is a partial payment to shareholders by a solvent corporation in the process of liquidation. In that situation, one would naturally refer to a liquidating distribution, not a liquidating dividend, though the phrase "liquidating dividend" doubtless is used in some circumstances.

It is important to recognize that a corporation may make a distribution even though it has no current earnings and no extra cash. A corporation may be able to go down to the bank, borrow money, and then turn around and make a distribution of that money to its shareholders. While that may not be wise, and may be inconsistent with statements made to the lender, it is not of itself illegal.

Payments to a shareholder in the form of salary, interest, or rent in this sense are not distributions at all since they are on account of services rendered or property supplied to the corporation by its shareholders rather than on account of the ownership of shares. However, in a more general sense, they do involve a distribution of corporate assets to the shareholder in question. Certainly, if the payments are so large as to bear no reasonable relationship to the value received by the corporation from the transaction to which they are attached, all or part of the payment may be viewed as a distribution on account of the ownership of shares.[71] Such transactions may be referred to as "informal" or "disguised" dividends or distributions.

§9.31 TAX TREATMENT OF DIVIDENDS AND DISTRIBUTIONS

Distributions by a C corporation out of "earnings and profits" of the corporation are taxable to the shareholders as dividends.[72] If the corporation has earnings and profits in the year the distribution is made, the distribution is a taxable dividend even if there is a deficit in accumulated earnings and profits carried over from earlier years. "Earnings and profits" is not itself a defined term in the Internal Revenue Code. It is not precisely equal to the taxable income of the corporation in all prior and the current years reduced by the amount of dividends previously paid out. Rather, it is a calculation of realized and undistributed economic profits. Various adjustments are required to move from the sum of all taxable income to earnings and profits, including for example, inclusion of gain on a transaction that is accounted for tax purposes under the installment or completed contract method of accounting. Prior distributions that are taxable as dividends reduce earnings and profits.

[71]See §9.38.
[72]I.R.C. §311.

Earnings and profits do not represent a fund. Rather, the concept is a test for determining when distributions are taxable to shareholders. A shareholder may not seek to avoid taxation of a distribution on a theory that the distribution was in fact "from" a source other than earnings and profits, e.g., loan proceeds. If the corporation has earnings and profits, the distribution is taxable as a dividend to the shareholders to the extent of earnings and profits without regard to its source.

If a C corporation makes a distribution that exceeds its earnings and profits (or when it has no earnings and profits), that distribution is not taxable to the shareholders but reduces the basis of their stock. Thereafter, if the distributions are greater than that basis (i.e., the nontaxable distribution reduces the basis to zero), the excess is taxable gain on the investment.

If a C corporation distributes property rather than cash, the amount of the distribution is measured by the fair market value of the property, and that value becomes the basis of the property in the hands of the shareholders. If the property has appreciated in value while owned by the corporation, the corporation is taxed on the amount of that gain upon the distribution, the former rule of *General Utilities*[73] that permitted such gain to avoid tax altogether having been repealed.[74]

Distributions by an S corporation are treated quite differently. Distributions reduce the basis of the shareholders' investment in the corporation, the shareholders already having included in their income for tax purposes their proportionate allocation of the corporation's prior income. However, an S corporation may have earnings and profits from its operations from earlier years while a C corporation, and certain kinds of transactions may trigger a tax at the corporate level even though the corporation subsequently has made the election to be taxed as an S corporation.

§9.32 TYPES OF DISTRIBUTIVE TRANSACTIONS

Several different and superficially unrelated transactions have the effect of making distributions to shareholders. In some states with older statutes, different legal rules may be applicable to different kinds of transactions in determining the lawfulness of a distribution. Such statutes are becoming less common, however, as states adopt modern statutes that apply a single legal standard to all distributions without regard to their form. The following types of transactions constitute distributions.

(a) *Distributions of Money.* The most common and best-known kind of distribution is a simple payment of money by the corporation to each

---

[73]General Utilities & Operating Co. v. Commissioner, 296 U.S. 200 (1935).
[74]I.R.C. §311(a), as amended in 1986. The gain has the same characteristic, e.g., ordinary or capital gain, as it would have had if the property had been sold.

shareholder, the amount of which is proportional to the number of shares owned by each shareholder.

(b) *Distributions of Property in Kind.* Property, unlike money, is usually not divisible into readily usable and discrete units. A distribution of undivided interests in a piece of improved real estate, for example, is likely to create problems of management and control thereafter. Further, undivided interests in property — for example, a 3/25ths or a 91/26,875ths interest in an apartment house — may be impossible to sell except to other owners of undivided interests in the property who may be interested in reassembling the ownership into salable form. Distributions of undivided interests in property are nevertheless sufficiently common for the corporate literature to distinguish between cash dividends and property dividends.

(c) *Distributions of Indebtedness.* A corporation may also distribute promises by it to make payments at some time in the future. The simplest way to do this is for the corporation to create instruments of indebtedness and distribute them to its shareholders. More commonly, the debt reflects a portion of the agreed-upon purchase price of shares to be repurchased by the corporation where the corporation lacks ready assets to pay the full purchase price and does not want to borrow funds from a commercial source for this purpose. The relationship between distribution-related debt and ordinary business indebtedness is discussed in Section 9.36.

(d) *Disguised or Constructive Dividends.* The question whether a specific payment is a dividend or is payment of interest, rent, salary, or other payment usually arises in the tax context in which a C corporation claims a deduction for the payment which is questioned by the Internal Revenue Service. The same question, however, may also arise in suits by shareholders who claim that payments to controlling shareholders, directors, or officers in effect constitute a disguised dividend which should be shared by all shareholders. The tests for such transactions outside of the tax context may be "conflict of interest," the "intrinsic fairness of the transaction," or "spoilation or waste." The tax-related litigation may be relied upon by shareholders complaining of specific transactions. The critical determinant under the tax law to determine if a specific payment is a dividend is whether the shareholder received more than an incidental, unpaid-for benefit from the transaction by virtue of her status as a shareholder. There are numerous cases involving transactions, such as the following: payment by the corporation of a debt actually owed by the shareholder, sale of property by the shareholder to the corporation at an excessive price, the sale of corporate property to the shareholder at a below-market price, corporate loans to the shareholder when there is no intention to repay the loans, excessive salary paid to the shareholder who is also an employee, and the furnishing by the corporation of benefits that are predominantly for the benefit of the shareholder (such as country club memberships or season tickets for sporting events) and only incidentally for the convenience of the corporation. These are eminently factual questions in the close corporation context.

(e) *Repurchases of Shares*. An important type of distributive transaction is the purchase by the corporation of its own shares. Indeed, transactions involving repurchases of shares are so common that the following sections are devoted to them.

§9.33 CORPORATE REPURCHASE OF SHARES

Superficially, a purchase by a corporation of its own shares may not be thought of as involving a distribution at all. It may appear to be the purchase of an asset rather than the making of a distribution. That analysis, however, confuses transactions in which the corporation repurchases *its own stock* and transactions in which it purchases stock *issued by another corporation*. The former is a distribution, the latter is an investment.

When a corporation buys back its own stock, it does not receive anything of value in the hands of the corporation. The remaining shareholders continue to own 100 percent of the corporate assets (now reduced by the amount of the payment used to reacquire the shares). A corporation cannot treat stock in itself that it has purchased as an asset any more than it can treat its authorized but unissued stock as an asset. One cannot own 10 percent of oneself and have one's total worth be 110 percent of the value of one's assets. This point is so fundamental that it may be well to re-read the last few sentences.

Stock issued by another corporation is entirely different. That does not create the same circularity problem. Shares of corporation B have value based on the assets owned by corporation B; if shares of corporation B are purchased by corporation A they are an asset in the hands of corporation A.

The fact that a repurchase of shares constitutes a distribution can be most easily appreciated by considering a proportionate repurchase of stock by the corporation from each shareholder. Assume that three persons each own 100 shares of stock in a corporation, its entire outstanding stock. The shareholders decide that each of them will sell 10 shares back to the corporation for $100 per share, or a total of $1,000 each. When the transaction is completed, each shareholder continues to own one-third of the corporation (now represented by 90 shares rather than 100 shares), the corporation is $3,000 poorer and the shareholders are each $1,000 richer. Clearly, there has been a distribution even though the transaction was cast in the form of a repurchase of stock rather than a direct distribution of assets by the corporation.

§9.34 TREASURY SHARES

Under most state statutes, the 30 shares reacquired by the corporation in the previous example are called *treasury shares*. Treasury shares are viewed as being held by the corporation in a sort of twilight zone until they are either retired permanently or resold to someone else in the future. Treasury shares are not an asset of the corporation even though they are salable and may be sold at some later time. Exactly the same thing can be said of every share of authorized but unissued stock.

Assume that the corporation in the example described above decides to resell the treasury shares to X (a nonshareholder) for $3,000. The interests of each of the three original shareholders have been diluted: There are now four shareholders owning shares in the ratio 90:90:90:30. The corporation could have paid the original shareholders a cash dividend of $1,000 each and then sold 33 shares of authorized but unissued stock to X for $3,000 with exactly the same economic result. (In this variation, the shares are owned 100:100:100:33 rather than 90:90:90:30; the percentage ownership interest, however, is as a practical matter identical.)

A repurchase of shares by the corporation is a distribution even if the corporation purchases only shares owned by one shareholder rather than proportionately from each shareholder. Such a transaction is a disproportionate distribution (i.e., one not shared proportionately by all shareholders). The corporation has made a distribution to a single shareholder equal to the purchase price it paid for the shares. This transaction is not all bad from the standpoint of the other shareholders, however, since it simultaneously increases their percentage interest in the corporation. For example, if the corporation with three shareholders in the above example repurchased all 100 shares owned by shareholder A for $10,000, the interests of shareholders B and C in the corporation are both increased from 33.3 percent to 50 percent. The assets of the corporation are reduced by the $10,000 purchase price paid to shareholder A to eliminate his or her interest in the corporation. Whether or not this is a "winner" for A or for B and C depends on the value of the assets in the corporation before the share repurchase.

§9.35 TAX TREATMENT OF SHARE REPURCHASES

The tax treatment of repurchased shares of C corporations reflects the reality that they are distributions. (Such transactions are called *redemptions* in the Internal Revenue Code.)[75] A redemption may be treated either as an *exchange* (that is, as a purchase of shares by the corporation) or as a dividend to the extent the corporation has earnings and profits. If the transaction is

[75]I.R.C. §317.

an exchange, only the gain is taxable to the shareholder and that gain is a capital gain and not ordinary income; if it is a dividend, the total purchase price is taxable as ordinary income (subject always to the earnings and profits requirement). The statute states that a redemption is an exchange if (a) it is not essentially equivalent to a dividend, (b) it involves a substantially disproportionate reduction of interest, or (c) it involves a "complete termination of interest."[76]

A redemption of the entire interest of shareholder A is not a distribution to shareholders B and C even though their percentage interest in the corporation has increased.[77] Shareholder A will of course recognize gain or loss on the transaction. In most S corporations, the redemption is treated as a tax-free return of capital up to the basis of the stock held by the taxpayer, and taxable gain to the extent the distribution exceeds the basis of the stock.[78]

§9.36 PRIORITY OF DISTRIBUTION-RELATED DEBT

If a corporation creates indebtedness as part of a distribution and the corporation is thereafter unable to discharge all of its debts, the question arises whether the indebtedness so created is on a parity with ordinary business or trade indebtedness, or whether shareholders who receive indebtedness as part of a distribution should be subordinated to such outside indebtedness. At first blush, indebtedness created as part of a distribution would seem not to be entitled to parity since, after all, it is part of a distribution that should be permitted only if all business creditors are paid first. The Model Business Corporation Act,[79] however, places all such debt on a parity with regular business indebtedness on this theory: The corporation, rather than distributing indebtedness directly to shareholders, could have borrowed funds from a third person and distributed the proceeds to the shareholders. The debt to the third person in that situation would certainly be on a parity with general trade indebtedness.[80] The creditors of the corporation are thus no worse off if indebtedness issued to shareholders is given parity with them

---

[76]Id. §302(b). In applying these standards, however, very broad attribution rules are applicable so that it is unlikely that a redemption within a family corporation can be taxed other than as a dividend. These very broad attribution rules are designed to prevent tax avoidance through the redemption of shares.

[77]Consult Rands, Closely Held Corporations: Federal Tax Consequences of Stock Transfer Restrictions, 7 J. Corp. Law 449, 456-457 (1982).

[78]This may not be true if the corporation has accumulated earnings and profits from earlier years as a C corporation.

[79]Model Business Corporation Act §6.40(f).

[80]The third-party creditor has simply made a commercial loan to the corporation, which is free to use the proceeds as it sees fit.

than if money is borrowed from third persons in order to make the distribution in cash. Further, a shareholder who accepts a distribution of indebtedness rather than insisting on cash should not be in a worse position than one who insists on cash knowing that the corporation has to borrow funds to make the payment being demanded.

§9.37 SHARE REPURCHASES IN C CORPORATIONS

Distributions in the form of repurchases of shares are very common in real life. In closely held C corporations, the elimination of one shareholder's interest in the corporation is almost routinely effected by a repurchase of shares by the corporation. Such a transaction permits the use of corporate rather than personal assets, has favorable tax consequences (if the attribution rules are carefully avoided), and does not affect the relative interests of the remaining shareholders. The alternative — having the shares be purchased by the remaining shareholders individually — requires the use of after-tax dollars, whereas the corporate repurchase of shares permits the use of corporate assets without there being a taxable distribution. Further, the corporation may fund its obligation in the event of the death of a shareholder with life insurance; mechanical problems are created if the number of shareholders is greater than two or three and each shareholder acquires insurance policies on the lives of the other shareholders. Finally, a corporate repurchase of shares avoids problems that are created if one or more shareholders are unwilling or unable to repurchase the shares allocated to them.

§9.38 LEGAL RESTRICTIONS ON DISTRIBUTIONS IN GENERAL

All state statutes contain provisions governing and restricting the power of corporations to make distributions or to pay dividends. These statutory provisions are confusing, sometimes internally inconsistent or self-contradictory, and often incomplete, in the sense of not addressing some recurring issues relating to distributions. Several factors contribute to this unfortunate state of affairs: (1) the historical development of these provisions, (2) the fact that these statutes serve several different and overlapping policies, and (3) there is considerable uncertainty about the wisdom and desirable scope of these policies.

Modern statutes contain two different types of prohibitions: (1) a capital protection provision that prohibits distributions that in some sense invade or reduce the permanent capital of the corporation, and (2) a provision prohibiting distributions that have the effect of rendering the corporation insolvent in the sense of being unable to meet its obligations as they mature.

307

The first test is usually referred to as the "balance sheet" test and the second as the "equity insolvency" test. These tests should be discussed separately.

§9.39 THE BALANCE SHEET TEST

Statutes regulate and limit distributions by imposing restrictions on the right-hand balance sheet entries that may be reduced by the payments.[81] An oversimplified balance sheet should make this relationship clear:

Assets		Liabilities	
Cash	$20,000	Bank loans	$30,000
Other	$40,000	Owners equity	
		Common stock	$20,000
		Earnings	
		current	$3,000
		accumulated	$7,000
Total	$60,000	Total	$60,000

In the Owners equity portion of the balance sheet, current earnings represent earnings of the present year while accumulated earnings represent earnings from previous years not distributed in the form of dividends. The Common stock entry represents what the shareholders paid for the stock when it was originally issued. Now let us assume that the corporation decides it wishes to distribute $6,000 to its shareholders. The payment of $6,000 will reduce the left-hand entry Cash by $6,000; the offsetting entry must be a reduction of some right-hand entry. The only real choices are current earnings, accumulated earnings, or Common stock. The legality of the distribution depends on what the state's distribution statute says about which right-hand accounts may be charged with the distribution and which may not. Since all state statutes permit the payment of dividends out of either current or accumulated earnings, the $6,000 payment is consistent with the balance sheet test in all states. This payment is still a dividend even though it is made in part out of accumulated earnings.

Now let us assume that rather than distributing $6,000 (which it clearly may do), the corporation wishes to distribute $15,000 to its share-

---

[81] Perhaps a word of explanation may be useful. A balance sheet restates a defined equality: *assets* − *liabilities* = *equity*. Hence, *assets* = *liabilities* + *equity*. If an asset item on the left-hand side of the balance sheet is reduced by a payment of cash, some item on the right-hand side must also be reduced (or another item on the left-hand side must be increased, as would be the case, for example, if the cash was used to purchase supplies or machinery). Distributions to shareholders must be reflected by a reduction in a right-hand account; since liabilities are not increased, only "equity" items remain. See §12.1.

holders. May it do so? It probably can afford it in the sense that even after paying out $15,000, the corporation will have assets of $45,000 and liabilities of only $30,000. That, however, is not relevant under the balance sheet test. What is important under that test is which right-hand account or accounts are to be reduced by $15,000. The current and accumulated earnings accounts can be reduced by $10,000 to 0 but the remaining $5,000 must be reflected as a reduction or invasion of capital. Another way of looking at this transaction is that the $15,000 payment represents a distribution of (a) $3,000 of this year's earnings, (b) $7,000 of accumulated earnings from previous years, and (c) $5,000 of capital.

State statutes vary widely as to whether a corporation may invade or distribute capital in this manner. Most modern statutes permit distributions of capital down to zero; older statutes, however, establish a variety of different standards or tests for establishing whether the distribution is permissible, and under most of them the invasion of capital would not be permitted.[82] The statutory penalty for making an illegal distribution is usually to make directors who voted for the distribution personally liable for the illegal portion of the distribution. Shareholders who receive the dividend knowing that it was illegal also may be personally liable.

This simple example makes two critical points. First, in order to control distributions, the balance sheet test places restraints on which right-hand entries may be reduced when a distribution is made. The right-hand entries in the balance sheet serve as a kind of valve or control on distributions of assets that appear on the left-hand side of the balance sheet. Second, the balance sheet test is not directly concerned with solvency, but rather with the preservation of announced capital. It is concerned with appearances: A corporation that says it has permanent capital of a specified amount on its balance sheet may not make a distribution of all or a portion of that capital to shareholders. This test harks back to an early era of corporation law where the corporation's capital was viewed as a cushion or trust fund for the benefit of subsequent creditors who may be induced to extend credit in reliance on the corporation's balance sheet.

Older statutes draw a distinction between permanent capital and surplus capital (with the permanent capital usually being defined as the aggregate sum of the par values of all shares issued by the corporation).[83] These statutes can easily be evaded by the manipulation of par value principles, either by adopting nominal par values initially or by subsequently amending

---

[82] As described below, if this corporation is incorporated in a par value state, and most of the original capital is contributed in the form of par value, the distribution would almost certainly be unlawful. If nominal par value is used, the excess of the amount contributed for stock over par value would be classed as capital surplus, and under most statutes that surplus may be reduced by the balance of the distribution if the proper procedures are followed. Under these circumstances, the distribution would be permissible.

[83] See §9.26.

articles of incorporation to reduce the par value of outstanding shares. As a result, these statutes are in fact largely ineffective in requiring minimum amounts of capital to be retained as a cushion. Indeed, these statutes give a deceptive picture of how much capital the corporation is required to maintain. Rather than providing protection to creditors, these statutes in fact become primarily rites of initiation for new corporation lawyers: When one learns how to avoid all meaningful restrictions on corporate distributions, one has proved one is a corporation lawyer.

The most modern statutes, largely developed in the last decade, recognize the impracticability of defining minimum amounts of capital, and freely allow the distribution of capital so long as after the distribution assets exceed liabilities plus preferential amounts payable in liquidation to holders of preferred shares. In these most modern statutes, greater reliance is placed on the equity insolvency test described below than on the balance sheet test in order to protect creditors.

No matter what specific tests are established in these balance sheet statutes, they all suffer from one major, indeed fundamental flaw. Chapter 12 on accounting principles makes it clear that the distinction between "capital" and "income" is a most slippery one indeed. Income and capital are not self-defining but are dependent on accounting principles adequate to handle a variety of complex and subtle issues such as the allocation of expense items to specific periods, the principles on which assets are to be valued, depreciation schedules, the time of recognition of asset appreciation and contingent liabilities, and the like. Different accounting principles may give widely varying answers as to what the income of the corporation during a specific period was, and therefore what the corporation's capital was at the end of that period. The creation of standard accounting principles by legislative fiat for all corporations, large and small, is a daunting task, and no state legislature has attempted to do so. It is basically up to the courts to decide what accounting principles must be followed.

Illegal dividend issues usually arise in suits to surcharge directors for approving improper dividends. That is a particularly brutal kind of litigation from the standpoint of the defendants, who are asked to restore to the corporation the amount of distributions made to shareholders out of their own personal pockets, even though they may have acted in perfect good faith in reliance on expert legal and accounting advice, and did not themselves receive any more than whatever portion of the distribution their shareholdings entitled them to. It is not surprising that courts tend to find a reason to uphold the legality of specific distributions out of sympathy with the defendants — often people of substance in the community — who are faced with substantial liability based on a misreading of the intricacies of financial accounting.

Recognition that elaborate balance sheet statutes fail almost entirely in their basic purpose is also evident from the behavior of creditors. They pay no attention to the elaborate statutory provisions ostensibly designed for their protection. Rather, they protect themselves in different ways: (1) they rely on credit reporting agencies and similar private organizations before extending unsecured credit to businesses, (2) they obtain purchase money security interests[84] when they sell goods on credit to businesses, (3) in the case of larger transactions, they negotiate elaborate loan agreements with debtors by which they obtain contract protection against unwise or improvident distributions of assets to shareholders, and (4) they require personal guarantees from shareholders.

§9.40 THE EQUITY INSOLVENCY TEST

All state statutes relating to distributions impose an equity insolvency test for distributions in addition to the largely ineffective balance sheet prohibitions described above. The equity insolvency test states that a distribution to shareholders is unlawful if it makes the corporation insolvent in the equity sense, i.e., unable to pay its obligations as they mature in the future.

At first blush, the equity insolvency test may sound like a variant of the balance sheet test for distributions: In fact it is based on a totally different approach. The balance sheet test is based on financial statements and accounting principles. The equity insolvency test is based on an examination of future cash flows and cash demands after the distribution. It requires the board of directors to determine whether the corporation has or will have available funds to discharge its near-future obligations as they come due if the proposed distribution is made. This test is easily stated but requires difficult estimates and projections in practice. The board of directors must make an examination of anticipated cash flows and future cash needs arising from the maturation of debts and liabilities to determine whether, after the contemplated distribution, the corporation will be able to meet its financial obligations in the regular course of business.

Despite the difficulty of application, it is generally recognized that the equity insolvency test provides meaningful protection to creditors. Properly applied, it requires directors to make meaningful estimates of future cash needs before authorizing distributions that may injure creditors.

The 1984 Model Business Corporation Act revises and rationalizes these complex rules about corporate distributions. First, it defines "distributions" in a manner to include all types of transfers of assets to shareholders on account of their shares.[85] Second, it adopts a liberal balance sheet test: A distribution is permitted unless, after giving it effect, "the corporation's

---

[84]A *purchase money security interest* gives priority to sellers of goods on credit to take back the goods if the buyer defaults.

[85]Model Business Corporation Act (1984) §1.40(6).

total assets would be less than the sum of its total liabilities. . . ."[86] There is no formal capital requirement under the Model Act that capital in some positive amount be retained. The equity test in the Model Act is defined in traditional terms: A distribution may not be made, if after giving it effect, "the corporation would not be able to pay its debts as they become due in the usual course of business. . . ."[87]

A series of safe harbors to protect directors from personal liability for improper distributions are also provided by the Model Act. First, in determining whether a distribution is lawful, the directors may base a determination "either on financial statements prepared on the basis of accounting practices and principles that are reasonable in the circumstances or on a fair valuation or other method that is reasonable under the circumstances."[88] Further, liability for an illegal distribution may be imposed only on directors who vote for or assent to the specific distribution, the liability only exists with respect to that portion of the distribution that exceeds the maximum amount of the distribution that could have been lawfully made, and only directors who failed to exercise due care as defined in the Model Act[89] in approving the distribution may be held liable.[90] The Model Act also contains detailed rules as to when the legality of a distribution is to be measured,[91] and imposes a two year statute of limitations on suits for illegal distributions.[92]

§9.41 SUITS TO COMPEL THE PAYMENT OF DIVIDENDS

In closely held corporations that are taxed as C corporations, distribution policies strongly tend in the direction of accumulation of surplus and no formal payment of dividends. Informal distributions in the form of tax-deductible salary, rent, or interest payments are common. The principal motivation, of course, is federal income taxation: The payment of a reasonable salary to a shareholder is deductible by the corporation and to that extent avoids the double tax on income that otherwise increases the tax cost of operating as a C corporation. Such deductions are allowed only to the extent that they are "reasonable," but that standard permits considerable flex-

---

[86]Id. §6.40(c)(2). If the corporation has issued preferred shares with a liquidation preference, that amount must also be retained within the corporation.

[87]Id. §6.40(c)(1).

[88]Id. §6.40(d).

[89]Id. §8.30.

[90]Id. §8.33(a).

[91]Id. §6.40(e).

[92]Id. §8.30(c).

ibility in distribution policy, often allowing the entire income of the corporation to be zeroed out to avoid all taxes at the corporate level.

Informal distributions of this type open the possibility of unfair treatment of minority shareholders or shareholders who do not participate in management, since they will not receive a proportionate part of the informal distribution. Even where the motive of the majority shareholder is not exclusionary, however, strict proportionality is unlikely, since the quantity and quality of services provided naturally vary from one individual to another. Further, strict proportionality may suggest to a revenue agent in a subsequent tax audit that all or a portion of the salary deductions claimed are in fact informal dividends. The result is likely to be accumulation of assets plus some informal distributions to some of the shareholders, a result that is most unattractive to the remaining shareholders.

The decision whether or not to pay dividends or make distributions theoretically involves business judgments by the board of directors as to whether it is prudent to preserve earnings for future needs or whether a distribution should be made and in what amount. Indeed, in many respects the decision whether or not to make a distribution is the classic example of a business judgment: Courts have long recognized that dividend decisions involve sensitive judgments about the future cash needs of the business both in terms of satisfying liabilities and making necessary investments in existing or new productive facilities. As a result, courts are loath to second-guess directors on such decisions, and within a broad range accept the decision of the board on such matters.

Directors also owe fiduciary duties to shareholders in connection with their stewardship of the corporation, and the decision to pay (or more commonly, to omit) dividends or distributions is evaluated within these broad duties. These duties may be phrased in terms of fair treatment of minority shareholders or of all classes of shares, or in terms of not favoring a class in which members of the board of directors have substantial personal interests. Tax considerations are not by themselves a justification to withhold all distributions. There is obvious tension between these fiduciary duties and the business judgment rule described in the previous paragraph. However, the existence of a relatively large number of cases in which courts have reviewed the dividend policy adopted by closely held corporations and ordered that a dividend be paid illustrates that often the fiduciary duty dominates.

A compulsory dividend is most likely to be ordered by a court where the minority shareholder can demonstrate: (1) actions by the majority shareholder that may be construed as constituting antagonism or bad faith against the minority, (2) the existence of liquid assets within the corporation in excess of the apparent needs of the business and apparently available for the payment of dividends, and (3) a policy of informal distributions to favored shareholders through salaries, loans, informal cash advances, and the like. When all is said and done, however, suits to compel the payment of dividends should be viewed as a long shot even in relatively egregious circumstances.

If a corporation has elected S corporation tax treatment, the corporate income is passed through to the shareholders for inclusion in their individual tax returns. There is no tax advantage in accumulating surplus and utilizing salary or similar accounts as a substitute for dividends. On the other hand, allocations of income to a shareholder for tax purposes does not necessarily mean there will also be the payment of a dividend or distribution. An S corporation may withhold distributions for exclusionary purposes, to "soften up" a minority shareholder in an effort to compel a distress sale. Indeed, if the corporation refuses to pay any cash dividends when it has substantial taxable income, minority shareholders may find it difficult or impossible to pay their personal tax bills swollen by the allocation of a substantial amount of corporate taxable income. In extreme cases, it may be necessary for minority shareholders to seek to revoke the S corporation election, if that is practical, or if it is not, to bring suit to compel the payment of dividends based on breach by the board of directors of its fiduciary duties to act in good faith and treat all shareholders equally. The usual pattern of S corporation distributions is to at least pay a dividend equal to the maximum tax that is due on the amount of income allocated to each shareholder pursuant to the S corporation election, though that practice is not always followed.

10

The Limits of Limited Liability and Corporateness

§10.1 INTRODUCTION

This brief chapter considers the extent to which the separate corporate existence is recognized in real life. The principal issue is of course whether the limited liability inherent in the corporate form will be recognized in specific situations; that is, whether one or more shareholders should be held personally liable for corporate obligations. However, the issue is broader than merely the potential liability of shareholders. It extends to a variety of issues that depend on whether or not a legal separation between the corporation and its owners will be recognized. Examples of such issues are whether service of process on the corporation is also service of process on a shareholder, whether a corporation is bound by a labor contract entered into by a subsidiary, or vice versa, or whether a contract entered into by a shareholder limiting her freedom of action also binds her corporation after its shares have been sold to a third person.

§10.2 LIMITED LIABILITY IN GENERAL

The desire for limited liability is, of course, typically a major force in causing closely held businesses to incorporate in the first place,[1] though today much the same protection may be obtained through the use of limited liability companies discussed in Chapter 6, and to a lesser extent by the use of limited partnerships and limited liability partnerships discussed in earlier chapters. However, the adoption of the corporate form of business does not of itself ensure that the shareholders will have limited liability. Indeed, in many small corporations it may not be practical to conduct business at all without at least some of the shareholders voluntarily assuming responsibility for some business debts. And, even where there is no voluntary assumption of corporate obligations, the shield of limited liability may easily be lost through carelessness or misconduct. The generic phrase for the imposition of liability on shareholders on these grounds is *piercing the corporate veil*.

§10.3 LIABILITY ARISING FROM PRE-INCORPORATION TRANSACTIONS: PROMOTER'S LIABILITY

When a new business is in the process of formation, someone must take the responsibility for assembling the various components: the physical facilities, the employees, the raw materials, the sales force, the managers, the working capital, the lines of credit, and so forth. The persons undertaking this responsibility are called the *promoters* of the enterprise. The word promoters may have a negative connotation in the minds of some readers,[2] but in real life promoters provide a useful — indeed essential — function of translating abstract ideas about a potential business into reality.

Very commonly, the promoters of a new business will be the principal

---

[1]This is not to suggest that limited liability is the sole reason to incorporate. The internal management structure of a corporation may be attractive, as may be the ability to raise capital by the issuance of shares. A business that is considering raising capital through a public offering of securities at some future time will almost inevitably elect the corporate form of business before that offering is made.

[2]I suspect that much of the opprobrium attached to "promoters" has resulted from situations in which the promoters take an unreasonably large portion of the equity of the business for their services, e.g., by issuing stock to themselves for their services while outside investors must pay cash for their shares. In addition, in the late Nineteenth and early Twentieth Centuries there were a number of promotions of huge businesses (involving the combination of many existing smaller businesses) in which inside participants received benefits vastly in excess of the value of their contributions.

shareholders in and managers of the business after it is underway. It is relatively easy in this situation for promoters inadvertently to incur personal liability for business obligations that are designed to be the responsibility of the corporation after it is formed. Where the business is to be conducted in corporate form following its inception, the promoters should always form the corporation as the first step in the promotion, and thereafter take all obligations or commitments in the name of that corporation. However, that is often not the way it is in fact done.

Even though the formation of a corporation is relatively simple and inexpensive, many promoters first test the waters by checking to see whether it is feasible to assemble the economic components of the business before actually forming the corporation. Where commitments are received before the corporation is actually formed, the promoters may record them in the form of agreements entered into (1) between the third party and the promoter individually, (2) between the third party and "ABC Corporation, a corporation to be formed," or (3) simply between the third party and "ABC Corporation" even though no attempt at incorporation had been made. In all of these situations, the promoter or person executing the agreement on behalf of the prospective venture is very likely to be held personally liable on the obligation. In the first situation, the promoter is a party to the contract and responsible for its performance.[3] In the second situation, a court is likely to refer to cases on "promoters' contracts" and conclude that since someone was intended to be liable, it must be the promoter. Cases involving this situation, however, may reach a result that no contract at all was intended if the third party intended to rely solely on the corporation for performance. In the third situation, the third party may be able to rely on common law concepts of "de facto corporations,"[4] or statutory provisions stating that liability should be imposed in such situations,[5] or the tort concept that the promoter, by executing a contract in the name of a nonexistent corporation, misrepresented its existence and is therefore liable for fraud.

Promoters' liability becomes a problem primarily when the promotion

---

[3]If the corporation is thereafter formed and assumes the contract, the promoter and the corporation are likely to be jointly and severally liable for the performance of the contract. The third party, of course, can agree to the substitution of the corporation for the promoter — a *novation* — but normally there is no reason for the third party to agree to this.

[4]The phrase "de facto corporation" is still widely used even though technically it relates to foul-ups in the formation process, e.g., a filing that is rejected by the secretary of state for technical reasons. The textbook definition of *de facto corporation* is that 1) there must be a statute under which the corporation may be formed, 2) a good-faith attempt at incorporation, and 3) actual user of the corporate franchise. A de facto corporation is valid against all third parties except the state, and therefore is "nearly as good" as a de jure corporation — a legally formed corporation.

[5]See, e.g., Model Business Corporation Act (1984) §2.04: "All persons purporting to act as or on behalf of a corporation, knowing there was no incorporation under this Act, are jointly and severally liable for all liabilities created while so acting."

aborts and the corporation never begins business. At this point, promoters face personal liability, or at least claims of personal liability on contracts entered into by the promoter that are now valueless. If the promotion is successful, on the other hand, the corporation normally assumes the obligations of these pre-incorporation obligations and discharges them. That raises another question: If the corporation is formed, is it automatically bound on the contract entered into in its name by the promoter, or may it decide that some contracts are simply "too rich" for its taste? Again, there is a black letter rule: The corporation is not automatically obligated on a pre-incorporation contract but must take an affirmative step to adopt the contract if it wishes to accept its benefits and assume its burdens. If the corporation does not like the pre-incorporation contract, it can reject it and the promoter again has to deal with the third party. This raises yet another question. What if the corporation does accept the contract? Does that let the promoter off the hook? At this point, the answer is not entirely clear. Adoption by the corporation arguably constitutes a novation and takes the promoter off the hook. However, it is also possible that a court may simply treat the corporation and the promoter as joint obligors.

§10.4 VOLUNTARY ASSUMPTION OF LIABILITY BY SHAREHOLDERS

Shareholders are usually not liable for the corporation's obligations on the theory that the corporation is "a separate legal entity." Further, an agent (who may well also be a shareholder) who commits the corporation to a transaction giving rise to a corporate obligation is not personally liable on that obligation under accepted agency principles if he is acting within the scope of his actual authority for a disclosed principal. Thus, abstractly the corporation is an easy route to the best of both worlds: entitlement to the fruits of the business if it is successful but little responsibility for its obligations if the corporation is unable to pay them.

   The reality of limited liability in small corporations, however, is often far different than the theory. Sophisticated creditors well understand the concept of limited liability. They will refuse to deal with a small corporation with limited assets unless the shareholders agree to be personally responsible for the corporation's obligations to those creditors. Sophisticated creditors are well aware that all corporate debt in the small corporation is essentially nonrecourse debt[6] from the standpoint of the shareholders. For many small corporations, then, the reality is this: When the sole shareholder goes to

---

[6]Nonrecourse debt is debt on which the borrower is not personally liable to repay; the creditor must look to some asset, fund, or other party for payment.

the bank to obtain a business loan, the bank officer says, "Your corporation does not meet our credit standards for a loan but we will be delighted to make the loan to your corporation if you personally guarantee its subsequent repayment." Further, for good measure the bank may require the spouse of the shareholder also to guarantee the repayment of the loan even though the spouse may be employed by an unrelated business and have no direct interest in or involvement with the corporation. The shareholder then has an unpleasant choice among three alternatives: 1) she can give up the corporate benefit of limited liability with respect to the bank loan, 2) her corporation can do without the loan, or 3) she can look for a loan elsewhere from someone who may have looser credit standards and not require a personal guarantee. And it is not only bank officers. It may be a landlord, a supplier of fixtures, a sophisticated purchaser of the product being manufactured and sold by the corporation, or any other potential creditor who has the sophistication and enough economic clout in the transaction to insist on personal guarantees. The fact is that important creditors are sophisticated and will usually refuse to deal with small corporations unless the shareholders personally guarantee the payment of the obligation or they otherwise have some assurance of repayment.[7] The protection against unlimited liability provided by the corporate form is thus not nearly as important as might first appear.

§10.5 TORT LIABILITY OF SHAREHOLDERS

The relationship between tort liability and corporate limited liability is quite different from contract liability where shareholder guarantees are almost routinely demanded by sophisticated creditors. If an agent of the corporation commits a tort while acting in the course of its business, general tort and agency principles make both the agent who commits the tort and the corporation itself personally liable.[8] These rules obviously provide the shareholder with significant protection against most tort liabilities. For example, if a delivery-truck driver for an unincorporated proprietorship or general partnership in the course of its business has a serious accident injuring a pedestrian or another driver, the proprietor and the partners are personally liable; if the business is incorporated, there is a good chance that

---

[7]Such assurance may be obtained in the case of inventory suppliers by assuring that the suppliers have a security interest in the inventory and the proceeds therefrom. Inventory suppliers may also require the corporation to place receipts in a special trust account to assure repayment. Other arrangements short of a personal guarantee may also satisfy creditors, for example, a letter of credit, a security interest in a specific asset, or an irrevocable proxy to vote the shares of the corporation in the event of default.

[8]See §2.7.

only the corporation (and the driver) will be liable, but the shareholders will be shielded from liability.

Protection of shareholders against tort liability, however, is not a sure thing. If a shareholder was involved in the tort in some way, she may be sued on the theory that she is a joint tortfeasor. This may be based on the argument that the shareholder failed to exercise due care in hiring the truck driver to begin with. However, a shareholder in a closely held corporation is also very likely to be named as a defendant in the law suit even if she had nothing directly to do with the accident or with the selection of the employee who committed the tort. The plaintiff's arguments may be based on various grounds that may be difficult to rebut easily on summary judgment: on the "piercing the corporate veil" theory discussed below; on a theory of negligent failure to direct, manage, or supervise; on a principal-agent theory (i.e., that the driver was the shareholder's agent as well as the corporation's)[9]; or possibly on other theories as well. It should not be surprising, therefore, that when small corporations purchase liability insurance, they usually purchase insurance well in excess of the net worth of their assets and they also may list the shareholders as "additional insureds" or "named insureds" on the policy to make sure that the shareholders are covered by the insurance.[10]

§10.6 AREAS WHERE CORPORATE LIMITED LIABILITY IS AN ADVANTAGE

The foregoing discussion does not mean that corporate limited liability is a snare and delusion without substance. Incorporation almost invariably does provide protection against important kinds of liabilities. It includes protection against tax claims.[11] It also includes claims from persons who deal with the corporation, but because of the small amount of the claims or the lack of sophistication, they fail to get personal guarantees from shareholders: employees, customers, small suppliers, and other contractual claims of vari-

[9]Such an argument would have particular force if the shareholder, in the past, has directed the employee to perform personal errands, e.g., picking her children up from day care.

[10]In addition, this makes sure that the insurance company will not compensate the injured tort victim and then sue the shareholder on a theory of subrogation to a claim by the injured party against the shareholder.

[11]However, persons charged with the responsibility of collecting and remitting taxes to the appropriate governmental unit may have personal liability if they fail to do so. Internal Revenue Code §6672 imposes a 100 percent penalty upon persons charged with administering withholding tax payments from employees' salaries if they fail to remit the funds to the Internal Revenue Service when required to do so. Small businesses often temporarily use amounts withheld as taxes as part of their working capital, in effect placing the treasurer or other responsible corporate employee in peril of a substantial tax liability if the business fails.

ous types. Limited liability may also protect against tort claims to the extent that the damages awarded the plaintiff exceed the available amount of insurance. These defenseless creditors may be placed into four rough categories: (1) those who are unsophisticated, (2) those who lack the economic power to demand guarantees, (3) those who are involved in such small individual transactions as not to justify the cost of seeking individual shareholder liability, or (4) those who have other means of claims collection, e.g., inventory suppliers who obtain security interests in the inventory and the proceeds thereof.

§10.7 UNCERTAINTIES IN THE CONTRACT CONTEXT

The following example illustrates the potential benefits (and uncertainties) that incorporation of a proprietorship may entail in a simple employment transaction. Assume first that the business is being conducted as an unincorporated proprietorship. The owner decides to hire a midlevel employee, a sales department manager, for example. She interviews several candidates; the most attractive candidate states that the terms of employment are basically satisfactory but that he wants at least a six-month employment contract if he is to leave his present position. Both he and the owner understand that an employment contract does not protect the manager from being fired for cause at any time, but that it does mean that if the manager is let go for any other reason within the six-month period, the business must pay the manager his salary for the remainder of that period (possibly reduced by whatever the fired employee may earn in substitute employment). The owner agrees and the parties shake hands on the deal. The agreement with the new manager clearly imposes personal responsibility on the proprietor for any unpaid salary owed to the manager during the six-month employment period; this agreement does not even have to be in writing to be enforceable.

Consider, next, how the very same transaction would be analyzed if the proprietorship has been incorporated. The proprietor is now wearing an agency hat in the negotiation representing the corporate employer, presumably her president or "sole director" hat. When she agrees to the terms proposed by the manager, it is very likely that only the corporation is obligated to pay the manager's salary for the six-month period, and, most importantly, that the proprietor is not personally liable. If the business becomes insolvent within the six-month period, the manager is out of luck.

Let us assume, further, that during the course of the negotiation, the owner says something that creates the impression that she is personally assuring the manager that his salary for six months is secure. Does that make any difference? Where the business is being conducted as an unincorporated proprietorship, the answer is that it obviously does not. The owner of the business is already personally liable on the obligation, and her promise adds nothing to that. In the case of the incorporated proprietorship, however, the answer is much more murky, and a lot may depend on precisely what was said. The corporation is a "separate entity," and the owner's assurance probably will be viewed as a promise to pay if the corporation doesn't. In other words, a suretyship relation may be created. However, a surety has a statute of frauds defense if her promise is not in writing and signed by the surety. Presumably, there is no such writing signed by the owner of the business. On the other hand, the manager might argue the "main purpose" exception[12] to the statute of frauds is applicable, which obviates the need for a writing, or that the owner's promise was an independent promise to induce the manager to join the business and not a suretyship promise at all. While nothing can really be certain in such a fluid and informal situation, the chances that the owner will be held personally liable are relatively small.

Of course, it would be an unusual sales manager who would have the temerity to request a six-month contract in the first place; it would be an extremely unusual (and sophisticated) sales manager to realize that in the case of the incorporated business he must request the sole shareholder to put that guarantee of the performance of the contract in writing. Of course if he did so, the contemplated arrangement becomes much less ambiguous, and the proprietor would have to decide whether or not to give her personal guarantee. An unsophisticated employee probably would not think about the possibility that the business might collapse within six months one way or the other.

§10.8 PIERCING THE CORPORATE VEIL IN GENERAL

The piercing the corporate veil doctrine is a broad set of amorphous principles that permits courts in some circumstances to ignore the separate existence of a corporation and hold a shareholder liable for a specific corporate obligation or, rarely, for all corporate obligations.[13] There are major intellectual difficulties with this doctrine. Perhaps in no other area of corporation law is there such a divergence between the rhetoric of opinions and the principles in fact being applied. Many years ago, Justice Cardozo com-

---

[12]This exception states that the statute of frauds is inapplicable if the main purpose of the transaction is to benefit the surety and not the debtor. On the facts described in the text this is a probable loser.

[13]A related principle permits a court to ignore the separate existence of related corporations, holding each liable for the obligation of the others. This may be referred to as "horizontal" piercing as contrasted with the "vertical" piercing described in the text. Essentially, the same standards are applicable in both types of cases.

plained that the doctrine was enveloped in the "mists of metaphor." That is true, but the problems are much more basic than simply the use of broad metaphors that explain nothing. Judicial opinions contain numerous affirmative lists of factors to be considered, lists that contain irrelevant factors or factors that have relevance only in certain limited classes of cases. In a word, this doctrine is a mess.

Probably the most accurate description of the test for piercing the corporate veil is that the court will ignore the separate existence of a corporation and hold a shareholder personally liable on the corporate obligation when necessary to "prevent an inequitable result" or when "justice requires." Obviously, however, these statements do not give very much guidance as to when it is reasonable to hold shareholders liable for corporate obligations and when it is not. Subsequent sections describe both the formal tests stated by courts and the considerations that rationally should go into an analysis of piercing issues.

The metaphor of piercing the corporate veil should not be taken too seriously. The issue is not "Is there a corporation?" or "Is there no corporation?" It is whether a specific shareholder who has been named as a defendant should be held personally liable on a corporate obligation. A corporation whose veil has been pierced is still a corporation; it is still required to pay franchise taxes, its name is still protected, and it may continue to conduct business, sue and be sued, and do all the other things that corporations normally do. It may continue to provide limited liability with respect to transactions not involved in the veil-piercing litigation. Furthermore, it is not at all clear that if one shareholder is held liable on a veil-piercing theory, other shareholders should automatically be held liable also. Shareholders not involved in inequitable or unjust conduct should not be held personally liable merely because some other shareholder did engage in such conduct.

The piercing the corporate veil doctrine is applicable exclusively to closely held corporations, usually corporations owned by one or two individuals; it is not a doctrine that is applied to a publicly held corporation.[14] A number of cases state that piercing is the exception rather than the rule and should occur only rarely, and in the most unusual and extreme situations. Finally, courts are in basic disagreement as to whether the piercing issue should be viewed as a question of fact, to be resolved by a jury, or a matter of equity, to be resolved by the court.

---

[14]However, there have been suggestions in recent theoretical literature that shareholder liability might be imposed on shareholders of both closely held and publicly held corporations on a proportional basis in connection with tort obligations. While arguably sound on the basis of abstract economic theory, there seems to be no practical way to implement directly such a proposal.

§10.9 GENERAL TESTS FOR PIERCING THE CORPORATE VEIL

The general principles formally applied by courts to determine whether shareholders should be held personally liable usually revolve around one of three different phrases: instrumentality, alter ego,[15] or identity. The *instrumentality* doctrine requires proof of "excessive" control by the shareholder/ defendant so that in some sense the corporation becomes purely an instrumentality of the shareholder and injustice can be avoided only by holding the share. The *alter ego* doctrine is applicable when there is such "unity of ownership and interest" between the corporation and the shareholder/ defendant that the separate existence of the corporation has ceased and recognition of the separate corporate existence would lead to an unfair or inequitable result. The *identity* doctrine is applicable where there is such unity of interest and ownership that the independence of the corporation had ceased, or had never begun, and adhering to the "fiction" of separate entity would serve only to "defeat justice and equity" by permitting the economic entity to escape liability arising out of an operation of one corporation for the benefit of the whole enterprise. After reviewing courts' attempts to define these doctrines, Dean Philip Blumberg comments that despite the different formulations, the doctrines are "essentially the same," and "interchangeable." They say little more than piercing requires a showing of domination of or control over the corporate form and a conclusion that recognition of the separate corporate form would lead to injustice or inequity. Obviously, these doctrines themselves provide little or no useful guidance as to when the separate corporate existence should be recognized and when it should not.

The problem with all of this traditional language defining the piercing the corporate veil doctrine is that it might easily apply to virtually every controlling shareholder in every closely held corporation. However, that doctrine has never been applied routinely to all controlling shareholders. Rather, it has been applied on a hit or miss basis to some corporations and not others, and to some shareholders and not to others. Unfortunately, the stated tests give no coherent basis for distinguishing the cases that do from the cases that don't.

§10.10 DETAILED TESTS FOR PIERCING THE CORPORATE VEIL

In addition to the general statements described above, many courts have listed a variety of detailed factors that they believe are relevant to piercing

---

[15] Alter ego means "second self."

the corporate veil. These lists include factors such as the failure to follow corporate formalities, gross undercapitalization, nonpayment of dividends, the solvency of the corporation at the time of the transaction, siphoning of funds of the corporation by the dominant stockholder, nonfunctioning of corporate officers or directors, absence of corporate records, and "the fact that the corporation is merely a facade for the operations of the dominant stockholder stockholders."[16] It is an unusual closely held corporation that does not flunk at least one of these tests. Virtually every incorporated proprietorship is a "facade," in a sense, and very few of them will have "functioning" boards of directors and officers.[17] Indeed, many of the recent developments in closely held corporations discussed in Chapter 8 in fact are designed to eliminate corporate procedural requirements as "meaningless formalities." It would be ironic if the desirable close corporation innovations turn out to lead to more pierced corporate veils.

Further, some of the listed factors seem to have nothing at all to do with whether a shareholder should be held liable for corporate obligations. The clearest illustrations of this are the commonly cited factors that the corporation has "failed to pay dividends" and that it has failed to "follow corporate formalities." These two factors are discussed immediately below.

From the standpoint of creditors — plaintiffs in suits against the corporation and its shareholders — a failure to pay dividends protects rather than injures. It protects because it leaves more assets in the corporation to satisfy claims of creditors. Further, close corporations can easily distribute assets to shareholders without declaring dividends. Hence, a "failure to pay dividends" as a test for piercing the corporate veil is both illogical and shows lack of understanding as to how close corporations actually operate.

The formalities test is equally flawed. It considers matters such as whether meetings have been held, shares have been issued, funds have been disbursed without authorization from the board of directors, and so forth. These factors usually have no relevance to shareholder liability for corporate obligations, at least absent any showing that the lack of formalities in some way misled the third party into thinking that a contract was being entered into by the shareholder and not by the corporation. One argument sometimes made is that if the shareholder fails to follow the corporation rules, third parties need not also. In effect, loss of limited liability becomes a penalty for failing to follow substantively meaningless requirements. One major objection to imposing this penalty is that its magnitude is based entirely on the happenstance of what claim is being asserted by the plaintiff

---

[16]This list is taken from a leading case involving piercing in a contracts context. De-Witt Truck Brokers v. W. Ray Flemming Fruit Co., 540 F.2d 681 (4th Cir. 1976). The case also involved a promise, not in writing, by the dominant shareholder that he would personally see that the creditor got paid if the corporation was unable to make payment.

[17]See, e.g., §9.21.

and is independent of what the corporation or the shareholder did or failed to do. There is no statutory authority for imposing liability on this basis. Indeed, Texas has adopted a statute affirmatively stating that personal liability should *not* be imposed on shareholders in contract cases solely because of the failure to follow formalities,[18] and many court decisions reach the same conclusion without the benefit of a statute. However, whether logical or not, in most states today there is a serious aspect to corporate formalities in view of the importance attached to them by the piercing the corporate veil doctrine. A failure to follow them may lead to the loss of the shield of limited liability, and the imposition of personal liability on some or all shareholders. Participants in closely held corporations should act accordingly.

§10.11 PIERCING IN TORT AND CONTRACTS CASES RECONSIDERED

The articulated tests for piercing, are basically unhelpful. It is more useful to examine the kinds of conduct that is likely to lead to the imposition of liability on shareholders, even though it must be confessed that cases go all over the place.

A basic distinction in the veil-piercing area is between claims based on contract (or on voluntary dealings between the corporation and the plaintiff) and claims based on torts (or on liabilities not arising through consensual transactions). Since the basic limited liability feature of corporations is well understood, persons entering into contracts with a corporation normally do not rely on the personal assets or wealth of the shareholders when deciding to deal with the corporation. In effect, they recognize that they are entering into nonrecourse transactions. Piercing the corporate veil in most contracts cases therefore gives the plaintiff a windfall in the sense of being able to hold liable a person on whose credit the creditor did not initially rely. If the plaintiff was unwilling to rely solely on the credit of the corporation, he should have demanded a personal guarantee from the shareholder. Further, if that demand was made and refused, the third party who thereafter deals with the corporation must be very well aware that he must look solely to corporate assets for recovery. Phrased another way, a contract creditor "assumes the risk" that the corporation might be unable to fulfill the contract when he dealt solely with the corporation. Depending on the specific facts, a contract creditor may also be met with the argument that the use of the corporate form was a part of the explicit allocation of risk of loss from the transaction. Piercing in such circumstances seems particularly unjustified.

[18]V.A.T.S. Bus. Corp. Act, art. 2.21(A)(3).

The same arguments are generally not applicable in most tort cases, where the plaintiff typically had no prior dealings with the corporation, and probably was desperately trying to avoid being involved with the corporation at all. In these cases, in which there is no prior dealing between the corporation and the plaintiff, the basic test for limited liability should be whether or not the corporation was in some sense "adequately" capitalized, and whether it acted appropriately in purchasing liability insurance to the extent it has assets available to do so. "Adequately" should be judged in light of the business it engages in: A corporation engaged in making nerve gas in downtown New York City should have more capital and carry more insurance than a grocery store whose primary risks are slip-and-fall cases. In other words, the "free" capital of a corporation should provide a "cushion" for possible tort claimants with the size of the cushion being dependent on how risky the contemplated business is. However, logically the test of adequacy should be based on likely or probable risks, not on the very worst case scenario, since no amount of capital could cover the very worst conceivable transaction — the delivery truck driver hitting a school bus and killing 55 children, for example. The test should be the reasonably foreseeable risk, or perhaps phrased differently, the amount of insurance an individual would wish to carry if he were personally involved in a business carrying those risks.[19] In this evaluation, liability insurance should count as capital since it provides funds for injured claimants.

Particularly dangerous in the tort context is a pattern that indicates that shareholders have intentionally distributed corporate assets to themselves while the corporation maintained only minimal insurance given the nature of the risks of the business. While easy to state in the abstract, the application of this test to specific situations also may be difficult.

What is surprising when one looks at decided cases is that despite the clear difference in underlying factual patterns between contract cases and tort cases, many courts reject any formal distinction between the two types of cases, applying nominally the same test in both contract and tort cases, and citing contract precedents in tort cases, and vice versa. To some extent, this may be due to the quite mistaken feeling that piercing is a corporation law issue which should be controlled exclusively by corporation law principles. Actually, it should not be; it is a fact-intensive examination of the circumstances to determine whether it is reasonable to hold shareholders personally liable for corporate obligations. While the length of the chancellor's foot should not be the sole criterion, basic notions of justice and equity are dominant.

---

[19]This standard seems attractive but is difficult to apply, since the amount of liability insurance an individual carries is only partially a function of the riskiness of his life style. Other factors, particularly the cost of insurance and the net worth of the individual that is being protected by insurance, are perhaps more important when deciding how much insurance an individual will elect to carry.

Many commentators have stated that it is easier for a court to pierce the corporate veil in torts cases than in contracts cases. The limited empirical evidence does not appear to bear this out,[20] though settlement practices by insurance companies and other factors may skew the statistics.

§10.12 CONFUSION OF ROLES

Despite the strength of the arms' length dealing and assumption of risk arguments against piercing the corporate veil in contract cases, there are situations where it is quite reasonable to impose liability on shareholders on contract claims. Cases regularly arise in which an agent dealing on behalf of the corporation (usually the principal or sole shareholder) does not clearly notify the plaintiff that he is acting as an agent of the corporation and not as an individual. The classic case is the construction company owned by a single shareholder; in talking about a remodeling project with home owners, he may say "I will do this" or "I will do that" without indicating that he plans to have his corporation enter into the contract.

In these cases, the contract presumably is presented to the third party showing a corporate form of execution. If the third party is at all sophisticated she should immediately insist that the shareholder guarantee the performance of the contract. The fact that this is not always done probably is a result of the fact that many third parties are not particularly sophisticated with respect to corporate dealings. In these cases, the piercing the corporate veil doctrine becomes essentially another exception to the statute of frauds provision relating to suretyship agreements.

Similar results may be reached in cases where the shareholder simply uses his corporation as a "name" in which his obligations are incurred, and makes no effort to actually operate the corporation except to enter into contracts. All the work is done by the shareholder or his agents without specifying that they are acting for or on behalf of the corporation. While the court may feel comfortable in finding liability based on the piercing the corporate veil doctrine, that appears to be unnecessary because under accepted agency principles the shareholder should be liable as a principal.

§10.13 FRAUDULENT CONVEYANCE CASES

Piercing the corporate veil also regularly occurs in cases where the shareholders in effect treat their corporation as a private piggy bank, shifting

---

[20]See Robert Thompson, Piercing the Corporate Veil: An Empirical Study, 76 Cornell L. Rev. 1936 (1991).

funds into and out of the corporation to suit their personal needs, and when the corporation ultimately fails, the money taken out substantially exceeds the money put back in. These transactions may be analyzed as fraudulent conveyances (transactions that defraud creditors), as commingling of business and personal transactions that shows a lack of corporate formalities, or as siphoning of assets designed to minimize corporate assets available for creditors that is unjust or fraudulent as to creditors. Many courts, however, appear reluctant to apply the rules with respect to fraudulent transfers, and appear more comfortable relying on the much more amorphous and vague tests for piercing the corporate veil. These cases are sometimes described as "stripping" or "denuding of assets" cases.

Any policy or practice which results in the diversion of assets from the corporation to the shareholders obviously increases the likelihood that the corporation will be unable to meet its obligations. Unless these transactions can be justified on the basis that the shareholders provided equal value in exchange for the assets diverted, they inevitably tend to harm creditors and cannot be justified on any plausible business ground. Liability on this theory may be justified in both contract and tort cases, since the fraudulent conveyance concept is designed to protect equally all creditors without regard to how the obligation arose. Liability may be applied on this theory even if the corporation had sufficient assets to perform the contract when it was commenced.

§10.14 PARENT-SUBSIDIARY CASES

Another class of piercing case involves the parent-subsidiary relationship. Many publicly held corporations conduct numerous businesses through departments or divisions rather than through subsidiaries. A "department" or "division" of a corporation is not a separate legal entity and the parent corporation is automatically responsible for liabilities created by that division. A *subsidiary* is a separate legal entity; usually the parent corporation owns all the outstanding shares, but that is not essential. If a subsidiary is unable to satisfy some obligation, recovery may be sought from the parent corporation on the basis of a piercing the corporate veil theory.[21] Some

---

[21]Other theories may also be possible. In the silicone breast-implant litigation, for example, arguments have been made that Dow Chemical Company, a 50 percent parent of Dow Corning Company (the manufacturer of the breast implants), should be held liable for a portion of the plaintiffs' claims because Dow Chemical had been involved in the testing of silicone products on living creatures and had negligently failed to warn Dow Corning of the potential dangers. Another theory may involve a corporate officer of the parent corporation performing duties as an officer of the subsidiary without clearly delineating that he was acting solely as an agent of the subsidiary.

cases suggest that the corporate veil of a subsidiary may be pierced either where it was necessary "to prevent fraud or other wrong" (the traditional test) or where "a parent dominates and controls a subsidiary" to the extent that its separate existence has disappeared. However, a laundry list of ten factors is cited in these cases as establishing "domination and control;" they include actions that tend to injure plaintiffs.[22] Mere domination and control, without conduct that injures or is likely to injure plaintiffs, does not appear to be enough to justify holding the parent corporation liable.

It is not clear that parent-subsidiary cases should be treated differently from cases in which the shareholders are individuals. It is probably true that the likelihood of confusion is greater when the shareholder is itself a corporation than when the shareholder is an individual. Also, a court may be more willing to pierce the corporate veil when the result is only that another fictitious entity becomes personally responsible for the liability than when an individual shareholder is involved. Finally, there may be an unarticulated feeling that a corporation-plus-subsidiary should be viewed as no different than a corporation that has divided its business into departments or divisions. Therefore, the parent corporation should not be able to hide behind the "veil" of its subsidiary. However, as indicated above, attempts to impose liability on a piercing the corporate veil theory merely because the parent-subsidiary relationship exists have been unsuccessful.

---

[22]Carte Blanche (Singapore) Pte., Ltd. v. Diners Club Intl., Inc., 2 F.3d 24 (2d Cir. 1993). A laundry list drawn from an earlier case, Wm. Passalacqua Builders, Inc. v. Resnick Developers South, Inc., 933 F.2d 131, 133 (2d Cir. 1991) was cited approvingly:

(1)   the absence of the formalities and paraphernalia that are part and parcel of the corporate existence, i.e., issuance of stock, election of directors, keeping of corporate records and the like,

(2)   inadequate capitalization,

(3)   whether funds are put in and taken out of the corporation for personal rather than corporate purposes,

(4)   overlap in ownership, officers, directors, and personnel,

(5)   common office space, address, and telephone numbers of corporate entities,

(6)   the amount of business discretion displayed by the allegedly dominated corporation,

(7)   whether the related corporations deal with the dominated corporation at arms' length,

(8)   whether the corporations are treated as independent profit centers,

(9)   the payment or guarantee of debts of the dominated corporation by other corporations in the group, and

(10) whether the corporation in question had property that was used by others of the corporations as if it were its own.

It may be suggested that this list includes some tests appropriate for tort cases, some appropriate for contracts cases, and some that seem to have no particular relevance to the piercing issue at all.

§10.15 OTHER PIERCING SITUATIONS

The issue whether the separate existence of a corporation should be recognized comes up in a variety of contexts unrelated to whether shareholders should be held personally liable for debts of the corporation. Typically, these situations involve corporations wholly owned by a single person or another corporation — alter egos in the most basic sense. A simple example is whether service of process on the corporation constitutes service on the shareholder who is not otherwise amenable to service of process in that jurisdiction. The typical answer is no, at least in situations where the parent is not otherwise amenable to service of process. Another type of case involves a contract by a corporation in which it agrees not to do something. May it form a wholly owned subsidiary to do what it is prohibited from doing? The usual answer is no, that it would constitute unfair dealing by the corporation.[23]

In some instances, the shareholder herself may seek to ignore the separate existence of her own corporation. An example is the well-known Minnesota case involving a statute that prohibited creditors from levying or foreclosing on agricultural land owned by individual farmers.[24] The farmer in question had conveyed his land to his wholly owned corporation but then successfully prevented the creditor from seizing the stock of that corporation or foreclosing on the land. This is an example of *reverse piercing*, since it is the shareholder, not the third party, who seeks to ignore the separate existence of the corporation. Many courts have expressed doubt about the appropriateness of reverse piercing, apparently taking the position that if a person forms a corporation she should take the bitter with the sweet and not argue that for some purposes the separate existence of the corporation should be ignored.

Piercing issues also arise under federal statutes of various types. A great deal of litigation has involved shareholder responsibility for environmental liabilities arising under CERCLA. A "federal law of piercing" has been developed in connection with certain federal programs.[25] It seems closely related to the state law described in general terms in this chapter.

---

[23] Usually, a court may reach the same conclusion by interpreting the corporation's agreement not to do something as covering "indirect" attempts as well as "direct" attempts to do what is prohibited.

[24] Cargill, Inc. v. Hedge, 375 N.W.2d 477 (Minn. 1985).

[25] See, e.g., United States v. Pisani, 646 F.2d 83 (3d Cir. 1981).

PART III

FINANCIAL TOOLS OF THE TRADE

11

Cash Flows, Income, and Leverage

§11.1 INTRODUCTION

The financial analysis of an investment begins with the premise that its value is the cash it provides to its owners at various times in the future. Payments by the owners to the firm, whether or not obligated, are viewed as negative cash payments by the owners. In this way, the financial analysis of a firm is essentially independent both of the form of business that has been adopted and the nature of the business the firm is engaged in. One may intuitively feel that the value of a business is what its various components and assets would be worth if the business were liquidated. Liquidation value is typically not how businesses are valued, however, because the "going concern" value — the value based on the cash it will return to the owners in the future — is usually greater than the liquidation value. This is why businesses are usually bought with a view toward their continuation, not with a view toward their liquidation.

This chapter considers whether primary attention should be paid to "income" or to "cash flow" in valuing a business and the differences between these two related concepts. It also discusses leverage.[1] Leverage explains why the use of debt in capital structures may improve the owners' return on their investment and why entrepreneurs usually desire to have their businesses borrow a portion of the capital needed to open and operate the business.

All of this is prefatory to a consideration of how one determines (or more accurately, approximates) the value of a closely held business, the topic of Chapters 13 and 14.

§11.2 METHODS OF ACCOUNTING

I begin with a brief discussion of fundamental accounting methods. The cash method of accounting for transactions is the simplest. An individual who begins his first job independent of his family will almost certainly open a bank account and record his financial affairs on the basis of deposits into that account and checks written on that account. That is cash-flow accounting in its simplest and most elemental form. If the amount in the bank account is greater at the end of the year than it was at the beginning, the individual feels he is better off, somewhat richer than when he began. This kind of simple accounting often gives an unrealistic picture of the success of the individual, in part because some kinds of cash receipts do not reflect an increase in his net worth.

For example, if you borrow $1,000 from your friendly banker and deposit the proceeds in your checking account, that account has increased by $1,000, but your liabilities have also increased by $1,000, and you are in fact no better off. If your account has $2,000 in it, and you owe your banker $1,000 (and these are your only assets and liabilities) your net worth is still $1,000. If you repay your banker the $1,000 you owe him, you still have a net worth of $1,000. While your assets have decreased, so have your liabilities, and your net worth is unaffected.

Small entrepreneurs may begin keeping track of business transactions in a separate book or separate ledger sheet, or (increasingly) by creating new accounts in a computerized personal finance program. Initially an entrepreneur, like the individual starting out in his employment, may simply record transactions when money is received or money is paid out. Profit or loss is calculated each month and year on the basis of the cash receipts and outflows of the business during the accounting period. These records are being kept on a *cash basis*. Cash basis record-keeping is little more than the entries in a check book.[2]

---

[1]See §11.9.

[2]One important objection to the cash method of accounting is that it is easily subject to manipulation. Some receipts and many payments of cash may be deferred from one ac-

The principal alternative method of accounting for profits or losses is on an *accrual basis*. The accrual method of accounting is almost universally used by large businesses and is used by most smaller businesses as well. Publicly held businesses must prepare their financial statements on the basis of "generally accepted accounting principles" (usually abbreviated as GAAP) which require the use of accrual principles. Any business that involves the manufacture, purchase, or sale of goods will use an accrual system because it much more reliably reflects income from one period to the next than the cash method of accounting; the Internal Revenue Code generally requires businesses that have an inventory component to adopt an accrual basis of accounting for tax purposes. The accrual method of accounting is summarized briefly below and discussed in some detail in Chapter 12.

The basic difference between cash and accrual accounting is that under the accrual method items of income and expense are recognized and taken into the accounting records when they are incurred, not when the actual payment or receipt of cash occurs. "Accounts receivable" and "accounts payable" must be established to record the amounts owed to and owed by the firm in connection with recognized transactions. Purchases of capital goods (e.g., a truck) are viewed as an exchange of one asset — cash — for another asset — the truck. The truck is then viewed as "being used up" over its expected life span, with deductions of annual depreciation being used to reduce earnings during the expected life of the truck. Purchases of raw materials are viewed also as an exchange of cash for raw materials, with the raw materials being treated as "inventory" — an asset — until they are used. Accrual accounting permits a much more accurate assessment of the actual earnings of a complex business than does the cash method. Modern computer software programs greatly simplify the creation and maintenance of accrual accounting systems for small businesses.[3]

Many service businesses — like law firms — traditionally have used the cash method of accounting. This is true even though the firm may be quite large with a very substantial flow of cash each month. The principal reason is that the cash method of accounting (unlike accrual accounting) provides

---

counting period to the next, thereby affecting the closing cash account but not affecting the wealth of the owner. One can pay the December rent either on December 29 or January 2 (assuming that books are being kept on a calendar-year basis); the landlord is likely to be satisfied in either event, but that decision clearly affects the amount of cash you have on hand as of December 31. This problem is particularly acute in firms that have a substantial inventory and are constantly engaged in purchasing raw materials and selling finished products for cash or on credit. In such businesses, decisions as to when bills are paid, when to replenish inventory and raw materials, and when to make payments on open lines of credit are largely discretionary with management and can be moved around to "smooth out" financial statements, if that is thought desirable.

[3] Indeed, the traditional study of "accounting" or "bookkeeping" is basically a study of the accrual system and all of its complications.

that fees that are billed are to be reported as income only when payment is received.

§11.3 CASH-FLOW ANALYSIS AND INCOME STATEMENTS

Most investors are accustomed to receiving income or profit-and-loss statements from the firms in which they invest that show the earnings (or lack thereof) on an annual, quarterly, or monthly basis. These statements are prepared in accordance with GAAP. In calculating income, they take into account as expenses a variety of noncash deductions. The most important noncash item is depreciation, though a number of other such items exist.

Modern cash-flow analysis is quite different from cash accounting. It works off the business's traditional accounting system. It therefore accepts principles of accrual accounting that eliminate the effect of the timing of payments and other transactions that do not increase the wealth of the owners. Cash-flow analysis differs from the analysis of income primarily in that it ignores depreciation and other noncash expenses that are included in traditional income statements. Cash-flow analysis is therefore a "purer" measure of value than income statements because it focuses exclusively on the cash that is made available to a business from its operations.

Cash flow and income statements thus are different; they look at the same business in two different ways. If the assumptions underlying the income statement are precise and accurate, and the time frame is sufficiently long, the two statements should come out exactly at the same place, because, in the last analysis, the only reason a business has value is the value of its cash flow. However, in real life, the time frame of many investors in businesses tends to be short rather than long, and perhaps even more importantly, the assumptions that underlie the noncash deductions are virtually never completely borne out.[4] This chapter considers the differences between these two types of analysis of the success of a business.

§11.4 AN EXAMPLE OF CASH-FLOW ANALYSIS

Consider a very simple business that consists of the purchase and ownership of a duplex house. The entrepreneur plans to buy a duplex which she expects to own and manage for three or four years and then resell when market conditions are favorable. This is purely a financial investment; she plans to rent out both sides of the duplex and manage the property herself (though managing a residential duplex is not very time-consuming). She locates a

[4]These points are discussed in §11.7.

338

suitable duplex and buys it partially for cash and partially with funds borrowed solely on the security of the duplex itself. She obtains, in other words, a nonrecourse loan for which she has no personal responsibility for most of the purchase price, but on which she must make the monthly payments if she is to keep the duplex. She then successfully rents out both sides of the duplex.

Three years later, the market for duplexes appears favorable and she decides to sell her entire interest in the duplex to some third party. During the three years she owns the duplex she dutifully records all transactions with respect to the duplex, viewing (as is customary) the duplex as a separate economic enterprise independent of her other income and expenses. The "Duplex Investment" financial statements are set forth in Tables 11-1 and 11-2. The notes following Table 11-2 describe how the various values of the rows in that table are obtained.

If a business produces more revenue in one year than the out-of-pocket disbursements necessary to operate the business in that year, it is said to have a positive cash flow. If disbursements exceed revenues, there is a negative cash flow. In the following example, the duplex had a small negative cash flow in the first year, presumably because of several nonrecurring expenses, but positive cash flows thereafter. Projects such as this with positive cash flows are generally self-supporting and usually do not need infusions of capital from the owner.[5] Here, the positive cash flow in the second and third years was sufficient to permit the owner to maintain an adequate cash reserve even after making the mortgage payments and withdrawing a total of $4,800 from the duplex's bank account for her own personal use.

Assume that our entrepreneur decides to sell the duplex after three

Table 11-1
Duplex Investment: Initial Investment

Purchase price	$120,000
Nonrecourse mortgage	$110,000
Equity required	$10,000
Total cash invested	
Equity required	$10,000
Closing costs	$4,000
Cash reserve	$1,000
Net investment	$15,000.

---

[5] There are situations, of course, where a positive cash flow may not be sufficient to cover necessary repairs or desirable improvements. If the duplex requires a new roof, for example, a modest positive cash flow might not be sufficient to pay for the necessary work. In effect, a negative cash flow has been created by the major repairs required.

Table 11-2
Duplex Investment: Summary of Three Years' Operations

Operating results	Year 1	Year 2	Year 3
Gross receipts	$15,000	$16,500	$18,000
Operating expenses [1]	$3,500	$2,800	$3,000
Net revenue [2]	$11,500	$13,700	$15,000
Mortgage payments [3]	$11,800	$11,800	$11,800
Net cash flow [4]	($300)	$1,900	$3,650
Withdrawals by owner [5]	-0-	$1,000	$3,800
Closing balance, cash account [6]	$700	$1,600	$1,000

Notes

[1] Operating expenses consist primarily of real estate taxes of $2,400 per year and liability and casualty insurance premiums. The owner manages the duplex herself, thereby holding other expenses to a minimum. Of course, managing a duplex does not ordinarily require a great deal of time.

[2] "Net revenue" equals gross receipts minus operating expenses and is computed before the monthly mortgage payments.

[3] It is assumed that the mortgage is a fixed-rate, 9 percent mortgage payable in equal monthly payments over 20 years. Standard amortization tables require that the fixed monthly payment on such a mortgage be $990 per month, or $11,800 per year, payable each month over the 20-year term of the loan. These monthly payments will reduce the unpaid balance of the loan to zero with the last payment 240 months later. To illustrate, the first such payment of $990 is composed of one month's interest on the unpaid $110,000 ($825) with the remaining $165 being allocated to principal, reducing the unpaid balance of the loan to $109,835. The second month's payment constitutes interest on the unpaid $109,835 ($823.76), with the remaining $166.24 being applied to reduce principal to $109,668.76. Each successive fixed payment of $990 is allocated first to the payment of interest on the balance outstanding at the beginning of the month and the excess is applied to reduce the unpaid principal. A level payment of $990 per month will reduce the principal to zero when the 240th payment is made. This is a classic example of *amortization*, which means to liquidate or extinguish an obligation by periodic payments.

[4] "Net cash flow" equals net revenue (row (2)) minus the mortgage payments (row (3)). This reflects the amount of cash made available to the owner each year by the duplex investment.

[5] Withdrawals by the owner consists of funds the owner believes may be prudently withdrawn and used for personal purposes. In this case, the amounts were withdrawn and used by the entrepreneur for purposes unrelated to the duplex.

[6] The "closing balance" is simply the amount in the duplex's bank account at the end of the year. It equals, in each year, the opening balance plus revenues minus expenses and minus amounts withdrawn by the owner during the year.

years subject to the nonrecourse mortgage. In other words, the entrepreneur and the purchaser agree that the mortgage on the property will not be paid off, but the property will simply be sold subject to that mortgage. Let us assume, first, that the sales price that is negotiated precisely equals her original equity investment ($10,000) plus the closing costs ($4,000) she incurred in order to buy the duplex originally. She has invested $15,000 of her own cash in this venture for three years. The cash flow made available by this investment is -$15,000 in Year 0, -$300 in Year 1, +$1,900 in Year 2, and +$18,800 in Year 3. It is possible to calculate her rate of return on this investment using an inexpensive hand-held calculator. It turns out to be a little over 11 percent per year. That is good, but hardly terrific in a hot real estate market.

One reason that the return is modest is the assumption that there was no increase in the market value of the duplex over the three years it was owned by the entrepreneur. It is not uncommon in many areas of the country for real estate values to increase by 5 percent or more per year during periods of active real estate markets. If our entrepreneur had purchased and resold during one of those periods, her return on the cash invested could have been much higher than 11 percent. For example, if the duplex had increased in value by 5 percent a year, the value of the entrepreneur's equity in the duplex would have increased by nearly $19,000, and the rate of return would have been about 18 percent per year.[6] This higher rate of return is the result of the leverage that arises from financing the purchase with $110,000 of debt capital and only $10,000 of equity capital.[7]

A negative cash flow of course means that the cash being generated by the project is not sufficient to cover its cash needs — and that is usually bad.[8] In many new ventures, a negative cash flow is anticipated during the first few years of operation and provision may be made for the necessary additional capital infusions in the original planning. In fact, that may be what our entrepreneur who purchased the duplex did, when she invested an extra $1,000 at the outset of the venture, an amount which easily cov-

[6]The original value of the duplex was $120,000. If it increases by 5 percent per year, the value will be $126,000 after one year, $132,300 after two years, $138,915 after three years. The value of the entrepreneur's equity would thus be about $29,000 (without taking into account the amortization on the mortgage over the three-year period).

[7]Leverage is discussed in §11.9. It arises in the above example because the 5 percent increase in value is based on the $120,000 market value of the duplex, but the holder of the mortgage is only entitled to a fixed monthly payment, As a result, the entire amount of the increase in value is allocated to the entrepreneur's equity interest in the duplex.

[8]It is "usually" bad because the investors may be required to make additional investments merely to preserve their current investment in the business. However, the events giving rise to a negative cash flow may also create tax losses that shelter other income from tax. These tax savings should logically be included in the cash-flow analysis. In some instances, the tax saving may be sufficient to change an apparent negative cash flow into a positive one, as was often the case with pre-1986 real estate investments.

ered the small negative cash flow during the first year. Of course, this small negative cash flow may not have been actually anticipated, but that is probably unimportant since the shortfall was relatively minor. Even where positive cash flows are anticipated during the first year, some cash reserve is usually necessary because cash flows during a single year may be "lumpy" and payments may come due before cash inflows are received to cover them. Thus, some initial working capital is necessary for even the simplest business.

The situation where a positive cash flow is confidently projected but fails to materialize and a significant negative cash flow is actually experienced may be disastrous. Let us assume that shortly after the entrepreneur buys the duplex, the real estate market in the community "tanks" and there are no tenants to pay the rent. The entrepreneur has a choice at that point: She can preserve her investment in the duplex only if she continues making those $990 per month payments on the mortgage for what may be an extended period. Or, she can default on the payments, "walk away" from the project, and allow the lender to foreclose on the mortgage. She thereby loses her entire $15,000 investment since the market value of the property will inevitably have plummeted when the real estate market in the community collapsed.[9] Since the original loan was nonrecourse, the entrepreneur's loss is probably limited to the amount she invested in the enterprise. However, typically, a misjudgment about cash flow is much more disastrous than simply the loss of one's capital investment. The duplex example is unrealistic in that it is very unlikely today that a lender would grant a nonrecourse loan on a single duplex.[10] Let us assume that the entrepreneur is personally liable on the mortgage, and the real estate market in the community collapses. The tenants move out to cheaper quarters, and the entrepreneur then faces disaster. The entrepreneur is personally responsible for the mortgage payments of $990 per month even though there are no rental payments to cover them. She then faces the painful and unexpected choice of either making an additional unplanned capital investment each month for a period that may continue for years or default on the mortgage. The result of a default on a full-recourse loan is not only foreclosure and a forced sale of

---

[9]As a result, the foreclosure sale is unlikely to produce enough to cover the balance of the mortgage. Hence, both the lender and the entrepreneur lose. There is a third possibility. She may negotiate with the lender for a temporary suspension of the monthly payments until conditions improve. Presumably, interest would continue to accrue even though payments are suspended. Foreclosure may be unattractive to the lender since it is unlikely to be able to rent or sell the duplex either.

[10]It does not help the investor to suggest that the duplex be placed in a corporation or other limited liability business form with minimal capitalization, and that a full-recourse loan be executed by that entity. If the lender is unwilling to make a nonrecourse loan directly to the entrepreneur, it will insist that the entrepreneur personally guarantee the payment of a mortgage executed by a limited liability entity.

the duplex into an unfavorable market, but also a likely suit by the lender against the entrepreneur for the deficiency. If the entrepreneur is unable to make this payment, she may be compelled to file for bankruptcy in order to obtain a discharge from the mortgage obligation and a "fresh start." Otherwise, assets acquired by her from future efforts may be seized by the creditor. The bankruptcy filing may also destroy her good credit standing and make it difficult for her to obtain credit for any purpose. Real estate speculation tends to be boom-or-bust; it is not uncommon for a speculator to go into bankruptcy, obtain a discharge, and then later return to speculation in real estate when her credit is restored.

§11.5 THE ADVANTAGES OF CASH-FLOW ANALYSIS

It is important to recognize that Table 11-2 (which does not take into account the hypothetical sale of the duplex at the end of Year 3 measures cash flow, not income. It simply compares the dollars coming in with the dollars going out, cash-in and cash-out. It is based on the entrepreneur's duplex checking account for the three years she owned the duplex.

Cash-flow statements unquestionably provide a useful picture of the performance of the business. They are easy to understand and analyze and they directly measure the ultimate source of value of any investment. Cash-flow statements are widely used by small closely held businesses in particular. Since a business is viewed as an entity that throws off cash from time to time, the value of that business may be estimated by determining the net present value of all predicted future cash flows. Businesses with an anticipated finite life, and relatively predictable cash flows such as our hypothetical duplex, are most likely to be valued on this basis.

§11.6 PROFIT-AND-LOSS STATEMENTS AND GAAP

For more than 60 years, all publicly held companies in the United States have been required to make public financial statements setting forth the results of their operations on the basis of profit-and-loss statements prepared in accordance with GAAP. GAAP is a somewhat loose set of principles that are designed to make periodic profit-and-loss statements reliable and comparable with other such statements. GAAP assumes that the business will continue in existence perpetually, or at least indefinitely. Chapter 12 introduces readers to the basic premises that underlie GAAP rules.

An *income statement* (or *profit-and-loss statement*, as it is usually called here) differs from a cash flow statement in that it takes into account all (or most) items of income or expense related to the business without regard to their effect on the available cash. Cash flow and income are in theory quite different concepts. This can be appreciated most easily by two examples drawn from the duplex investment discussed in the last section.

In the cash-flow analysis in Table 11-2, the entire mortgage payment each month was deducted from the available cash because it obviously is a required payment to an outside party, and that payment indisputably reduces the cash available to the venture. However, that payment consists of two components, and only the interest component really reflects part of the cost of operating the duplex. The principal component of the monthly payment (the portion of the payment that exceeds the interest component) reduces the mortgage on the duplex and therefore increases the value of the equity of the entrepreneur in the duplex.

The repayment of a loan is not an expense of doing business in the same way as paying interest on a loan. As pointed out earlier, if you owe X $1,000 and have $2,000 in the bank, (and these are your only assets and liabilities) your net worth is $1,000. If you repay X the $1,000 you owe him, you still have a net worth of $1,000. While your assets have decreased, so have your liabilities, and your net worth is unaffected. However, if you must pay $50 in interest for the use of the borrowed money, that $50 is truly a cost of the business that is an expense of doing business.

Exactly the same thing is true of the entrepreneur in the duplex example. The cash-flow statement treats the entire monthly mortgage payment as a reduction of cash (which it clearly is) but takes no account of the fact that a portion of that payment reduced the mortgage on the duplex and thereby increased the owner's net worth by that amount. When one calculates a profit-and-loss statement for our entrepreneur, the calculation should exclude the portion of each monthly payment that reflects a repayment of principal. Many other types of cash payments similarly do not affect the profitability of a business and are treated differently in profit-and-loss statements than in cash-flow statements.

A second important difference between cash-flow and income calculations is that in the cash-flow analysis no account is taken at all of the fact that the duplex itself has a limited life — perhaps 20 years (if it is constructed the way most speculative duplexes are constructed) — and gradually wears out. If we assume for simplicity that the duplex wears out at a constant rate over 20 years,[11] the net worth of the entrepreneur should decline by 5 percent of the original value of the duplex each year, other things being equal. In a broad view, this decline in value is certainly a cost of operating the duplex and some deduction from income should be taken to reflect this wearing out of the duplex: If the duplex cost $100,000 to build

---

[11]The actual wearing out of the duplex is probably not monotonic, as suggested in the text. Its depreciation in value is likely to be relatively small during its first years, and then it will decline more rapidly as its ages. For simplicity, however, I assume that it declines at a constant rate.

($20,000 being the value of the lot on which it is built), one-twentieth of its cost each year — $5,000 per year — might be viewed as an estimate of this reduction in value. This type of expense is of course called *depreciation* and is one of several expenses that do not involve a reduction of available cash flow.

There are other expenses that may be treated differently when calculating cash flow and when calculating the income from the duplex, but the two adjustments discussed above are the most important differences between cash-flow and income statements for real estate investments, and adequately show how an income statement differs from a cash-flow statement.

Table 11-3 is an income statement for the three years the duplex was owned by the entrepreneur.

Table 11-3
Duplex Investment: Income Statement

	Year 1	Year 2	Year 3
Gross receipts	15,000	16,500	18,000
Operating expenses	$3,500	2,800	3,000
Depreciation	5,000	5,000	5,000
Interest	9,800	9,500	9,100
Total expenses	$18,300	$17,300	$17,100
Net income (loss)	(3,300)	(800)	900

The numbers in parentheses of course represent losses. Thus, from a traditional income statement approach, this duplex investment was not a success. It has shown a net loss in two of the three years of operation; it is awash in red ink.[12] Further, even though earnings are improving, it is quite possible that the duplex's operations will never be significantly above the break-even point from an income standpoint.

§11.7 CASH-FLOW AND INCOME STATEMENTS COMPARED

The previous sections set forth a simplified illustration of a business which has a positive cash-flow statement and a highly negative income statement. This section considers which is "right," the cash-flow statement or the income statement?

In a sense, both are. Most persons investing in duplexes do not expect

---

[12]Red ink is an alternative way of showing a negative number on financial statements; even though separate colored ink is rarely used today, the name has stuck.

to own them for 20 years or more; they hope that inflation and improvements in the real estate markets will more than cover any depreciation in the value of the duplex, and that they will ultimately be able to sell the duplex at a break-even price or at a profit. Viewed in this light, the cash-flow statement is more realistic, since the owner actually has the use of the cash flow during the period she owns the property. The profit-and-loss statement is more theoretical and approximate since it assumes that the duplex is "wearing out" in an economic sense. From the standpoint of the short-term owner, the income statement does not reflect the real value of the investment and is an artificial construct. One can make spending decisions on the basis of positive cash-flow figures but one cannot determine how much is available to spend from an income statement prepared on the basis of GAAP accounting principles.

In the long run, the income statement and the cash-flow statement will come out exactly the same if they are both correctly calculated. If our entrepreneur owns the duplex for 20 years, the mortgage is paid off when due, and the building wears out as expected and is in fact replaced precisely at a cost of $100,000, the two statements should show exactly the same net result. These assumptions, of course, are completely unrealistic. Even if the duplex does wear out at the predicted time (itself a very dubious assumption) and is replaced (also a dubious assumption), the cost of replacement will certainly not remain constant at precisely $100,000, given the effects of inflation over a long period of time. The profit-and-loss statement, by including a depreciation deduction for the duplex, is necessarily assuming that these events will happen; the cash-flow statement does not make any of these questionable assumptions.

In the last analysis, the value of a business is the discounted value of its future cash flows. Complex businesses that report results of operations on the basis of GAAP profit-and-loss statements regularly use various types of cash-flow projections for a variety of internal purposes. For example, estimates of cash receipts are necessary in order to assure that the business will have cash on hand sufficient to cover expected outflows of cash in the near future if expensive emergency borrowings are to be avoided. Cash-flow analysis may also be utilized for the purpose of determining whether a specific investment is justified. For purposes of planning whether or not to make a specific investment in new plant or equipment, or whether to purchase a new line of business, a firm will normally use some kind of cash-flow analysis. In deciding whether to make a short-term commercial loan, a lender normally also looks only to cash flow, since, after all, its loan will be repaid only if dollars are available to do so.

Finance theorists and economists view cash flows as the ultimate source of value, and tend to deprecate income statements prepared on the basis of GAAP accounting. However, America's public-owned enterprises are all required to report the results of their operations in the form of GAAP income statements, not cash-flow statements.[13] Anyone reading a financial newspaper such as the *Wall Street Journal* must be struck by the total acceptance of earning statements rather than cash-flow statements in financial reporting and analysis.

For example, in late 1992, a manufacturer of computer components, Comptronix Corporation, announced that its three top officers had conspired to overstate accounting profits apparently by creating fictitious sales transactions, and that the corporation might be required to issue restated financial statements. The corporation also announced, however, that the fictitious transactions did not materially affect the corporation's cash flow (as one would expect by the nature of the fraud disclosed). Nevertheless, the announcement had an immediate devastating impact on the market price of Comptronix stock: in one day it plummeted to $6.125 per share, losing $13.875 per share, a decline of 72 percent in a single day. Of course, part of that decline might be attributable to the market's concern that fraud had apparently been committed by top-level managers. But apparently the major portion of the decline was attributable to the fact that Comptronix had announced a steady increase in earnings over the last couple of years, which presumably the market had capitalized in the process of establishing a share price. The information that the accounting records had been manipulated indicated that the reported earnings did not exist. But this example clearly indicates that the trading markets consider earnings to be the principal determinant of success of an enterprise.

From the standpoint of our duplex entrepreneur, she will almost certainly keep her records on a cash-flow basis. On the other hand, she will also have to prepare a profit-and-loss statement each year in order to complete her federal income tax return. However, she will measure the success or failure of the duplex investment on the basis of its cash flow until she successfully sells it.

§11.8 TAX SAVINGS AS POSITIVE CASH FLOW

Duplexes were a common tax shelter before the tax rules were dramatically changed in 1986. If this duplex had been purchased before 1986, the entrepreneur would have had an additional positive cash flow element not mentioned in the earlier discussion. Prior to 1986, losses on commercial real estate investments were deductible from income for tax purposes. Thus, our entrepreneur would calculate the profit or loss for tax purposes on the basis of an income statement very much like that shown in Table 11-3. She would then claim a loss for tax purposes for the years of negative income

---

[13]Information as to the sources and dispositions of funds — a kind of cash-flow statement — however are part of the required disclosures of publicly held businesses.

without regard to what the cash-flow statement showed. This tax loss could be used to offset her other income, e.g., from her medical practice or from investments. Deductible losses are very desirable since they lead to a reduction in the entrepreneur's total tax bill; in effect, losses shelter other income from taxation. The tax saving that arises from this sheltering effect logically should be viewed as a positive cash-flow item in assessing the attractiveness of the investment to begin with.

Before 1986, these tax savings were another positive element of cash flow arising from the duplex investment, and, indeed, the market price of $120,000 paid by our entrepreneur presumably reflected these anticipated tax savings. If the tax loss were big enough, the resulting positive cash-flow item might be sufficient to make attractive an investment that from a purely economic standpoint promised only a negative cash flow.

The 1986 Tax Reform Act closed off this attractive feature of real estate investments, at least for higher income taxpayers, and thereby undoubtedly contributed to the decline (or collapse) of real estate values during the late 1980s. Under current tax rules, a loss from a duplex investment would be classified as a "passive loss" and might not be deductible at all.

§11.9 LEVERAGE IN COMMERCIAL REAL ESTATE

Commercial real estate is a traditional boom or bust industry. Historically, participants seem to be either getting rich quickly or filing for bankruptcy. Indeed, the same individual may find himself in both of these positions within very short periods of time. The principal reason that commercial real estate has this characteristic is that it is an ideal vehicle for leveraged transactions. The simple duplex acquisition in this chapter is an example of a leveraged transaction since the great bulk of the purchase price of the duplex was borrowed.

Leverage is a very simple idea. Most loans are at fixed interest rates so that the cost of the borrowed capital is a known and fixed amount. If the return on the investment (per dollar of total investment) is greater than the cost of the borrowed capital, the rate of return on the investor's equity in the project is enhanced by the difference. On the other hand, if the return on the investment (per dollar of total investment) is less than the cost of the borrowed capital, the return of the entrepreneur suffers, since the fixed cost of the borrowed capital must be met in any event. The presence of debt in a capital structure is thus a two-edged sword. It increases risk on the downside as well as increasing return on the upside.[14]

The goal of a person purchasing commercial real estate differs from that of a person considering the purchase of residential real estate. The goal

---

[14]Again, however, the downside effects might be ameliorated by tax savings.

in purchasing residential real estate is largely personal satisfaction, finding a good place to live given the constraints of the person's financial resources. In contrast, the goal of a person purchasing commercial real estate is usually purely economic, based on the hoped-for financial return in light of the required investment, and is usually (though not always) unrelated to personal considerations of taste or aesthetics.

In the freewheeling days of the 1970s and 1980s, banks, savings and loan associations, and other commercial lenders were anxious to make commercial real estate loans. The atmosphere was totally different than it is in the 1990s. Because of the collapse of the savings and loan industry and economic problems in the banking industry in the late 1980s, the government has imposed (at least as this is written in 1996) severe restrictions on commercial real estate loans. This cautious attitude limits the availability of leveraged transactions. The following discussion and the examples used were entirely realistic in the 1980s, but may not be realistic in the late 1990s. On the other hand, it is quite possible that the good old times in the real estate industry, at least from the standpoint of commercial real estate developers, will return again in the near future.

The ability of commercial real estate to generate cash flows usually makes a "bootstrap" acquisition possible: By borrowing most of the cost of the land and improvements, the developer of the property may use the later cash flows to repay the loans and thereby pay for the land and improvements with virtually no personal investment. When acquiring commercial real estate it is customary to persuade a lender to lend money to finance the project primarily by developing estimates of the later cash flow that show that it will be sufficient to repay the loan. These estimates may be in the form of computer-generated spread sheets or documents with titles such as projected cash flow or pro forma cash projections.

Because commercial real estate loans are typically made or refused primarily on the basis of projected cash flows, analysis of these projections is usually vital to the success of a contemplated project. The question asked by a commercial real estate developer is not primarily "Is this a good project?" but rather "Can I persuade a lender that this is such a good project that they should make a large loan on it?" To a very substantial extent, decisions whether or not projects will go forward are made by the sources of possible financing, not by the developer itself. For this reason, the developer of commercial real estate often seeks to obtain letters of intent from potential tenants — particularly the major ("anchor") tenants — in order to improve the reliability of the cash-flow projections in the eyes of possible lenders. Such letters are usually not binding in a legal sense, but are indications of interest in the project.

There is no traditional minimum cash down payment required for a commercial real estate project. If the projected cash flows are high enough, a developer may be able to persuade one or more lenders to lend 100 percent, or even more, of the acquisition and development cost of the project. Generally, it is in the interest of the developer to obtain the largest loan possible since that makes the project self-sufficient and reduces the amount of personal capital the developer initially has to invest in the project. After all, the duplex purchaser in the previous sections had to come up with $15,000 in cash; even so, she was heavily leveraged because she was able to borrow $110,000, but doubtless she would have preferred to invest an even smaller amount if she could have obtained a larger mortgage. If a loan for 80 percent of the purchase price is desirable, then a 90 percent loan is even better, and a 100 percent loan may be ideal from the standpoint of the entrepreneur. In the 100 percent mortgage case, the entrepreneur owns a project with essentially a zero capital investment. However, even where a capital investment is required of the entrepreneur, if the cash flows develop as planned or, even better, if they exceed the original estimates, the entrepreneur may be able to recoup his or her original investment in a relatively brief period of time. She will then own a project (subject of course to the lenders' interest) that may be worth millions of dollars with a zero capital investment. It is like magic — making money for oneself using other people's money. Many real estate fortunes have been made on the basis of the simple principle of borrowing as much as possible and then making the project a success. On the other hand, many real estate fortunes have been lost just as quickly, when projected cash flows fail to materialize in highly leveraged transactions. For this reason, nonrecourse loans are the jewels of the commercial real estate industry.

Most lenders are concerned that the developer does not get a totally free ride and they therefore do not usually give 100 percent mortgages. Indeed, banks, savings and loan institutions, and many other financial lenders are constrained by statute, regulation, or internal policy to make only first lien mortgages that cover no more than a designated fraction of the value of the project. The difference between the amount of the first mortgage and the estimated cost of the project has to come either from the developer as a large capital investment or from other lending sources. The usual pattern of commercial real estate financing is first to obtain a first mortgage from one of these lenders. This mortgage may be a traditional fixed interest rate, level-payment mortgage, or it may be an adjustable-rate mortgage the payments on which vary with changes in interest rates. Nevertheless, it is for a long term and provides a significant fraction of the needed financing at relatively low interest rates.

Junior mortgages from different sources, usually called second or third mortgages depending on their priority are then sought. Projected cash flows from a commercial project are usually sufficient to justify more than a single mortgage on the project. The developer may obtain several junior mortgages that in the aggregate exceed 100 percent financing in specific situations even if the senior lender refuses to fund more than 70 or 80 percent of the anticipated cost of the project. Because the junior mortgages in this type of situation are more risky, a junior lender insists on a higher interest rate and may insist on receiving a percentage of the equity ownership as a condition to making a risky junior loan. This is often referred to as a "piece of the action."[15]

Leverage is an essential element of speculation that drives a free-enterprise economy. It appears in various guises throughout the economy. For example, a corporation is utilizing leverage whenever it finances expansion of its productive capacity by issuing debt securities that carry fixed interest rates rather than selling additional shares of common stock. Do you see why? There is nothing inherently wrong in taking risks; there is obviously nothing inherently wrong in borrowing other persons' capital to invest in one's own business. Many of America's most famous entrepreneurs could never have established huge and successful businesses unless they had been able to borrow money to enable their businesses to grow. They became rich in part because of the benefits of leverage, or to put it more crudely, by using other people's money.

An example may be useful. Assume that the project cost $1 million and was financed by a $800,000 loan and $200,000 of equity. Assume also that the interest rate on the debt is 6 percent per year, but the venture earns eight cents on each dollar of capital — debt and equity combined — that is invested in the enterprise. The $200,000 of equity earns $16,000; the return on the debt capital is $64,000, $48,000 of which represents interest payable to the lender, and $16,000 of which is available to the entrepreneur. Because of leverage, the entrepreneur's return has been precisely doubled. If the enterpreneur can squeeze an additional two cents per dollar invested out of the venture (to a total of ten cents per dollar invested), the return on equity as a result of the leverage will be increased by $32,000, while the return on the equity portion of the investment itself is increased only to $20,000 — another $12,000 of free cash flow! As earnings of a leveraged business increase, the yield on the equity capital increases much more quickly than if the same business were not leveraged with debt capital. On the down side, if the profitability of the business declines, the income may not be sufficient to cover the interest cost of the debt, creating losses for the equity owners even though the business operations (before the payment of interest) was profitable. For example, if the return per dollar invested is only three cents, the entrepreneur will owe $48,000 in interest, but the total return on the project will be only $30,000 each year. That is not good.

---

[15]Second and third mortgages are for shorter terms and carry higher interest rates than first mortgages to reflect the additional risk of default. They may also involve a variety of devices, such as balloon payments or variable interest rates that are designed to reduce the risk of default by matching payment obligations with likely cash inflows.

§11.10 EBITDA AND EBIT

Real estate transactions lend themselves to cash-flow analysis because the future cash flows are easy to predict and the uses to which cash is to be put — payments on real estate mortgages and other expenses — are limited. Once one moves to a complex business that maintains an inventory of raw materials and goods for resale, cash transactions become numerous and individually less meaningful. As a result, one cannot realistically use a checking account approach when making a cash-flow analysis of such businesses. Rather, a profit-and-loss statement will usually be prepared following most generally accepted accounting principles. It is then possible to "back in" to a type of cash-flow analysis by estimating cash flows from the accounting statements.

EBITDA (earnings before interest, (income) taxes, depreciation and amortization) is an interim calculation based on a profit-and-loss statement that roughly approximates the cash-flow capacity of the enterprise before the costs of capital are taken into account and before deductions of noncash items from earnings. Depreciation and amortization are traditional significant noncash items that reduce earnings but do not involve a reduction of cash. Thus, adding back these items tends to reflect the cash flow of the basic business.

The exclusion of interest and income taxes from EBITDA is based on a different theory. Earnings calculated in accordance with GAAP assume that the firm has a specific capital structure since interest on long-term capital is an expense deducted from earnings. The greater the amount of debt carried by a business — the more the leverage — the lower will be the accounting earnings because of higher interest payments. The lower the accounting earnings, the lower will be the firm's tax bill. Correspondingly, the lower the debt carried by the firm, the greater will be the amount of equity capital needed by the business, and the higher its income tax obligations. The exclusion of interest payments and taxes when calculating EBITDA means that it represents a good estimate of the raw earning power of the business's assets before the cost of capital is taken into account.[16]

EBIT (earnings before interest and taxes) is used by persons considering the purchase of a going business as an estimate of earning power of the business. The use of EBIT permits the purchasers to consider how to recapitalize the business as part of the acquisition, that is, how much leverage should be built into the capital structure of the acquired business. It is not itself an estimate of cash flow.

In many firms, employees are awarded incentive compensation if the firm does well. "Doing well" may be defined in terms of EBITDA rather than

---

[16]Income from unrelated business operations may also be excluded from EBITDA on the theory that they do not reflect the earning capacity of the business itself.

352

accounting earnings, because it more closely reflects the success in improving the efficiency of the business of the enterprise.

§11.11 THE PERMANENT NATURE OF DEBT

Most of the capital of an established business may be in the form of loans from outside parties. In other words, the amount of debt incurred by a firm may be greater than its equity capital, which consists of the original capital for issuance of equity interests plus retained earnings.

A business primarily capitalized with debt is deemed "highly leveraged" for the reasons discussed above. Some of this debt may be short-term, requiring the business to raise large amounts of capital at regular intervals. The owners may view these short-term cash obligations as a sword hanging over their heads. However, while it is true that the business must generate a sufficient cash flow to service this debt, an established business usually is able to "roll over" debt before it matures. *Rolling over* debt simply means that the business is able to obtain new loans (either from the same lender or from another lender) to pay off the old debts before they mature.

Indeed, most successful businesses roll over debt quite routinely as it matures, a process that can go on indefinitely so long as the business appears to remain profitable. Thus, borrowed funds may be (and should be) viewed as a part of the permanent capitalization of the business. From the standpoint of the business, the loans are paid off only when the millennium comes and the firm goes out of business.

§11.12 THE DEBT/EQUITY RATIO

Because debt of an established business is appropriately viewed as a permanent investment in the enterprise, one can meaningfully speak of "debt capital" and "equity capital." One can also readily grasp the concept of the *debt/equity ratio*, which is simply the ratio of debt to equity.[17] A corporation with four times as much debt as equity has a debt/equity ratio of 4:1. Businesses with high debt/equity ratios tend to be more risky than similar businesses with lower ratios, because the interest cost to carry the debt takes up a larger portion of the earnings from operations (before deducting interest on debt). On the other hand, a business heavily capitalized with debt is highly leveraged, and if the business is successful, the return to the equity holders will be significantly increased over what the return would have been if the business had been financed solely with equity capital.

[17]See §9.26.

Debt/equity ratios are discussed in a number of different business contexts. In a C corporation, the shareholders may contribute a portion of the needed capital in the form of debt rather than equity. Historically, one of the factors taken into account in determining whether the debt should be reclassified as equity for income tax purposes is the "inside" debt/equity ratio, the ratio of shareholder-owned debt to equity. The "outside" debt/ equity ratio compares the total indebtedness of the business with the equity capital invested in the business, and is a measure of the creditworthiness of the business.

12 Generally Accepted Accounting Principles

§12.1 INTRODUCTION: THE FUNDAMENTAL ACCOUNTING STATEMENTS

This chapter describes the fundamental principles that underlie the two basic modern accounting statements — balance sheets and profit-and-loss statements — prepared in accordance with generally accepted accounting principles. It deals with the accepted methods of treating several commonly recurring accounting problems in a complex enterprise that utilizes the accrual method of accounting. These principles are widely applied when accounting for the operations of both closely held and publicly held businesses.

This chapter assumes some knowledge about the relationship between balance sheets and profit-and-loss statements. The starting point of the whole subject of accountancy is a very simple equation:

$$\text{Equity} = \text{Assets} - \text{Liabilities}$$

Equity in this equation has nothing to do with the historical courts of equity or with notions of fairness or simple justice: It means ownership or net worth. This equation simply states that the net worth of a business is equal to its assets minus its liabilities.

A *balance sheet* is the most fundamental financial statement: It is simply a restatement of this fundamental equation in the form:

Assets = Liabilities + Equity

A balance sheet is a presentation of this equation in a chart form:

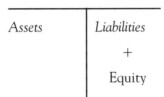

Every balance sheet, whether it is for General Motors or the smallest retail grocery store, is based on this format. The asset side of a balance sheet is always referred to as the left-hand side and the liability/equity side is always referred to as the right-hand side.

There are several fundamental premises underlying financial accounting that should be stated at the outset. First, financial accounting assumes that the business that is the subject of the financial statements is an entity independent of other businesses that may be owned by the same persons.[1] The equity referred to in that business's balance sheet is limited to the person's investment in that single business. Second, all entries have to be in terms of dollars. All property, tangible or intangible, shown on a balance sheet, must be expressed in dollars, either historical cost or fair market value or some other consistent method of valuation. Third, many "assets" or "liabilities" of a business are not reflected at all. A person's friendly smile may be an asset in a sense, but will not appear on a balance sheet since a dollar value cannot be attached to a smile.

Similarly, a company may have a reputation for sharp practices or questionable dealings; while that reputation is doubtless a liability in a sense, it is not the type of liability that appears on a balance sheet. A liability for accounting purposes is also different from the concept of a liability in the legal sense. A *liability* in the balance sheet sense is a *recognized* debt or obligation to someone else, payable in a reasonably ascertainable amount either in money or in something reducible to money. Contingent liabilities

---

[1]Of course, a single business may have many units. If the entrepreneur discussed in Chapter 11 owned several duplexes, she might consider them to be a single business. However, if the entrepreneur owned some duplexes and also was a practicing lawyer with an active practice, she would probably view herself as the owner of two separate businesses with each having its own set of financial statements.

are booked only when it is reasonably clear that the contingency will in fact occur and the amount of the liability can be reasonably estimated. In the case of litigation filed against the firm, that means an unfavorable outcome must be highly probable and the amount can be reasonably estimated.[2]

Further, a balance sheet has to balance. The fundamental accounting equation itself defines an equality: The two sides of the balance sheet restate that equality in somewhat reorganized form. A balance sheet therefore is itself an equality and the sum of the left-hand side of the balance sheet must precisely equal the sum of the right-hand side. If a balance sheet doesn't balance, somewhere the accountant has made a mistake. Finally, every transaction entered into by a business must be recorded in at least two ways if the balance sheet is to continue to balance. This last point underlies the concept of that mysterious subject, double entry bookkeeping, which is the cornerstone on which modern accounting is built.

Some transactions affect only the balance sheet. For example, if a new company (that has just started business with $10,000 in cash provided by the owner) purchases a used truck for $3,000 in cash, that transaction will be evidenced by an decrease in the asset denominated as cash and an increase in another asset, Trucks, or more likely Machinery and Equipment:

Assets		Liabilities	
Cash	7,000		
Trucks	3,000	Equity	10,000
	$10,000		$10,000

However, most transactions that a business enters into are of a different type: They involve ordinary business operations leading to a profit or loss in the current accounting period. Let us take a simple example: The business involves hauling things in the truck for customers. The day that it opens for business, it hires a truck driver at a cost of $200 per day to drive the truck and pick up and deliver for it. During that first day, the truck driver works very hard and for long hours making deliveries for which the business is paid $500. It is simple to create a profit-and-loss statement or income statement for the business for the one day of operation. "Profit and loss" and "income" are synonyms for this purpose. The basic formula is:

$$\textbf{Income} = \textbf{Revenues} - \textbf{Expenses.}$$

[2]However, disclosure of material litigation that is pending must be disclosed in a note to the financial statements if it is not booked as a liability. If the litigation threatens the continued existence of the firm, the auditor's opinion should refer specifically to the litigation as a qualification of the opinion itself.

Obviously, the business had income of $300 ($500 of revenue minus $200 of expense for the truck driver) for its first day of operation. There may have been other expenses as well that arguably should be charged to that first day of operation, but for simplicity we are ignoring that possibility.

At first glance, the income statement appears to have nothing to do with the balance sheet described above. However, one should not jump too quickly to conclusions. It is possible to create a new balance sheet to reflect each of these transactions as well:

First, the payment of the $200 to the truck driver involves a cash payment of $200 by the business; it is easy to record that. But where should the offsetting entry be? The balance sheet cannot look like this:

Assets		Liabilities	
Cash	6,800		
Used truck	3,000	Equity	10,000
	$9,800		$10,000

Something is obviously wrong since this balance sheet does not balance. There has to be an offsetting entry. It certainly should not be an increase in value of the truck. Perhaps one could view the services as an asset something like the truck, but that does not make much sense since the services are transient and performed at the time the payment is made. One could perhaps argue that no balance sheet should be created until the payment to the truck driver is offset by whatever he earns during the rest of the day, but that cannot be correct either, because the balance sheet must balance after every transaction, not just at the end of a sequence of transactions. The only possible solution is to reduce "owner's equity" by the payment:

Assets		Liabilities	
Cash	6,800		
Used truck	3,000	Equity	9,800
	$9,800		9,800

Second, the $500 payment for the services rendered:

Assets		Liabilities	
Cash	7,300		
Used truck	3,000	Equity	10,300
	$11,300		$11,300

Admittedly, these two balance sheets are not very helpful in showing the relationship between the balance sheet and the income statement. What is needed is a segregation of income items within the equity account so that the permanent investment and the transient changes are shown separately. If we take as the period of time the one-day period in which the truck driver was hired and his services were performed, the following balance sheet at the end of the period is much more illuminating:

Assets			Liabilities	
Cash	7,300			
Used truck	3,000		Equity	
			Original capital	10,000
			Earnings	300
	$10,300			$10,300

The important point is that the statement of income or profit and loss should itself be viewed as a right-hand entry on the balance sheet.

The balance sheet is a static concept showing the status of a business at a particular instant in time while the income statement describes the results of operations over some period of time: daily, monthly, quarterly, or annually. In a sense, the balance sheet is a photograph, the income statement a motion picture. However, the income statement for a period provides the bridge between the balance sheet at the beginning of the period and the balance sheet at the end of the period because positive income items (revenues) increase the owner's equity account while negative income items (expenses) reduce that account. Logically, the balance sheet is the basic document around which all financial statements are constructed while the income statement is a bridge between successive balance sheets.

§12.2 SUMMARY OF BASIC GAAP PRINCIPLES

GAAP requires that transactions be taken into the bookkeeping records ("booked" is the verb traditionally use) when their primary economic impact occurs, not necessarily when cash is received or disbursed. Assume that a seller sells goods on credit. The customer pays for the goods several months later. On the cash basis, the transaction would be recorded in the month the payment was made; on the accrual basis, the transaction would be recorded in the month the sale was made. The credit aspect of the transaction would be recorded on the asset side by an increase in "accounts receivable," i.e., a debt owed by someone to the seller. Costs or expenses are taken into the accounts when the benefit occurs, which is typically when the revenues to which they relate are earned. In other words, the general goal of the accrual system is the matching of expenses with corresponding revenues wherever that is possible. The cost of the goods sold would be booked as an expense (a reduction in the inventory account is the offsetting entry) in the same period that the sale is booked.

Certain kinds of indirect expenses cannot be allocated to specific revenues, and they are booked as time passes independent of revenues. Examples of indirect expenses that are accrued on the basis of time are interest on borrowed funds or rent that must be paid. Similarly, revenues such as interest or rent received cannot be allocated to a specific transaction and are viewed as earned simply by the passage of time.

One of the complexities of the accrual system is that cash receipts or expense payments that are received or paid in accounting periods other than the one in which they have their primary impact, are viewed as creating assets or liabilities on the balance sheet; these assets or liabilities are "parked" on the balance sheet and "booked" (that is, treated as revenue) or "written off" (that is, taken as expenses) in the year in which they are "recognized" for accounting purposes. A simple example is where a business leases out space to a third party and receives two months' rent in advance. In order to record that transaction, a new balance sheet account, called "prepaid rent," must be created to record that payment; at the end of each month during which the rent was actually earned, earnings would be increased by the rent and the prepaid rent account would be reduced by the same amount.

Because revenue is not accounted for until the transaction occurs (or time passes, in the case of rental income), any receipts or payments of cash allocable to other accounting periods are treated as balance sheet entries. Prepaid expenses are treated as assets and unearned receipts are treated as liabilities (as in the case of the prepaid rent). People sometimes find it difficult to accept that the prepayment of an expense item creates an asset while the receipt of unearned income creates a liability. This relationship may be appreciated intuitively by noting that the prepayment of an expense is indistinguishable in principle from the purchase of an asset such as a truck.

Another important aspect of accrual accounting is that the acquisition of machinery, buildings, or other long-lived assets is viewed as the purchase of an asset that is "capitalized" and its subsequent depreciation over its estimated useful life. For example, if a new truck has an estimated life of five years, one-fifth of the cost may be viewed as an expense — depreciation — each year over the next five years. Indeed, in one sense, all assets on a balance sheet (other than cash) are expenses waiting to be written off some appropriate future accounting period.

Accrual accounting presents a more realistic picture of how the business is doing than cash accounting. However, it is more complex and requires the accountant or bookkeeper to make judgments on difficult questions, such as "What is the estimated useful life of the truck purchased last month?"

§12.3 ACCOUNTING FOR LONG LEAD-TIME BUSINESSES

The accrual system works best for firms that carry inventories and have large numbers of profitmaking or loss-creating transactions during each accounting period. In other types of businesses, however, traditional accrual accounting sometimes results in the bunching of income, making accounting results incomparable from one year to the next.

A classic example of this latter type of business is an airplane manufacturer with a contract to build an airplane that involves two years of design and construction work before the first plane is delivered. An airplane involves a long lead time since costs must be incurred for an extended period before revenues are received. If the contract for the plane involves, say, a $60 million payment when each plane is delivered, the airplane manufacturer, if it follows simple accrual accounting principles, will show no income — but huge losses as expenses mount — during the two-year development phase and will record its first revenue with the sale of the first plane in the third year of the contract. Since the development expenses will have been written off in the presale phase, earnings in later years will be overstated. This basic pattern is very common. It may be present in the development of software for computers, the production of motion pictures, heavy construction projects, and other business activities that involve development periods of more than one year.

The accrual system avoids this distortion of earnings by permitting the *capitalization of expenses*. If the airplane manufacturer follows conventional accrual principles, it will "capitalize" development expenses (that is, treat them as an asset much like prepaid rent rather than as expenses) and show zero income during the development years, followed by profits in the years during which the planes are sold. The capitalized development expenses are written off as planes are sold.

If it appears likely from the outset that the project will be profitable, it may be more realistic to allocate a portion of the ultimate profit to each of the two developmental years in which much of the work is done as well as capitalizing those development costs. In this way, the business would show a profit during the start-up years even though it had no revenue in those years! Is there anything wrong in "leveling out" the earnings record over such a cycle? The application of an accrual accounting system to such firms is not without controversy. The accountant takes pride in treating recognition issues conservatively, and refusing to recognize income unless it is certain to be earned. The difficulty with our hypothetical airplane manufacturer is that it is usually not possible to determine that the airplane being developed will in fact be salable until after sales begin. The proposed accounting treatment may be based more on optimism and hope than on reliable prediction. In effect, the company is gambling on its ability to design and produce an airplane that will be attractive to customers when it is available, a kind of gambling crucial in an entrepreneurial economy. To book profit throughout the developmental period assumes away the reality of the risk.[3]

Accounting on a basis other than traditional accrual principles is nevertheless well-accepted in some industries. For example, many companies engaged in commercial construction report income on a percentage of contract completion basis that spreads anticipated profits over the lifetime of the contract. Sellers of large consumer or commercial equipment on credit over several years may report income on the installment basis rather than using the point of sale as the time of realization of income.

Deciding what is the most appropriate time for revenue recognition is often a matter of judgment. To take one real-life example, consider whether in the trading-stamp industry revenues should be recognized when the stamps are sold to merchants for distribution to retail customers, or when the stamps are presented for redemption, which is the first time that the costs of providing the redemption goods are known.

§12.4 DEPRECIATION, DEPLETION, AND AMORTIZATION

Depreciation, depletion, and amortization in an accounting context all refer to essentially the same process: the allocation of the cost of a long-lived asset to consecutive accounting periods as expenses to reflect the gradual using up of the asset. Depreciation is associated with the process of writing off plant and equipment; the word *depletion* refers to the gradual exhaustion of natural resources through the process of capture and development; amortization involves intangible assets with a limited life, (such as copyrights or patents) and deferred charges (such as organizational expenses, research and development costs, or "dry holes" in oil and gas exploration). In a sense, the writing off or expensing of long-lived assets is similar to any prepayment of future expenses: The purchase of a truck, for example, can be seen as a prepayment to ensure the availability of the truck over the balance of its useful life in much the same way that the advance payment of two years' rent creates an asset account — prepaid expenses.

---

[3]The manufacturer, of course, has some idea of the potential market before designing a new airplane. For example, it may have solicited nonbinding "orders" for the plane from customers and hence have a good idea that a market will exist for the plane when it becomes available.

§12.5 DEPRECIATION: THE BASIC CONCEPTS

Assume that a business purchases a used truck for $3,000. This purchase leads to the opening of an asset account on the balance sheet for the truck with an entry of $3,000, the purchase price (historical cost) of the truck. To calculate the depreciation of this asset following its acquisition requires the following steps: Someone (presumably an accountant) estimates (1) the useful life of the truck, and (2) the scrap or resale value of the truck, if any, at the end of that period. Assuming that straight-line depreciation is being followed, the difference between the original cost and the scrap value is then divided by the number of years of the truck's estimated useful life. That amount is treated as the annual expense of "using up" the truck, and reduces earnings by that amount. For example, if the useful life of the truck is estimated to be five years and the resale value of the truck at the end of that period is zero, straight-line depreciation accounting requires that the business include as an expense, in each of the next five years, $(\frac{\$3,000 - 0}{5})$, or $600 per year. At the same time, a new balance sheet account is created (Less: Accumulated Depreciation) that appears as a deduction or offset against the asset account: As each depreciation deduction is taken as an expense, this new account is increased by the same amount. (This type of negative asset account is sometimes called a *contra account*.) After two years have gone by, the contra account will be $1,200 and the "book value" of the truck will be $1,800.

There are several important points to make about this simple example: First, the contra account, usually labeled Less: Accumulated depreciation, is purely a bookkeeping entry. There is no separate fund or separate account in the corporation's assets marked "depreciation account" or "depreciation reserve" that contains $1,200, and there are no funds set aside to help pay for the truck's replacement when it wears out. Rather, the $1,200 is simply the sum of two $600 items taken as expenses; some such entry is necessary in order to make the balance sheet balance. But, mustn't there be an extra $1,200 somewhere? In a sense there is, since the two deductions for depreciation made annual earnings smaller than they would have been had no depreciation been claimed. Somewhere in the balance sheet there are offsetting items, but this is not a fruitful line of inquiry since there is no way to say where they are. What is important for our purposes is that the business has not in fact squirreled away $1,200 in a special account or fund.

Second, the truck will of course gradually wear out, and will presumably have to be replaced. However, depreciation deductions do not affect this process in a direct way. The only real economic effects depreciation deductions have on a business are that they (1) reduce reported earnings without being a drain on the business's current cash flow, and (2) reduce the business's tax bill (assuming that the Internal Revenue Code permits the particular depreciation deduction to be calculated and claimed in the way proposed). This tax consequence arises because depreciation is a deductible expense item for tax purposes, and larger depreciation deductions mean lower income subject to tax, and therefore lower taxes. Arguments for faster depreciation deductions are usually motivated to some extent by self-interest since faster write-offs mean larger current tax deductions. Even though the accumulated depreciation account is not a fund created to provide for a replacement for the truck when it wears out, one often hears arguments that larger amounts should be deductible from income to reflect increases in replacement costs because of inflation, or because the American manufacturing plant is wearing out, or because the American economy is consuming its own capital. While legitimate arguments may be made about what kinds of depreciation deductions should be permitted to reflect inflation, most such arguments are based on a selfish unstated premise, namely that it is desirable from the interests of the speaker for the United States to reduce the amount of income taxes it collects from his or her business. Unfortunately, this self-interest colors much of the theoretical debate over depreciation.

Third, after two years, the book value of the truck has been reduced to $1,800 on the books of the business through two depreciation deductions of $600 each. *Book value* simply means the value of the truck as shown on the books of the business. Is there any relationship between this book value and what the truck is actually worth after two years? The answer is probably not. If the current market value of the truck is in fact $1,800, it is purely by chance. Trucks do not usually decline in value at a steady rate precisely equal to that originally estimated by an accountant. Furthermore, the starting value for the depreciation calculation was the cost of the truck two years ago: What has happened to the used truck market in the meantime? Indeed, there is no reason to believe that the business originally paid precisely the fair market value of the truck when it bought it: It could have paid too much, or it could have gotten a bargain. But that does not matter. For accounting purposes, the value of the truck when it is purchased is its cost. Certainly, the depreciation calculation takes none of these factors into account. What then does the book value represent? It represents historical cost reduced by some arbitrary number of expense deductions, and not a whole lot more. It may or may not be a reasonable approximation of the resale value of the truck. When the business sells the truck, it probably will be at a price different from its book value; the gain or loss on that transaction is reflected in income or retained earnings at that time.

Fourth, does the truck disappear after its value has been reduced to zero on the books of the business? Of course not. If the truck still has economic value it may continue to be used in the business. In this case, the original estimate of the useful life of the truck was too conservative — the truck was written off more quickly than its useful life actually warranted.

Once the truck has been fully depreciated — i.e., reduced to its estimated scrap or resale value — no further depreciation deductions are available to the business for that truck if it continues to be used in the business thereafter.

This traditional way of handling depreciation has one justification: It requires that costs of certain assets be allocated in an orderly and verifiable fashion to different accounting periods. Whether or not the specific allocations to specific periods are accurate may be less important than that they be done on a systematic basis that approximates the useful life span of the asset.

§12.6 ACCELERATED DEPRECIATION SYSTEMS

In the foregoing discussion, it has been assumed that annual depreciation deductions will be calculated by dividing the depreciable value of the property by its expected life. This type of depreciation is called *straight-line depreciation* since the amount of the deduction for depreciation each year is constant over the life of the asset.

Accelerated depreciation systems involve placing relatively larger amounts of the depreciation deductions in the early years of the asset's life. These systems are to a large extent tax-oriented, because the increased deductions generated by these systems in the early years of the life of the asset, if accepted for federal income tax purposes, create significant tax benefits that are strong incentives to adopt the systems. In some circumstances, however, these systems may be independently justified from an accounting standpoint because, by loading most of the depreciation charges in the early years of the asset's life, they more closely approximate actual market values for assets such as automobiles or trucks, which typically depreciate in value very rapidly during their early years of use. The most popular accelerated depreciation system are the sum of the digits method[4] and the *declining balance* method.[5]

---

[4]In this method, the depreciation deduction is calculated each year by creating a fraction in which the numerator equals the number of years of useful life remaining and the denominator equals the sum of all the useful years of life of the asset. For example, for the truck with a five-year useful life expectancy, the denominator is $5 + 4 + 3 + 2 + 1$, or 15; in the first year, the numerator is five (and the fraction is $5/15$ or $1/3$); in the second year, the numerator is 4 (and the fraction is $4/15$); in the third year, the numerator is 3 (and the fraction is $3/15$ or $1/5$), and so forth. The internal logic of this system is not as important as the accelerated pattern of deductions that it creates.

[5]In this method, a stable fraction or percentage is applied to the current book value of the asset (historical cost minus previous depreciation deductions), rather than to original cost less salvage value. (Salvage value is not considered when applying the declining balance method.) The fraction or percentage is usually a multiple of the straight-line depreciation

§12.7 DEPLETION AND AMORTIZATION

The calculation of depletion of natural resources is usually made on the basis of estimates of the total recoverable resources in the field or ore body. The original purchase price or cost of the asset is divided by the estimated recoverable resources in the field or ore body to determine the cost per unit (per barrel, per ton, or whatever the appropriate measure is). Then, as each unit is captured and recovered, the cost is shown as Less: Accumulated Depletion, much the same way as depreciation is shown.

The amortization of intangible assets and deferred charges follows a similar pattern, though the issues are more controversial. Relatively few problems are created by amortization of traditional intangible assets such as patents, copyrights, and trade names that are purchased or developed internally so that the cost of acquisition or development can be readily established. Serious problems, however, are created by the capitalization and amortization of research and development (R&D) costs, the drilling of "dry holes" in connection with the successful exploration of oil and gas, and start-up expenses for a variety of new businesses or enterprises.

If a firm expends funds for R&D, for example, GAAP requires that it treat the expenditures as expenses in the year incurred unless it can show that the expenditures will lead to marketable products. If the firm can prove this connection, it may capitalize the expenditures and write them off in future years against those products. While R&D expenditures directed toward a specific product or project are almost always capitalized, basic or general research often cannot be allocated with any precision, and should

---

rate. Thus, if the asset has a five-year life, the straight-line depreciation rate is 20 percent per year. The double declining balance method applies twice the 20 percent rate, or 40 percent per year. For example, a $3,000 truck depreciated over five years by the double declining balance method would lead to the following depreciation deductions in the first five years:

Cost (less depreciation)	Rate	Depreciation deduction
$3,000	40%	$1,200
(3,000 − 1200) = 1800	40%	$720
(1,800 − 720) = 1080	40%	$432
(1,080 − 432) = 638	40%	$259.20
(638 − 259.20) = 378.8	40%	$151.52

The 150 percent declining balance method would entail the use of a 30 percent rate on a five-year asset. The declining balance method, like the sum of the digits method, results in very substantial deductions in early years. In the above example, the double declining balance method results in a write-off of 40 percent of the cost of the truck in the first year, compared with the 33 percent maximum write-off obtainable under the sum of the digits method.

therefore be expensed when incurred.[6] While this treatment is not entirely consistent with the basic notion that expenses should be recognized when the revenue to which they relate is recognized, the possibility of manipulation and foul play in financial statements was so great that an objective and relatively bright-line rule was thought appropriate.

In this area, there is a real risk that capitalized expenses shown as assets on a balance sheet in fact have a zero value.

§12.8 HISTORICAL COST ACCOUNTING IN LOSS SITUATIONS

Assets are generally recorded in the financial statements at historical cost. What, if anything, should be done if the current market value is less than they cost. This problem arose in the late 1980s and early 1990s, when real estate values declined significantly in some areas of the country. Developers went broke and much of this property was foreclosed upon by lenders. At the time, federally insured savings and loan associations and banks were permitted to record the values of foreclosed real estate properties at historical cost rather than current market value. However, the result was that the true financial position of these financial institutions was completely hidden: their assets in fact were worth so much less than their book value that many institutions were actually insolvent in real life even though their books showed positive equity.

This problem became so serious that banking regulations were modified to require institutions to write down the value of properties from historical cost to current market values, when that value was substantially below historical cost. This process, known as *marking to market* creates accounting losses that do not reflect a decline in cash reserves. Historical cost accounting may present a highly unreliable picture of a business in a down market.[7] Conservative accounting principles require that assets that have declined in value be marked down to market value.

§12.9 ACCOUNTING FOR INVENTORY

Inventory includes (1) all finished goods awaiting sale, (2) all goods in various stages of production beginning with (and including) raw materials, and

---

[6]An argument can be made that all research expenditures should be immediately expensed without regard to the probability that a marketable product will be forthcoming as a result of the research.

[7]A mark to market principle is generally applicable to inventory that has declined substantially in value.

(3) all goods on hand that are ultimately consumed in the production of goods. Accounting for inventory is complex primarily because tremendous variation exists from industry to industry and from business to business as to the nature and variety of items maintained in inventory. Furthermore, some forms of accounting for inventory artificially reduces current earnings.

Control of inventory costs is a major component in determining whether or not a business is successful. Problems of pilferage or shortages are most likely to involve inventory. Unaccountable losses of inventory — whether due to pilferage, failure to maintain adequate records, spoilage, or other causes — are also called, somewhat charitably, "shrinkage."

Goods that are manufactured or purchased are usually stored (or parked) in the inventory account on the balance sheet until they are taken into the expense account of the income statement. Practical considerations, however, require most businesses to adopt artificial conventions for estimating inventory costs since it is not practical or cost justifiable for most businesses to keep track of each inventory item as it wends its way through the manufacturing process and even if it were, this tracking alternative readily lends itself to manipulation. It is usually not practicable or desirable to try to match specific cost inputs directly with specific sales. The most common conventions are FIFO (first-in first-out) and LIFO (last-in first-out), discussed in the following section.

The most widely used inventory systems require businesses to record additions to inventory as they occur on the balance sheet but determine the cost of goods sold only at the end of each accounting period. This determination is usually made in the following way. The cost of goods sold for a period is determined at the close of the period by the following basic formula:

(1)   **Cost of goods sold = value of opening inventory**
+ additions to inventory − value of closing inventory

All of these amounts are of course recorded in dollars. The value of both the opening inventory and the closing inventory are determined by taking physical counts of what is on hand at the end of an accounting period and then assigning it a dollar value under FIFO or LIFO. In other words, an essential part of the year-end auditing process is a physical count of inventory. The value of the inventory at the end of one period (the closing inventory) becomes, of course, the value of the inventory at the beginning of the next period (the opening inventory) so that only one physical count per year is necessary.

The physical inventory count and the manner of valuing that inventory are absolutely critical steps in the determination of the profitability of the business. That should be evident from the following formula:

(2)   Gross profit = net sales − cost of goods sold

This formula reveals that every change in the number of dollars attributed to cost of goods sold leads to a dollar-for-dollar increase or reduction in the gross profit of the business. Further, formulas (1) and (2) are obviously interrelated; one can substitute formula (1) into formula (2) to yield this:

(3)   **Gross profit = net sales − value of opening inventory − additions to inventory + value of closing inventory**

(Remember your high school algebra about the effect of minus signs on other minus signs.) The implications to be drawn from formula (3) are these: First, every change in the number of dollars attributed to closing inventory also means a dollar-for-dollar change in gross profit. Second, the higher the value of the closing inventory, the lower the cost of goods sold and the higher the gross profit. Correspondingly, the lower the value of the closing inventory, the higher the cost of goods sold and the lower the gross profit.

These calculations do not attempt to trace what specific inventory items were actually consumed during the period in question, but simply subtract the value of closing inventory from all inventory available to the business during the period (opening inventory plus additions to inventory for the period). Since the increase of closing inventory by one dollar increases gross profit by one dollar while the decrease of closing inventory by one dollar decreases gross profit by that amount, the manner of assigning dollar value to closing inventory items significantly affects reported earnings.

§12.10 FIFO AND LIFO

FIFO determines the value of closing inventory by assuming that the earliest items in inventory are always sold first. FIFO has certain advantages. For one thing, it actually conforms with the physical inventory practices of many businesses, which follow the principle that because of spoilage, staleness, or obsolescence, the oldest items should always be sold first. Second, since inventory is always composed of the last-acquired items, the value of closing inventory on the balance sheet is likely to reflect closely the current market value of inventory items. In this sense, FIFO improves the reliability of the balance sheet since the important inventory item reflects the most current prices at which inventory was actually purchased.

LIFO proceeds on the opposite assumption to FIFO, namely that the last items are always sold first. No account is taken of the sequence of actual subtractions from inventory in applying either FIFO or LIFO. It is probably true that LIFO does not accurately reflect the way in which most businesses in fact consume inventory (i.e., disposing of the last first), but it is certainly true of some businesses.

The advantages of LIFO over FIFO arise because of the general inflationary trends that have persisted in the American economy since World War II. Inventory replacement costs have generally risen and rarely fallen. This is the context in which the choice between FIFO and LIFO must realistically be evaluated.

The major real-life advantage of LIFO is that, since 1939, businesses may use LIFO in calculating their federal income tax liability. Because of general price inflation that has existed in the American economy since World War II, companies using LIFO generally value the goods sold at a higher value than companies using FIFO; as a result, LIFO provides tax savings over FIFO. Indeed, if one assumes that inventory costs increase steadily, FIFO maximizes the business's taxes while LIFO minimizes them. The argument has been strongly made that every business should shift from FIFO to LIFO simply because of this tax saving.

Further, the tax savings arising from LIFO are permanent as a practical matter. Theoretically, the tax saving arising from LIFO will be lost when the low-cost LIFO inventory is totally liquidated; at that time FIFO and LIFO should have led to the same total cost of goods sold. This, however, totally ignores the time value of money: The immediate reduction of taxes through LIFO is worth much more than the future increase in taxes when the LIFO inventory is consumed, come the millennium, when the business liquidates. Obviously, most companies go on for years or centuries without totally liquidating inventory: They reduce taxes by the LIFO election immediately and (apparently) permanently.

LIFO tends to cause reported earnings to reflect accurately the most current cost of goods sold, since LIFO uses the most recent inventory costs in determining cost of goods sold. FIFO tends to make the inventory value shown on the balance sheet relatively current but overstates earnings. LIFO emphasizes the accuracy of the income statement over that of the balance sheet — consistent with modern thinking about the relative roles of the two statements. The major disadvantage of LIFO is that the cost of inventory as shown on the balance sheet tends to become increasingly obsolete if, as is usually the case, the business maintains a stable or increasing inventory over several years. If a stable inventory is assumed, the LIFO inventory will always carry the value it had as of the date on which the LIFO election was made! In other words, it is quite possible that a 1996 balance sheet reflects inventory costs based on, say, 1939 product prices.

A second major problem with LIFO arises when, by reason of a strike or shortage, a LIFO inventory must be partially consumed in a later accounting period to keep up current production or sales. The inventory so consumed is on the books at an artificially low price, so that earnings are inflated solely because of the method of accounting for inventory costs. One possibility is that businesses be allowed to replenish LIFO inventories without adverse accounting or tax consequences when the depletion was in some sense involuntary.

A final observation may be made about the choice between FIFO and LIFO in inflationary periods. Irrespective of the inventory valuation system adopted, profits are going to be inflated during inflationary periods simply from price increases occurring during the period between the time of purchasing inventory and the time of recording it as an expense. The profit recorded by a business is in part its normal operating profit from whatever business it is in and in part an abnormal trading profit caused by price increases during the manufacturing or resale process. LIFO tends to minimize the amount of this artificial profit, but does not eliminate it entirely. Elimination would require a radical shift to a current value system for valuing inventory consumed during the accounting period. Such a proposal seems impractical and has never been adopted. But LIFO is more sensitive to the effect of inflation on income statements than is FIFO.

§12.11 FINAL THOUGHTS ON HISTORICAL COST AND VALUE

The numbers appearing in financial statements are of course in terms of dollars. The basis on which dollars are assigned to various assets in the accounting system involves historical cost. This is not a common meaning of "value." Value usually means the price established by transactions between willing buyers and sellers in some market. It might also mean the value of the asset to the user, or the cost of reproducing or replacing the asset. The one thing it most certainly does not usually mean is what the asset cost, perhaps years earlier. And yet that is precisely the definition accounting typically uses. To an accountant, value means historical cost.

The use of historical cost as the basis for accounting can be justified on several pragmatic grounds: Most importantly, it fits in easily with the intricate systems of accounts created under the principles of double entry bookkeeping. Also, it is objective and easily verifiable. Indeed, the use of historical cost is so basic to the modern accounting system that even assets whose current market values may be determined without difficulty are nevertheless recorded at cost. The current market value of a portfolio of marketable securities, for example, may be determined by a single telephone call to a securities broker. Yet the value of appreciated securities is always shown at cost on the financial statements though it is customary to show their current market values as a parenthetical addition to the balance sheet as part of the description of the account.[8]

A corollary of the basic historical cost principle is that a business should not record appreciation in the value of assets until that appreciation has been realized by sale or disposition of the asset. In the course of law school, you may run into instances in which a business decided to record (or book) unrealized appreciation, and a court decided that it was lawful for the business to do so. The best known example of this is *Randall v. Bailey*,[9] where a corporation recorded unrealized appreciation on its books in order to improve its dividend-paying ability. Of course, generally accepted accounting principles may not have anything to do with the question of what lawfully may be done. Therefore, cases such as *Randall v. Bailey* do not really bear on the issues of modern accounting principles. Some statutes embody undefined accounting concepts and in the absence of legislative direction, one should probably not assume that the legislature intended to require all businesses to follow GAAP in the application of these statutes.[10] In any event, the write-up of unrealized appreciation permitted in *Randall v. Bailey* does not conform to GAAP, but sometimes occurs today in businesses that are not required to prepare GAAP financial statements.[11]

Theoretically, one could abandon historical cost and develop an alternative accounting system that immediately recorded unrealized appreciation. Abstractly, such a system is neither right nor wrong, neither legal nor illegal. However, it would be a risky accounting system, because asset values that go up can also go down, as was vividly demonstrated by real estate prices in the 1980s and 1990s in many areas, and there is a serious risk that unless there is a more or less continuous review, asset values might be significantly overstated at times and understated at others.[12] Whether or not such a system would provide useful information to owners and creditors is doubtful.

Generally accepted accounting principles do contain a couple of important qualifications to the historical cost principle. The first is that GAAP assumes that the business is a going concern. If an auditor concludes that the business is contemplating liquidation or is otherwise unlikely to survive,

[8]If the securities have declined in value, however, the loss should be reorganized in the current year and the securities booked at their current market value.

[9]23 N.Y.S.2d 173 (1940).

[10]Section 6.40 of the Model Business Corporation Act (1984) authorizes the use of any "reasonable" accounting system for the determination of the lawfulness of dividends. The choice of accounting system is to be made by the board of directors of the corporation.

[11]A write-up of assets occurs routinely in transactions known as leveraged buyouts.

[12]Of course, a person deprecating the use of historical cost might rejoin that using historical cost leads to a system in which the recorded value is unlikely ever to equal current value.

he or she should insist that the basis for reporting values be changed from historical cost to current liquidation values in order to assess the availability of assets to cover liabilities. As a practical matter, that change usually results in a significant mark-down in values and the elimination of many assets from the balance sheet. For example, organizational expenses may be capitalized and viewed as an asset only if the business is a going concern: It is obvious that these expenses have little or no inherent market value if the business is to be liquidated.

A second major qualification is embodied in the principle that assets the firm holds for resale should be valued at the lower of cost or market. In other words, if the market value of inventory or marketable securities is clearly less than their original cost, those assets should be immediately written down to current market value.

The principles outlined in this section are sometimes cited as illustrating the conservatism of the accounting profession in assigning values to assets. This may be so, but it should be recognized that this conservatism has its costs in the form of financial statements that largely reflect historical relationships, not current values. In periods of inflation, the use of historical costs undervalues assets more often than it overstates them. At least this has been true during most of the period since World War II. As a result of the accountant's conservatism the book values of businesses are likely to be understated.

How to Read and Use Financial Statements

§13.1 INTRODUCTION

Corporate lawyers are often expected to examine and analyze unfamiliar financial statements of closely held businesses on behalf of clients. This process requires familiarity with the way in which financial statements are prepared, how useful information can be squeezed from them, and the ability to recognize signs of trouble ahead. This chapter provides an introduction to this rather arcane art.

The assessment of financial statements for closely held businesses is complicated by the fact that there is no requirement that GAAP principles be used. As a result, any assessment must consider not only the numbers on the financial statements themselves but also who prepared them and the principles that were followed in generating the numbers.

The analysis of financial statements is usually the responsibility of accountants and other experts trained in financial analysis. Moreover, a lawyer's examination of financial statements for an unfamiliar business may be supplemented by expert advice obtained from nonlegal sources. However, in the routine representation of business clients, lawyers are normally involved in transactions in which the financial position of another entity is important but expert advice cannot practically be obtained. As a result, lawyers must have some knowledge of financial statements.

§13.2 USES OF FINANCIAL STATEMENTS

When examining financial statements, one must always keep in mind the purpose of the examination. What are you or your client proposing to do? Likely alternatives are: (1) lending money to the business, (2) buying from, selling to, or otherwise dealing with the business, (3) making an investment in the business, or (4) buying the business outright. The attitude you take toward the financial statements must depend to a large degree on what is the nature of the proposed transaction and your client's exposure to loss in the event the other party runs into unexpected financial difficulties or is unable to perform as contemplated.

§13.3 SHORT-TERM TRANSACTIONS

If the proposed transaction involves lending money to or entering into commercial transactions with the business on a relatively short-term basis, an extended analysis of financial statements is seldom required. The question usually is simply whether the business is likely to be able to repay the loan or pay for the goods or services being provided. At the most, an analysis of cash flow over the period of the loan should be sufficient. But probably more useful would be a credit check through one of the commercial credit reporting agencies that provides information about bill-paying history. In addition, useful information about specific companies may be obtained from a variety of publications such as Standard & Poor's Corporation Records, Moody's Industrial Manual, and the Value Line Industrial Survey.

The risk of nonpayment may often be reduced or eliminated by simple protective measures: obtaining a lien or security interest in the debtor's property, requiring the principal shareholders or owners of the debtor to guarantee personally the payment of the debt, or requiring the debtor to provide a letter of credit from a responsible financial institution assuring that payment will be made when required upon the submission of appropriate documents. If personal guarantees are being relied upon, it is essential to obtain financial statements of the guarantors as well as of the principal debtor.

In deciding what the risk of nonpayment is, the financial statements of the debtor should be examined to determine whether the transaction is of such a magnitude that it may strain the normal resources of the debtor. If so, a relatively short-range cash-flow analysis may be requested in order to determine how the debtor contemplates raising the necessary funds to complete the transaction. Even where the risk appears to be a substantial one, your client may be able to protect itself by structuring the transaction so as to limit risk by, for example, providing that your client may suspend performance if payments are not made at specified intervals.

§13.4 LONG-TERM INVESTMENTS

Decisions whether or not to make a long-term investment in another business (either of debt or equity) are almost always preceded by an investigation into the nature and quality of the business. Market share, the quality of top-level personnel, and the attractiveness of product lines are important nonfinancial areas of inquiry. Expert analysis of the financial statements is also an important part of this investigation. A long-term investment usually involves a relatively passive interest in the business. Financial statements, prepared on the basis of GAAP or otherwise, will be the principal source of information for evaluation of earning potential or longer-term cash flows. In this situation, one must always be alert for danger signals indicating that the business is not as financially healthy as the financial statements might indicate.

In making a financial analysis, one should try to obtain financial statements (usually shortened simply to "financials") for at least the last five years (if the business has been in existence that long) to study trends not apparent from current financial statements only. A declining rate of growth or a rate of growth smaller than the industry as a whole are signs of possible trouble. Many danger signals, however, cannot be detected solely from the financial statements themselves. They include unusual turnover of key personnel, changes in auditors, and a gradual slowdown in the rate of payment of liabilities.

§13.5 ACQUISITION OF THE BUSINESS

If your client is proposing to acquire control of the business, a basic question is whether the client wants to acquire specific assets or ownership of the legal entity that is currently conducting the business (through the purchase of shares of stock if the entity is a corporation or by assignments of interests from the owners, if the business is a partnership, limited liability company, or other unincorporated form). The principal risk when acquiring the entity itself is that there may be unknown liabilities of the firm that go with the firm and may be asserted in the future, for example, tax liabilities arising from prior years' operations, undisclosed product liability claims that may surface after the firm is acquired, or environmental claims arising from prior operations that may be asserted sometime in the future.

Because of these risks, an asset purchase transaction is usually more attractive than a purchase of the business entity itself. An asset purchase transaction permits your client to designate which specific business liabilities it will assume and agree to pay, and which it will disaffirm, leaving them the responsibility of the seller. However, an asset purchase transaction does not avoid all unpleasant surprises because even excluded claims may be asserted on theories of "de facto merger," "mere continuation," or some related theory grouped under the general rubric of *successor liability*.[1] However, this risk may be acceptable to your client, since a carefully structured asset transaction, combined with an express exclusion of all but specific listed liabilities,[2] is likely to avoid the actual imposition of liability on subsequent claims.

In addition to successor liability, other matters of financial concern are whether the book value of assets as reflected in the financial statements of the business significantly overstates their market value, whether the cash flows of the business appear to be sufficient to finance future growth, and whether claims may be asserted by third parties against specific business assets. Land records and UCC filings must be examined to determine whether recorded claims or liens exist. Given the methods of valuing inventory described in sections 12.9 and 12.10, consideration must be given as to whether the actual value of the physical inventory approximates its book value. This requires that an actual physical count be made at the time of the closing, together with an examination by a person familiar with the trade to ensure that the inventory is merchantable. Obviously, one cannot

---

[1] Claims may be asserted against the purchaser in these asset transactions because the selling entity typically distributes the proceeds of the sale to its owners and then dissolves shortly after the asset transaction is completed. In some cases, courts have insisted that an asset purchaser also take responsibility for product liability or environmental clean-up claims despite express provisions that such liabilities are not being assumed by the purchaser. The so-called bulk sales law also may lead to the inadvertent assumption of liabilities if proper notice is not given to the creditors of a business. If such liability is imposed, the purchaser presumably has an action against the selling entity for breach of warranty, for whatever that is worth.

[2] Normally, an asset purchaser will assume liabilities "incurred in the ordinary course of business." Disputes may arise in the future as to whether specific liabilities are included within this general language.

378

hope to resolve these issues solely from an examination of the financial statements.

When a business is being purchased, one can often reduce the scope of risk in various ways. For example, it may be possible to require the seller to warrant the essential accuracy of the financial statements and the absence of material off-book liabilities. A right to rescind the entire transaction may be negotiated if these warranties turn out to be false after the transaction is closed. The absence of undisclosed liabilities may be made a condition to closing, giving the purchaser an opportunity to make a more complete investigation and withdraw from the transaction if such liabilities are discovered. The disbursement of funds at the closing may be conditioned upon the completion of a physical count of the inventory and the certification by an expert that the inventory is merchantable and approximates in value its book value.

Negative factors such as inventory shortage or the existence of undisclosed or contingent liabilities may affect only the amount of consideration being paid for the business. In some circumstances, however, the problems discovered may be so significant as to call into question the soundness of the entire transaction.

§13.6 GAAP AND NON-GAAP FINANCIAL STATEMENTS

A major purpose of the mandatory principles set forth in GAAP is to ensure comparability of public financial statements. In addition, there are standards for independence of the auditor and the depth of his or her audit that permit a person to deal with GAAP financial statements with some degree of confidence. However, one should not overstate the degree of reliability of financial statements on the basis of a clean certificate by an outside auditor.

Even though GAAP is designed to ensure that operating results have a large degree of comparability, it is important to recognize that GAAP, like accounting generally, is not a set of mathematical principles that can be inferred from a limited number of axioms. Rather it comprises judgmental principles established in an effort to make financial statements useful to persons who use them. A fair amount of discretion may exist as to how certain transactions are treated for accounting purposes. Where transactions are material, a reference to the way they are treated should appear either in the auditor's statement or in the notes to the financial statements. Management rather than the outside auditor usually makes these discretionary decisions, though the outside auditor has a voice in the matter, and in some instances that voice may be decisive. Significant disagreements between a business and its outside auditors as to how a transaction should be treated under GAAP do not occur often, but the fact that they occur at all reveals that even fundamental accounting notions may be subject to challenge and that accounting principles are neither right nor wrong in any absolute sense. Like legal principles generally, the application of GAAP in a specific situation involves exercise of judgment.

Many closely held businesses use professional accounting services but do not prepare financial statements on the basis of GAAP. Rather, such statements may incorporate GAAP treatment of some assets or transactions, particularly the accrual system for recording transactions, but depart from GAAP in other respects. One must consider the effects of the deviations from GAAP on both the value of assets and the income statement or cash flow of the business.

It should not be assumed that there is a consistent bias in the direction of overstating assets or income in non-GAAP statements. Often, closely held businesses adopt accounting principles in an effort to minimize income rather than to maximize it. For example, many closely held firms follow a policy of expensing as many asset acquisitions as possible, with a view toward reducing current income and current federal income taxes. Excessive salaries payable to the major equity owners of the business who control day-to-day operations may appear as expenses even though comparability may require that many of these salary payments be treated as distributions. Similarly, expense accounts may reflect hidden compensation. In these instances, the reported earnings of the closely held corporation may be significantly understated. Moreover, even the assumption that a single accounting system has been consistently applied by a closely held corporation in the past must be investigated.

Finally, as a kind of ultimate caveat about accounting systems generally, it is important to recognize that all accounting principles, whether or not GAAP, involve not only flexibility and discretion, but also conventions and assumptions about honesty and good faith. Financial statements are usually prepared to put the best possible face on management's performance and management has the preponderant voice on which accounting conventions are adopted. There have been numerous incidents in the past in which outside auditors have given "clean" GAAP opinions on optimistic financial statements even though shortly thereafter the business collapsed from over-expansion or unwise business decisions.

Further, no accounting system provides complete protection against hidden or sophisticated fraud or theft. There are many dishonest ways to cook the books even if they are nominally kept on a GAAP basis. A major fraud in 1979, for example, was based on rigging the inventory count at the end of the accounting period by counting four boxes of sutures as 44, three boxes of gauze pads as 33, and so forth.[3] In a more recent case, a manufac-

---

[3] As described in §12.9, overstating the closing inventory for a period also overstates gross profit for that period. In the case discussed in the text, management planned to "de-

turer of computer disk drives was discovered to have shipped bricks rather than disk drives in an effort to book an increase in orders billed during the accounting period. Even though outside auditors participated in the physical count of inventory in both of these cases, they did not notice these discrepancies.[4] There are many other instances in which even major and massive frauds were being actively pursued by insiders unknown to the outside auditor. Obviously, even the finest GAAP financial statements cannot guarantee the honesty and probity of their creation.

§13.7 ADJUSTING THE NUMBERS IN FINANCIAL STATEMENTS IN GENERAL

It may be desirable to make adjustments in financial statements before (or as part of) the analysis of them. There is nothing magical or correct about numbers simply because they are written down in an official-appearing and certified set of financial statements. Indeed, the reliability and usefulness of financial statements is not improved merely because they appear in an attractive format in an annual report printed in three or four colors and containing a glowing report from management. It is surprising how reluctant many people are to subject attractively printed financial statements to the same skeptical scrutiny they would routinely give typed or handwritten financial statements. The gift wrapping is not important: It is what is inside that counts.

When examining financial statements, it is important to read carefully the notes that are appended. If the statements depart from GAAP, both that fact and the manner in which they were prepared usually appears in the notes.[5]

In deciding what adjustments should be made, one must always keep in mind the issue that is being addressed. For example, if one is considering buying the business, adjustments might eliminate entirely intangible assets such as goodwill from the balance sheet.

---

stroy" the nonexistent inventory thus created at some later date, but the scheme collapsed because one of them went to the SEC in an effort to avoid prosecution.

[4]One would expect such a blatant fraud to collapse of its own weight, and indeed, ultimately it did. The accounting firm settled a malpractice claim based on this fraud by agreeing to pay a substantial amount.

[5]The notes to financial statements often provide useful insight as to how the financial statements were prepared and the conventions that were followed in their development. Accordingly, they should receive at least as much attention as the statements themselves.

§13.8 READJUSTING ASSET VALUES TO REFLECT CURRENT MARKET VALUES

Assume that you are considering financial statements of a company that has been continuously in existence since 1953. On its balance sheet is the enigmatic entry "Land: $300,000." Such an entry should be a red flag for further investigation and possible adjustment since that $300,000 is a cost figure, and it may reflect either a purchase more than 40 years ago when land was selling for a fraction of what it is today or a purchase last week at or above current market values.

If the company owns marketable securities, the balance sheet should set forth by parenthetical notation a recent estimate of the current market value of the securities. It may be appropriate to substitute these market values for the cost figures for analytic purposes. It may also be appropriate to substitute up-to-date market values from the *Wall Street Journal* or similar sources for those appearing in the parenthetical notation on the balance sheet (which states figures as of the close of the accounting period).

Other asset adjustments that should be considered include an upward adjustment in value if inventory is calculated on a LIFO basis and a readjustment of the machinery and equipment account if accelerated depreciation schedules have been used. If accelerated depreciation schedules are being used, an upward adjustment to earnings may also be justified. On the downside, a machinery and equipment account may include all sorts of obsolescent or useless assets that should be written off to zero because their usefulness is exhausted and their resale value nonexistent. It may include office furniture and the like that will be scrapped if the transaction goes through.

Inventory may be theoretically valued at the lower of cost or market, but additional write-downs may be appropriate for obsolescent or stale items that the sellers have not gotten around to writing off. Adjustments of these types usually require a detailed investigation of specific asset accounts by a person intimately familiar with the type of business involved.

§13.9 ELIMINATION OF NON-ASSET ASSETS

Balance sheets often contain items that have zero realizable value. The most common items of this type are "goodwill," "organizational expense," "capitalized promotional expense," and "capitalized development costs." It may be appropriate to eliminate these items entirely from the balance sheet, reducing retained earnings by the same amount.

The problem of non-asset assets is not limited to intangible assets. Investments in subsidiary corporations or other businesses may have a zero realizable value and yet be recorded on the books as being worth the amount invested in them. Even traditional asset accounts such as fixed assets or inventory may contain positive values for worthless property. Usually, a detailed investigation is necessary to determine the extent of overstatement in these accounts.

§13.10 RECOGNITION OF VALUES NOT RECORDED IN STATEMENTS

When purchasing or investing in a firm, one is naturally concerned about overstated or unsalable assets. However, understatements of value are also common. For example, self-developed product lines with strong consumer name recognition may in fact be worth millions of dollars, dollars that appear nowhere in the financial statements. A well-recognized trade name such as "Coke" or "Dow" may have tremendous market value but may be recorded on the financial statements as having a nominal value, if it is recorded in the financial statements at all. The reason is that such values are not the types of value recorded under traditional accounting principles.

Usually a seller of a business will be quick to point out hidden values in the business. However, it is quite possible that the present owners may be unaware of the existence of these values.

§13.11 ADDITION OF NON-BOOK LIABILITIES

Most businesses have at least some material liabilities that are not reflected in the balance sheet. These items include future obligations under pension and profitsharing plans, litigation in process that is being actively contested, potential future product-liability claims, commitments under fixed contracts such as firm long-term leases and employment contracts, responsibility for cleaning up hazardous waste sites, and potential tax liabilities arising out of ongoing audits of earlier years' operations. Some of these items may be referred to in the notes to the financial statements: If not, it is usually difficult for an outsider to learn of their existence. A warranty should be sought to the effect that no unrecorded liabilities exist except those specifically described in writing. It may be appropriate to increase book liabilities to reflect these off-book liabilities or to make an appropriate adjustment to the terms of the contemplated transaction to take account of their existence.

Of course, responsibility for some or all of these undisclosed liabilities may be avoided if the purchase transaction is cast as a sale of assets rather than a sale of the legal entity that conducts the business. However, many undisclosed liabilities may relate to the core business itself, and may be assumed inadvertently as part of obligations incurred in the ordinary course of business.

In the modern era of large tort judgments for product defects, a separate inquiry is often made about possible product-liability claims that may arise from sales of products many years earlier. This is true even if a purchase of assets is contemplated, because there is some risk that these liabilities may be found to follow the business assets despite a disclaimer to the contrary. In many jurisdictions, product-liability claims are not barred by the statute of limitations, which begins to run only when the injury occurs. The adequacy of insurance for such risks should also be investigated. Most insurance against liabilities of these types is written on a "claims made" basis that may require insurance to be maintained indefinitely even if the portion of the business manufacturing the products in question is discontinued.

Where product-liability claims are likely, it may be necessary to place a portion of the purchase price in escrow to cover undisclosed claims or claims that exceed some estimated amount. The seller may be willing to agree to indemnify the purchaser against undisclosed or understated claims to the extent they exceed some specified amount. That amount is usually referred to as a "cushion."

§13.12 ADJUSTMENTS TO INCOME STATEMENTS

Changes in accounting principles or practices may be used to artificially inflate current earnings or current cash flow. For example, recent changes in the estimated lives of assets subject to amortization or depreciation may be lengthened to reduce depreciation deductions and increase apparent income. Discretionary costs such as advertising or research may be reduced or deferred to create or preserve an apparent improvement in earnings. Of course, reduction or deferral of such items may be unwise from a longer-term perspective. Professional or expert analysis of the financial statements and the underlying accounting records is usually necessary to determine whether changes of these types have occurred, and whether they materially affect the results of operations.

In a closely held business, accounting policies may be adopted in an effort to minimize apparent income for tax or other purposes. Upward adjustments to reflect income consistently with GAAP principles may therefore be appropriate. The most likely adjustments are to capitalize items that were expensed in the financial statements, to restore to earnings amounts distributed to the owners of the business in the form of excessive salaries or fringe benefits, and to eliminate the effects of excessively rapid depreciation write-offs. Again, the sellers of the business are likely to point out and emphasize these desirable features.

§13.13 DANGER SIGNALS

When examining financial statements, it is helpful to determine the degree of skepticism that is justified. Financial statements are a little like onions; there are deeper and deeper layers, and one can spend almost infinite amounts of time in reviewing them. When one or more danger signals are present, an increased degree of skepticism is justified and a somewhat greater investment of time warranted.

The quality of financial statements can sometimes be gauged by examining estimates or predictions made in earlier years, and then comparing the predictions with the actual financial or operating results for those years. While some optimism is understandable and justified, repeated examples of excessive optimism may justify an increased degree of skepticism about the financial statements generally and future predictions in particular.

One common danger signal is a phenomenal growth in earnings in relatively recent accounting periods. It is always possible that the business has dramatically improved the efficiency of its operations and the control of its costs or discovered a new line of activity that produces phenomenal profits. It is also possible, however, that the growth in levels of profits has been helped along significantly by filling a limited demand, or by the use of accounting gimmicks or adjustments that overstate earnings. If earnings growth appears too good to be true, it probably isn't true.

Another danger signal is a company that has changed auditors in the recent past. It is always possible that the original auditor was unsatisfactory for entirely appropriate reasons. It is also possible, however, that the change in auditors was made because the auditor was doing its duty. While any recent change in auditors merits some inquiry, it is definitely a danger signal if it happens more than once. The company may well be opinion shopping, seeking to find an auditor who is willing to accept desired accounting treatment of some material items.

Yet another danger signal is a company that has engaged in unlawful conduct in the past or has the reputation for "sharp" business practices. While the conduct may have occurred in the distant past or the reputation may be unjustified or based on tough, but legitimate bargaining tactics, additional caution is justified when examining the financial statements of such a business.

Financial statements of a company that has difficulty in obtaining financing or has accepted significant and unusual restrictions on its management prerogatives in loan agreements should also be examined skeptically. This means that at some earlier time apparently sophisticated lenders declined to deal with the company at all or agreed to lend money to the company only if it accepted unusual and onerous restrictions. There probably was a good reason for the earlier lenders to do this, and the same problem may exist today.

§13.14 FLIMFLAM IN THE BOOKS

Financial statements nominally prepared in accordance with GAAP are subject to manipulation that may extend to outright fraud and misrepresentation. This process is colloquially described as "cooking the books" or "engaging in creative accounting." Fraudulent financial reporting consists of intentional or reckless conduct, either by act or omission, that results in materially misleading financial statements. Usually it involves intentional overstating of assets, improperly recognizing revenue, or improperly deferring the recognition of costs. Fraud may be practiced by using fictitious transactions to hide thefts or by adopting non-GAAP accounting principles without disclosing them. Income statements may be overstated by rigging inventory counts, by the creation of fictitious assets, by omitting liabilities from the balance sheet, or by capitalizing expenses that should be treated as current expenses. Sales to wholly owned affiliates at attractive prices may be booked as sales to independent outside parties. Sales may be booked immediately even though goods have been shipped on approval or subject to buy-back guarantees that are likely to be exercised. Depending on the sophistication of the persons engaged in the wrongful conduct, it may be difficult or impossible to discover that the books have been cooked without tracing specific transactions. Major thefts may often be hidden in the books of a large and complex business in a way that may escape detection for long periods of time. Often, however, successful frauds are based on relatively simple techniques, such as the recordation of nonexistent sales or the manipulation of inventory accounts to hide thefts. The development of computerized accounting systems does not prevent the cooking of books; it simply requires a different kind and degree of sophistication to cook them successfully.

Of course, persons who misappropriate business assets or fraudulently misrepresent the financial condition of a business usually face criminal charges at the federal or state level if they are apprehended.

At a higher level of social acceptability are discretionary decisions that have the effect of improving the appearance of profitability and the attractiveness of the business as a financial investment. The goal of management may be to improve the salability of the firm over time; this is furthered by creating the appearance of a stable history of growing earnings. Erratic earnings are not as likely to be highly capitalized by a potential purchaser as steady and predictable increases.[6] A fair amount of smoothing out and improving of earnings may be accomplished by discretionary decisions; for example, by booking income at an early stage of the sales process even though additional costs may later be incurred. Businesses may also improve the earnings picture by "hiding" expenses, e.g., by viewing them as nonre-

---

[6]Capitalization of earnings valuation method is discussed in Chapter 14.

curring and extraordinary, and charging them directly against retained earnings.

Another common accounting-oriented strategy is "taking a bath" during one bad accounting period. It is usually desirable, if a business is going to have a bad year in any event, to lump as many write-offs in that period as possible so that a return to predictable increases in profits becomes inevitable in the following year. Taking a bath in this fashion is a widely followed and attractive strategy.

Taking a bath involves discretionary decisions to take as many losses as possible within a single accounting period that is going to show losses anyway. Smoothing out income involves discretionary allocations of income and expense items to specific periods to stabilize reported earnings. Many of these decisions may be consistent with GAAP principles because businesses have a considerable amount of discretion regarding when to book transactions and when to recognize losses. For example, businesses often have assets or whole lines of business which can only be disposed of at a loss; the timing of the disposition is discretionary. Similarly, intangible assets or capitalized expenses that can never be fully recovered may be written off at a time which is to some extent at the discretion of management. Bad debts or obsolete inventory may similarly be written down or off on a discretionary basis.

Companies have sometimes engaged in transactions near the end of their fiscal year primarily in order to improve the closing figures. The company may make big shipments from inventories at bargain prices near the close of the accounting period in order to be able to book the sales. In effect, the company may be "borrowing" from next year's sales, booking 13 months of sales in a single year, as it were. Manipulation of the mix of inventory between raw materials and finished products may increase closing inventory (thereby increasing gross margin) at the expense of the following year. A company with cash-flow problems may borrow money on December 28 in order to show a large amount of cash on hand at the close of the fiscal year. Of course, that cash is only temporarily resident in the company's accounts and may disappear on January 3. These tactics are known as "window dressing" and shade off into actionable fraud or deception.

§13.15 FINANCIAL PROJECTIONS

GAAP statements, of course, reflect what happened in the past. Typically, the person contemplating an investment in an enterprise is not so much interested in the past as what is likely to happen in the future. Projections into the future are what is needed in order to evaluate the desirability of many proposed financial transactions.

It is of course possible to make projections based on trends as they appear to exist from the financial statements themselves. Unaudited interim financial reports, if available, may be analyzed to determine whether the trends appear to exist. Annual reports of publicly traded corporations now must contain a discussion by management of anticipated developments and trends in the industry. A discussion of industry trends by the management of publicly held companies in the same industry may provide useful insights as to the outlook for a closely held firm in that industry. Industry participants are inevitably more familiar with market conditions and trends than an outsider, and simple interviews may be useful.

Many investments may be more accurately evaluated by an analysis of expected cash flows than of projections of profits or loss. This is particularly true of short-term and tax-oriented investments. Short-term extensions of credit usually contemplate repayment from relatively predictable future cash flows and are not usually dependent on long-term profitability, while tax-oriented investments must consider tax savings or costs as well as traditional income or loss calculations.

A cash-flow statement or financial analysis that includes projections of future developments should be viewed skeptically. It is very easy to project continued growth and continued improvement in sales, rents, or fees indefinitely into the future, but those projections may not be realistic. Cash-flow projections that extend far into the future are obviously less reliable than short-term cash-flow projections based on results of operations in the recent past, and indeed may be inherently unreliable. In addition, the relationship of the person making the projections to the business under investigation should be considered.

§13.16 ESTIMATES OF CASH FLOW FROM INCOME STATEMENTS

As cash-flow popularity has grown, techniques of estimation from traditional financial statements have become more sophisticated. Discussions of EBIT (earnings before interest and taxes) and EBITDA (earnings before interest, taxes, depreciation and amortization) in the literature are increasing.[7] Further, cash flow may itself be subdivided into different types based on the objectives of the person making the estimate.

A simple formula to estimate cash flow from an income statement is:

Cash flow = net income + depreciation + depletion + amortization − maturing debt obligations

[7]See §11.10.

A potential purchaser of a business may wish to estimate how much debt a particular business can carry on the assumption that the business will be "leveraged up" to the maximum. In this scenario, interest payments will equal or exceed taxable income, reducing income tax liabilities to zero. He will consider *operating cash flow*, determined as follows:

$$\text{Operating cash flow } = \text{ cash flow } + \text{ interest expense}$$
$$+ \text{ income tax expense}$$

The potential purchaser works from operating cash flow because it plans to restructure the current capital structure of the business and eliminate all taxable income through interest deductions.

On the other hand, an investor in the enterprise may analyze *free cash flow*, defined as follows:

$$\text{Free cash flow } = \text{ cash flow } - \text{ expected capital expenditures}$$
$$- \text{ preferred dividends}$$

The investor is concerned about free cash flow if he is assuming that the current operations and financial structure will not be materially changed by his investment. Free cash flow is available to satisfy obligations owed to him. (Chapter 14 describes how one estimates the value of a business from projections of future cash flow.)

§13.17 RATIO ANALYSIS

Traditional methods of analysis of financial statements involve the use of ratios of various elements of the balance sheet and income statement. These techniques are particularly useful for determining the creditworthiness of an enterprise, but also are regularly used by financial analysts for other purposes as well. The following discussion includes only the most widely used ratios.

Tables 13.1 and 13.2 are a simplified balance sheet and income statement from which the numbers set forth in the examples are derived.

1. Net Working Capital. A basic question is whether a business has sufficient economic strength to continue in operation for a reasonable period. Current assets are defined to be those that involve cash, cash equivalents, and assets that should be reduced to cash within a year, while current liabilities are defined to be those that come due within a year. A simple measure of short-term stability of the business is to ascertain that current assets exceed current liabilities. The difference is called *net working capital:*

$$\text{Net working capital } = \text{ current assets } - \text{ current liabilities}$$

Table 13-1
Balance Sheet — X Company
December 31, 1995

ASSETS			LIABILITIES		
Current Assets			Current Liabilities		
Cash	50		Accounts Payable	75	
Securities	20		Bank debt	155	
Accounts					230
Receivable	100				
Inventories	200		Long-term debt		250
		370			480
Long-term assets			SHAREHOLDERS' EQUITY		
Land	30		Common stock (800 shares)	40	
Plant/ Equipment	500		Retained earnings	380	
		530			420
TOTAL ASSETS		900	LIABILITIES/EQUITY		900

Table 13-2
Income Statement — X Company
Year ending December 31, 1995

SALES		1000
EXPENSES		
Cost of goods sold	600	
Selling costs	170	
Depreciation	60	
Interest	16	
Operating Costs		846
PRETAX INCOME		104
Income taxes		44
NET INCOME FOR YEAR		60
Less Dividends Paid		25
ADDITION TO RETAINED EARNINGS		35

X Company has net working capital of $370 − $230 = $140. A negative net working capital indicates actual or potential financial difficulty in the short term. A business with negative working capital may improve its position by raising additional equity capital — selling more stock — or by borrowing long term. Of course, the purchasers of stock or long-term lenders have to assess the possibility that improved working capital will actually have a favorable effect on operational results: It may turn out that additional working capital is only a temporary expedient. If it is, the new capital investment or long-term loan should not have been made: It turned out to be throwing good money after bad.

A corporation that has adopted the LIFO method of accounting for inventory almost certainly understates its current assets because inventory is carried on the balance sheet at a historical figure that is usually less than current value. Whether or not this is material obviously depends on the circumstances.

2. The Current Ratio. A widely used measure of the adequacy of working capital is the *current ratio*, which is the ratio between current assets and current liabilities:

$$\text{Current ratio} = \frac{\text{current assets}}{\text{current liabilities}}$$

X Company's current ratio is 370:230, or 1.6:1. As a broad rule of thumb, a solid current ratio for an industrial company is 2:1. However, lower current ratios may be entirely adequate for many businesses. In general terms, the smaller the inventory levels required and the more easily collectible the amounts receivable, the lower the current ratio that is acceptable. Again, the election of the LIFO method of accounting for inventory may understate the current ratio and give the impression that smaller inventory levels are required than is in fact the case.

3. The Acid Test. Bankers and others considering short-term loans to a business often rely on quick asset analysis. *Quick assets* are assets that can be used to cover an immediate emergency. They differ from current assets in that they exclude inventories. Quick assets are obviously never greater than current assets.

$$\text{Quick assets} = \text{Cash} + \text{marketable securities} + \text{current receivables}$$

$$\text{Net quick assets} = \text{Quick assets} - \text{current liabilities}$$

$$\text{Quick assets ratio} = \frac{\text{quick assets}}{\text{current liabilities}}$$

The quick assets ratio is usually referred to as the *acid test*. X Company has quick assets of only $170 [$370 − 200]; net quick assets of − $60 [$170 − $230]; and a quick assets ratio of 0.74:1 (170/230).

A quick asset ratio of 1.0 or better shows that a company is able to meet its current liabilities without liquidating inventory. Ratios of less than 1.0 do not necessarily signify danger, however. An analysis of anticipated cash flow over the period of the loan may show that the company is able to repay the loan without difficulty despite a ratio of less than 1.0. It all depends on how promptly liquidation or turnover of inventories occurs.

4. Book Value of Shares. Book value of shares is an important concept that simply means the value of those shares calculated from the books of the company using the values shown on its books. Shares of closely held corporations have a book value even though the shares have never been bought or sold and no one has any idea of their value. Book value also does not mean liquidation value or "real" value, since the financial statements are constructed on historical cost rather than current market value of assets. The book value of X Company's common shares is computed simply by subtracting liabilities from the book value of assets and dividing by the number of outstanding shares:

$$\text{Book value} = \frac{\text{assets} - \text{liabilities}}{\text{number of shares}}$$

Book value therefore equals $900 − $480 divided by 800, or 420 divided by 800, or $0.525 per share. Exactly the same mathematical result may be reached by adding together the capital contributed by the common shareholders and retained earnings, and then dividing that sum by the number of outstanding shares.

5. Income Analysis in General. For most analytic purposes, information about past earnings and prospects of future earnings is more useful than information about property and assets. An old axiom is that assets are worth only what they can earn. Assets that have no earning capacity are salable only for scrap. Hence, more reliance should usually be placed on the income statement ratios described below than the balance sheet ratios described above. Actually, income statement ratios is not an entirely accurate term, since income statement analysis often involves ratios between items appearing on the balance sheet as well as on the income statement.

6. Operating Margin. Perhaps the simplest analytic tool is the *operating* (or *profit*) *margin*, which is simply the ratio of pretax income to gross sales:

$$\text{Operating margin} = \frac{\text{Pretax income}}{\text{Gross sales}}$$

Interest on long-term debt may be added back to pretax income on the theory that this interest really represents a part of the cost of capital rather than an operating cost. In the case of X Company, the profit margin is 104/1000 or 10 percent, if interest is included in the calculation of income, and approximately 120/1000 or 12 percent, if interest is excluded from income. The calculation is approximate because a portion of the interest expense of $16 presumably represents interest on current liabilities.

Operating margin is a basic measure of the profitability of a business. Generally, increases in sales cause dramatic improvements in the profit margin since some costs (e.g., rent and main office expenses) are fixed and do not rise or fall in proportion to volume. Correspondingly, a decrease in sales volume may cause a disproportionately large decline in the operating margin.

7. Net Profit Ratio. The *net profit ratio* is simply the ratio between the bottom line and gross sales:

$$\text{Net profit ratio} = \frac{\text{Net income}}{\text{Gross sales}}$$

In the case of X company, its net profit ratio is 60:1000 or 6 percent, not a stellar performance.

8. Earnings per Share. Another fundamental measure of profitability, which is of particular interest to shareholders, is *earnings per share*, computed as the net income divided by the number of shares outstanding:

$$\text{Earnings per share} = \frac{\text{Net income}}{\text{Outstanding shares}}$$

In the case of X Company, each share of common stock earned $0.075 (60/800). Earnings per share obviously are not the same thing as dividends per share; considerably greater weight is given to earnings per share because dividends are discretionary with the board of directors.

9. Return on Equity. The ratio of net income to net worth is *return on equity*:

$$\text{Return on equity} = \frac{\text{Net income}}{\text{Net worth}}$$

X Company's return on equity is 14 percent (60/420). This is one of the more widely used ratios since it describes how much the company is earning on each dollar of shareholders' investment. When applied to GAAP statements, it is also broadly comparable from company to company and from industry to industry even though it is affected to some extent by the accounting conventions that have been adopted. It also may be subject to manipulation. Management that desires to preserve a high return on equity may decide to forego current investments that have immediate returns smaller than the current return on equity even though the investments increase the earnings per share and have great potential for future income. These problems may sometimes be discovered by the use of operating margin and net profit ratio, as well as return on equity as measures of overall success of operations.

10. *Return on Invested Capital.* Return on invested capital is analogous to return on equity but treats long-term debt as capital:

$$\text{Return on capital} = \frac{\text{Net income} + \text{interest}}{\text{Net worth} + \text{long-term debt}}$$

X Company's return on capital is:

$$\frac{60 + 16}{420 + 250} = \frac{76}{670} = 11\%$$

This ratio is a broad measure of the effective deployment of capital assets. Like return on equity, when applied to GAAP statements it is broadly comparable from company to company and from industry to industry.

Numerous other ratios may also be devised. For example, in a manufacturing or retail business an important — often critical — factor is whether the company's inventory is too large for its level of operations and whether inventory turns over quickly or is sluggish. Inventory turnover varies widely from industry to industry, and to a lesser extent from company to company within a single industry. Inventory comparisons therefore are most useful on a historical basis for a single company. The most accurate measure of inventory turnover would compare average inventory during the accounting period with cost of goods sold. However, average inventory is not usually available from financial statements, and it is therefore customary to use closing inventory. Unfortunately, the use of LIFO reduces substantially the usefulness of all ratios based on closing inventory, which is carried on the books under LIFO at an artificially low value.

The ratios described above are the most general, the most important, and the most widely used. All of these analytic tools, of course, are not to be used mechanically and their usefulness largely depend on the quality and reliability of the financial statements to which they are applied, and the sophistication of the user.

14

Valuation of a Closely Held Business

§14.1 INTRODUCTION

This chapter deals generally with the question of what a specific business is worth. The words "valuation" and "appraisal" are virtually synonymous and are used interchangeably in this chapter. The appraisal of the value of a business means the same thing as a valuation of the business.[1]

---

[1] In corporation law there also exists a narrow statutory appraisal right or right of dissent and appraisal designed to protect minority shareholders against certain types of potentially abusive transactions specifically defined in the statutes. This statutory appraisal right has nothing to do with the subject of this chapter.

The valuation techniques discussed in the later sections of this chapter require familiarity with concepts discussed in earlier chapters, cash-flow analysis (Chapter 12) and financial statement analysis (Chapter 13).

§14.2 VALUATION OF FIXED CASH FLOWS

The logical starting point for a discussion of valuation is to consider the present value of the right to receive a fixed and completely determinable series of future payments. Further, we assume that there is an ironclad guarantee that the payments will actually be made on a timely basis. First, what is the right to receive $1,000 a year from now worth today? Assuming that there is no risk that the payer will default, is it not clear that the right is worth something less than $1,000? For if one had $1,000 today, one could invest it for a year in a riskless investment and thereby earn one year's interest in addition to the original $1,000. Thus, $1,000 payable a year from now has to be worth somewhat less than $1,000 in hand today. Second, how much less? One way that such a question can be answered is to approach it from the point of view of a hypothetical investor: If that investor can make 12 percent per year on her money in a riskless investment, how much should she pay today for that right to receive $1,000 in one year? So phrased, the issue becomes an algebraic calculation:

$$x + 0.12x = 1,000$$

$$1.12x = 1,000$$

$$x = 1,000/1.12 = 892.86$$

To such an investor, the right to receive $1,000 one year from now is worth precisely $892.86. But, it may be rejoined, why choose a 12 percent return? Why not, say, an 8 percent return, in which case the calculation becomes

$$x + .08x = 1,000$$

and the value of the right to receive $1,000 in 12 months becomes $925.93. Of course, there is no one single rate of return that is correct in an absolute sense. But the basic process by which the *present value of future payments* is to be ascertained should be clear. The process involves *discounting* the future payments to their present value. Discounting in this context simply means reducing. Another phrase that describes this basic process is determining the *time value of money*. This calculation is in effect the reverse of determining what a present investment will be worth at some future time.

Three basic points should be evident from these simple examples. First, since interest rates are positive, a dollar to be paid in the future is *always* worth less than one dollar today. Second, the higher the interest rate applicable to the transaction, the lower is the current value of a right to receive a future payment. Higher interest rates mean greater risk. In other words, the greater the risk of an investment, the higher must be the interest rate to induce investors to make that investment. Hence, finally, the *riskier* the investment, the lower the current value of a future payment based on that investment.

Following the same line, what is $1,000 payable two years in the future worth today? If we again assume a 12 percent interest rate, we simply need to determine what amount must be invested today to yield $892.86 one year from now, and we will then have the answer, since we already know that $892.86 is the amount that we must invest today to earn $1,000 one year from now. A simple calculation[2] leads to the figure $797.19 as being the present value of the right to receive $1,000 two years from now.[3] A formula to determine the present value of a future payment due in n years is

$$PV = \frac{FV}{(1 + i)^n}$$

where PV equals present value; FV equals future value; I is the interest rate; and n the number of periods over which interest is calculated.

Despite the apparent mathematical certainty of this formula, it is important to recognize that the precise calculation of the present value of a series of future payments depends not only on the applicable interest or discount rate but also on the number of subperiods within the period over which interest is compounded. In other words, in order to get mathematical precision as to what a series of future payments is worth, one must know both the applicable discount rate and whether interest is to be compounded within the two year period, on a monthly, quarterly, semiannual, or annual basis.

Two more tables based on the 12 percent discount rate might be helpful before returning to the application of the time value of money to business valuations. Table 14-1 is the present value of $1,000 payable n years in the

[2] $1.12x = 892.86$; $x = 797.19$.
[3] It will be noted that this assumes that the investor receives the interest owed on the transaction at the end of the first year, and that amount is then added to the initial investment for reinvestment during the second year. If one posits monthly payments of interest, the calculation would require treatment of the year as consisting of 12 periods and the monthly interest rate being one-twelfth of the annual rate, so that interest is added to principal each month. The calculation in the text is a *compound interest* calculation, since the interest due from a prior period is added to the previous principal at the beginning of the next period.

future while table 14-2 is the present value of a stream of payments of $1,000 each payable at the end of each year for n years in the future. Such a stream of constant payments is usually called an *annuity*.

Table 14-1
Present Value of $1,000 Payable in N Years
12 percent Discount Rate

Number of years	Value of $1,000
1	$892.90
2	797.20
3	711.80
4	635.50
5	567.40
10	322.00
25	58.80
50	3.50
100	0.01

Table 14-2
Present Value of Annuity of $1,000
Payable in N Years
12 percent Discount Rate

Number of Years	Value of Annuity
1	$892.90
2	1,690.10
3	2,401.90
4	3,073.30
5	3,604.80
10	5,650.20
25	7,843.10
50	8,304.50
100	8,333.30

These two tables are obviously closely related. Indeed, Table 14-2 is simply the sum of the prior rows of Table 14-1: the value of an annuity running for two years equals $892.90 + 797.20 = $1,690.10; the value of an annuity for three years equals $1,690.10 + 711.80 = 2,401.90, and so forth. These tables make two basic points. First, future payments payable far into the future are worth very little, and second, an infinite stream of payments — a perpetual annuity — is not worth an infinite amount. Mathematically, the present value of a perpetual stream of payments is finite; it comes to a limit. This is a result, of course, of the rapid drop off in the present value of payments increasingly far in the future. For example, a perpetual annuity of $1,000 per year at 12 percent per year is worth precisely $8,333.33. How do I know that this is the case? Intuitively, it is easy to see that this must be the right answer because if you start with an investment of $8,333.33 and invest it at 12 percent per year, that investment will yield precisely $1,000 per year forever (8,333.33 × .12 = $999.999) without ever consuming a penny of the $8,333.33. How did I determine that $8,333.33 is the right answer? There is a very simple formula for the present value of a perpetual stream of constant payments. Such a stream equals precisely the reciprocal of the discount rate:

$$\frac{1}{\text{discount rate}}$$

In the above hypothetical, 1 divided by 0.12 equals 8.333; 8.333 times $1,000 equals $8,333.33.

The above examples use a 12 percent discount rate. What is the present value of a perpetual annuity that is capitalized at 20 percent? The answer is easy: 1 divided by 0.2 equals five; the present value of a perpetual annuity capitalized at 20 percent is five times the amount of the annual payment. What if it is capitalized at 5 per cent? Answer: 1 divided by 0.05 equals 20, so the present value is twenty times the annual payment. As one should intuitively expect, the lower the discount rate, the higher the present value.

§14.3 VALUATION OF UNCERTAIN CASH FLOWS

In theory, a business may be viewed as just a series of future cash flows to be received by the owner or owners at various times in the future. The above analysis of present values of future cash flows permits valuation of such a stream of payments if the amount and timing of the future cash flows is known and a suitable capitalization ratio can be ascertained. At that point, the calculation of value of future cash flows becomes a simple mathematical exercise. The problem of valuations in real life is that one cannot know with certainty what the future cash flows will be or what is the "correct" capitalization rate. Typically, the only reliable information about the business that is available is a set of financial statements for the recent past. Many industries, furthermore, are dynamic and changing; what happened last year is not a reliable guide about what will happen next year. While capitalization of expected future cash flows or earnings is certainly the most common technique used to value businesses, the basic cause of uncertainty is the reliability of the information used in the calculation. "Garbage in, garbage out" is perhaps the major concern in valuation problems in real life.

Further, some businesses should be valued in more reliable ways than by a capitalization of future cash flows. Some businesses are worth more if they are liquidated than if they remain in business. A scrap-metal business located on a piece of land that has become extremely valuable because of changes in the surrounding community is a classic example.

Yet another problem arises when only a small part of an enterprise is to be valued. A shareholder owning 100 shares of IBM common stock in fact owns an infinitesimally small portion of a very large business. It would be silly to value these 100 shares on the basis of a valuation of the worth of the entire IBM enterprise based on its cash flow; one simply looks up the value of 100 shares of IBM in the local newspaper for the day in question. Many businesses, of course, are not publicly traded the way IBM stock is traded on the New York Stock Exchange, yet very commonly there have been sales of ownership interests in the business at various times in the past; when we are valuing a minority interest in that business, at least some weight should be given to these earlier transactions.

§14.4 THE BASIC TEST FOR VALUING A BUSINESS

There is general agreement as to the fundamental standard by which the value of a business is ascertained. Valuation is an attempt to determine the *fair market value* of the business, which in turn is defined as the price that would be established by a buyer and a seller in an arms' length negotiation for the purchase and sale of the business, with both parties ready, willing, and able to enter into the transaction, each under no compulsion to enter into the transaction, and each having essentially complete information about the relevant factors.

While this fundamental standard is relatively easy to state, it gives little guidance as a practical matter in every case where the business is closely held and there have been no recent sales of the business itself. Indeed, the "ready, willing, and able" test in one sense completely begs the basic question because it gives no clue as to what techniques should be used by the hypothetical buyer and hypothetical seller in determining what price to offer and what price to accept for a closely held business that has not previously been the subject of a sale.

Valuation problems arise primarily in the context of a closely held business. As indicted above, a publicly held business such as IBM differs from a closely held one in the valuation context primarily because there exists an ongoing market for ownership interests in publicly held businesses.

§14.5 EXPERT BUSINESS APPRAISERS

Valuation of a business is a factual and business-related issue, not a legal issue. Many persons and firms call themselves valuation or appraisal experts;

they hold themselves out as familiar with valuation techniques for businesses and competent to estimate values of businesses of various types. These persons are retained regularly to provide opinions or recommendations on questions of valuation, or to serve as expert witnesses in litigation on valuation disputes. However, valuation is far from an exact science and the conclusions of even sophisticated "experts" can be suspect.

Indeed, it is easy to be cynical when discussing valuation experts. Every person in business is familiar with stories in which valuation opinions were given primarily on the basis of what the person paying for the opinion wanted to hear. The necessary points of view are usually not conveyed by such crass statements as "I want you to come out with a high value," or "I want an opinion that this business is worth between $20 million and $30 million," or "I want an opinion that $21 per share is a fair price for the rest of the stock." Rather, they may be effectively communicated simply when the proposed transaction or reason for the appraisal is described to the person retained to give a valuation opinion. After all, it does not take a genius to realize that sellers usually want high valuations and buyers low valuations, or that minimization of taxes is the goal of an estate seeking a valuation of a closely held business. It is also not unknown for a person dissatisfied with one opinion to commission a second opinion from a different, and perhaps more sympathetic, source.

Among the many individuals and organizations that consider themselves competent in business valuation matters are the following:

1. **Accountants** and **accounting firms** regularly make valuation studies and recommendations on valuation issues. They may prepare studies and recommendations for the benefit of management decision-making on investment or divestment issues that involve substantial valuation questions. A company, for example, has decided to sell off a line of business on which it is currently losing money but which it believes can be turned around with different management. The price to be placed on that line may be based on a report and recommendation by the company's outside auditors. The company's internal accounting staff probably has essentially the same expertise as the outside auditor and also may make a study and report, or may review the outside auditor's report and make an independent recommendation. The report of an outside accounting firm is usually obtained both as a check on the conclusions of the inside auditors and because an internal recommendation may be viewed as being more subject to the domination of management than the same recommendation from the outside auditor.

2. **Investment banking firms** also regularly make valuation recommendations or give opinions relating to value, particularly with regard to transactions involving the purchase or sale of interests to the general public. The expertise of investment banking firms in the valuation area rises from their historical role of establishing prices for the sale of equity interests to the general public in connection with raising of equity capital. The establishment of such public issue prices is tricky: The price must be low enough to

attract outside capital and yet not so low as to anger existing equity owners because of the dilution caused by issuing new interests at bargain prices. During the 1980s, investment banking firms were heavily involved in the takeover business, and in that connection prepared numerous fairness opinions that a proposed price for a business was a fair one. Target management in turn employed another investment banker to opine that the proposed price was wholly inadequate. These opinions sometimes became the subject of litigation, involving judges in the tricky business of valuation and appraisal.

3. Similar valuation expertise may reside in employees of so-called **full-service securities brokerage firms,** that is, firms that provide a variety of advisory and related services in addition to the simple execution of securities transactions. These integrated firms may provide services similar to investment banking firms for issuers or purchasers of securities; in addition, they regularly provide investment advice that necessarily involves valuation questions. These firms also have information immediately at hand to value portfolios of securities.

4. Independent firms that describe themselves as **management consultant firms** also provide valuation services. These firms may employ persons with experience in accounting and auditing as well as management decision-making, areas where valuation expertise is likely to develop.

5. Valuation or appraisals of specific income-producing properties such as commercial real estate may be prepared by real estate brokerage firms or individual **real estate brokers.** Valuation may be based on estimated cash flows. However, a widely used method of estimating the market value of commercial real estate is based upon recent sales of similar nearby properties — *comparables*, as they are usually called. Persons actively engaged in buying and selling commercial real estate in the community usually have a feel for the market and are likely to be familiar with prices being paid for other commercial properties in the area and the comparability of those other properties to the property in question. Other methods of estimating value — replacement cost and prior sales history — may also be utilized. The use of these methods of valuation for commercial real estate projects is questionable.[4]

6. **Auction** or **brokerage firms** may specialize in the purchase and sale of substantial commercial assets such as heavy construction equipment, and may provide valuation opinions in some situations. These valuations may be based on capitalized future cash flows, but more likely will be based on liquidation values, that is, based on the assumption that the operating assets

---

[4]In an "overheated" real estate market, the use of comparables and similar valuation methods tends to fuel speculation rather than concentrating on the present value of probable future cash flows. Replacement cost, for example, may be relevant for fire insurance purposes but has little to do with earning capacity.

are to be broken up and sold or auctioned off individually. For some types of secondhand equipment there may be published blue books or catalogues used in estimating value.

7. **Business brokers,** usually working on a nationwide scale, specialize in the listing of existing businesses for sale and in locating persons who are both interested in acquiring such businesses and have the financial resources to do so. Most of the businesses listed are relatively small, but that is not always the case: Some very large firms may list themselves (or large specific lines of business they are interested in disposing of) with these brokers. These brokerage firms of course have extensive experience with business valuation matters, though like brokers generally, their principal interest is the commission upon the completion of the sale, which typically runs about 5 percent of the purchase price of a small or medium-sized business. In addition, many brokers demand an initial retainer up front to make sure the seller is in fact interested in selling and not merely testing the waters to see what his or her business is worth.

§14.6 THE VAIN SEARCH FOR THE "ACTUAL VALUE" OF A BUSINESS

Those unfamiliar with the valuation process often labor under the entirely mistaken apprehension that businesses have a "real" or "actual" value, and that the goal of the valuation process is to find that value. Valuation is not an exact science, nor is it a search for the Holy Grail of value. Rather, it is a study of competing approaches that lead to inconsistent results and of estimates and approximations based on incomplete and sometimes unreliable information. Valuation issues are interesting and challenging precisely because there is no single number that can be pointed to as the value of a business. At best, there is a range of possible values that might be assigned, and at worst there are wildly varying approximations as to what an appropriate value is, with the approximations based on quite different approaches as to how value should be measured in the specific case. Intuitively, these alternative approaches toward valuation may seem to be equally plausible. Further, the uncertainties of the valuation process are usually so great that high or low valuations may be plausibly argued for even when following the same basic technique of valuation.

A number of different adjectives may be associated with the word value, for example, "fair" value, "market" value, "book" value, "liquidation" value, and "replacement" value. Some of these phrases refer to specific and meaningful concepts — for example, book, liquidation, and replacement value all refer either to specific numbers in connection with a business or to a specific method of calculating a value in connection with that business. Other phrases, such as "fair" value, "real" value, "true" value, and "actual" value, have no inherent meaning at all. At best, these phrases are merely synonyms for the basic definition of value, namely the price on which a willing buyer and willing seller agree. Basically, there is no objective answer to the question "What is this business really worth?"

There is some advantage in exploring further unarticulated lay notions of value. Many individuals have had the experience of selling a used car, where value means "resale value" which can be easily approximated simply by looking it up in the "blue book," by going to several used car dealers and asking for price quotations, or by advertising the car oneself and seeing what offers come in. These are appropriate ways to measure the value of goods that are reasonably standardized and are recognized objects of trade. The problem is that businesses are rarely like used cars; they are not at all standardized, each one is unique, there is no authoritative blue book, and there is usually not an active market with many buyers and sellers. A value may have to be assigned to a business where there are no sales that are even remotely comparable.

A second lay approach toward value is to assume that value really means liquidation value, that is, what the assets could be sold for if the business were closed down and the assets broken up and sold. For an individual, this would be the answer to the question, "What are my worldly assets worth?" or, in more pessimistic terms, "How large would my estate be if I died today?" A business can certainly be valued in this way. However, in almost every situation, liquidation of the business is not contemplated by anyone, and what is being valued is not a mass of isolated assets but something that has value because it has produced cash flow in the past and has (presumably) greater potential of producing cash flow in years to come. The use of liquidation value in most situations is therefore illogical because it values the business in a way that does not address the actual value-producing ability of the business.

Whatever the reason for the notion that a business has a real or actual value, students regularly rely on this notion in law school classes when valuation issues are first discussed. One also finds traces of it in opinions of presumably sophisticated judges who argue, for example, that a transaction should be set aside because a price for shares of closely held stock was set entirely arbitrarily and did not reflect real, actual, or true value. Since there is no such thing as "true" value in an objective sense, this reasoning simply is assertion of a conclusion and not analysis. (It does not necessarily follow, of course, that the court was wrong in setting aside the transactions in question in these cases; what is being criticized here is the reasoning, not necessarily the result.)

There are different valuation techniques that may be used to analyze value, and each technique may yield significantly different numbers. These techniques are described in the following sections of this chapter: The point here is that it is considerably more accurate to envision the ultimate "value" of a business as a range than as a specific number. For the same reason, the valuation opinions of even sophisticated individuals with extensive backgrounds in valuation techniques usually may be impeached, or at least shaken, by a lawyer familiar with valuation techniques and their limitations.

§14.7 VALUATION BASED ON INCOME STREAMS

Usually, the value of a business lies in its ability to provide a future stream of net cash. The simplest and most direct way of measuring value therefore is to estimate what this stream will be in the future and assign a value to it, using the techniques described in this chapter on discounting future payments back to present value.

Essentially the same valuation technique may be applied to income flows rather than cash flows. Usually, reliable estimates of future net cash flows are not available, and the only available information is conventionally prepared income statements for prior accounting periods. Of course, it may be possible to convert a conventional income statement into a cash-flow statement.[5] However, in many businesses, the transition to a cash-flow approximation will not lead to a significantly improved estimate of value. One may reach approximately the same estimates of the value of the business by capitalizing estimates of future income flows based on conventional income statements rather than first converting them to estimated cash flows. In other words, net income computed on the basis of traditional accounting principles is widely used for valuation purposes rather than estimated net cash flows. Indeed, this method of valuation is well-established. It is usually described as the capitalization of income or earnings.

In the following discussion the phrase "income or cash flow" is used to describe the stream of future payments that are capitalized to estimate the value of the business generating those payments.

§14.8 SUMMARY OF THE CAPITALIZATION PROCESS

It will be recalled that the valuation of a steady stream of payments in the future requires knowledge of two variables: the size of the payments in each period, and the appropriate capitalization rate to use to discount those future payments to present value.

The capitalization rate is a function of two variables: the going or market interest rates for riskless loans in the economy at the time, and the degree of risk presented by the specific business. Where constant perpetual payments are involved — that is, the stream of payments is assumed to re-

---

[5]This process is described earlier as calculating EBITDA. See §11.10 and §13.16.

main fixed in amount and continue permanently in the future — the present value of the stream is equal to the reciprocal of the interest rate multiplied by the payment:

$$\text{Present value} = \text{Payment} \times \frac{1}{\text{discount rate}}$$

The reciprocal of the interest rate (1/interest rate) is called the *capitalization factor* or *multiplier*. Table 14-3 shows how one can quickly develop a table of reciprocals that show what the capitalization factor is for a variety of discount rates.

Table 14-3
Capitalization Factors

Discount Rate	Capitalization Factor
100%	1
50%	2
33.33%	3
25%	4
20%	5
16.66%	6
12.5%	8
10%	10
8%	12.5
7%	14
6%	16.67
5%	20

In the context of a going business, a value can be obtained simply by estimating the future income or cash flow of the business, selecting a discount rate, and multiplying by the reciprocal set forth in Table 14-3. Thus, if a business's estimated future income is $120,000 per year, and it is determined that an appropriate discount rate is 10 percent, that business is worth $1,200,000 (10 × $120,000 = $1,200,000). If the estimated future income were $90,000 per year, the value would be $900,000. If the business were considerably riskier and the appropriate discount rate were 20 percent, the company would be worth precisely half as much: 5 × $100,000 = $500,000. The riskier the business, the higher the discount rate, the smaller the capitalization factor, and the lower the value placed on the stream of income or cash flow. If it were so much less risky that the appropriate discount rate was 6 percent, the business would be worth $1,666,667, and so forth. It is apparent that accurate assessments of both anticipated income (or cash flow) and discount rate are essential if the valuation so obtained is to be reliable. However, it should also be apparent that in real life, information about both variables creates serious problems.

§14.9 ESTIMATES OF FUTURE INCOME OR CASH FLOWS

For some businesses, the size of future income or cash flows can be estimated with a fair degree of reliability. For example, the rental income of a shopping center may be based on long-term leases that provide a reasonable basis for estimating future cash flows (though the standard practice of charging rent based in part on a percentage of gross sales may be a complicating factor). Much the same thing may be true of a hotel or an apartment house in which vacancy rates can be estimated based on experience or historic patterns. Such businesses, however, probably are unusual; the more common characteristic is that future income or cash flows are highly erratic, uncertain, and problematic.

In some instances, projections of future income or cash flow prepared by management may be available. These estimates may be used as the projection of earnings into the future. There is a risk, however, that these estimates may be overly optimistic.

For most businesses, historical information is available as to how the business fared in the recent past. Table 14-4 shows the income pattern of a hypothetical business:

Table 14-4
Income of X Company

Year	Net income after taxes
1992	$100,000
1993	120,000
1994	180,000
1995	210,000
1996	160,000

Such information may be available in early 1997 as to income for the previous five years. Again a caveat may be necessary: These are "book earnings" and adjustments may be necessary to more accurately reflect the true earning capacity of the business. See section 13.12. Assuming that this is unnecessary (i.e., the income stream described above has already been suitably adjusted), can one draw an inference about what future income will be from this historical data? One might take the average earnings over these five years, which is $154,000 (100,000 + 120,000 + 180,000 + 210,000 + 160,000 = 770,000 ÷ 5 = 154,000), and conclude that this number is a reasonable estimate of the average earnings of the business in the future. One can then choose an appropriate discount rate (e.g., 12.5 percent) and conclude that the value of the business is $1,232,000 ($154,000 × 8). (Where the 12.5 percent discount rate comes from is discussed below.)

It is easy to raise objections to the reliability of this process. First of all, is it realistic to assume that the earnings will average $154,000 per year *forever*? What about the period beginning three years from now? Ten years from now? Certainly, as the time frame lengthens, the uncertainties and inaccuracies of present predictions must also increase. That is true, but there are two plausible countervailing comments. As pointed out in an earlier section, mathematically, the contribution to value made by those later years is relatively small in contrast to the contribution of the next few years, where presumably the estimate is more reliable. In other words, most of the overall value is represented by the next five, more reliable years, and a relatively small amount is represented by the assumption that earnings will average $154,000 from the year 2001 on. Hence, one might conclude that the calculation should not be materially changed if the $154,000 assumption were extended to the infinite future or, alternatively, that a different assumption were made about the income in these later years.

Secondly, while it is true that uncertainties increase the further into the future we look, it also is as likely that the current estimate will understate future earnings as it is that they will overstate them. If the probability of an upside error and of a downside error are roughly of the same order of magnitude, the current estimate will not be materially changed. Clearly, we are engaged in an impressionistic and not a scientific inquiry, and there is a gamble in it from the perspective of both sides.

On the other hand, the seller of the contemplated business (interested, obviously, in a high valuation) might legitimately complain that the $154,000 average figure used in the above calculation gives undue weight to the first two years (1992 and 1993), which are the most remote from the present. After all, in the last three years of the five-year period (1993-1996), earnings never were below $160,000 and yet future earnings are estimated at only $154,000. It is more reasonable, it might be argued, to use only the average earnings of the last three years, which places the estimated earnings at $183,333 per year. The overall value of the business, using a 12.5 percent discount rate, would then be $1,466,664. In response, it might be argued that the significant decline in earnings in 1996 is a warning that conditions giving rise to the steady increase in earnings before 1996 may have changed, and that the average earnings in the future should in no event be viewed as being greater than those in 1996 ($160,000). Along the same line, earnings arguably should be less than $160,000 if the downward trend can be expected to continue. Obviously, analysis of causes of the 1996 decline is of central importance in this debate.

Let us assume a somewhat different pattern of earnings for the period 1991-1995 with no change in average earnings for the period:

1991	$100,000
1992	120,000
1993	160,000
1994	180,000
1995	210,000

This rather minor adjustment gives a dramatically different appearance to the future of the business. The seller might well argue that the estimate of average income in the future should build in a growth factor. For example, the seller might argue that the trend of growth in current earnings should be extrapolated into the future, for example:

1995 (actual)	210,000
1996 (estimated)	240,000
1997 (estimated)	270,000
1998 (estimated)	300,000

If this analysis is accepted, and the average of these four projections ($255,000) is taken as the anticipated income or cash-flow stream, the value of this business at a 12.5 percent discount factor becomes $2,040,000. At the very least, the trend might justify the use of the results for 1995, or $210,000, as estimated future income. If the 12.5 percent discount factor is applied to this figure alone, the value of the business is $1,680,000.

All this may be entirely too subjective for many people. There exists a well-developed theoretical model for analysis of future cash flows under conditions of uncertainty. This analysis essentially involves the assessment of likely future cash-flow outcomes, the assignment of probabilities to each outcome, and the weighting of all possible results with the probability that that result will occur. The end result of this process is a single number that represents the value of the probable outcome given the uncertainties worked into the analysis. This analysis is often presented in the form of a "decision tree" that may help in making sure that major contingencies are not overlooked.

For example, assume that last year's income or cash flow was $210,000 and management can reasonably anticipate that there is a 25 percent chance that income or cash flow will be $200,000, a 25 percent chance it will be $250,000, and a 50 percent possibility that it will be $300,000. The present value of this array is $262,500 (.25 × 200,000 + .25 × 250,000 + .5 × 300,000).[6]

---

[6]One cannot assume that all identical present values are equally attractive. People tend to be risk-averse and to prefer closely grouped arrays over more risky alternatives. For instance, an array of a 25 percent chance of $100,000, a 25 percent chance of $150,000, and a 25 percent chance of $650,000 also has a present value of $262,500. However, the risk that the actual return will be less than $150,000 is 75 percent, certainly much less attractive than the hypothetical in the main text above.

The isolation of possible outcomes and the assignment of specific probabilities to each outcome gives a satisfying specificity to the entire operation. However, even if all major contingencies are isolated in the decision-tree analysis (itself a dubious assumption), the assignment of probabilities to them usually involves so much guesswork and is so uncertain that it is doubtful that the use of this technique in real life situations provides a materially improved estimate of future events than is provided by the much more impressionistic analysis based on a mixture of historical results and generalized predictions about future trends set forth above. And the danger of assigning hard numbers to estimates is that the conclusion may appear to be more specific, and therefore more reliable, than it actually is.

§14.10 SELECTION OF CAPITALIZATION FACTOR

Recall that the interest rate used to discount future payments back to present values in effect describes a measure of the risk that the payments will not occur (as well as the general costs of borrowing money in the economy as a whole). The determination of what discount rate to use in valuing a business appears at first glance to involve variables even more uncertain than the determination of the anticipated income or cash flow of the business. Indeed, one might argue that the multiplication of one gross approximation by an even grosser approximation must inevitably yield "garbage," that is, a figure so unreliable that it should not be used at all.

The capitalization factor choice is not as bleak as that, however. Usually, the discount rate to be used in valuing a business can be established from the actual relationships between average earnings or cash flows and sales prices of similar businesses in the recent past rather than from a "market interest rate plus additional risk" assessment. Persons familiar with the purchase and sale of businesses are also generally familiar with actual sales prices of businesses that have been sold in the recent past and the estimated earnings or cash flows used in the negotiations leading to those sales. Statements such as "Companies in which the personal services of the owners are an important income-producing factor generally sell at two times earnings or less," or "Steel companies generally sell for about eight times earnings," or "Companies developing computer software that have marketed at least one successful product generally sell for at least fifteen times recent cash flows," are all meaningful statements that provide useful signposts for the selection of an appropriate capitalization factor for a noncomparable business in the same or related industry. If a small or medium-sized company has a stable cash flow and a good track record, a "quick and dirty" estimate of sale value is four to six times annual pretax cash flows. In addition, the quarterly editions of the magazine *Mergers and Acquisitions* contain data on the actual sales prices of businesses that sold for more than $1 million.

Information about income or cash flow about these businesses may also be publicly available or be obtained by inquiry.

In addition, for publicly traded securities there is readily available information about price/earnings ratios.[7] The price/earnings ratios are not precisely identical to capitalization factors because the price/earnings ratios of publicly traded stocks reflect a multitude of investment decisions for small blocks of stock not affecting the control of the business, while capitalization ratios assume that control of the business itself is being bought and sold. In other words, the price/earnings ratio of publicly held companies, as usually computed, reflects only the investment value of securities and not any premium that represents the control factor. Use of price/earnings ratios as the capitalization factor for valuation purposes for closely held businesses therefore may underestimate to some extent the value of the company being appraised. However, in view of all the uncertainties inherent in the valuation of a closely held business, this concern does not appear to be a serious one. In any event, the two are closely related, and price/earnings ratios are routinely used as estimates of capitalization ratios.

In an ideal situation, one may be able to find a publicly held corporation that is similar in most important respects to the closely held business being valued. If the two businesses are roughly comparable, then one can apply the price/earnings ratio of the publicly held stock as a ballpark estimate of the appropriate capitalization ratio for the closely held company being valued. Again, it must be remembered that we are not dealing here with precise scientific data but with an impressionistic analysis establishing a range of values.

Unfortunately, however, there is usually no publicly held corporation that is a close match for the firm being valued. The most common problem of noncomparability is that the publicly held corporation has substantial business operations in several different industries while the closely held firm being valued is active in only a single industry. In this situation, one may use a composite price/earnings ratio for all the publicly held companies in the industry, if that is available. That composite ratio may be an appropriate capitalization factor for a business active only in the same industry on the theory that the averaging of price/earnings ratios for different publicly held companies tend to cancel out the effect of different multiple operations in different industries. Also, the notes to the financial statements of one or more of the publicly held corporations may contain sufficient breakdowns and information on the results of operations in the industry in question to make possible the calculation of a separate price/earnings ratio for those operations alone.

In selecting an appropriate capitalization ratio, it may be appropriate

---

[7]The *price/earnings ratio* is the ratio between the market price per share and the earnings per share of the publicly held stock for the last available accounting period.

413

to adjust an industry-wide price/earnings ratio to reflect unique aspects of the company. For example, if the company appears to have a more obsolete plant than the comparable company or the industry average, a reduction in the capitalization ratio may be appropriate. The following hypothetical analysis is typical: "The best-managed companies in this industry sell for nine times earnings. The company being valued is certainly not among the most efficient. A downward adjustment in the capitalization ratio is therefore appropriate." There are two problems with such an adjustment, however. First, it is relatively easy to say that an "appropriate" adjustment should be made, but there is almost never any criterion for determining what that adjustment should be. If the base ratio is nine times earnings, should the appropriate capitalization ratio for the corporation with a somewhat obsolete plant be eight times earnings? Eight and one-half times? Eight and three-quarters times? Such differences in the capitalization ratios may have substantial effects on the overall value of the business. The difference between eight and one-half and eight times earnings, for example, may easily involve millions of dollars. The second problem is the risk of double counting a negative factor. If the lack of efficiency is used first to justify a reduction of anticipated future earnings or cash flow, and used a second time to reduce the appropriate capitalization ratio, it is likely that the double use of the same negative factor will overstate its importance.

Logically, an adjustment of this nature probably should be made in the expected income or cash-flow determination rather than the discount rate because changes in capitalization rates have more substantial impact on the total valuation figure. Double counting of such an item may in any event be avoided if the analysis follows a standard decision tree approach.

§14.11 EVALUATION OF ANALYSIS OF INCOME OR CASH FLOW

What then should be said about the capitalization of earnings or cash-flow approach? It is the most popular method of valuation of closely held businesses that are being purchased because of their potential earnings or cash flows. It is also widely used in valuation disputes generally, such as those relating to the value of closely held stock for gift and estate tax purposes. Indeed, despite its drawbacks, the capitalization of earnings or cash flow is generally believed to be the most reliable method of estimating the value of a business anticipated to be in existence indefinitely.

The following sections briefly discuss other methods of valuation that may be used, either in conjunction with or as a substitute for, discounted cash-flow or income analysis.

414

§14.12 VALUATION BASED ON ASSET APPRAISALS

Asset valuations may enter into the calculation of the value of a business in many circumstances. The most obvious situation is where the goal of the purchaser is in fact to liquidate the business — a "bust-up transaction," as it is sometimes called. In closely held corporations, such transactions may occur if the present owners fail to recognize that the corporation is worth more liquidated than it is as a going entity.

Another situation in which liquidation values may enter into the valuation of a business is where the purchaser's basic goal is obtaining the use of one specific valuable asset or line of business and he or she plans to dispose of the balance of the assets in some way after the sale is completed. In this situation, the buyer is likely to value the business by taking the value of the desired asset or line of business (determined by capitalizing its contemplated cash flow or income) and adding to it an estimate of the liquidation value of the remaining assets.

If the business being acquired has assets that the purchaser believes to be unnecessary for the successful continuation of the business (or if the assets duplicate under-utilized property that the purchaser currently owns), the purchaser may again simply add the liquidation value of those assets to the value based on capitalized earnings for the balance of the business to determine the total price he or she is willing to offer. Similarly, if the company being valued has cash or marketable securities in excess of its needs, the buyer may increase the price by the amount of the excess cash or cash equivalents which, if the purchase is successful, may be withdrawn without adversely affecting the operation of the acquired business. In effect, the buyer is paying cash for cash or cash equivalents.

In many of these situations, the seller may be aware of the existence of the excess assets and will exclude them from the sale or will distribute them to the owners of the business before the sale takes place.

The calculation of liquidation value becomes very difficult on an asset-by-asset basis for any substantial business. Estimates of net asset value are usually made in such situations by using book values and then making adjustments for assets such as land, marketable securities, and LIFO inventories. When lines of business are salable as units, traditional income or cash-flow analysis may be applied to appraise those lines with the resulting value being treated as net asset values for each particular line.

Assets may also be valued on the basis of an estimate of what it would cost to replicate the plant and operations of the business rather than what the assets of the corporation would bring upon dissolution, an asset valuation based on replacement cost rather than liquidation value. Such a figure is usually estimated when a business is contemplating expanding into a new area of operation, and is choosing between the alternatives of building a plant from scratch or buying an existing company that owns a plant then in operation. However, replacement cost, like liquidation value, is generally not an appropriate way to measure the value of an ongoing business, since normally the purchaser would not view the business as equal in value to what a brand-new plant created from scratch would cost. Indeed, in the case of many mature businesses the replacement cost of a plant greatly exceeds the value based on future net cash flows. The only reliable indication of value in that situation is the capitalization of estimated cash flows.

§14.13 BOOK VALUE

Book value means the value of the residual interest in the business according to the financial records of the business. *Residual* means what remains after subtracting liabilities from assets. It is an accounting concept rather than a true measure of value. Since financial records are normally kept on the basis of historical cost, book value usually does not reflect either the earning capacity of the business or the current value of its inventory and capital assets. Furthermore, book value is calculated from the balance sheet, which is sometimes used in accounting as a place to park revenues waiting to be taken into income or expenses waiting to be written off, a fact that should not inspire confidence in the reliability of book value as a measure of value.

Despite these deficiencies, book value is almost always calculated as part of the valuation process, and may be relied upon to a greater or lesser degree in that process. There are several reasons for this. First, it is very easy to calculate book value from the financial records of the business. Second, book value tends to increase with the success of the business, so that it is not automatically made obsolete simply by the passage of time. Third, shareholders may view book value as a floor under the price for shares and resist proposed sales for less than book value. On the securities markets, a stock that is selling for less than book value is often viewed, somewhat irrationally, as a questionable investment. Even though these attitudes are not strictly logical, they do reveal that book value, based as it is on historical cost and the weaknesses of accounting principles in determining value of trade names on consumer product recognition, is given some weight in the valuation process.

One problem with book value is that it may be significantly affected by accounting conventions that do not themselves affect the earning capacity or assets of the business. For example, if there are two identical companies, one using LIFO and the other using FIFO to reflect inventory costs, the book value of the FIFO company should be higher than the book value of an identical company using LIFO.[8] Thus, if book value is relied upon,

---

[8]See §12.10 and §12.11. Since LIFO uses the oldest prices to calculate the value of inventory, the discrepancy is likely to widen in periods of inflation the older the prices are actually used to value the LIFO inventory.

adjustments may be necessary to offset the use of these accounting conventions.

§14.14 PRIOR PURCHASES AND SALES

This section considers the relevance of prior sales of the business, or more commonly, prior sales of interests in the business, in determining the value of the business. In considering prior sales, one should sharply distinguish between a closely held business where there is no regular market for the shares of the business, on the one hand, and businesses whose shares are publicly traded, on the other. One should also distinguish between a form of business such as a general partnership which grants a right of exit to any participant and business forms such as corporations or limited liability companies that generally do not grant a minority owner the right to "put" the interest back to the business at a "fair" valuation.

When valuing a business, one sometimes discovers that a negotiated sale of the entire business occurred at some earlier time. A sale of the entire business in the fairly recent past, in an arms' length transaction between sophisticated individuals, is considered practically conclusive evidence of value as of the time of the sale. Indeed, where a retrospective valuation is involved, such as the value of a gift for tax purposes made several years ago, one happily uses an arms' length sale occurring years after the gift was made, as providing a reliable basis for going back and estimating the value of the business at the earlier time when the gift was made. In these determinations, adjustments made to that negotiated sales price are limited to adjustments required by changes that occurred in the business between the time the sale took place and the earlier or later date on which the value is to be ascertained.

When valuing the overall business, what weight, if any, should be given to a voluntary negotiated sale of a minority interest — a 10 percent interest, say — that does not involve control considerations by a minority shareholder? This question has no fixed answer if the business form does not permit an automatic right of exit. It depends entirely on the circumstances. If the circumstances of such a sale comes close to the valuation ideal (ready buyer, ready seller, etc.) it may provide the best objective evidence of actual values of interests in the corporation. However, many negotiated sales do not approach this ideal. Thus, a sale between family members under circumstances that indicate a motive for the transaction may have been partially to make a gift is given little or no weight. A sale to the firm itself or to the majority owner of the business may appear to be at arms' length but may actually be a situation in which the minority shareholder was under considerably greater compulsion to sell than the purchaser was to buy. Thus, the circumstances underlying each specific sale have to be examined carefully.

Of course, a perfect arms' length transaction rarely exists, and useful information about value may often be obtained from a transaction that does not meet this ideal. For example, an arms' length sale by a 10 percent shareholder in a closely held corporation to the majority shareholder at a price that was clearly bargained over, should be given some weight even though it appears that the seller was in some financial distress and needed cash for personal reasons. Absolute perfection in the bargaining process is not required. On the other hand, if it appears that in a similar transaction (1) there were unsuccessful attempts by the seller to find other potential purchasers, (2) the seller needed cash urgently for personal reasons or to avoid bankruptcy, or (3) the sale took place at a price set by the buyer on a take-it-or-leave-it basis, that sale is not a very reliable indication of value. It all depends on an estimate of how close the actual transaction comes to the theoretical ideal described in section 14.4.

In many other commercial contexts, a price negotiated at arms' length is given some weight in assessing the fair market value of an asset even though defects existed in the negotiation process. One need only think of transactions taking place at rug bazaars, at country auctions, and in a host of everyday transactions in which it is unlikely that the ideal conditions of perfect knowledge and lack of compulsion are present. The same thing is true of isolated arms' length sales of interests in closely held firms as well.

When the value of an entire business is estimated from isolated sales of minority shares, an appropriate adjustment should be made to reflect the discounts normally applied to such shares for lack of marketability and the minority status of such shares.[9]

§14.15 VALUATION BASED ON A MIXTURE OF METHODS

It is customary, when valuing a business, to make estimates of value based on different approaches or assumptions. For example, a person preparing a valuation opinion might assemble the following estimates of value:

1. Straight book value, without adjustment for accounting conventions.
2. Adjusted book value, with adjustments for LIFO accounting convention, appreciation in marketable securities, and elimination of non-asset assets.
3. Capitalized earnings, assuming mildly pessimistic long-term projections for the industry as a whole and average projections for the business's market position within the industry.

[9]See §14.17.

4. Capitalized earnings, assuming average growth projections for the industry as a whole but assuming a gradual improvement in market position of the business being evaluated within the industry.
5. Capitalized cash-flow projections eliminating all depreciation deductions and assuming the debt/equity ratio is increased from 25 percent to 60 percent.
6. Estimated resale value of physical assets (obtained by using balance sheet assets excluding intangible assets and making adjustments for inventory valuation, marketable securities, land, and excess depreciation on plant and equipment taken in earlier years).

After making these six calculations, the results may be tabulated and the degree of disagreement considered. If all are within a relatively narrow range, it is likely that a number will be selected within that range and an optimistic report prepared stating that "all signs point to a value within the range of . . ."

If the numbers vary widely, the general rule should be that the most reliable estimate in the eyes of the person doing the study should be adopted. However, it is always tempting to take an average of the values, and view that average as the best estimate of value. This is a somewhat muddled approach because the averaging process involves combining discrete numbers — apples and oranges, as it were. The decision to take the arithmetic mean of book value, liquidation value, and value based on capitalized earnings estimates, for example, has little theoretical justification since each is based on an inconsistent assumption of what will happen to the business. If the business is worth more as a going enterprise than if it were liquidated, it makes no sense to even consider the liquidation value as affecting the value of the enterprise. The fundamental valuation standard also does not appear to contemplate an averaging of different estimates of value, but the temptation to combine disparate figures into a single number is strong. Even if the highest and lowest estimates of value are discarded, and the remaining estimates averaged, the same basic problem exists.

§14.16 CONTRACTUAL RESTRICTIONS ON TRANSFER

Interests in closely held businesses are very commonly made subject to buy-sell or option arrangements that require an owner desiring to sell her interest to sell or offer to sell to the firm.[10] These contractual provisions are an essential aspect of planning for the management and control of closely held

[10]See, for example, §§8.27-8.32. This is likely to be the case in connection with corporations or limited liability companies. Restrictions on assignments of partnership interests are also common.

businesses and are as much for the benefit of the holders of minority owners as they are for the controlling owners. A question that often arises is the extent to which the existence of these transfer restrictions should affect the value of the minority interests subject to the restrictions.

If the contractual restriction on transfer obligates a solvent business (or its owners) to purchase the shares at a specified or determinable price, one would normally expect that the contract price is the value of the interest being sold. If the contractual restriction is in the form of an option to purchase (rather than a firm obligation to purchase) at a specified or determinable price, one would expect that the option price would put a cap on the valuation of those shares but that lower valuations might be determined, since there is no assurance that the shares will actually be sold at the contract price. In this situation, the mere existence of the option arrangement may have an adverse affect on the valuation of the shares since a potential purchaser cannot be assured that the option will not be exercised.

As a practical matter, the valuation of shares subject to contractual restrictions on transfer regularly arises in a tax context upon the death of a shareholder. Property owned by a decedent takes a stepped-up basis on the death of a taxpayer for income tax purposes and is valued at current market value for estate tax purposes. A provision in the Internal Revenue Code addresses squarely how the existence of restrictions on transfer affect the valuation of the shares.

§14.17 DISCOUNTS FOR LACK OF MARKETABILITY AND OTHER FACTORS

This section deals primarily with valuation issues as they pertain to the value of a minority interest in a firm, rather than to the overall value of the firm itself. At the outset, it assumes that the aggregate value of the business has been established by expert opinion, prior sales transactions, analysis of net present value, or judicial decision.

Once the value of the business itself has been determined, the value of a minority interest would appear to be calculable simply by multiplying that value by the percentage of the total firm that the minority interest represents. Unfortunately, however, life is not that simple.

When valuing interests in a firm, there is no inherent reason why the value has to be allocated proportionately to each party's interest in the firm. Indeed, the earlier discussion of the value of control should make it clear that proportional allocation is usually not realistic.[11] Owners of minority interests in a firm may not be able to participate in management and may receive little or no financial return from their investment, while owners of

[11]See §§8.20-8.21.

the controlling interest may receive substantial salary and other "perks" from the firm. The usual manner of handling these differences between otherwise identical interests in a firm is not by setting up a dual price structure, but by a system of discounts and premiums that reflect the marketability or value of the specific interests. A "discount" is simply a justification for knocking off a portion of the percentage value of the interest; A "premium" is an additional amount added to the proportionate value of one specific interest because of control or other considerations.

There are a large number of discounts that have received some degree of judicial or professional acceptance in the corporate context. They should be applicable without significant adjustment in limited liability companies and other business forms where there is no automatic guarantee of exit. These discounts tend to arise during negotiations as arguments over valuation. Since they have some degree of judicial recognition, however, they must be considered. The following listing is not complete, but includes the ones most likely to be encountered in practice.

1. *Minority interest discount.* For the reasons discussed earlier, minority interests in closely held corporations sell at substantial discounts from control shares. The discount from gross per share value for minority interest status may be substantial, ranging from as low as 50 percent to as high as 90 percent.
2. *Loss of key person.*
3. *Small company business risk.*
4. *Inability to obtain financing.*
5. *Unaudited financial statements.*
6. *Blockage.* Large interests in a business may be more difficult to dispose of than smaller interests. This phenomenon regularly appears in securities which are thinly traded in public markets; it may also arise in connection with the disposition of interests in closely held businesses. A 40 percent interest in a business may be more difficult to dispose of because of the lack of buyers than, say, a 10 percent interest. The valuation of a large minority interest in a business may therefore involve a discount for *blockage*.

The precise character of these discounts is less important than an appreciation of their niche in the valuation process.

§14.18 VALUATION BASED ON SUBSEQUENT PERFORMANCE OF THE BUSINESS

When a business is being sold for cash to an independent purchaser, differing valuations of the business may create an impasse: The gap between the lowest price the seller is willing to accept and the highest price the buyer is willing to offer may be unbridgeable by negotiation. This gap is usually traceable to differing assumptions about what the future holds for the business. The parties agree that the price should be ten times future earnings, but they disagree on what the future earnings are likely to be: The seller sees a high probability of continuing improvement in earnings or cash flow with relatively little risk while the buyer, naturally more cautious, sees cloudier skies with greater probability of disappointing results. This impasse threatens to kill the deal entirely, and yet it involves the valuation issue exclusively.

Devices exist that may enable the parties to bridge the gap between these inconsistent expectations and forecasts. These devices basically set the initial contract price at the buyer's price but defer the final determination of the sales price until after the post-sale operations of the business can be evaluated. The buyer commits to the conservative price he is willing to pay and agrees to pay an additional amount at the end of one or two years if earnings exceed an amount stated in the agreement (basically this amount is the buyer's conservative prediction of income or cash flow). If the operations are more successful than this stated amount, the seller is entitled to an addition to the purchase price computed on the actual post-sale earnings. This contingent payment based on actual post-sale results largely eliminates the impasse over valuation, since if the buyer's more pessimistic forecasts turn out to be accurate, no further payment is due, while if the business is as successful as the seller expects, the ultimate purchase price will be based on the seller's estimate. These devices are sometimes called *workout agreements* because a portion of the purchase price is earned or worked out after the transaction is closed. They have nothing to do with business workouts in the near-insolvency context. Agreements of this type permit transactions to close immediately without requiring consensus on the true value of the company at the time of the closing. The usual period for the workout is three years or less following the closing, though longer workout periods are of course possible.

Workout agreements involve complex negotiation and complex drafting, particularly where the parties have no reason to trust the other side's good faith. The seller may be unwilling to accept the unsecured promise of the buyer that the additional purchase price will be paid when it becomes due a year or two after the sale has closed. The seller may request that the workout payment be placed in escrow with a stakeholder to assure the seller that the payment will be made promptly if it is earned. The buyer may resist this proposal if he or she proposes to use the cash-flow generated during the workout period to pay the additional purchase price. The escrow arrangement, of course, ties up independent funds for a significant period of time. There may also be detailed negotiation over the terms on which the business is to be conducted during the workout period. The most basic concerns are from the seller's standpoint, who wishes to ensure that the purchased business has a fair shot of earning the workout. The two parties must decide whether the buyer or the seller is to manage the purchased business until the workout period ends, how much additional capital is to be provided by the buyer during the workout period, at what times and in what amounts, and a host of other business issues such as limitations on salaries, on inter-business transactions the buyer may have with the purchased business, and so forth. Usually, the seller proposes to run the business during the workout period. If this is acceptable to the buyer, the buyer may nevertheless seek protection against artificial changes in business operations, such as reduction of deferrable expenses, which the seller may quietly institute in order to improve earnings during the workout period and thereby earn the workout payment.

Even though the development of a workout agreement may involve difficult negotiations and complex issues, the advantage of permitting negotiations to come to a settlement without requiring either party to accept the valuation assumptions of the other, should be obvious. The workout concept is practical principally in connection with transactions involving the sale of businesses. It cannot ordinarily be used in other types of transactions to avoid valuation controversies.

Glossary

ACCELERATED DEPRECIATION SYSTEMS permit larger amounts of depreciation deductions with respect to an asset in the early years of the asset's life. These systems, if accepted for federal income tax purposes, create significant tax benefits for the firm. The most popular accelerated depreciation systems are the sum-of-the-digits method and the declining balance method.

ACCOUNTS RECEIVABLE in accounting systems is an asset account which reflects a debt owed by someone to the firm.

ACCRUAL BASIS is the accounting system almost universally used by modern business. Generally accepted accounting principles require the use of accrual principles for any business that involves the manufacture, purchase, or sale of goods. Under the accrual system of accounting, items of income and expense are recognized and taken into the accounting records when they are incurred, rather than when the payment or receipt of cash occurs.

ACCUMULATE AND BAIL OUT is a tax strategy for C corporations which involves minimization of taxable dividends followed by sale of the stock in a transaction that qualifies for capital gain treatment.

ACID TEST is a financial test that measures the immediate debt paying capacity of a business. The acid test is current liabilities divided into quick assets.

ACTION FOR ACCOUNTING (or for a **FORMAL ACCOUNT**) in partnership law is the traditional legal remedy available to a partner to establish the rights and obligations of the partners within a partnership.

ACTUAL AUTHORITY (also described as **EXPRESS AUTHORITY** or simply by the words **AUTHORITY** or **AUTHORIZED**) arises from the manifestation of a principal to an agent that the agent has power to deal with others as a representative of the principal. The actions of an agent within the scope of his actual authority without more bind the principal.

ADOPTION is a contract doctrine providing that a newly formed corporation is not automatically obligated on pre-incorporation contracts but must take an affirmative step to adopt the contract if the corporation wishes to accept its benefit and assume its burdens.

ADVANCEMENTS OF EXPENSES in corporation law are payments made by the corporation to officers or directors who are named as defendants in litigation to permit those defendants to present an effective defense, to obtain skilled legal assistance, to engage in pretrial discovery, and so forth.

AGENCY is the "fiduciary relation which results from the manifestation of consent by one person to another that the other shall act on his behalf and subject to his control, and consent by the other so to act." Restatement of Agency, Second.

AGENT is a person who acts for a principal and is subject to control by that principal.

ALLOCATIONS in partnership agreements determine how profits or losses are to be divided among the partners. This allocation is also called the partner's **DISTRIBUTIVE SHARE.**

ALTERNATIVE MINIMUM TAX (AMT) is a separate tax structure independent of the regular tax system designed to limit the use of a variety of different tax exclusions, deductions, or credits that are available to individual and corporate taxpayers.

AMORTIZATION relates to the accounting treatment of intangible assets (such as copyrights or patents that have a limited life) and to deferred charges (such as organizational expenses, research and development costs, or "dry holes" in oil and gas exploration). Amortization involves the gradual write-off of these assets by charges against income.

AMT is an acronym for the **ALTERNATIVE MINIMUM TAX.**

APPARENT AUTHORITY arises from the manifestation of a principal to a third party (directly or indirectly) that another person is authorized to act as an agent for that principal.

APPRAISAL is a means to determine what a specific business is worth. A statutory right of "dissent and appraisal" is a totally different provision designed to protect minority shareholders against certain types of abusive transactions that are specifically listed in the corporation statutes. See **DISSENTERS' RIGHTS.**

ARTICLES OF INCORPORATION in most states is the document filed with the appropriate state agency to form a corporation. The articles of incorporation must contain specific information about the corporation, its name, purpose, and duration, the number of shares it may issue, and so forth. The articles of incorporation may also provide rules of governance for the corporation. Terminology with respect to the basic document filed to form a corporation is not uniform in all states. In the Model Act and statutes of most states this basic document is called the articles of incorporation. In Delaware and other states it is called the **CERTIFICATE OF INCORPORATION.**

ARTICLES OF ORGANIZATION is the document filed with the appropriate state official to create a limited liability company.

ASSET ACQUISITION is the purchase of the assets of a business that is being acquired. An asset acquisition transaction permits the purchaser to designate which specific business liabilities it will assume and agree to pay, and which it will disaffirm, leaving them the responsibility of the seller.

ASSIGNMENT OF AN INTEREST IN THE PARTNERSHIP under the 1914 UPA transfers only the partner's financial interest in the partnership. In the 1994 UPA, these transactions are referred to as "transfers" of the "partner's transferable interest in the partnership."

ASSOCIATION TAXABLE AS A CORPORATION is an unincorporated association taxable as a corporation under the Internal Revenue Code. An association taxable as a corporation and its owners are different taxable entities and each is separately subject to tax, first at the level of the organization on the income earned by it at corporate tax rates, and second, at the level of the owners on distributions made to them out of the earnings and profits of the association.

AT WILL means that a relationship can be terminated at any time by a party without liability to other parties.

AUTHORITY in the law of agency refers to three quite different, but interrelated, sources: actual authority, apparent authority, and inherent authority.

AUTHORIZED CAPITAL of a corporation is the number of shares of various classes that the corporation is authorized to issue.

BALANCE SHEET is the fundamental financial statement. It is simply a restatement of the fundamental accounting equation in the form:

Assets	Liability + Equity

BALANCE SHEET TEST is a test for the validity of corporate distributions. It prohibits distributions that invade or reduce the permanent capital of the corporation.

BLANK SHARES in corporation law are a class of preferred shares from which the board of directors is authorized to carve one or more series of shares and set the financial terms of each series.

BLOCKAGE refers to the fact that large interests in a business may be more difficult to sell or dispose of than smaller interests. This phenomenon usually appears in securities which are thinly traded in public markets; it may also arise in connection with the disposition of interests in closely held businesses.

BOARD OF DIRECTORS of a corporation has the general power to manage the business and affairs of the corporation. This power is almost plenary, extending to all facets of the business of the corporation, including decisions as to the payment of dividends, the election of officers to manage the day-to-day business of the corporation, and so forth.

BOND is a transferable, long-term debt instrument secured by a lien or mortgage on specific corporate property. The word "bond" may also be used in a more generic sense to refer to both bonds and debentures.

"BOOKED" refers to taking transactions into the bookkeeping records of a business.

BOOK VALUE means the value of the asset as shown on the books of the business at that time.

BOOK VALUE OF SHARES means the value of corporate shares calculated from the books of the corporation using the values shown in those books. Book value of a business means the value of the residual interest in the business according to the financial records of the business. Residual means what remains after subtracting liabilities from assets. Book value is an accounting concept rather than a true measure of value.

BOOTSTRAP ACQUISITION means an acquisition that is financed by borrowing most or all of the purchase price.

BROAD NON-LIABILITY STATUTE refers to a type of limited liability partnership statute that protects all innocent partners from personal responsibility for partnership liabilities.

BUSINESS in general is defined as any kind of profitmaking endeavor excluding only employment in which one person works for and under the direction of another. A profitmaking endeavor in turn is an enterprise or activity that promises to throw off money in the future to its owners. The economist uses the word **FIRM** to refer to the same concept.

BUSINESS FORM generally refers to whether a business is conducted as a proprietorship or one person corporation (in the case of a one-owner business), or a partnership, limited partnership, corporation, limited liability company, or some other form (in the case of a multi-owner business).

BUSINESS JUDGMENT RULE establishes the standard for imposing liability on corporate directors for failing to exercise "due care." A reasonable approximation of the scope of this rule holds that directors are not personally liable for the consequences of decisions they make if the following are true: (1) they have no personal interest in the transaction itself, (2) they make the decision in good faith and on the basis of an investigation or inquiry into the facts and circumstances that they deem to be appropriate under the circumstances, and (3) the decision has some rational relationship to the best interests of the corporation. In addition, in making the inquiry or investigation, directors may rely on other directors, on committees of the board of directors, on officers or employees of the corporation, or on experts (such as lawyers or accountants), if they have confidence in their judgment.

BUSINESS PLAN is (usually) a document that describes the rights and responsibilities of each person involved in a new business venture. A business plan may be a relatively formal written document prepared by a lawyer, or it also may be a sketchy memorandum written on a paper napkin, or even an entirely oral understanding.

BUY-SELL AGREEMENT is a contract that requires the corporation (or other shareholders) to purchase the shares owned by a shareholder in specified circumstances. A buy-sell agreement is a type of share transfer restriction.

BYLAWS are adopted by a corporation to provide detailed rules governing its internal operations. Bylaws are binding on the corporation, its shareholders, officers, and directors. They constitute an internal set of rules for the governance of the corporation, dealing in some detail with such matters as elections, notices, size of the board of directors, restrictions on the transfer of shares, and a host of similar matters.

CALL is an option that requires the other party to sell shares or other property at a price specified in the contract.

CAPITAL ACCOUNTS in partnership accounting refer to the basic ownership accounts of each partner. Each partner's capital account is increased by (1) the amount of money contributed by that partner, (2) the fair market value of property contributed by that partner to the partnership (net of liabilities), and (3) allocations to that partner of partnership income and gain. Each account is decreased by (1) the amount of money distributed to that partner by the partner, (2) the value of property distributed to the partner, and (3) allocations to that partner of partnership expenditures, loss, or deductions.

CAPITALIZATION of a corporation is based on the number of shares actually issued and the capital received therefor. Compare **AUTHORIZED CAPITAL.**

CAPITALIZATION FACTOR in the valuation process is the reciprocal of the discount rate used in valuing a business. It can be established from the actual relationships between average earnings and sales prices of similar businesses in the recent past or from a "market interest rate plus additional risk" assessment.

CAPITALIZATION OF EXPENSES in the accrual accounting system treats development expenses as an asset (much like prepaid rent) rather than as expenses to be deducted from current income.

CAPITALIZED PROMOTIONAL EXPENSE is an example of an asset that may appear on a balance sheet but have zero realizable value.

CASH-FLOW ANALYSIS is a valuation process that works off the business's traditional accounting system. Cash-flow analysis differs from income analysis primarily in that it ignores depreciation and other noncash expenses that are included in traditional income statements. Cash-flow analysis is therefore a "purer" measure of value than income analysis because it focuses exclusively on the cash that is made available to a business from its operations.

CASH METHOD of accounting is based on the receipt or payment of cash. Transactions are taken into the firm's accounts only when cash is received or paid. This system of accounting may give an unrealistic picture of the success of a business because it is easily manipulated, but some substantial service businesses, including law firms, may use the cash method of accounting. Individual income taxation is also based on the cash method of accounting.

CASH-OUT MERGER in corporation law is a merger that requires some shareholders in one or more of the corporations to accept cash rather than an interest in the continuing entity.

C CORPORATION is a corporation subject to income taxation under Subchapter C of the Internal Revenue Code as a taxable entity separate from its shareholders.

CERCLA is an abbreviation for the Comprehensive Environmental Response, Compensation, and Liability Act.

CERTIFICATE OF INCORPORATION is a formal document issued by the filing authority when it accepts articles of incorporation for filing. In Delaware and some other states, the basic document filed with the state to form a corporation is called the Certificate of Incorporation.

CERTIFICATE OF LIMITED PARTNERSHIP is the document that is filed with the state filing authority to form a limited partnership.

CHARGING ORDER in partnership law is the device by which an individual creditor of a partner levies upon the partner's interest in the partnership.

CHECK THE BOX are proposed regulations that make the selection of tax treatment of unincorporated business entities entirely elective. The organization simply "checks" a box to determine the type of tax treatment it prefers.

CLOSE CORPORATION means a corporation with relatively few shareholders and no ready market for its shares.

CLOSE CORPORATION STATUTES authorize corporations meeting specific statutory definitions to abandon the traditional corporate structure and adopt radical management structures. These statutes also permit corporations to adopt special remedies for deadlock and oppression.

CLOSELY HELD BUSINESS generally is a business with a few owners.

COMMON SHARES are the fundamental units into which the proprietary interest of a corporated is divided. The basic rights of common shares are: (1) they are entitled to vote for the election of directors and on other matters coming before the shareholders, and (2) they are entitled to the net assets of the corporation (after making allowance for debts and senior securities) when distributions are to be made, either during the course of the life of the corporation or upon its dissolution.

CONDUIT TAXATION (or **PASS THROUGH TAXATION**) is based on the principle that the unincorporated association is not a separate taxable entity. Rather, the various tax consequences are passed through to the owners, who must include gains, losses, income, deductions, and so forth in their individual returns.

CONTINUATION AGREEMENTS in partnerships eliminate the right of a withdrawing partner to compel winding up and termination of the partnership following a dissolution or dissociation.

CONTINUITY OF LIFE is a corporate attribute. A corporation remains in existence even though the persons who are shareholders may change from time to time.

CONTRA ACCOUNT in accounting practice is an account that appears as a deduction or offset against an asset account. "Less accumulated depreciation" is an example of such an account.

CONTRACT PARTNERS are partners in a law firm who have only limited participation rights in profits and no obligation to contribute toward losses. The partnership agrees to indemnify these partners against liabilities or losses. A contract partner presumably is a partner and not an employee. However, if a contract partner is compensated solely on a salary basis (or on the basis of salary plus year-end bonus of a specified amount), she may argue that she is not truly a partner because she is not sharing in profits. A contract partner is also referred to as an **INCOME PARTNER.**

CONTROL BLOCK is a block of shares in a corporation that has the power to determine who will manage the corporation. Control blocks are usually sold as a unit and rarely broken up.

CONVERSION RATIO with respect to convertible corporate securities determines how many shares of common stock a preferred shareholder receives upon the exercise of the conversion privilege.

CONVERSION SECURITIES are the securities into which a convertible security may be converted.

CONVERTIBLE DEBENTURES are debt securities issued by a corporation that may be converted into equity securities, almost always common shares, on some predetermined ratio.

COOKING THE BOOKS is a slang phrase describing manipulation of accounting transactions that may extend to outright fraud and misrepresentation.

CORPORATION SERVICE COMPANIES are companies providing incorporation or filing services, primarily to lawyers. These companies, for a fee, will prepare and file articles of incorporation, limited partnership certificates, and other documents. They also may provide additional services to complete the formation of a corporation.

CREATIVE ACCOUNTING is a slang phrase describing manipulation in accounting statements that may extend to outright fraud and misrepresentation.

CUMULATIVE DIVIDENDS relate to dividend rights of preferred shares in a corporation. If a dividend is cumulative, an omitted dividend in any year is carried forward and both it and the current year's preferred dividend must be paid in full before any common dividends may be declared in either year. Unpaid cumulative dividends are not debts of the corporation, but a continued right to priority in future earnings.

CURRENT ASSETS in financial analysis are, cash, cash equivalents, and assets that will be reduced to cash within a year.

CURRENT LIABILITIES in financial analysis are liabilities that will come due within a year.

CURRENT RATIO is the ratio between current assets and current liabilities.

DBA (or **D/B/A**) stands for "doing business as."

DEADLOCK in corporation law is created when there is equally divided voting power, usually tie votes for the election of the board of directors. Directoral deadlocks may arise where there is an even number of directors and the voting structure permits each shareholder or faction to elect precisely the same number of directors as the other shareholder or faction.

DEBENTURE is an unsecured transferable corporate obligation. See **DEBT SECURITIES.**

DEBT/EQUITY RATIO is normally defined as the mathematical ratio between a corporation's debts to its shareholders and the shareholders' equity. For example, a corporation capitalized by its shareholders with $10,000 of common stock and $90,000 of loans from the shareholders to the corporation has a debt/equity ratio of 9:1. This ratio is the "inside ratio." The debt/equity ratio may also be calculated by using all corporate liabilities, including those owed to third persons, compared to shareholders' equity. This is the "outside ratio." For purposes of the thin-capitalization doctrine, the inside ratio is typically used. For purposes of financial analysis, the outside ratio is used (and, indeed, loans by shareholders to the corporation may be viewed as a kind of permanent investment in the corporation).

DEBT SECURITIES are transferable fixed obligations by the issuer to pay the face amount of the instrument at a specific date in the future and interest in specified amounts at specified times in the interim. Debt securities include **BONDS** and **DEBENTURES.**

DE FACTO CORPORATION is a concept at common law protecting shareholders from personal liability for defectively formed corporations in limited circumstances. It requires a statute under which the corporation could be formed, a good-faith attempt to incorporate, and actual use of the corporate franchise. A de facto corporation is valid against all third parties except the state, and therefore is "nearly as good" as a de jure corporation — a legally formed corporation. The phrase "de facto corporation" is also sometimes used to refer to any defectively formed corporation.

DEFINED BENEFIT PLAN is an employee benefit plan in which contributions are based on an actuarial computation to provide each employee with a pension of a specified amount upon retirement.

DEFINED CONTRIBUTION PLAN is an employee benefit plan in which the amount of the contribution is based on the employer's profits or the employee's salary.

DE JURE CORPORATION is a validly formed corporation. A de jure corporation is formed even though there may have been a failure to comply with minor directory statutory requirements.

DELAWARE GENERAL CORPORATION LAW (GCL) is the most influential state corporation statute. Many innovations first adopted in Delaware find their way into statutes of other states which adopt the substance, if not the precise language of the Delaware statute.

DELECTUS PERSONAE in partnership law is the principle that partners may choose who may participate with them in the partnership.

DEPARTMENT (or **DIVISION**) of a large corporation is not a separate legal entity. The parent corporation is thus automatically responsible for all liabilities created by the department or division.

DEPLETION in accounting practice refers to the gradual exhaustion of natural resources through the process of capture and development. Calculation of depletion of natural resources is usually made on the basis of estimates of the total recoverable resources in the field or ore body. As each unit is captured and recovered, the cost is shown as "Less: Accumulated Depletion" in much the same way as depreciation.

DEPRECIATION in accounting practice is associated with the process of writing off assets such as plant and equipment. A portion of the original cost of the asset is viewed as being "used up" each year and taken as a current expense.

DERIVATIVE SUIT is a suit brought in the name of a corporation by one or more shareholders, usually against the directors or officers of the corporation for misconduct or gross negligence. Derivative suits may also be brought by limited partners in the name of the limited partnership against the general partners.

DISCLOSED PRINCIPAL in agency law is a principal whose identity is known to the third party at the time the transaction with an agent is entered into.

DISCOUNTING TO PRESENT VALUE means reducing the face amount of a future obligation to its equivalent in current dollars.

DISSENTERS' RIGHTS (or **RIGHT OF DISSENT AND APPRAISAL**) is a statutory remedy that permits a nonassenting shareholder to an amendment of the articles of incorporation or a merger to reject the consideration offered for his shares and obtain an independent judicial valuation of his shares. This remedy is available only in specified classes of transactions.

DISSOCIATION is the act of withdrawal by a partner under UPA (1994). Every partner has the power to dissociate at any time. The word "dissolution" is used for the same concept in UPA (1914).

DISSOLUTION in UPA (1914) is defined not as the terminal event in a partnership's existence, but rather as the "change in the relation" among partners that occurs when a partner ceases to be a partner. In corporation law, it is the event terminating the existence of the corporation for most purposes. Compare **EVENTS OF WITHDRAWAL.**

DISTRIBUTION in corporation law is a general term referring to any kind of payment (in cash, property, or obligations of indebtedness) by the corporation to one or more shareholders on account of his ownership of shares. In partnership practice, it is the amount that a partner actually receives from the partnership. A distribution may be greater or less than the partner's allocation.

DISTRIBUTIVE SHARE. See **ALLOCATION.**

DIVIDEND is a special type of distribution: a payment to shareholders by the corporation out of its current or retained earnings in proportion to the number of shares owned by the shareholder.

DIVIDEND PREFERENCE with respect to preferred shares means that the shares are entitled to receive a specified dividend each year before any dividend may be paid on the common shares. A dividend preference may be described either in terms of dollars per share (the "$3.20 preferred") or as a percentage of par or stated value (the "5 percent preferred"). A dividend preference does not mean that the shareholder is entitled to the payment as a creditor. A preferred dividend is still a dividend, and may be paid only if the corporation has available surplus from which a dividend may be paid and the board of directors elects to declare a dividend. The board may decide to omit all dividends, common and preferred.

DIVIDEND RECEIVED DEDUCTION is a tax deduction available only for corporate shareholders. This deduction ranges from a 100 percent deduction for dividends paid to an affiliated corporation that owns 80 percent or more of the voting power and value of the corporation's stock to a 70 percent deduction for dividends paid to corporations owning less than 20 percent of the stock.

DOUBLE TAXATION in tax law arises in connection with dividends paid by C corporations. The corporation is first taxed directly on its income calculated under the corporate rate schedule. The amount of any dividend paid to a shareholder is subject to a second tax at the shareholder's personal income tax rate.

DOWNSTREAM CONVERSION in corporate law is the right to convert preferred stock into common stock (or debt into preferred or common stock) at the option of the holder.

DUTY OF CARE is a basic duty of directors when exercising their managerial powers in a corporation. In some states, the duty of care is a common law duty. Many states follow the MBCA and define this duty as requiring actions in "good faith, with the care an ordinarily prudent person in a like position would exercise under similar circumstances, and, in a manner he reasonably believes to be in the best interest of the corporation." See also **BUSINESS JUDGMENT RULE.**

EARNINGS AND PROFITS is a corporate tax concept that determines when distributions to shareholders are taxable to the shareholders as dividends. It is not a defined term in the Internal Revenue Code. Rather, it is a calculation of realized and undistributed economic profit.

EARNINGS PER SHARE in accounting practice is the net income of a corporation divided by the number of outstanding shares.

EBIT in accounting practice stands for "earnings before interest and taxes." It is used by persons considering the purchase of a going business as an estimate of the earning power of the business independent of its current cost of capital.

EBITDA in accounting practice stands for "earnings before interest, taxes, depreciation and amortization." It is an interim calculation based on a profit-and-loss statement that approximates the cash flow of the enterprise before the costs of capital are taken into account.

EIN is an acronym for **EMPLOYER IDENTIFICATION NUMBER.**

EMPLOYEE AT WILL is an employee who does not have a contract for a specific term of employment. Either employer or employee is theoretically free to terminate the relationship at any time without cause and without liability to the other party.

EMPLOYEE SHARE OWNERSHIP PLAN (ESOP) is an employee benefit plan that permits employees to acquire shares of a corporate employer.

EMPLOYER IDENTIFICATION NUMBER (EIN) is a number issued by the Internal Revenue Service to employers to record filings and transactions involving tax withholding for employees.

ENTREPRENEUR is an owner of a business who is personally involved in its management and who shares in its profits or losses. Entrepreneurship combines both ownership and management.

EQUAL OPPORTUNITY RULE is a proposed rule that would require controlling shareholders who plan to sell their shares to a third party to first offer the opportunity proportionately to minority shareholders. This rule has never been adopted in part because it would deter many desirable sales of control transactions.

EQUITY in accounting practice means ownership or net worth. The equity in a business is equal to its assets minus its liabilities.

EQUITY INSOLVENCY TEST is a test for the validity of corporate distributions. It prohibits distributions that have the effect of rendering the corporation insolvent in the sense of being unable to meet its obligations as they mature.

EQUITY PARTNER is a general partner in a law firm which also has contract or income partners.

EQUITY SECURITY refers to common and preferred shares.

ESOP is an acronym for **EMPLOYEE SHARE OWNERSHIP PLAN.**

ESTATE TAX FREEZE is a device to minimize estate taxes after the death of business owners. A freeze may involve limited partnerships or corporate recapitalizations in which interests shift without a transfer. These arrangements have been largely closed off by amendments to the Internal Revenue Code.

EVENTS OF WITHDRAWAL of a general partner in a limited partnership are similar to the corresponding dissolution provisions with respect to general partnerships.

FAIR MARKET VALUE means the price that would be established by a buyer and a seller in an arms' length negotiation for the purchase and sale of a business, with both parties ready, willing, and able to enter into the transaction, each under no compulsion to enter into the transaction, and each having essentially complete information about the relevant facts.

FIDUCIARY RELATIONSHIP means that the fiduciary is accountable to the beneficiary for any profits arising out of the transactions he is to conduct on the beneficiary's behalf. The fiduciary also breaches his duty to the beneficiary if he acts either to benefit himself or someone else other than the beneficiary. The fiduciary also may not act adversely to the interest of the beneficiary or assist an adverse party to the beneficiary. A fiduciary also may not compete with the beneficiary concerning the subject matter of the relationship.

FIFO in accounting practice is a method of determining the value of closing inventory by assuming that the earliest items in inventory are always sold first. FIFO stands for "first in first out." In periods of inflation, FIFO improves the reliability of the balance sheet since the value of inventory reflects the most current prices at which inventory was actually purchased.

FINANCIALS is a short-hand reference to financial statements.

FINANCING STATEMENT is the document that must be filed under Article 9 of the Uniform Commercial Code to create a security interest in most types of property.

FIRM. See **BUSINESS.**

FORMAL ACCOUNT is the traditional judicial remedy available to a partner used to establish the rights and obligations of the partners within a partnership following its dissolution. See **ACTION FOR ACCOUNTING.**

FREE CASH FLOW in accounting practice equals cash flow plus expected capital expenditures minus preferred dividends.

FREEZE-OUT is an oppressive tactic in corporations in which a controlling shareholder prevents all payments from the corporation to minority shareholders in an effort to persuade them to sell their shares to the controlling shareholder at an unreasonably low price. This tactic is also known as a **SQUEEZE-OUT.**

FUNDAMENTAL TRANSACTIONS in corporation law include amendments to articles of incorporation, mergers, consolidations, sale of substantially all the assets of the corporation, mandatory share exchanges, and dissolution.

GAAP is an acronym for **GENERALLY ACCEPTED ACCOUNTING PRINCIPLES.**

GCL is an acronym for the **DELAWARE GENERAL CORPORATION LAW.**

GENERALLY ACCEPTED ACCOUNTING PRINCIPLES (GAAP) are a loose set of accounting principles designed to make periodic financial statements of publicly held corporations reliable and comparable with similar statements of other companies. GAAP assumes that the business will continue to existence perpetually, or at least indefinitely.

GENERAL PARTNERS in a limited partnership are unlimitedly liable for the debts of the business to the same extent as partners in a general partnership without limited partners.

GENERAL UTILITIES DOCTRINE was a tax principle that provided that a C corporation was not subject to tax on the distribution of appreciated property to shareholders. This doctrine was legislatively repealed and such distributions are now taxable to the corporation to the extent of the appreciation.

GmbH is a German business form similar to American limited liability companies.

GOODWILL appears on balance sheets in order to reflect asset purchases at higher than fair market value. Goodwill on balance sheets is shown as an asset but may have zero realizable value.

GUARANTEED PAYMENTS in partnership law are fixed payments required by the partnership agreement to be made to specific partners.

HAIG-SIMONS is a theory of income taxation policy that states that an individual should be taxed only on her accretion of wealth rather than on source-based rules.

HANDSHAKE PARTNERSHIP is an informal partnership governed by the default rules of the applicable partnership statute.

HIGH QUORUM REQUIREMENT in corporation law is a provision that requires more than the statutory minimum of attendance by shareholders or directors to constitute a valid meeting.

HISTORICAL COST in accounting practice means acquisition cost and is the basis on which dollars are assigned to various assets in the financial statement.

INCIDENTAL AUTHORITY in agency law is authority to do incidental acts that relate to an authorized transaction.

INCOME PARTNER. See **CONTRACT PARTNER.**

INCOME STATEMENT is a basic accounting statement that differs from a cash-flow statement in that it takes into account all (or most) items of income or expense related to the business without regard to their effect on the available cash. The income statement is also called a **PROFIT-AND LOSS STATEMENT.**

INCORPORATED PROPRIETORSHIP means a corporation in which one individual owns all outstanding shares.

INDEMNIFICATION of directors means that a corporation has agreed to reimburse a director named as a defendant in a lawsuit complaining of some action taken while a director for her expenses regarding the litigation. In some cases, a director may also be indemnified for amounts paid in settlement of litigation.

INDEPENDENT CONTRACTOR in agency law is a "person who contracts with another to do something for him but who is not controlled by the other nor subject to the other's right to control with respect to his physical conduct in the performance of the undertaking." Restatement of Agency, Second.

INHERENT AUTHORITY in agency law arises from the agency itself and without regard to actual, apparent, or incidental authority. Inherent authority may be viewed as authority arising by implication from the actual authority granted to the agent.

INTEREST IN A PARTNERSHIP consists of the right of each partner to receive distributions when and as they are made. A partner's interest in the partnership is analogous to the interest of a holder of shares in a corporation. It reflects the partner's general ownership interest in the business and not the ownership of any specific asset.

INVENTORY in accounting practice consists of (1) all finished goods awaiting sale, (2) all goods in various stages of production beginning with (and including) raw materials, and (3) all goods on hand that are ultimately consumed in the production of goods.

INVOLUNTARY DISSOLUTION in corporation law is a statutory remedy for deadlock, oppression, or waste of corporate assets.

JINGLE RULE in partnership law states that partnership creditors have priority over individual creditors with respect to partnership property and individual creditors have priority over partnership creditors with respect to individual property. Bankruptcy law does not follow the jingle rule.

JOINT AND SEVERAL LIABILITY in partnership law (and elsewhere) means that suit may be brought against one or more partners for the entire claim without bringing suit against all of them simultaneously.

JOINT LIABILITY in partnership law (and elsewhere) means that all the partners must be named as defendants and served with process if the claim is to be pursued.

JOINT STOCK COMPANY is a common law unincorporated business form developed in England as a commercial substitute for the royal corporate charters that created the City of London and the great universities of Oxford and Cambridge. Joint stock companies have limited recognition in the United States,.

JOINT VENTURE is a partnership that has a limited and more narrow business objective than a general partnership, e.g., a partnership that engages in a single transaction such as the purchase and resale of a specific piece of real estate. Partnership rules are generally applicable to joint ventures, the major difference being in the scope of the actual and apparent authority that each joint venturer possesses.

JUNIOR PARTNERS are partners who have limited managerial rights under a partnership agreement which provides for "senior" and "junior" partners.

KINTNER REGULATIONS are the regulations long used by the Internal Revenue Service to determine the tax treatment of an unincorporated business entity. The Kintner regulations listed four critical "corporate" characteristics that were to be considered in determining whether an entity should be classified as a partnership or as an association taxable as a corporation — continuity of life, centralization of management, limited liability, and free transferability of interests.

LEGAL FORM of a business refers to whether the business is organized as a corporation, partnership, limited liability company or other form.

LEVERAGE is an economic principle that explains why the use of debt in capital structures may improve the owners' return on their investment. Most loans are at fixed interest rates so that the cost of the borrowed capital is a known and fixed amount. If the return on the investment (per dollar of total investment) is greater than the cost of the borrowed capital, the rate of return on the investor's equity in the project is enhanced by the difference. Leverage increases risk on the downside as well as increasing return on the upside.

LEVERAGING UP is a phrase that refers to the fact that a potential purchaser of a business may finance the purchase by debt usually to the greatest extent possible.

LIABILITY in accounting practice means a recognized debt or obligation to someone else payable in a reasonably ascertainable amount. Contingent liabilities are booked only when it is reasonably clear that the contingency will in fact occur and the amount of the liability can be reasonably estimated.

LIFO in accounting practice is a method of determining the value of closing inventory by assuming that the last items in inventory are always sold first. LIFO does not accurately reflect the way in which most businesses in fact consume inventory (i.e., disposing of the last first) but it is popular because it reduces taxable income in periods when prices are rising.

LIMITADAS of various types are similar to American limited liability companies. They include the *sociedad de responsabilidad limitada* (S.de R.L. of Mexico) and the Portuguese *sociedate por quotas responsibilitidade limitada*.

LIMITED LIABILITY COMPANY (LLC) is a hybrid business form that became popular in the United States in the 1990s. Its attractiveness arises from its combination of desirable tax and business features: almost complete internal flexibility coupled with limited liability for all of its owners and pass through tax treatment of a partnership. An LLC is free to develop its own organizational and management structure and, at least to some extent, its own governing rules and principles. Default rules for LLCs are drawn in part from corporation law, from general partnership law, and from limited partnership law.

LIMITED LIABILITY LIMITED PARTNERSHIP (LLLP) is a limited partnership in which the general partners have elected to become a limited liability partnership. In an LLLP, the limited partners have no liability for the firm's obligations under the limited partnership statute, while the general partners have personal liability only to the extent provided by the LLP statute.

LIMITED LIABILITY PARTNERSHIP (LLP) is for most purposes a general partnership. It differs from a general partnership only in that some (or all) partners are by statute not personally responsible for certain partnership liabilities. See **BROAD NON-LIABILITY STATUTE.**

LIMITED PARTNERS are investors in a limited partnership having no personal liability for the debts of the partnership. Limited partners traditionally are not expected to participate in the day-to-day management of the partnership.

LIMITED PARTNERSHIP ASSOCIATION is a Nineteenth Century business form created in Pennsylvania, Michigan, New Jersey, Ohio, and Virginia. These variant partnership forms have apparently been rarely used during the Twentieth Century, though a modern resurgence in their use appears possible.

LIMITED PARTNERSHIP (LP) differs from a general partnership in that there are two classes of partners: (1) one or more general partners who have the same rights, obligations, and duties as general partners in a general partnership, and (2) one or more limited partners, who are investors in the partnership but who are not personally liable for the debts of the partner and who are not expected to participate in the day-to-day management of the partnership.

LIQUIDATING DISTRIBUTION in corporation law is a distribution that is a partial payment to shareholders by a solvent corporation in the process of liquidation.

LIQUIDATION PREFERENCE in corporation law means that one or more classes of preferred shares are entitled to receive a specified distribution from corporate assets in liquidation (after provision has been made for corporate debts) before the common shares are entitled to receive any liquidating distribution.

LITIGATION COMMITTEE is a committee of directors of a corporation charged with the responsibility of determining whether a derivative suit that has been filed is in the best interest of the corporation or should be dismissed. Members of a litigation committee are independent directors not involved in the claims involved in the suit.

LLC is an acronym for **LIMITED LIABILITY COMPANY.**

LLLP is an acronym for **LIMITED LIABILITY LIMITED PARTNERSHIP.**

LLP is an acronym for **LIMITED LIABILITY PARTNERSHIP.**

LP is an acronym for **LIMITED PARTNERSHIP.**

MANAGERIAL EMPLOYEE in a business is a high-level employee typically in charge of a department or division who oversees the activities of a number of lower-level employees. A managerial employee is nevertheless an employee.

MANAGER-MANAGED LIMITED LIABILITY COMPANY is an LLC that has elected to be governed by managers who are similar to directors of a corporation and have similar powers and duties. Inactive members of a manager-managed limited liability company are analogous to shareholders of a corporation or to limited partners in a limited partnership. Managers may be chosen by the members in a manner similar to the way directors are chosen by shareholders in a corporation.

MARK TO MARKET in accounting practice means using current market values of an asset rather than historical cost. Conservative accounting principles require that inventory that has declined in value be marked down to market value. Mark to market is also used elsewhere, e.g., for marketable securities generally and to reflect declines in real estate values for savings and loan associations.

MASTER in agency law is a principal who "employs an agent to perform service in his affairs and who controls or has the right to control the physical conduct of the other in the performance of the service." Restatement of Agency, Second.

MASTER LIMITED PARTNERSHIP is a type of limited partnership in which the limited partnership interests are publicly traded on the public securities markets. The units of public trading may be depository receipts for limited partnership interests rather than the limited partnership interests themselves.

MBCA is an acronym for the **MODEL BUSINESS CORPORATION ACT** (1984).

MEMBER-MANAGED LIMITED LIABILITY COMPANY is an LLC managed in a manner similar or identical to that of a partnership. Each member of a member-managed limited liability company is an agent of the limited liability company for the purpose of its business.

MEMBERS of an LLC are the owners of the firm.

MERGER is an amalgamation of two or more corporations: a traditional merger of Corporation A into Corporation B means that Corporation B is the surviving corporation and that shareholders of Corporation A become shareholders in Corporation B on some predetermined ratio. Mergers may also involve elimination of some shareholders by cash payment. Mergers of unincorporated business forms are also permitted in many states.

MINORITY INTEREST DISCOUNT is a reflection of the fact that minority interests in closely held corporations sell at substantial discounts from shares owned by the controlling shareholder. A discount for minority interests in the valuation process is well accepted and may be substantial, ranging from as low as 50 percent to as high as 90 percent.

MODEL BUSINESS CORPORATION ACT (1984) **(MBCA)** is a product of the Committee on Corporate Laws of the American Bar Association. The first Model Act was first published in 1950; important amendments were made in 1969. A major revision and recodification was completed in 1984.

MULTIPLIER is the reciprocal of the interest rate used to discount future cash flows to present value.

NARROW NON-LIABILITY STATUTES refers to the original type of limited liability partnership statute. These statutes protect "innocent" partners from personal responsibility for liabilities created by errors, omissions, negligence, incompetence, or malpractice committed by other partners or by employees supervised by other partners. In other respects, all partners in this type of LLP have the same rights, duties, and responsibility for other types of liabilities as partners in a general partnership. The definition of "innocent" varies from state to state, but typically includes all partners who (1) did not themselves commit the act of malpractice, (2) did not have the responsibility of overseeing the persons who committed the act of malpractice, or (3) were not aware of the act of malpractice or did not take reasonable steps to correct it.

NATIONAL CONFERENCE OF COMMISSIONERS ON UNIFORM STATE LAWS (NCCUSL) is an organization consisting of commissioners appointed by the governors of each state. The major function of NCCUSL is the development and approval of uniform legislation. NCCUSL also works to obtain the enactment of such legislation.

NCCUSL is an acronym for the **NATIONAL CONFERENCE OF COMMISSIONERS ON UNIFORM STATE LAWS.**

NEGATIVE CAPITAL ACCOUNTS in partnership law reflect money potentially owed by a partner to the partnership.

NEGATIVE CASH FLOW of a business means that the cash being generated by the business is not sufficient to cover its current cash needs. In some new ventures, a negative cash flow may be anticipated during the first few years of operation and provision may be made for the necessary additional capital infusions in the original planning.

NET PROFIT RATIO in accounting practice is the ratio between the net profit and gross sales.

NET WORKING CAPITAL in accounting practice is a measure of short-term stability of a business. It is the amount by which current assets exceed current liabilities.

NEXUS OF CONTRACTS THEORY is a model of the corporation as a bundle of contracts entered into by the managers of the enterprise with providers of labor, services, raw materials, capital, and contractual commitments of various types. In this model, the managers are viewed as the essential glue that fits together all the various contributors to the firm in the most efficient way, while the shareholders are the contractual suppliers of residual capital, the group whose contract entitles them to the residual profits of the business and requires them to assume the primary risk of loss since all other providers to the corporation have priority in payment over them.

NOMINAL PAR VALUE is a par value of perhaps one cent, ten cents, one dollar, or ten dollars when shares actually are to be issued at a significantly higher price. Nominal par value is a device minimizing the risk of watered share liability.

NONCUMULATIVE DIVIDENDS disappear each year and need not be made up in later years if they are not paid. See **CUMULATIVE DIVIDENDS.**

NONRECOURSE LOAN is a loan in which the creditor agrees to look only to the specific property for repayment and to voluntarily release its right to seek a personal recovery against the borrower.

NO PAR SHARES in corporate law are shares issued under traditional statutes that are stated to have no par value. However, before no par shares are issued the board of directors must establish the consideration for which such shares are to be issued, and that determination by the board essentially substitutes for the provision in the articles of incorporation establishing a par value.

OFFICERS of a corporation are selected by the board of directors. Their principal functions are to execute and carry out the decisions of the board of directors and to conduct the business on a day-to-day basis. Traditional officers are a president, one or more vice presidents, a secretary, and a treasurer, though the 1984 Model Act and many modern statutes do not require designated offices. In publicly held corporations, officers typically have broad power to manage the business under the oversight of the board of directors.

OPERATING AGREEMENT in an LLC sets forth the basic managerial roles in the LLC. They are analogous to corporate bylaws but have binding force. The operating agreement may also be called **REGULA-TIONS** in some states.

OPERATING CASH FLOW in accounting practice equals cash flow plus interest expense plus income tax expense.

OPERATING MARGIN in accounting practice is the ratio of pre-tax income to gross sales. It is also known as the **PROFIT MARGIN.**

OPPRESSION in close corporations is a comparative term that assumes a minority shareholder has a certain minimum economic return or right of participation that he is now being deprived of by the controlling shareholders' conduct. This minimum return or right of participation is usually judged, where applicable, by the terms on which the minority shareholder originally invested in the corporation or the promises which induced him to invest. Courts have given varying definitions to this term, e.g., conduct that "substantially defeats the expectations that objectively viewed were both reasonable under the circumstances and were central to the minority shareholder's decision to join the venture," "burdensome, harsh and wrongful conduct," or "a visible departure from the standards of fair dealing, and a violation of fair play on which every shareholder who entrusts his money to a company is entitled to rely."

ORGANIZATIONAL EXPENSE in accounting practice may appear as an asset on a balance sheet but has zero realizable value.

PARTIALLY CUMULATIVE DIVIDENDS are usually cumulative to the extent earned; that is, the dividend is cumulative in any year only to the extent of actual earnings during that year.

PARTIALLY DISCLOSED PRINCIPAL in agency law is a principal whose identity is unknown but the third person knows that the agent is in fact acting for someone else.

PARTICIPATING PREFERRED SHARES are preferred shares entitled to an original preferential dividend but if a specified dividend per share is paid on common shares, the participating preferred becomes entitled to additional distributions on some predetermined basis.

PARTNERSHIP is a business form that is a logical extension of a proprietorship: It is an unincorporated business in which there is more than one owner. UPA (1914) defines a partnership to be the relationship that exists among persons who are "co-owners of a business for profit."

PARTNERSHIP AT WILL is a partnership in which there is no agreement as to how long it is to continue. Such a partnership may be dissolved by a partner at any time without liability to any other partner.

PARTNERSHIP FOR A TERM (or **DEFINITE UNDERTAKING**) is a partnership dissolvable by any partner but one in which premature dissolution may make the dissolving partner liable for breach of contract.

PARTNER'S TRANSFERABLE INTEREST IN THE PARTNERSHIP is the phrase used in UPA (1994) to describe a partner's "interest in the partnership" as used in the 1914 Act.

PAR VALUE for shares of stock goes back to ancient times. The par value is a per share amount selected for each class of shares when the corporation is formed (or when articles of incorporation are amended to authorize a new class of shares). Par value is part of the definition of the security itself. For example, the shares issued are "common shares with a par value of $x." The original purpose of par value was to define the issuance price of shares in order to guarantee each investor that all other investors are paying the same amount per share.

PASS THROUGH TAXATION See **CONDUIT TAXATION.**

PIERCING THE CORPORATION VEIL is a corporate doctrine that is in fact a broad set of amorphous principles permitting a court in some circumstances to ignore the separate existence of a corporation and hold a shareholder liable for corporate obligation. A court may also ignore the separate existence of related corporations, holding each liable for the obligation of the others. This may be referred to as "horizontal" piercing.

PREEMPTIVE RIGHTS is a corporate principle that states that current shareholders have a right to purchase their pro rata portion of new shares proposed to be issued. The purpose of preemptive rights is to maintain voting power within the corporation. Preemptive rights were originally viewed as an inherent part of the concept of owning shares but are now viewed as an optional right that the governing corporate documents may grant or deny, or may grant on a qualified basis.

PREFERRED SHAREHOLDERS' CONTRACT describes the provisions relating to preferred shares in basic corporate documents. This usage reflects that rights of preferred shareholders are generally limited to those set forth in this "contract" and that preferred shareholders have relatively few rights outside of those granted expressly to them by the basic corporate documents.

PREFERRED SHARES are equity securities created by provisions in the articles of incorporation (or in other publicly filed documents). In effect, preferred shareholders are granted limited economic rights carved out of the rights of common shareholders; they are "preferred" since some economic right of the preferred shareholders, either a right to distributions or a right to share in the surplus on dissolution, or both, must be satisfied ahead of the rights of common shareholders.

PREPAID RENT in accounting practice is an asset account created when the business receives rent in advance. Then, in each month during which the rent is actually earned, earnings are increased by that month's rent and the "prepaid rent" account on the balance sheet is reduced by the same amount.

PRESENT VALUE OF FUTURE PAYMENTS describes the process of discounting the future payments to their present value.

PRINCIPAL in agency law is the person for whom an agent is acting.

PROFESSIONAL CORPORATION is a business form that enables professional firms to incorporate within the limits of the ethical proscriptions applicable to those professions. In some states, these entities may be known as "professional service companies," "professional associations," or by other names. Professional corporations provide benefits for shareholders in the form of limited liability and some modest fringe tax benefits.

PROFIT AND LOSS and income are synonyms. Income in accounting practice equals revenues minus expenses.

PROFIT-AND-LOSS STATEMENT See **INCOME STATEMENT**.

PROFIT MARGIN See **OPERATING MARGIN**.

PROMOTER'S CONTRACTS are contracts entered into by a promoter on behalf of a corporation in the process of formation. Many promoter's contracts are executed by the promoter individually or in the name of "ABC Corporation, a corporation to be formed."

PROPRIETORSHIP is a business owned by a single individual in his individual capacity.

PROTOTYPE LIMITED LIABILITY COMPANY ACT is an LLC statute proposed in 1992 by a committee of the American Bar Association.

PURPORTED PARTNER is a person who has the power to affect partnership relations as a partner even though there is in fact no agreement either to be co-owners or to share profits. These are situations in which a person represents either that he is a partner with another person or that he is a member of an existing partnership when in fact that is not the case. If another person relies on the representation, partnership-type liabilities may be imposed on the purported partner. If the other persons in the purported partnership make similar statements, they also may be liable as though a partnership existed.

PUT is an option to compel a corporation or a third person to buy shares or other property at a predetermined or determinable price.

QUICK ASSETS is an accounting term referring to current assets that can be used to cover an immediate emergency. Quick assets are cash and current receivables but exclude inventories.

RECONSTITUTION of a limited partnership occurs under RULPA when the sole remaining general partner withdraws, and within 90 days all the remaining partners agree in writing to continue the business of the limited partnership and to appoint one or more new general partners.

REDEEMABLE SHARES are shares that may be acquired by the corporation, at the option of the corporation, upon the payment of a fixed amount for per share. Such shares are also called "callable" shares. The redemption price may be a matter of negotiation between the corporation and an investor at the time the preferred shares are issued. The price is usually established at a level somewhat higher than the consideration originally paid by the investor for the preferred shares, but tied to the original issue price. For example, if preferred shares are issued for $100 per share, they may be made redeemable at $105 or $110 per share.

RED INK refers to negative numbers on financial statements. Colored ink is rarely used today in financial statements but the phrase is still used.

REGULATIONS in an LLC. See **OPERATING AGREEMENT.**

RESPONDEAT SUPERIOR is a Latin phrase that means "let the master respond."

RETURN ON CAPITAL in accounting practice is the ratio of net income plus interest paid to net worth plus long-term debt.

RETURN ON EQUITY in accounting practice is the ratio of net income to net worth.

RIGHT OF DISSENT AND APPRAISAL. See **DISSENTERS' RIGHTS.**

RIGHT TO PARTICIPATE IN THE MANAGEMENT OF A PARTNERSHIP is defined as a property interest in UPA (1914).

ROLLING OVER DEBT means obtaining new loans (either from the same lender or from another lender) to pay off old debts as they mature.

ROLL-UP is a partnership transaction in which a number of pre-existing partnerships are merged into one master limited partnership. Such transactions are now governed by federal statute.

RULPA is an acronym for the **REVISED UNIFORM LIMITED PARTNERSHIP ACT.**

RUPA is an acronym for the **REVISED UNIFORM PARTNERSHIP ACT OF 1976 WITH 1985 AMENDMENTS.**

SAFE HARBOR statutes or regulations set forth a general legal standard but also list certain specific actions that automatically fall within that general standard. Actions that do not fall within the safe harbor provision continue to be governed by the general legal standard.

SCHEDULE B is the tax schedule in form 1040 on which an individual taxpayer lists his personal deductions.

SCHEDULE C is the tax schedule in form 1040 on which an individual taxpayer reports income or loss from individually owned businesses.

The income or loss of each business is added to or subtracted from the taxpayer's other income to establish taxable income. A separate Schedule C must be filed for each business.

SCHEDULE C-EZ is a tax schedule available for the very smallest proprietorships, those that have no employees and less than $25,000 in gross receipts.

S CORPORATION ELECTION permits most corporations with less than 75 shareholders to elect to be taxed in a manner that allows income to be passed through the corporation and be taxed directly to shareholders. Subchapter S tax treatment is similar to (but in some respects significantly different from) the conduit tax treatment applicable to partnerships and other unincorporated entities.

SECTION 531 is an Internal Revenue Code penalty tax applicable to corporations "formed or availed of for the purpose of avoiding the income tax with respect to its shareholders or the shareholders of any other corporation, by permitting earnings and profits to accumulate [beyond the reasonable needs of the business] instead of being divided or distributed."

SECURITY for purposes of federal and state securities regulation is generally defined as a "financial interest the gain from which is dependent on the efforts of others." Limited partnership interests are "securities" under this definition but general partnership interests usually are not.

SECURITY INTEREST in goods is a lien created under Article 9 of the Uniform Commercial Code. A security interest is obtained by the execution of a security agreement and the filing of a financing statement as required by Article 9 of the Uniform Commercial Code.

SELF-DEALING TRANSACTION is a personal transaction between a director and the corporation. The classic example is director who sells a piece of land to his corporation at a price that may or not may be fair.

SELF-EMPLOYMENT CONTRIBUTIONS ACT OF 1954 is a statute that imposes a tax on Schedule C income equal (in 1995) to 12.4 percent of proprietorship income up to $61,200 for old age survivors and disability insurance (OASI), and an additional uncapped 2.3 percent for Medicare.

SENIOR PARTNERS in a partnership have general power to govern the affairs of the partnership under a partnership agreement which provides for "junior" and "senior" partners.

SERIES OF PREFERRED SHARES are created by the board of directors of a corporation acting alone if specifically authorized by the state corporation statute and by the corporation's articles of incorporation. The articles of incorporation must in effect create a class of preferred shares without any substantive terms and specifically authorize the board of directors to create (or "carve out") series from within that class from time to time and to vary the substantive terms of each series at the time it is created as appropriate for market conditions then existing.

SERVANT in agency law is an agent the details of whose performance is determined by the principal (the master). A more modern term for this relationship is **EMPLOYEE.**

SHAREHOLDERS of a close corporation are the residual claimants to the assets and income of the corporation. Shareholders have only limited management participation rights. Shareholders generally may act in their own self-interest and owe no fiduciary duty to the other shareholders or to the corporation.

SHARE TRANSFER RESTRICTIONS include (1) option arrangements, by which a shareholder who wishes to sell or dispose of her shares must first offer them to the corporation or the other shareholders, (2) mandatory buy-sell agreements, (3) rights of first refusal, (4) consent requirements that permit the board of directors of the corporation to reject a potential purchaser, or (5) prohibitions against the transfer of shares to specific persons or classes of persons.

SHIELD OF LIMITED LIABILITY is the protection against personal liability provided by various business statues.

SQUEEZE-OUT. See **FREEZE-OUT.**

START-UP BUSINESS is a new business just getting underway. The prototype start-up business is the entrepreneur with a good idea attempting to translate it into a viable and profitable business.

STRAW PARTY is a person without financial resources who agrees (usually for a nominal fee) to execute liability-creating documents on behalf of another. A corporation without substantial assets is an example of a straw party.

STRIPPING of assets, i.e., transferring of assets to shareholders, is one of the amorphous and vague tests for piercing the corporate veil.

SUBSIDIARY in corporate law is a separate corporation, a majority or all of the outstanding shares of which are owned by the parent corporation. If a subsidiary is unable to satisfy its obligations, recovery may be sought from the parent corporation on the basis of a piercing-the-corporate-veil theory.

SWING SHARES are shares that determine which of two factions have control of the management of the corporation. Swing shares may sell at a premium, since the purchaser of the swing shares in effect captures the value of the control element within the corporation.

TAKING A BATH is a slang accounting phrase that describes the common practice of a business facing a bad year in any event to lump as many write-offs in that period as possible so that a return to predictable increases in profits becomes inevitable in following years.

TAX CLASSIFICATION refers to whether an unincorporated entity is to be taxed as an "association taxable as a corporation" under the Internal Revenue Code or as a partnership.

TEFRA is an ancronym for the Tax Equity and Fiscal Responsibility Act of 1982. This statute essentially eliminated the federal income tax benefits that had been the subject of the professional corporation battle for 20 years.

TENANCY IN PARTNERSHIP is the phrase used in UPA (1914) to describe the relationship between partners and partnership property. Property held as tenancy in partnership must be used solely for the benefit of the business and is usually referred to as "specific partnership property."

TERMINATION is the event that marks the end of the partnership's business under UPA (1914).

THINLY CAPITALIZED in corporate law means that most of the capital of a business is provided in the form of debt and only a small portion is in the form of equity.

TIME VALUE OF MONEY is a phrase that describes the process of discounting future payments to their present value.

TRADE NAME is an assumed name under which a business is conducted. A trade name is lawful so long as it does not deceive the public, is not misleadingly similar to the name of a competing business, and is not otherwise used in a fraudulent or deceptive manner.

TREASURY SHARES in corporate law are shares that were originally lawfully issued and then reacquired by the corporation. Treasury shares are viewed as being held by the corporation in a sort of twilight zone until they are either retired permanently or resold to someone else in the future. They are viewed as being continuously "issued" and held in the corporation's treasury for purposes of the technical rules of issuing shares but not issued for purposes of a quorum, voting, or dividends. Treasury shares are also not assets of the corporation even though they may be sold at some later time.

UCC-1 FILINGS are financing statements required by Article 9 of the Uniform Commercial Code to be filed to perfect security interests in collateral.

ULLCA is an acronym for the **UNIFORM LIMITED LIABILITY COMPANY ACT**, a statute approved by NCCUSL in 1996. ULLCA may already be too late in the day, since all but a handful of states had already enacted LLC statutes when ULLCA was approved.

ULPA is an acronym for the **UNIFORM LIMITED PARTNERSHIP ACT** (1916).

UNDISCLOSED PRINCIPAL in agency law is a principal whose existence is not know to a third party dealing with the agent under the belief the agent is acting on his own behalf.

UPA is an acronym for the **UNIFORM LIMITED PARTNERSHIP ACT** versions of which were approved in 1914 and 1994.

UPSTREAM CONVERSION in corporation law is a right to convert common shares into preferred shares, or common or preferred shares into debt securities.

VALUATION is the process of determining the fair market value of a business or asset. Appraisal and valuation are synonymous.

WATERED SHARES in corporation law are shares issued for less than par value or for less than the consideration determined by the board of directors as the price for the shares. Much of the corporate jurisprudence of the last century was devoted to stamping out this perceived evil.

WINDING UP of a partnership is the practice of liquidating assets and discharging liabilities following dissolution or dissociation if the partnership is to be terminated.

WINDOW DRESSING in accounting practice are transactions entered into near the end of a fiscal year primarily in order to improve the appearance of the balance sheet. Window dressing may involve big shipments from inventories at bargain prices near the close of the accounting period in order to be able to book the sales. Alternatively, a company with cash-flow problems may borrow money on December 28 in order to show a large amount of cash on hand at the close of the fiscal year. Of course, that cash is only temporarily resident in the company's accounts and may disappear on January 3. Window dressing may shade off into actionable fraud or deception.

WORKOUT AGREEMENT in connection with a sale of a business makes a portion of the purchase price payable based on earnings after the transaction is closed. The buyer commits to a conservative price and agrees to pay an additional amount at the end of one or more years only if earnings exceed an amount stated in the agreement. This contingent payment based on actual post-sale results may eliminate an impasse over valuation, since if the buyer's more pessimistic forecasts turn out to be accurate, no further payment is due, while if the business is as successful as the seller expects, the ultimate purchase price will be based on the seller's estimate.

ZERO OUT in tax law means reducing taxable income of a C corporation virtually to zero by making payments of salary, rent, interest, and the like to shareholders. Such payments are deductible by the corporation for tax purposes.

Index

Freeze-outs, 230, 231
Full-service securities brokerage firms, 404

Galler v. Galler, 252
General partnerships
  actions for an accounting, 96, 97
  admission of new partners, 83, 84
  agency law, 69, 70
  allocations vs. distributions, 88
  assignments, 81, 82
  bankruptcy, 80, 81
  business plan, 53
  capital accounts, 86-88
  charging orders, 78, 79
  classification issues, 57-59
  continuation agreements, 93-95
  creditors, 79-81
  dissociation, 95, 96
  dissolution and winding up, 90-93
  dissolution without winding up, 93-96
  economic/business characteristics, 54, 55
  entity vs. aggregate concepts, 62, 63
  fiduciary duties, 71-73
  handshake partnerships, 59-61
  introduction, 52, 53
  Kintner regulations, 85, 86
  legislation/statutes, 56, 57
  liability of partners, 74, 75
  limited partnership, compared, 100, 101
  management, 71, 77
  oppression, 242
  partnership, defined, 57-59
  partnership agreements, 64-69
  property rights, 76-78
  purported partners, 61, 62
  start-up, 53
  taxation, 69, 84-86
  termination, 88-93
  voting power, 71
  who may be partners, 63, 64
Generally accepted accounting principles
    (GAAP)
  amortization, 366
  balance sheet, 356, 357
  basic principles, 359-361
  capitalization of expenses, 361
  conservatism, 373
  depletion, 362, 366
  depreciation, 362-365
  going concern assumption, 372, 373
  historical cost, 367, 371-373
  honesty/good faith assumption, 380
  income statement, 357-359
  inventory, 367-371
  judgmental principles, 379
  lower of cost or market, 373

marking to market, 367
revenue recognition, 362
unrealized appreciation, 372
General Utilities doctrine, 267 n.11, 302
Going concern assumption, 372, 373
Going concern value, 335
Gross profit, 369
Guaranteed payments, 68

Handshake partnerships, 59-61
Hiding expenses, 386
Highly leveraged business, 353
Historical cost, 367, 371-373

Identity doctrine, 324
Income statement ratios, 392
Income statements
  adjustments to, 384
  basic formula, 357
  cash-flow statement, contrasted, 343-347
  estimates of cash flow, 388, 389
  GAAP, 357-359
Incorporated proprietorships, 213-218,
    321, 322
Independent contractor, 14
Inside debt/equity ratio, 296 n.56, 354
Instrumentality doctrine, 324
Integration proposals, 269
Invested capital, 279
Investment banking firms, 403, 404
Investment contract, 140

Jingle rule, 80, 81
Joint ventures, 62

Keogh plans, 257 n.134
Kiddie tax, 267 n.13
Kintner regulations, 85, 86, 118, 119, 137

Leverage, 341 n.7, 348-351
Liability, 356
LIFO, 369-371
Limited liability — corporations, 315, 316
  advantages, 320, 321
  personal guarantees of corporate
      debt, 318, 319
  piercing corporate veil. *See* Piercing cor-
      porate veil
  preincorporation transactions, 316-318
  tort liability of shareholders, 319-321
Limited liability companies (LLCs)
  corporations, compared, 126-129